The
TRIUMPH OF MUSIC

The
TRIUMPH

OF MUSIC

Tim Blanning

The Rise of Composers, Musicians and Their Art

Belknap Press of Harvard University Press / Cambridge, Massachusetts 2008

Copyright © 2008 by Tim Blanning
All rights reserved
Printed in the United States of America

Cataloging-in-Publication Data available from the Library of Congress
Library of Congress catalog card number: 2008026753
ISBN-13: 978-0-674-03104-3

This book is dedicated to all those students and colleagues with whom I have worked in Cambridge and elsewhere, especially Derek Beales, Jonathan Steinberg, Chris Clark and Roderick Swanston

Contents

Preface

Among the many attractions of being a member of the Faculty of History at the University of Cambridge is the relative freedom to construct courses as one sees fit. During the past two decades I have taken advantage of this to introduce a musical element into the curriculum by creating courses on music in European society and culture and on Richard Wagner and German history. In the process I have learned a great deal, both from the students and from three colleagues with whom I have worked successively—Derek Beales, Jonathan Steinberg and Chris Clark. I have also benefited immeasurably from the wit and wisdom of Roderick Swanston at the numerous music festivals for which he and I have lectured. It is to these four scholars that this book is dedicated. Each very generously read a first draft of this book and made numerous immensely helpful criticisms.

But I have also incurred a number of other debts, institutionally, to the various libraries in which I have worked over the years, most notably the Seeley Historical Library and the University Library in Cambridge, the music department of the Bibliothèque National in Paris, the Staatsbibliothek in Munich, the Nationalbibliothek in Vienna and the Kunstbibliothek and the Staatsbibliothek in Berlin. I am also grateful to the numerous societies and other institutions that have given me the opportunity to expose my views on 'the triumph of music' to public debate and criticism.

Although so many individuals have helped me in various ways that I cannot thank them all, I do wish to find room for the following: Robert Alexander, Tony Badger, Sally Beales, Mark Berry, Charles Blanning, Susan Boehmer, Ben Buchan, Vicki Cooper, John Deathridge, Linda Fritzinger, Mary Gallacher, Eric Hobsbawm, John Kulka, Gerald Levy, Cecilia Mackay, Arthur Marwick, Kirsty McCluskey, Barry Millington, Sean Milmo, John Mole, Michael O'Brien, Christopher Page, Claire Preston, Martin Randall, Donald Sassoon, Claudia Schneider, Hagen Schulze, Paul Scott, Brendan Simms, David L. Smith, Ian Stevenson, Simon Winder, and Andrew Wylie. Last but not least, my wife, Nicky, has repeatedly sacrificed her own scant leisure time to allow me to get on with the research and the writing. I could not have finished without her invariable love, support and good humour.

Tim Blanning
Cambridge, May 2008

The
TRIUMPH OF MUSIC

Introduction

In modern times, three British monarchs have reigned long enough to celebrate a golden jubilee: George III in 1809, Queen Victoria in 1887 and Elizabeth II in 2002.[1] All three marked the occasion with a church service. King George contented himself with a private affair in the chapel at Windsor. Queen Victoria attended a Service of Thanksgiving at Westminster Abbey, where she heard her late husband's setting of the 'Te Deum' and another of his compositions, the anthem 'Gotha'. The present queen went to St. Paul's Cathedral for a similar event, albeit without the prince consort's music, and was told by the archbishop of Canterbury that 'unlike so much in the modern world, this relationship, the one between Sovereign and people, has grown stronger and deeper with the passage of time'. For these three monarchs—heads of the Church of England and devout Christians all—the religious service may well have marked the highpoint of the jubilee celebration. For the subjects of George and Victoria, however, it was more likely the ox roasts, free beer and fireworks that went down best.

Plenty of food and drink were consumed in 2002 also, but for the majority of Queen Elizabeth's subjects the climax was the great openair pop concert held in the grounds of Buckingham Palace on Monday, 3 June. Although the limited space meant that only the 12,500 people who had been successful in a ballot could attend, a million more watched it on giant

Party at the Palace—the Queen's Jubilee Concert, 3 June 2002.

screens in the Mall and the royal parks, while another 20 million in the United Kingdom and more than 200 million worldwide watched it on television. A hundred thousand copies of the CD were sold within a week, and untold millions more have watched the concert on DVD since. Together with the classical concert (Prom at the Palace) staged the previous Saturday, the Party at the Palace (as the event was officially known) gave the jubilee a public impact greater than any previous royal occasion.

The DVD revealed many good moments: an Atomic Kitten constantly threatening to pop out of her dress without ever quite succeeding; the once satanic Ozzy Osbourne, former lead singer of Black Sabbath, growling 'God Save the Queen' as he left the stage after performing his anthem 'Paranoid'; the comely Rachel Stevens looking somewhat nonplussed when seized by Cliff Richard during their performance of 'Move It'—just to mention three. Undoubtedly the highlight, however, was the concert's opening, with Brian May playing 'God Save the Queen' on the roof of Buckingham Palace. Although the Queen herself perhaps did not make the fullest possible use of the opportunities presented by the event—she arrived shortly before the end sporting ear plugs and was visibly unamused by the proceedings—most commentators concluded that it had been a mighty public relations coup. Even self-confessed republicans were impressed.

Typical was the reaction of the columnist India Knight, who was in Ireland on the evening of the concert:

> I idly switched on the television while I ran a bath. The first thing I thought, with a sort of kick of excitement around the stomach, was: 'Oh my goodness, how fabulous is this?' The second thing was: 'It's Brian May and his horrible hair playing the guitar on the roof of Buckingham Palace, ergo it can't be fabulous, ergo I need to get a grip, sharpish.' I was supposed to go to the pub, but watched the concert instead, mesmerised—the same grandad-friendly concert I had been sniggering about for weeks: Rod Stewart, Ozzy Osbourne, Paul McCartney, the remaining members of Queen, the exact opposite of cool. And yet it was fantastic. More fantastic still was the sight of one million people waving their flags and roaring their approval: every time the camera panned to them. I felt choked.

Her story was published under the title: 'So Help Me, I'm a Patriot'.[2] If that seems a little impressionistic, one could add the more hard-headed response of Hans Petri, the managing director of Opus Arte, the company responsible for marketing the DVD, who found himself overwhelmed by orders from would-be distributors: 'When they saw that picture of Brian May on the roof of the palace, they just all went through the roof', he said.[3] For once, the application of the overworked adjective 'iconic' to Brian's performance seems justified.

The event attracted a great deal of attention, of course, but none of the millions of words that flowed—so far as I can tell, at least—tried to place it in its historical context, apart from the occasional brief reference to the two previous royal jubilees (or three, if Queen Victoria's diamond jubilee of 1897 is included). This book will show how the concert was the culmination of three centuries of musical development. Of course other occasions could have been chosen, but the Prom and Party at the Palace serve very well as a starting point, because present on those two June evenings were at least four of the five essential ingredients that have fused to ensure

Brian May performs 'God Save the Queen' at the opening of the Jubilee Concert, 3 June 2002. 'Brian May's hair should instantly be declared a national monument' proclaimed *The Daily Mirror.*

the triumph of music (and which the five chapters that follow will take up in turn).

First was the elevated status of the musician. No group of comparably famous and rich creative artists working in fields other than music could have been assembled. Almost everyone who appeared was a household name, several were knights or dames, and most were very rich. *The Sunday Times* 'rich list' included Sir Paul McCartney with a fortune of £760m, Sir Elton John with £170m, Sir Tom Jones with £150m, Ozzy Osbourne with £100m, Brian May with £55m, Roger Taylor with £50m, John Deacon with £50m, Sir Cliff Richard with £40m (almost certainly a serious underestimate), Annie Lennox with £30m, and so on. How things have changed since 1781, when Mozart was literally booted out of the service of the archbishop of Salzburg 'with a kick to my arse'.

In addition to the status of the performers, the place and the space for this occasion were also significant. The address may have been Buckingham Palace, but access was not controlled by the owner-occupier. This was a public event, less a concert than an *al fresco* party, as the audience got into the swing of things and gradually became participants rather than spectators. Moreover, the space was not bounded by the palace walls but spilled out into the surrounding boulevards and parks to become a mass phenomenon. And this was made possible only by technology, especially by the amplification of sound and the transmission of images. Without them, not even Tom Jones would have been audible and visible to more than a few hundred people. With them, even the softly singing, self-effacing Corrs could be heard and seen by tens of millions. As we shall see, place, space and technology worked together to take music out of the palace and into the public sphere.

The messages that were broadcast from the stage were various but not incoherent. Without too much of a stretch of the imagination, they could be gathered under a single umbrella labelled 'liberation', whether it was for women (Annie Lennox and 'Sisters Are Doing It for Themselves'), the young (Queen's 'Radio Ga Ga'), ethnic minorities (Paul McCartney's 'Blackbird', Aretha Franklin's 'Respect'), gays (Sir Elton John's 'I Want Love'), lovers (Bryan Adams' 'Everything I Do'), or the elderly (Sir Cliff Richard's contributions).

The only aspect of the concert that appeared to be at odds with music's triumphant progress relates to its purpose. As a royal celebration it looked to have much in common with the great festivals of the Habsburg or Bourbon monarchs, where the purpose of music was to represent the power of the patron. The expressive capacity that has allowed music, over the course of four centuries, to leapfrog the other arts to pole position may not have been obvious in the 2002 festivities: Emma Bunton cooing her way through 'Baby Love' or Tom Jones belting out 'Sex Bomb' was very much at the commercial end of the spectrum. Yet the performances of, among others, Queen's 'Bohemian Rhapsody', Eric Clapton's 'Layla' and Paul McCartney's extracts from The Beatles' *Sergeant Pepper's Lonely Hearts Club Band* and *White Album* were sufficient reminders of music's ability to operate at a higher level by diving deeper into the human psyche and expressing what is found there in a way that has universal appeal.[4] Indeed, as more than one journalist pointed out, it was not clear who was being honoured most—the Queen, or the kings and queens of pop.

Status, purpose, places and spaces, technology, and liberation—these are the five categories I will explore to explain music's march to cultural supremacy. What follows is an exercise in social, cultural and political history, not musicology—no technical knowledge of music is required. It is not intended to be a history of music and is necessarily selective in the illustrations that have been chosen. Apologies are offered in advance to fans of, say, Puccini (a *very* sensitive group) or the Sex Pistols (ditto) for not giving their heroes more attention. Although I have placed heavy emphasis on the late eighteenth and nineteenth centuries, because that was when many of the great changes occurred, every chapter concludes with a section bringing the story up to the present day. A date chart at the end provides a chronological thread and places musical events in their general historical context.

Advancing a simple thesis always carries with it the dangers of reductionism. I am well aware that all the phenomena I discuss also had an impact on other branches of the creative arts, but I shall argue that music benefited most.

1

Status

'You Are a God-Man,
the True Artist by God's Grace'[1]

The Musician as Slave and Servant

Most of recorded history has made a sharp discrepancy between the status of music and the status of musicians. In ancient civilisations, music was venerated as a medium ideally suited both to convey divine commands and to give thanks for them. In pharaonic Egypt, any alteration of the traditional chants was strictly prohibited, for the good reason that their composer was the god Osiris. The last of the Psalms of the Old Testament exhorts the faithful to praise the Lord with brass, woodwind, strings and percussion.

In the more anthropocentric culture of classical Greece, it was humans who revealed the power of music, most famously Orpheus, who saved his fellow Argonauts on their way home with the golden fleece by outsinging the Sirens. Lyric poetry (poems sung to a lyre) was an integral part of Greek tragedy from the very start. That was why Nietzsche called his first masterpiece *The Birth of Tragedy from the Spirit of Music.* In the *Poetics* Aristotle identified music as one of tragedy's six essential components (the others being plot, character, diction, thought and spectacle). So powerful an influence did Plato ascribe to music that it formed the basis of his educational scheme. In book two of *The Laws*, he expounds it through a conversation between an Athenian stranger and a Cretan, Cleinias:

ATHENIAN STRANGER: Shall we begin, then, with the acknowledgment that education is first given through Apollo and the Muses? What do you say?

CLEINIAS: I assent.

ATHENIAN STRANGER: And the uneducated is he who has not been trained in the chorus, and the educated is he who has been well trained?

CLEINIAS: Certainly.

ATHENIAN STRANGER: And the chorus is made up of two parts, dance and song?

CLEINIAS: True.

ATHENIAN STRANGER: Then he who is well educated will be able to sing and dance well?

CLEINIAS: I suppose that he will.

In *The Republic* Plato was even more emphatic: 'Musical training is a more potent instrument than any other, because rhythm and harmony find their way into the inward places of the soul, on which they mightily fasten'. For that reason, he demanded—with his usual lack of equivocation—that no changes in musical forms should be allowed. If they were, the very existence of the regime might be jeopardised, for 'when modes of music change, the fundamental laws of the state always change with them'. In his totalitarian utopia, all aspects of musical activity were to be strictly regulated.

Those who followed in Plato's footsteps down through the centuries may not have shared his *dirigisme* (although we shall meet his wagging finger again when we look at the moral panics excited by rock 'n' roll in the 1950s), but they did share his assessment of music's power. St. Basil the Great (c. 330–c. 379) observed in his *Homily on Psalm 1* that the Holy Spirit had provided 'the delight of melody' to help humankind turn from its natural bent for pleasure to the straight and narrow path of an upright life: 'He mingled with the doctrines so that by the pleasantness and softness of the sound heard we might receive without perceiving it the benefit of words, just as wise physicians who, when giving the fastidious rather bitter drugs to drink, frequently smear the cup with honey'. Among those who testified to the accuracy of this insight was St. Basil's near-contemporary and fellow saint, Augustine (354–430), who wrote of his baptism: 'The music surged in my ears, truth seeped into my heart, and my feelings of devotion overflowed, so that the tears streamed down—but they were tears of gladness'.[2]

As the cultural coherence of the Middle Ages began to dissolve, music retained its elevated status. In *The Book of the Courtier* (1528), Baldassare Castiglione spoke through the count to urge its importance: 'I shall enter into a large sea of the praise of music and call to rehearsal how much it hath always been renowned among them of old time and counted a holy matter; and how it hath been the opinion of the most wise philosophers that the world is made of music, and the heavens in their moving make a melody, and our soul framed after the very same sort, and therefore lifteth up itself and (as it were) reviveth the virtues and force of it with music'.[3]

This kind of encomium could be replicated at will, but one further example will suffice. It is a good one, not least because it stems from Shakespeare. In the final act of *The Merchant of Venice* Jessica tells Lorenzo that she is never merry when she hears sweet music, which prompts the following neo-Platonic response:

> The reason is, your spirits are attentive:
> For do but note a wild and wanton herd,
> Or race of youthful and unhandled colts,
> Fetching mad bounds, bellowing and neighing loud,
> Which is the hot condition of their blood;
> If they but hear perchance a trumpet sound,
> Or any air of music touch their ears,
> You shall perceive them make a mutual stand,
> Their savage eyes turn'd to a modest gaze
> By the sweet power of music: therefore the poet
> Did feign that Orpheus drew trees, stones and floods;
> Since nought so stockish, hard and full of rage,
> But music for the time doth change his nature.
> The man that hath no music in himself,
> Nor is not moved with concord of sweet sounds,
> Is fit for treasons, stratagems and spoils;
> The motions of his spirit are dull as night

And his affections dark as Erebus:
Let no such man be trusted. Mark the music.

In fact, by that time (the mid-1590s) music had been long under attack from the more extreme wing of the Protestant reformers. Although fond of music, Calvin was deeply uneasy about its power, suspecting that it was conducive to 'unbridled dissipations', 'immoderate pleasure', 'lasciviousness and shamelessness', to mention a few of its attractions, and 'just as wine is funnelled into a barrel, so are venom and corruption distilled to the very depths of the heart by melody'.[4] All he would allow, therefore, was the unaccompanied congregational singing of psalms. So deep was the aversion to instrumental music he inspired in his followers that, three years after his death, they had the organ pipes of his church melted down to serve as flagons for the communion service. Calvin's compatriot Ulrich Zwingli banned any form of music whatsoever.

This hostility to music was founded on an ingenious interpretation of the Old Testament's revelation of God's words, from whose rich store of contradictory utterances almost any position could (and can) be justified. So Martin Luther, on the other hand, with the authority that came from someone who had translated the entire Bible, took the view that God positively encouraged music-making, proclaiming that 'one of the most beautiful and magnificent gifts of God is music'. He called on both ecclesiastical and secular authorities to promote it. In particular he advocated joyous song as a prophylactic against temptation: 'The Devil is a sad spirit and makes people sad and therefore he does not like gaiety. That is why he flies from music as far as he can, and does not stay when people sing, especially religious songs'.[5] The hymns that Luther wrote in his inimitable German vernacular and the music he composed—and he very likely *did* compose the tune for his most famous hymn 'Ein feste Burg ist unser Gott' ('A Mighty Fortress Is our God')—was music to be sung by the whole congregation, a microcosm of the priesthood of all believers that made up the Lutheran church.[6]

As well as being a conduit for the Word of God or a weapon against the Devil, music was also prized in early modern Europe for its healing qualities. Paraphrasing the Dutch physician Lemnius, Sir Robert Burton wrote in his *Anatomy of Melancholy* that music is 'a roaring-meg against melancholy, to rear and revive the languishing soul; affecting not only the ears, but the very arteries, the vital and animal spirits, it erects the mind, and makes it nimble'.[7]

In short, with the exception of the grim Franco-Swiss reformers, Europeans have always cherished music—especially when performed collectively (whether by Athenians, Jews, medieval monks, Protestant congregations or whomever). Individual performers were quite a different matter. In many ancient civilisations, the actual musicians were also slaves, or—in the case of Persia—prostitutes. As late as the twentieth century, according to the French polymath Jacques Attali, Islam forbade the faithful to eat at the same table as musicians.[8] In his *Politics* Aristotle commended music as a crucial part of a liberal education, but he set strict limits on the performing skills to be acquired, for 'we call professional performers vulgar; no freeman would play or sing unless he were intoxicated or in jest'. To acquire musical skill for its own sake, he argued, was unacceptable. Only when music was internalised as part of a programme of moral improvement was it permissible:

> Thus then we reject the professional instruments and also the professional mode of education in music (and by professional we mean that which is adopted in contests), for in this the performer practices the art, not for the sake of his own improvement, but in order to give pleasure, and that of a vulgar sort, to his hearers. For this reason the execution of such music is not the part of a freeman but of a paid performer, and the result is that the performers are vulgarized, for the end at which they aim is bad.[9]

The Romans took the same line. Boethius (c. 480–c. 524 AD) was prepared to recognise as true musicians only philosophers who approached music at the level of theory. Instrumentalists he dismissed as 'servants . . . who do not make any use of reason and are altogether lacking in thought' and composers as songsmiths motivated 'not so much by speculation and reason as by a certain natural instinct'.[10] This emphasis on the theoretical aspects of music went back to the Greeks, especially to Pythagoras (569–475 BC), who was less concerned with the sound or structure of music than with its relationship to the heavenly bodies, each of which sent forth its own characteristic sound as it orbited the earth.[11] This 'music of the spheres' was still binding man and universe in Shakespeare's day. Immediately before the passage from *The Merchant of Venice* quoted earlier, Lorenzo tells Jessica:

> There's not the smallest orb which thou behold'st
> But in his motion like an angel sings,
> Still quiring to the young-eyed cherubins;
> Such harmony is in immortal souls;
> But whilst this muddy vesture of decay
> Doth grossly close it in, we cannot hear it.

While music remained part of the immutable divine order, its earthly servant would remain just that, whether as an anonymous member of a group or as an individual composer-performer. (A composer was almost invariably a performer, although not *vice versa*.) At the royal courts of the Middle Ages, the most prestigious group of musicians were the clergy who comprised the chapel choir. They were supported by lay minstrels performing lighter secular music designed more for recreation and with a correspondingly lower status. Although some of the early troubadours were of knightly rank, most came from the margins of polite society. An examination of fifteen troubadours by the historian Christopher Page revealed their diversity: five were clergymen of some kind, four were poor knights or the sons of poor knights, three were the sons of townsmen, and two had previously been artisans.[12]

In medieval Florence both the teaching and composing of music were performed by clerics coming from at best an artisan background.[13] The most celebrated composer of the late fifteenth century, Josquin des Prez, was a cleric who served in the households of a number of princes, including the duke of Anjou, King Louis XI of France, Cardinal Ascanio Sforza, and the duke of Ferrara, before seeing out his days as provost of the collegiate church of Notre Dame in Condé-sur-l'Escaut. However, he does appear to have had a clear sense of what his talent was worth, and an attitude to match. In 1502 one of the duke of Ferrara's agents recommended the appointment of Heinrich Isaac rather than Josquin: 'To me [Isaac] seems well suited to serve Your Lordship, more so than Josquin, because he is more good-natured and companionable, and will compose new works more often. It is true that Josquin composes better, but he composes when he wants to and not when one wants him to, and he is asking 200 ducats in salary while Isaac will come for 120—but Your Lordship will decide'.[14]

Indeed he would—and that was the problem. The duke of Ferrara might give, but he might equally well take away. The fickleness of princely patrons was discovered by Claudio Monteverdi (1567–1643) when he was dismissed abruptly by the duke of Mantua in 1612, leaving him unemployed and with just twenty-five *scudi* to his name. Or so he claimed. In reality his fame was already such that a new patron was soon knocking on his door. In the following summer he moved to the republic of Venice to become director of music *(maestro di capella)* of St. Mark's Basilica. When the Mantuans tried to woo him back seven years later, Monteverdi clearly enjoyed the opportunity to decline at some length, in a justly famous letter that revealed what a musician wanted (and still wants).

First, money: Venice paid him 400 ducats, and he could earn 200 more for freelance work, whereas in Mantua he had earned appreciably less and, moreover, had to go cap-in-hand to the ducal treasurer to beg for payment ('I have never in my life suffered greater humiliation of the spirit').[15] Second, security: in Venice his appointment was permanent and not affected by sudden changes such as the death of a ruler. Third, control: as *maestro di capella* he decided who was hired and fired and directed all other matters relating to the employment of his subordinates, right down to the choristers. Fourth, respect: 'There is no gentleman who does not esteem and honour me, and when I go and perform, whether church music or chamber music, I swear to Your Excellency that the whole city runs to listen'.

Monteverdi's sharply contrasting experiences with his patrons would seem to suggest that a republic offered a musician the most favourable working and living conditions. Confirmation might be sought in the career of Johann Sebastian Bach (1685–1750), who, after serving two princes, chose to spend the last twenty-seven years of his life employed by the town council of Leipzig, which, if not a self-governing republic like Venice, being part of the Electorate of Saxony, did control its own cultural affairs.

At least the duke of Mantua had not tried to prevent Monteverdi from moving to Venice. North of the Alps, that appears to have been quite common. In 1721 Christoph Graupner was unable to accept the position of cantor at the St. Thomas school in Leipzig simply because his current employer, the landgrave of Hessen-Darmstadt, refused to let him go.[16] When Bach tried to leave the employment of the duke of Weimar in 1717, on receipt of a more attractive offer from the prince of Anhalt-Cöthen, he was sent to prison. As the official record put it: 'On November 6th, the *quondam* concertmaster and organist Bach was confined to the County Judge's place of detention for too stubbornly forcing the issue of his dismissal and finally on December 2nd was freed from arrest with notice of his unfavourable discharge'.[17] Composers, singers and musicians working for princes were treated like the liveried servants they were and could count themselves lucky if they were not required to double as valets or footmen. Overwhelmed by gambling debts, in 1753 the young Carl Ditters fled from Schlosshof near Vienna to a new position in Prague. To no avail, for his master, Prince Joseph Friedrich von Sachsen-Hildburghausen, had him arrested and sent back.[18]

Surely the acme of princely autocracy was Frederick the Great of Prussia (ruled 1740–1786), whose musical regime has been described aptly by Thomas Bauman as 'an astonishing instance of artistic despotism'.[19] He paid the piper and he called the tune, specifying arrangement, orchestration, key and tempo into the bargain. As he wrote to his *directeur des spectacles,* Graf von Zierotin-Lilgenau: 'The singers and the musicians are subject entirely to my choice, together with many other objects connected with the theatre, which I order and pay for myself'.[20]

One singer who felt the full force of this attitude was Gertrude Elizabeth Mara (*née* Schmeling), one of the greatest sopranos of her day. As she recorded in her autobiography, in 1774 she received from London the kind of offer Prussian singers could only dream of: 1,200 guineas for twelve evenings, plus 200 guineas travel expenses and a benefit concert. At first Frederick gave his permission, although insisting that her husband stay behind in Berlin as a guarantee that she would return, but then reneged at the last moment. When the couple tried to escape to fulfill the engagement, they were arrested at the gates of Berlin and her husband was imprisoned for ten weeks. In 1780 she fell ill, but Frederick refused to allow her to go to a Bohemian spa for a cure: 'But now I began to feel the weight of slavery. Not only was I having to bury my fame and fortune with him [Frederick] but also now my health', so this time the Maras planned their flight carefully. Describing her emotions on waking up for the first time in the safety of Bohemia, she wrote: 'A magnificent morning awaited my awakening; there was a lawn in front of the house, so I had my tea served there and felt completely happy—*O Liberté!*'[21]

If Frederick was exceptionally autocratic, the subservient status of even the greatest singers and composers was the rule in courts large and small. The primer commissioned by Empress Maria Theresa for the education of her son Ferdinand contained a table illustrating the social hierarchy; it placed musicians at the very bottom, along with beggars and actors.[22] In 1771 she added her own gloss in reply to Ferdinand's request for advice as to whether or not he should employ the fifteen-year-old musician Wolfgang Amadeus Mozart:

> You asked me whether you should take the young Salzburger into your service. I can't think why you should, for you don't need a composer or any other useless people for that matter. But if you think it will give you pleasure, I shan't stand in your way. I only give you my opinion because I don't want you lumbering yourself with good-for-nothing folk. However, you must certainly avoid giving these people honorary titles as if they were in your service. For it brings service itself into disrepute when these people roam around the world like beggars.[23]

In 1761 when Prince Paul Anton Esterházy, one of the richest and most powerful magnates in Maria Theresa's dominions, offered Joseph Haydn a position as his deputy director of music, he presented the twenty-nine-year-old Haydn with a contract that spelled out very precisely not just his duties but also his conduct and his dress. When Haydn and the other musicians performed before the prince, they were always to appear 'neatly in white stockings, white linen, powdered, and either with pigtail or hairbag, but otherwise of identical appearance'. In 1766 the distribution of new winter-weight livery prompted the following grovelling address from Haydn: 'The most welcome arrival of my patron's name day (which may Divine Grace let Your Serene Highness spend in perfect well-being and happiness) causes me not only to offer to Your Serenity in dutiful submission six new divertimenti, but also to kiss the hem of your robe'.[24]

The most obtrusive signal that Haydn was to become the prince's servant, and his alone, appeared in clause four of his contract, which stated: 'The said *Vice-Capel-Meister* shall be under permanent obligation to compose such pieces of music as his Serene Princely Highness may command, and neither to communicate such new compositions to anyone, nor to allow them to be copied, but to retain them wholly for the exclusive use of his Highness; nor shall he compose for any other person without the knowledge and gracious permission of his Highness'.[25] While Haydn was obliged to see out his probationary period of three years and give six months' notice if he decided to leave at the end of it, the prince was 'free at all times to dismiss him from his service'. This was the kind of unequal agreement that prompted Rousseau to denounce all contracts as swindles. In fact, it was more like a feudal bond between lord and vassal. This was shown by the details of Haydn's remuneration, which included substantial payments in kind—wine, firewood, wheat, rye, semolina, beef, salt, lard, candles, cabbages, beans and a pig.[26]

Musically, this relationship found expression in the 126 pieces for baryton that Haydn composed between 1765 and 1778. Derived from the viola da gamba, the baryton has up to seven gut strings that are bowed and ten additional metal strings inside an open neck that resonate sympathetically and can also be plucked from behind. Cumbersome and difficult to play it may have been, but it was the favourite instrument of Prince Nicholas Esterházy, who succeeded his brother as head of the family in 1762. So whatever Haydn may have thought of it, he was obliged to compose a regular supply of appropriate music—indeed, he was chided in 1765 for not producing enough.[27] Without Haydn's compositions, no doubt the baryton would have been consigned to the museum a long time ago.

A more distinguished musical illustration of Prince Nicholas Esterházy's power over his musicians is to be found in Haydn's Symphony No. 45 in F-sharp Minor (*The Farewell Symphony*). The main Esterházy residence was an enormous palace-cum-office-block at Eisenstadt, fifty kilometres south of Vienna, built in the 1660s. Prince Nicholas, however, became increasingly attached to a hunting lodge on the Neusiedler lake, which he turned into a not-so-miniature version of the Habsburg palace of Schönbrunn. Calling it Esterháza, he lavished both time and money on renovating the lodge, and spent more and more time there. Although its musical resources were second to none, including an opera house seating five hundred and no fewer than 126 guest rooms for aristocratic visitors, no humbler accommodations to house the wives and families of the prince's retainers could be found anywhere.[28]

That the prince went to Esterháza for peace and quiet can be inferred from his estates manager's report in 1772: 'I have communicated to all the musicians by word of mouth your high order that none of the wives and children of the musicians are to be allowed to be seen at Esterháza'.[29] His assurance that 'there was no one who did not agree to the terms of the high order' was then challenged by Haydn's symphony. Just when the fourth movement, marked *presto,* appears to be drawing to a close, what is in effect a fifth movement, marked *adagio,* begins. As the simply orchestrated lilting melody wends its way, instructions written on the score direct one musician after another to cease playing (although not before he has drawn attention to his skill with a solo passage), snuff his candle and leave the room. After a hundred bars or so, only Haydn and his second-in-command were left to bring the work quietly to a close. According to an anecdote circulating at the time, the prince was not offended by this progressive withdrawal of labour but commented, 'If they all leave, then we must leave too', and he ordered a return to Eisenstadt.[30]

As this subtle stratagem implies, Haydn was a good-natured, easygoing sort of person who enjoyed an amicable if subservient relationship with his employer. What did annoy him, however, were the restrictions on his freedom of movement. Summoned back to Esterháza from Vienna in February 1790, he wrote bitterly to his close friend Maria Anna von Genzinger, the wife of the Esterházy physician: 'Well, here I sit in my wilderness—forsaken—like a poor waif—almost without any human society—melancholy—full of the memories of past glorious days'.[31] In May he complained that 'I have to put up with many annoyances from the Court here which, however, I must accept in silence', the greatest source of irritation being the prince's refusal to allow him to go to Vienna. By the end of June he had worked himself into a rage of self-pity: 'Again, I find that I am forced to remain here. Your Grace can imagine how much I lose by having to do so. It really is sad to be a slave, but Providence wills it so. I'm a poor creature! Always plagued by hard work, very few hours of recreation, and friends'.[32]

Handel, Haydn and the Liberation of the Musician

Salvation came to Haydn courtesy of God and Mammon. On 28 September 1790 Prince Nicholas died after a short illness, and his son and successor, Prince Anton, promptly disbanded the opera company and the orchestra, leaving Haydn all the leisure time in the world in which to enjoy his comfortable pension in Vienna. Or in London. Back in 1785 *The Gazeteer and New Daily Advertiser* of London had lamented:

> There is something very distressing to a liberal mind in the history of *Haydn*. This wonderful man, who is the Shakespeare of music, and the triumph of the age in which we live, is doomed to reside in the court of a miserable German prince, who is at once incapable of rewarding him, and unworthy of the honour . . . Would it not be an achievement equal to a pilgrimage, for some aspiring youths to rescue him from his fortune and transplant him to Great Britain, the country for which his music seems to be made?[33]

As it turned out, kidnapping proved unnecessary. The German-born but London-based impresario Johann Peter Salomon was touring the Rhineland looking for talent when he learned of Prince Esterházy's death. Hurrying to Vienna, he burst in on Haydn with the words, 'I am Salomon of London and have come to fetch you. Tomorrow we will arrange an *accord*.'[34] Indeed they did, and on 1 January 1791 the two men arrived in the richest city in Europe, the Eldorado of musicians. Haydn was already well known to the English musical public through publication. This did not necessarily mean printing. As with most composers of the period, Haydn's music first began to circulate in manuscript copies, which found their way into the collections of numerous Austrian monasteries and French, Italian and German aristocratic connoisseurs. Publication of any kind was contrary to Prince Esterházy's formal monopoly of Haydn's output, as laid down in the contract of 1761. Always honoured more in the breach than in the observance—Haydn's music was first advertised for sale in 1768, in manuscript only—the clause was dropped in the revised contract of 1779.[35]

By that time his music was readily available for purchase across Europe. Haydn was fortunate that his career coincided with a massive expansion of music printing and publishing. Although printing had been possible since the late fifteenth century, not until the middle of the eighteenth did something approaching a mass market begin to develop. This was an integral part of a much wider phenomenon—the emergence of a public sphere. The growth of literacy and the reading revolution associated with it, the

From the Breitkopf and Härtel thematic catalogue (1763).

expansion of towns and the promotion of urban values, the rise of consumerism and the commercialisation of leisure, the proliferation of voluntary associations such as reading clubs, choral societies and masonic lodges, the improvement of communications and postal services—all of these developments combined to create a new kind of cultural space into which musical entrepreneurs eagerly moved.[36]

Publishing houses had operated in Amsterdam, Paris, Leipzig and London by the end of the seventeenth century, but the numbers multiplied after 1750.[37] Just to list the foundation dates of firms specialising in the printing or sale of music gives some idea of the scale of the change: Breitkopf of Leipzig (1745), Hummel of Amsterdam (1753), Robert Bremner of Edinburgh (1754), Venier of Paris (1755), Chevardière of Paris (1758), Longman and Broderip of London (1767), Schott of Mainz (1770), André of Offenbach (1771), Artaria of Vienna (1767), Torricella of Vienna (1775), John Bland of London (1776), Forster of London (1781), Hoffmeister of Vienna (1783), Birchall and Beardmore of London (1783), Bland and Weller of London (1784), and so on.[38] In the view of most publishers, engraving offered the best combination of elegance and economy, although Johann

The Duke of Alba by Goya (1795).

Gottlieb Emmanuel Breitkopf's invention of an improved movable type process in 1754–55 allowed much larger print runs and consequent economies of scale. His application of commercial techniques—catalogues, advertising, distribution networks, mailorder—allowed him to build up a major enterprise that employed over a hundred workers on the printing side alone.[39]

Through publishers such as these, as well as by word of mouth among connoisseurs, Haydn began to establish an international reputation. As early as 1763 Breitkopf was listing a harpsichord di-

Franz Joseph Haydn by J. E. von Mansfeld.

vertimento by Haydn in his catalogue, to be joined two years later by eight string quartets. In 1764 two Parisian publishers—Chevardière and Venier—were advertising four string quartets and a symphony, respectively. In 1765 Hummel of Amsterdam advertised six string quartets in the *Amsterdamsche Courant*—pieces that were also available in the same year from Robert Bremner's shop in London, situated in the Strand opposite Somerset House.[40] Over the next two decades, an ever-increasing stream of Haydn's compositions found their way to the international market, sometimes in manuscript but increasingly in printed editions. Especially successful was the set of six keyboard sonatas (Hob. XVI: 21–6) published in 1774 and dedicated to Prince Esterházy, which were soon reprinted in Paris, London and Amsterdam.[41] By the 1780s Haydn was composing music for patrons all over Europe: masses, quartets and operas for the countess-duchess of Benavente and Osuna and the duke of Alba in Spain, and six *Paris Symphonies* for the Concert de la Loge Olympique in Paris, to cite just a few examples. A very fine visual illustration of Haydn's international fame can be seen in Goya's portrait of the duke of Alba, who is holding a book of the composer's *Four Songs with Pianoforte Accompaniment*.[42]

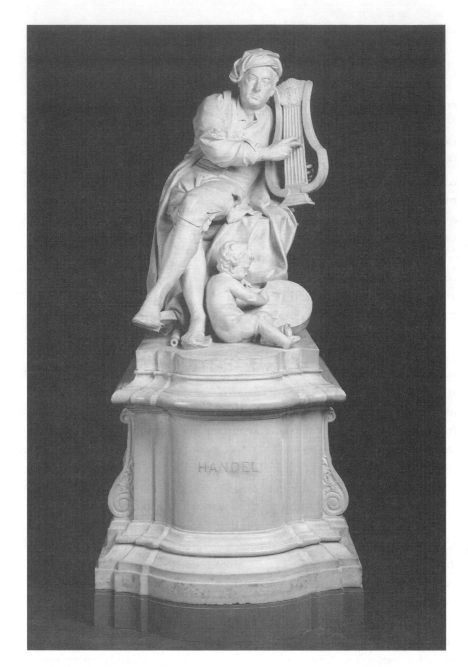

Handel by Louis François Roubiliac.

Handel Monument by Louis François Roubiliac, Westminster Abbey.

In London, rumours were constantly flying that Haydn was about to put in a personal appearance to direct a series of concerts. In November 1782 the *Morning Herald* recorded that 'the *musical world* are rather alarmed, lest the celebrated *Haydn* should decline visiting England'.[43] In the following year the *Morning Post* announced joyfully but erroneously that 'the great Hayden' was indeed set to appear in the autumn.[44] Although restricted to the narrow Vienna-Eisenstadt-Esterháza triangle, Haydn was well aware of his growing fame and did all he could to promote it. In 1781 he commissioned the celebrated artist J. E. von Mansfeld to paint his portrait, which was then engraved, reproduced and advertised for sale by the Viennese publishing house Artaria, with which Haydn had teamed up the previous year.[45] The result was immensely flattering, omitting any trace of his nasal polyp or smallpox scars.

In short, by the time Haydn really did reach London on New Year's Day, 1791, the musical public was ready and waiting. It had already shown its willingness to embrace German-speaking musicians by taking Handel to its ample collective bosom. Indeed, Handel's success during the half-century he spent in London (1710–59) was an early demonstration of how a musician could become rich and famous through the public sphere. He was the first composer and musical impresario who made a fortune from a paying public.[46] When he died in 1759, Handel left an estate valued around £20,000, which made him a millionaire by present-day standards.[47] Riches were accompanied by high status. When he first arrived in London, he was referred to as 'retainer to the elector of Hanover', but by the time he died Handel was fêted by king, aristocracy and country. Never dependent on any one of these, he benefited both materially and socially from all three. A private man who never married, Handel drew his few close friends from the upper ranks of society.[48]

One highlight of Handel's highly successful career was the erection of a full-length life-size statue at Vauxhall in 1738, the largest pleasure garden in London, by its entrepreneur, Jonathan Tyers. His choice of the unknown immigrant sculptor Louis François Roubiliac was an inspired act of good luck or good judgment. Roubiliac's creation, which shows Handel in relaxed posture and dress, plucking a lyre in the style of Orpheus, became one of the most celebrated of all musical statues.[49] It was intended to be both an act of homage to a cultural hero and a reminder of the soothing power of music.

The Vauxhall statue was Roubiliac's first commission; his last was to be Handel's monument in Westminster Abbey, completed in 1761. This is much more formal, as befits the setting and occasion, showing an angel poised aloft, playing a harp, as Handel writes down the notes of 'I Know That My Redeemer Liveth' from *Messiah*.[50] By also including the 'Hallelujah Chorus' in this work, Handel has probably been responsible for more praise of his God than any other individual. That he should be honoured by such a prominent tomb in Westminster Abbey testifies to his personal status and the growing sacralisation of his art. Shortly after he died, he was also the revered subject of the first book-length biography ever devoted to a musician.[51] Twenty-five years after his death, Handel enjoyed an apotheosis in the form of five commemorative concerts in Westminster Abbey and the Pantheon on Oxford Street. The main event at the former was attended by George III (whose favourite composer was Handel), several members of his family and a large number of the peerage and gentry. As William Coxe observed, the commemoration was 'the most splendid tribute ever paid to posthumous fame' and 'an honour to the profession, the nation and to the Sovereign'.[52]

Haydn must have known of Handel's success in the great metropolis, but even so he was overwhelmed by the warmth of his own public welcome. He wrote home: 'My arrival caused a great sensation throughout the whole city, and I went the round of all the newspapers for three successive days. Everyone wants to know me. I had to dine out six times up to now, and if I wanted, I could dine out every day'.[53] After the first concert, on 11 March, the *Morning Chronicle* reported:

> SALOMON'S CONCERT.
>
> The First Concert under the auspices of HAYDN was last night, and never, perhaps, was there a richer musical treat.
>
> It is not wonderful that to souls capable of being touched by music, HAYDN should be an object of homage, and even of idolatry; for like our own SHAKSPEARE [sic], he moves and governs the passions at his will.
>
> His *new Grand Overture* was pronounced by every scientific ear to be a most wonderful composition; but the first movement in particular rises in grandeur of subject, and in the rich variety of air and passion, beyond any even of his own productions.[54]

Charles Burney recorded in his memoirs: 'Haydn himself presided at the piano-forte; and the sight of that renowned composer so electrified the audience, as to excite an attention and a pleasure superior to any that had ever, to my knowledge, been caused by instrumental music in England. All the slow middle movements were encored; which never before happened, I believe, in any country.'[55] Lionised by English society, from the king and prince of Wales on down, Haydn also made very large sums of money: within six months he was able to remit nearly 6,000 gulden to Austrian banks (between five and six times his annual salary from Prince Esterházy).[56] According to his contemporary and biographer, Griesinger, his two visits to London yielded a net profit of 15,000 gulden.[57]

Haydn's fame and fortune in London provides a good illustration of how the commercialisation of an art form could influence its content. This was not so much a question of artistic resources as of patronage. At the Esterházy palace of Eisenstadt, Haydn had at his disposal a magnificent concert hall appreciably larger than the Hanover Square Rooms, the venue of the Salomon concerts in London.[58] But much more important was the relative size of the orchestras he wrote for. At Eisenstadt and Esterháza in the 1770s, Haydn was writing symphonies for three first and three second violins, one viola, one cello, one double bass, one bassoon, two oboes and two horns—fourteen players in all.[59] As each one of these was a permanent charge on the princely exchequer, even as rich a magnate as Prince Esterházy could not afford a larger band. In London, Salomon could draw on a much larger pool of professional musicians who could be hired by the season or even by the concert, and so he was able to provide Haydn with an orchestra of between fifty and sixty members.[60] Significantly, only in the other great European metropolis, Paris, could such forces be matched on a regular basis.

Yet even this discrepancy does not wholly explain the striking stylistic development revealed by the symphonies Haydn wrote for Paris and London in 1784–85 and 1791–95 respectively. A popular explanation is that Haydn's sense of writing for a large public spurred him on to greater things. The *doyen* of Haydn studies, H. C. Robbins Landon, has stated:

> The London public of the last decade of the century deserves part of posterity's gratitude for eliciting the expansion of ex-

pressive boundaries in Haydn's last twelve symphonies. The music reflects the atmosphere of *fin de siècle* London: assured, disputatious, intriguing, eccentric, open-minded yet sensitive. Haydn respected and nurtured his public, they, by adulation, encouraged him to a degree and in a manner no other city could have done (and certainly no individual) to further his propensity for musical argument and entertainment.[61]

This is certainly a plausible hypothesis and can be supported by references to Haydn's frequent and fervent expressions of gratitude to his admiring London audiences. Through publication, Haydn caught the attention of the public, and this allowed him to escape the gilded cage that was Esterháza to freedom in the London public sphere. His liberation might also be placed in a wider historical context in which the public concert is presented as both a cause and a symptom of the victory of the middle classes, as Peter Schleuning has pointed out. Yet this was probably not the whole story, either in the particular case of Haydn or more generally.

In an autobiographical letter written in 1776, Haydn recorded that in 1761 he had moved from the service of the bankrupt Count Morzin to become *Kapellmeister* of Prince Esterházy, 'in whose service I wish to live and die'.[62] And that was just what he did. As his visits to London in 1791–92 and 1794–95 demonstrated, he could easily have made a good living as a freelance musician working for the anonymous public. Yet he chose to see out his days as the loyal servant of the Esterházys. He never explained why, but perhaps it was because his patron supplied most of the requirements Monteverdi listed earlier: a comfortable if not princely income, security, control and prestige. Perhaps most important was the consideration that he was in sole command of a large musical establishment of high quality which provided him with everything a composer needed: instruments, space, a superlative library of books and musical scores, an excellent orchestra and unlimited rehearsal time.

The quality of the musical forces at his disposal can be inferred from the music he asked them to play. Just to take one example: in the slow movement of Symphony No. 51 in B-flat, the horn player is asked to go from the highest note of his instrument's range to a whole series of stopped and overblown notes at the very bottom—and all this, of course, without the assistance of valves. And how many modern composers, apart from those working with purely electronic devices, can have their creations performed at once under their own direction?

Haydn was well aware of the advantages he enjoyed: 'My Prince was content with all my works, I received approval, I could, as head of an orchestra, make experiments, observe what enhanced an effect, and what weakened it, thus improving, adding to, cutting away, and running risks. I was set apart from the world, there was nobody in my vicinity to confuse and annoy me in my course, and so I had to be original.'[63] One must wonder whether he could have created the extraordinarily original symphonies of his so-called *Sturm und Drang* period of the late 1760s and early 1770s if he had been writing for the public of London or Paris and not for the discerning and tolerant Prince Nicholas Esterházy. I cannot be alone in preferring the stark emotional vitality of these earlier works to the more polished Paris and London symphonies.[64]

Perhaps more than any other eighteenth-century composer, Haydn managed to have the best of both worlds, aristocratic and public. By the last decade of his long life, he had become a cultural icon of the Habsburg monarchy, a process encouraged by his composition of a national anthem. On 27 March 1808, to mark his seventy-sixth birthday, the aristocratic concert society led by Prince von Trauttmansdorff organised the crowning glory of his career in the form of a gala performance of his oratorio *The Creation* in the main hall of the University of Vienna. By the time Haydn's carriage arrived, the crowd waiting outside was so large that the police had to take action to maintain order. After being greeted by a reception committee including Prince Lobkowitz, Prince Esterházy and Beethoven, Haydn was carried into the hall in an armchair, to tumultuous reception and shouts of 'Long Live Haydn!' Before the performance began, he was presented with two verse eulogies, one in German, the other in Italian, prompting him to burst into tears.

After the orchestral introduction and a brief recitative, the chorus sings the following:

> And the spirit of God moved upon the face of the water;
> And God said:
> Let there be light!
> And there was light!

The apotheosis of Haydn on 27 March 1808, originally painted by Balthasar Wigand on a box.

The passage is sung *pianissimo* until 'light' is reached for the second time, at which point chorus and orchestra suddenly blaze out *fortissimo.* This is always a spine-tingling moment; on this occasion, the audience broke into applause so thunderous that the performance had to be halted, while Haydn 'the tears streaming down his pallid cheeks and as if overcome by the most violent emotions, raised his trembling arms to Heaven, as in prayer to the Father of Harmony', as the *Allgemeine Musikalische Zeitung* put it.

This surely was one of the most memorable musical moments of modern Europe. The event was recorded pictorially by the miniaturist Balthasar Wigand, at the request of Princess Esterházy, who presented the result to Haydn.[65] At the beginning of his career, Haydn became famous because he was the *Kapellmeister* for the Esterházys; by the time he died, the Esterházys were famous because their *Kapellmeister* was Haydn. He died on 31 May 1809 when Vienna was under French occupation, but not before giving Napoleon the opportunity to pay his respects by having an honour guard posted outside the dying man's door.[66]

Mozart, Beethoven and the Perils of the Public Sphere

In following Haydn's life to its conclusion, we have skipped over a composer of at least equal stature but much less happy fortunes. To be the slave of such a benign and musically gifted autocrat as Prince Nicholas Esterházy was one thing. To be subject to Hieronymus Count von Colloredo, archbishop of Salzburg, was quite another. The contrasting experiences of the two supreme musicians of the second half of the eighteenth century illustrate well the randomness of life as a creative artist under the old regime. For all his occasional grumbles, Franz Joseph Haydn lived and died a loyal servant of his patron. Wolfgang Amadeus Mozart famously did not. His emancipation from Colloredo, deemed by some to be nothing less than 'a declaration of war between the new bourgeois world and the old regime of artistic production', demonstrated emphatically that he did not find the bars on his particular cage to be gilded in the slightest.[67]

In Mozart's opinion, his patron was unappreciative and miserly, conferring neither material benefit nor prestige. He angrily wrote to his father from Vienna in March 1781:

> What you say about the Archbishop is to a certain extent perfectly true—I mean, as to the manner in which I tickle his ambition. But of what use is all this to me? I can't subsist on it. Believe me, I am right in saying that he acts as a *screen* to keep me from the notice of others. What distinction, pray, does he confer upon me? Herr von Kleinmayr and Bönike [archiepiscopal officials] have a separate table with the illustrious Count Arco. It would be some distinction if I sat at that table, but there is none in sitting with the valets who, when they are not occupying the best seats at table have to light the chandeliers, open the doors and wait in the anteroom *(when I am within)*—and with the cooks too![68]

Not unreasonably, Mozart concluded that his employer was trying to treat him like a piece of property. As he went on to complain in this letter, his request for permission to play at a charity concert of the Society of Musicians, where he would have had the opportunity to win 'the favour of the Emperor and of the public', was turned down flat. Haydn might have composed another *Farewell Symphony*, but Mozart was not Haydn. He was not Haydn because he was a generation younger (born in 1756), had travelled extensively in Europe as a child prodigy, was encouraged in his social aspirations by his ambitious father and possessed a much less phlegmatic temperament. He kicked hard against the pricks and was duly chastised. In June 1781, after a blazing row about the date on which he should leave Vienna to return to Salzburg, Mozart was ejected from the archbishop's service in the most literal possible way.

In a letter to his father, he described what happened when he went to present a petition to the chief steward, Count Arco: 'Instead of taking my petition or procuring me an audience or advising me to send in the document later or persuading me to let the matter lie and to consider things more carefully—*enfin*, whatever he wanted—Count Arco hurls me out of the room and gives me a kick on my arse. Well, that means in our language that Salzburg is no longer the place for me, except to give me the favourable opportunity of returning the Count's kick, even if it should have to be in the public street.'[69]

So Mozart went freelance. He was well placed to do so, being able to draw on four main sources of income: commissions for new works, ticket sales from concerts at which he performed as a pianist, royalties from publishers, and music lessons. In addition, in 1787 he was appointed imperial chamber composer, a sinecure which paid 800 gulden annually. Volkmar Braunbehrens has estimated that his total salary was roughly equivalent to that of a senior civil servant.[70] It was a good thing that he commanded this kind of earning power, for he liked to live well in comfortable accommodations, to maintain his own horse and carriage and to dress like an aristocrat. When the pianist-composer Muzio Clementi first met Mozart, he assumed that he must be a courtier, so elegant was his attire.[71]

Mozart liked to consort with nobles, and he derived most of his income from them. If only the greatest magnates could afford to maintain their own orchestras on a permanent basis, many more could form ensembles when the need arose from the large pool of freelance musicians living in the capital.[72] The high level of musical education enjoyed by the Viennese nobles made them unusually receptive to innovative music of high quality. During his first year as a freelance musician in Vienna, Mozart gave concerts at the residences of Countess Thun, Count Cobenzl, Prince Galitzin and Archduke Maximilian Franz (Emperor Joseph II's brother). As he proudly told his father, 'If you really believe that I am detested at Court and by the old and new aristocracy, just write to Herr von Strack, Countess Thun, Countess Rumbeck, Baroness Waldstätten, Herr von Sonnenfels, Frau von Trattner, *enfin,* to anyone you choose'.[73] A year later he wrote of Prince Galitzin: 'I am engaged for all his concerts. I am always fetched in his coach and brought to his house and treated there most magnificently'.[74]

These noble connoisseurs also played a crucial role in promoting the success of the other main vehicle for new music—the 'academy' or benefit concert mounted by a composer-performer acting as his own impresario. Mozart's success in attracting noble support for his subscription concerts got him off to a flying start in the capital. The list of 176 subscribers was nothing less than 'a roll call of the higher nobility, with room left over for luminaries of the lesser nobility and state bureaucracy'.[75] Fifty percent were from the high nobility, forty-two percent from the lesser nobility and only eight percent from the bourgeoisie. In other words, whether Mozart was performing in palaces or public rooms, the audience consisted mainly of nobles. It was with them in mind that he wrote the symphonies, serenades, vocal works and—above all—the piano concertos which made up his programmes. As his copious correspondence with his father during these years make clear, he kept eyes and ears fixed firmly on what his customers wanted.

Mozart showed that a gifted and energetic musician-composer could do well in the public sphere—but only when times were good. When they took a turn for the worse in the late 1780s, he may well have envied the security that Haydn's position in the Esterházy household gave him. Why he experienced the acute financial problems that forced him to move four times in eighteen months to ever cheaper accommodation and to solicit loans from friends is still not entirely clear. Speculation that he incurred debts from gambling has never been substantiated. What is clear is that his wife Constanze suffered a long illness, beginning in 1788, which necessitated heavy expenditure on doctors, medicine and spells at a spa. Even more serious was the war with the Turks that began in the summer of 1787 and led to a mass exodus of noble army officers to their regiments and a correspondingly sharp contraction of Vienna's cultural life. To make matters worse, this coincided with a Europe-wide economic recession.[76] It turned out to be a temporary blip. The end of the war in the summer of 1790 returned the situation to something approaching normal, encouraged by the death of the turbulent Joseph II and the accession of his eirenic brother Leopold. In the last year of his life Mozart was once again earning substantial sums, which allowed him to pay off his debts and, among other things, to send his son to an expensive private school.

The first performance of *La Clemenza di Tito* in Prague on 6 September 1791 and of *The Magic Flute* in Vienna later the same month showed Mozart at the height of his powers in both *opera seria* (grand opera sung in Italian) and *Singspiel* (popular ballad-opera sung in German). Never had his international reputation stood higher, as invitations from European capitals from London to St. Petersburg and the offer of pensions from groups as diverse as the merchants of Amsterdam and the magnates of Hungary demonstrated.[77] He may have been buried without ceremony—as was the custom at the time—but his achievement was recognised in public and private and his memory was venerated.[78] If he had not been carried off by rheumatic fever at the age of thirty-five, most likely he would have enjoyed a degree of material success and prestige at least comparable to that achieved by Haydn. The enthusiastic reception accorded to *The Magic Flute* pointed the way.

What Mozart and Haydn had in common was the massive contribution they made to raising both the status of music, by the quality of their compositions, and the status of the musician, by their demonstration of what could be achieved in the rapidly changing social and cultural conditions of the late eighteenth century. Their musical heir, Ludwig van Beethoven, built on their achievement. In the year that Haydn died, Beethoven was offered a post at the court of Westphalia, the new kingdom created by Napoleon for his brother Jerome. Beethoven was sensible enough not to accept but also shrewd enough to use it to improve his material conditions in Vienna. It is some measure of both his personal standing and the importance now attached to music that three aristocrats should have clubbed together to guarantee him an annual income of 4,000 gulden, payable for life, for as long as he remained in Austria. In the contract they paid tribute to his 'extraordinary talent and genius as a musical artist and composer'. This had prompted them to free him from the mundane cares of earning a living so that he might devote himself solely to creating 'great and sublime works ennobling the arts'.[79] Also revealing was the nature of the relationship he enjoyed with his three benefactors—Prince Lobkowitz, Prince Kinsky and the Archduke Rudolph (Emperor Francis I's brother), for it was more akin to friendship than patronage.

This was the only sort of relationship that Beethoven would accept. In twenty-first-century parlance, Beethoven had *attitude*. It was not just the revolutionary originality of his music and his phenomenal pianistic skills that forced contemporaries to view him as so much more than a musician. It was also his behaviour, his way of life, his clothes, even—one might almost say especially—his appearance. The number of people who actually experienced Beethoven at first hand was very small, but his image was broadcast far and wide. He was the first musician to become the centre of a cult, a legend in his own time. In the year that Beethoven died, the fourteen-year-old Richard Wagner heard one of his symphonies (the Seventh) for the first time and was bowled over. But what threw him into a characteristically Wagnerian frenzy of enthusiasm was not just the sounds he heard in the Leipzig Gewandhaus but also 'the added impact of Beethoven's physiognomy, as shown by lithographs of the time, as well as the knowledge of his deafness and his solitary and withdrawn life. There soon arose in me an image of the highest supernal originality, beyond comparison with anything'.[80]

The visual projection of a musician's image is today so integral a part of his or her work that it is taken for granted. Just imagine Elton John or Beyoncé trying to operate in a world without the means of visual representation. Yet for most of recorded history musicians have not been depicted as individuals at all, but were rather subsumed in symbolic images of music *per se* as Orpheus, Apollo, King David, Pythagoras, Saint Cecilia or 'Lady Music'.[81] Not until the later part of the fifteenth century did independent portraits of specific musicians begin to be painted, the finest being Hans Memling's portrait of the Flemish singer-composer Gilles Joye in 1472.[82]

By no coincidence, the first musician to be celebrated visually by contemporaries was Claudio Monteverdi, who was operating in the relatively public musical world of Venice and whose fame was his alone, not a reflection of a great princely patron. Bernardo Strozzi's portrait of 1640 is no

Monteverdi by Bernardo Strozzi (1640).

less eloquent for presenting him simply and directly, eschewing any Baroque representation. This same iconic image reappeared on the frontispiece of Giovanni Battista Marinoni's poetic tribute, published three years later to mark Monteverdi's funeral. The latter was a public event, as the obituarist recorded: 'The news of such a loss turned all the city to sadness and mourning, and was accompanied not by singing from the choir of singers of San Marco, but by their tears and weeping.'[83]

Employment by a city rather than a prince was no guarantee of visual recognition, however, as the example of Johann Sebastian Bach demonstrated. Although Bach was the greatest composer of his and perhaps any other age, only one undisputed contemporary portrait of him exists, painted in three versions by Elias Gottlob Haussmann in 1746–50 toward the very end of Bach's life. The first version was commissioned by the composer himself, to fulfill the conditions of joining Lorenz Christof Mizler's

Johann Sebastian Bach by Elias Gottlob Haussmann (1746).

Corresponding Society of the Musical Sciences, a private and very exclusive club with only thirteen other members (Handel had been the twelfth to join). The second and third versions were probably painted for his sons Carl Philip Emmanuel and Wilhelm Friedemann, respectively.[84] And that was that. Not the least reason that J. S. Bach seems so much more remote than the next generation of composers is the difficulty of visualising him. As the very different pictorial history of his exact contemporary, Handel, shows, an urban setting was not enough. What was needed was an urban environment with the depth and breadth to sustain a demand for a visual image.

The catalogue of the exhibition staged at the National Portrait Gallery in London in 1985 to mark the tricentenary of Handel's birth opened with the resounding claim: 'Images of Handel abound. He was portrayed

George Frederick Handel by Thomas Hudson (1756).

more often than any other great composer of his century and perhaps of any century'.[85] The images are as revealing as they are numerous. A simple juxtaposition of Haussmann's portrait of Bach with Thomas Hudson's second portrait of Handel is more eloquent than a paragraph of prose. In the former, Bach is depicted as a simple burgher, dressed in a plain blue jacket and white linen, holding the highly technical piece of music he presented to Mizler's society, namely, a triple canon in six parts (BWV 1076). Handel, on the other hand, is very much the gentleman, sitting on the terrace of his mansion, resplendent in a silk suit, and with gold everywhere—on the elaborately embroidered brocade of his jacket, on the buckles of his shoes, on the handle of the cane he grasps and on the hilt of the sword he wears at his waist. In front of him stands not a technical piece accessible only to his fellow musicians but the score of *Messiah,* an oratorio that was performed in public—and could even be performed *by* the public—and exemplified his achievement of fame and fortune in a metropolitan public sphere.

London was also responsible for the pictorial discrepancy between Haydn and Mozart. The latter's image has been reproduced more often than any other musician working in the classical tradition, thanks to the vigorous promotion of the Mozart 'brand', beginning in the late nineteenth century with the marketing of confectionery bearing his name. Just the number of times his image has adorned *Mozartkugel*—balls of pistachio-flavoured marzipan covered in nougat with an outer layer of chocolate—must run into billions. Yet his pictorial legacy is surprisingly sparse. Although estimates vary, the best guess is that only twelve contemporary portraits of him have survived.[86] And several of those have little value, either aesthetically or as likenesses. The best one, painted by his brother-in-law Joseph Lange in 1789–90, was left unfinished, whereas the most frequently reproduced one—by Barbara Krafft—was not painted until nearly thirty years after Mozart's death.

Haydn of course lived more than twice as long as Mozart, but even so both the quantitative and qualitative superiority of his contemporary portraits is striking. Their provenance also demonstrates Haydn's enviable capacity for having the best of both the aristocratic and public worlds. The first portrait, painted in 1768, was probably commissioned by Prince Esterházy and shows Haydn in his employer's livery. The best, painted by Thomas Hardy in 1792, was commissioned by the London music publisher John Bland, who of course then had it engraved, reproduced and put on sale.[87]

Also of high quality and also produced in London was the portrait painted by John Hoppner for the prince of Wales. It is both sad and revealing that the best-known picture of Mozart performing, by Michel Barthélemy Ollivier, shows him as a child prodigy playing in the Parisian salon of the prince de Conti, whereas Haydn's equivalent is Balthasar Wigand's painting at the performance of *The Creation* a year before his death.

This brings us back to Beethoven, and Wagner's emotional response to his appearance. While Haydn or Mozart had admirers, Beethoven had fans—and significantly, the word derives from 'fanatic'. The sonic gulf that separates even the final symphonies of Mozart and Haydn from the *Eroica* is mirrored in visual representations. Beethoven's fans wanted to know what their hero looked like, and the publishing houses of Vienna were only too happy to oblige. Across Europe, music lovers could see that Beethoven's appearance matched his compositions—passionate, indomitable, exciting, untamed, above all *original*. What was more, he could be viewed in three dimensions, for Franz Klein took a life mask in 1812 and then used it as the basis for a wonderfully expressive portrait bust. Contemporaries had many reasons to feel that they knew Beethoven better than any previous musician, but this unprecedented visual access was certainly one of them.

Much can be learned about an artist's standing during his life by the manner in which his death is marked. In the case of Beethoven, it is thrown into sharper relief when compared with events following Mozart's demise a generation earlier. No one knows exactly when Mozart was buried, not even the day. According to his widow, Constanze, he died at 1 A.M. on 5 December 1791. At 3 P.M. on the following day or on the day after that (the surviving documents are not clear), the body was taken to St. Stephen's Cathedral, where it was blessed in front of the Crucifix Chapel and was then transported on a hearse through the Stuben Gate, then along the Landstrasse to the new cemetery of St. Marx.[88] The actual interment may have taken place on the same day—the 6th or 7th depending on which authority one follows, or more likely on the 7th or 8th, given the lateness of the hour. If some of the crasser myths surrounding Mozart's obsequies have been exploded, the fact remains that it was a very muted send-off. No one was present at the graveside, apart from the sexton and the priest, and no gravestone was erected to mark the spot.

How different was the treatment of Beethoven thirty-six years later. As he lay dying, presents—including cash—flooded in from all over Eu-

Mozartkugel advertisement.

rope. His last words before slipping into unconsciousness were 'Pity, pity—too late'—his disappointed reaction to the arrival from Mainz of a case of his favourite Rhine wine.[89] When he died at around 5:45 P.M. on Monday, 26 March 1827, his friends had already selected an appropriate plot in Vienna's Währing cemetery. Once he was officially pronounced dead, they set about arranging an autopsy, preserving Beethoven's physical likeness for posterity through a drawing and a death mask by Joseph Danhauser, and safeguarding his possessions. They also kept a vigil alongside the 'polished oak coffin which rested on ball-shaped gilded supports' and which was surrounded by eight candles, as the throngs of those wishing to pay their last respects filed past.

Three days later the funeral took place, beginning at three in the afternoon. Formal invitations had been issued, and a school holiday had been declared by the authorities.[90] As the coffin was carried down into the courtyard of the House of the Black-Robed Spaniard, nine priests from the Schottenstift intoned a blessing and a choir drawn from the Italian Opera sang a chorale by Anselm Weber. So dense had the crowd become that the procession had great difficulty starting off, as one can see from Franz Stober's cele-brated painting. (That a visual ac-

Beethoven by Franz Klein (1812).

count of his funeral was deemed necessary was itself significant.) When eventually it did get going, a second choir sang the *Miserere* to trombone accompaniment. Along the road, so many people 'from all classes and es-tates', as a report in *Berliner Allgemeine Musikalische Zeitung* put it, had gathered that the procession to the church of the Holy Trinity in the Alser-gasse took one-and-a-half hours to cover the 500 yards.[91] One of the thirty-six torch bearers was Franz Schubert. After the funeral service, the cortège, still numbering in the thousands, formed up again for the journey to the Währing cemetery.[92] The contrast with Mozart's last journey could hardly have been more stark. At some point between the death of Mozart and the death of Beethoven, the status of the musician had been transformed.

This was not all. At the gates of the Währing cemetery, the classical actor Heinrich Anschütz delivered an oration written by Austria's most celebrated dramatist, Franz Grillparzer. This last episode distinguished Beethoven's funeral from anything that had gone before. But if this was the first grand funeral for a musician in continental Europe, it had been antici-pated in London, where Handel had been given a tremendous send-off back in 1759. The service in Westminster Abbey before a packed congregation of 3,000 had included a great deal of music sung by the combined choirs of the Chapel Royal, St. Paul's Cathedral and the abbey itself.[93] The difference was that Handel's had been an exclusively religious service, as was appropriate for a man of such deep piety. Grillparzer's funeral oration for Beethoven, on the other hand, did not mention God at all. The only deity recognised was music *per se* and its high priest, Beethoven. At some point between 1759 and 1827, music had been sacralised.

We shall come back to this in the next chapter. Here, it is Beethoven's impact as a role model that must be addressed. He refused to conform not only to the conventional musician-patron relationship, he also turned his back on the public. He would accept a pension, board and lodging from Prince Lichnowsky—but only if he could live as a member of the family.[94] One of Beethoven's pupils, Carl Czerny, referred to the prince as 'Beethoven's friend . . . he treated him like a friend and a brother and persuaded the whole of the high nobility to support him.'[95] Beethoven dedicated several works to the emperor's brother, Archduke Rudolf—the Fifth (*Emperor*) Piano Concerto, op. 73, the *Archduke Trio,* op. 97, and the *Missa Solemnis,* op. 123, among them—but he did so as teacher and friend, not as supplicant.

At this point, allowance must be made for myth-making. So potent was the image Beethoven projected to his contemporaries that some of them could not resist embroidering, gilding and even inventing. A good example was the 'incident at Teplitz'. According to Bettina von Brentano, in 1812 Beethoven and Goethe were walking together in the park at the Bohemian spa Bad Teplitz when they encountered the Emperor Francis I and his family, including Archduke Rudolf. Ever the suave courtier, Goethe stepped to one side, bowing deeply, whereas Beethoven stayed defiantly upright, saying, 'Keep hold my arm, they must make room for us, not we for them', and kept on walking, brusquely pushing his way through the imperial party.[96] Unfortunately, the letter from Beethoven to Bettina von Brentano, which allegedly described this incident, has not survived. She herself did not refer to it until twenty years later. It may well be true, for Goethe did meet Beethoven at Bad Teplitz and did comment on his 'utterly untamed personality', while Beethoven did criticise Goethe for being too much the courtier. For an understanding of Beethoven's contemporary impact, this does not matter very much. It was just one of many similar anec-

Beethoven's funeral procession in 1827 by Franz Stober.

dotes making the rounds of educated Europeans, designed to illustrate his craggy independence and contempt for convention.

Yet if Beethoven was prepared to accept high society only on his own terms, he was equally distanced from the general public. Although his growing deafness cut him off from most social intercourse, he lived in amongst the Viennese and knew what was happening to the city's musical culture. It changed rapidly during his thirty-five years there, in response to two complementary developments. On the one hand, the great magnates such as Prince Lichnowsky and Prince Lobkowitz were experiencing intense financial pressure as a result of the wars of 1787–1815. Among the first casualties were their musical establishments. As early as 1795 a musical periodical could report that only Prince Schwarzenberg's orchestra was still in existence; by 1800 they were all gone.[97] On the other hand, the ever-accelerating growth of the city's population created a correspondingly larger musical public. So a group of impresarios emerged to feed its appetite, organising public concerts for anyone who could afford the price of a ticket.

These paying audiences were given what they wanted, and that was easy listening in the form of plenty of variety, good tunes, regular rhythms and pieces that were not too long or demanding.[98] Concerts such as the marathon organised by Beethoven at the Theater an der Wien on 22 December 1808, which included his Fifth and Sixth Symphonies, Fourth Piano Concerto and Fantasia for Piano, Chorus and Orchestra, op. 80, ceased to be viable. Increasingly, public concerts took the form of pot-pourris, mainly comprising popular overtures, operatic arias and dance tunes, with at best a single movement of a symphony or a concerto. In particular, the enduring craze for dance music led to the reorchestration of even choral music and oratorios into waltz or polka time to allow toes to tap, the *non plus ultra* surely being the 'Stabat Mater Quadrille'.[99]

Long and loud were the complaints from composers that the public did not appreciate them but preferred the jaunty tunes and rumpty-tumpty orchestration of Italian opera. Although deeply disapproving of all this, a critic writing in the *Allgemeine Musikalische Zeitung* put his finger on the impetus that lay behind it: the music developed by Haydn, Mozart and Beethoven and their followers had become too complex for the general public, who had turned to the Italians for simple enjoyment.[100] Italians liked to put it another way: 'Teutonic accompaniments do not constitute a guard of honour for the melody, but a police escort'.[101] To the hour came the man, and the man was Rossini. As Stendhal commented: 'Light, lively, amusing, never wearisome, but seldom exalted—Rossini would appear to have been brought into this world for the express purpose of conjuring up visions of ecstatic delight in the commonplace soul of the Average Man'.[102]

This disdain was echoed by the music critics, who lamented that popularisation had degenerated into vulgarisation. In 1820, shortly after Beethoven had composed the Hammerklavier Sonata in B-flat, op. 106, which convinced some contemporaries that he was mad as well as deaf, the influential *Allgemeine Musikalische Zeitung* complained that the flood of piano transcriptions of popular operatic arias was killing off the sonata, for which a special musical orphanage should be established.[103] So when in 1824 a group of noble connoisseurs persuaded Beethoven to give a concert after a gap of ten years, they appealed to his patriotism, lamenting that foreign taste had taken over in Vienna.[104] Beethoven's own comment on the prevailing fashion for Italian opera, conveyed two years later in a conversation with Hummel, was characteristically pithy: 'It is said *vox populi, vox dei*—I never believed it'.[105]

Rossini, Paganini, Liszt—the Musician as Charismatic Hero

During Beethoven's last years, the *vox* of the *populi* was not so much calling as shrieking for Italian opera, especially for Rossini. When the latter visited Vienna in 1822, the *Allgemeine Musikalische Zeitung* reported: 'It was really enough, more than enough. The entire performance was like an idolatrous orgy; everyone there acted as if he had been bitten by a tarantula; the shouting, crying, yelling of "viva" and "forza" went on and on'.[106] Six years later, an English visitor complained that 'the people of Vienna are Rossini mad, but they are mad not only for him, but mad for his worst imitators: with good ears they tolerate the worst of music'.[107]

Not only in Vienna but across Europe, Rossini bestrode the musical scene like a colossus. His stupendous success was the clearest possible sign that the musical public sphere had come of age. In his own country, moreover, this sphere was wide enough to embrace a large section of the urban population. The English poet William Rose reported from Venice in 1819 that Rossini's arias were sung by workmen 'with as much passion as the most *tolerolo* tunes are bawled about in England'. His friend and fellow expatriate Lord Byron, who knew a thing or two about popular adulation, wrote at about the same time, 'There has been a splendid opera lately at San Benedetto—by Rossini—who came in person to play the harpsichord—the people followed him about—crowned him—cut off his hair "for memory"—he was shouted for and sonnetted and feasted—and immortalised much more than either of the emperors'.[108]

As this last comment suggests, public hero worship was taking the musician into spheres previously reserved for kings and generals. In 1824 Stendhal published his *Life of Rossini*, which begins: 'Napoleon is dead; but a new conqueror has already shown himself to the world; and from Moscow to Naples, from London to Vienna, from Paris to Calcutta, his name is constantly on every tongue. The fame of this hero knows no bounds save those of civilisation itself; and he is not yet thirty-two! The task which I have set myself is to trace the paths and circumstances which have carried him at so early an age to such a throne of glory.'[109] Rossini's earnings were in proportion: in just one season in London in 1823 he is reputed to have earned £30,000 net, a substantial fortune by the standards of the time.[110] So rich was he by the end of the decade that he could spend the next forty years in opulent retirement, never writing another opera. He appears to have been well aware of his status, informing George IV when they met that 'His Majesty was then standing between the two greatest men in Europe—Rossini and Wellington.'[111]

Rossini was a charismatic musician who could establish a direct relationship with the audience, and this, according to Stendhal, was the secret of his fame. In the recent past, the words 'charisma' and 'charismatic' have been so debased by overuse and careless application to any public figure that catches the attention of journalists as to become little more than synonyms for 'glamour' and 'glamorous'. But originally 'charisma' meant simply 'gift from God', and its modern usage stems from Max Weber's tripartite categorisation of legitimate authority into traditional authority, legal authority, and charismatic authority. Traditional authority derived its legitimacy simply from having existed since time out of mind ('the authority of the eternal yesterday', as he poetically put it). Legal authority was based on a contract between ruler and ruled. Charismatic authority stemmed from 'the extraordinary and personal gift of grace (charisma), the absolutely personal devotion and personal confidence in revelation, heroism, or other qualities of individual leadership'.[112] In early modern Europe, charisma was deemed to derive directly from God, bestowed at the sovereign's coronation in the form of the sacramental anointing. That was why French kings, for example, went straight from the coronation ceremony to heal the sick of 'the King's evil' (scrofula) through touching, for they were now *rois thaumaturges*, equipped with miracle-working powers.

With the French Revolution's radical secularisation of political authority, this external source of charisma was discarded. Now charisma became a purely internal quality, derived exclusively from the personal qualities of the individual. The first modern autonomous charismatic leader was Napoleon Bonaparte, who started with nothing, believed in nothing, achieved everything and ended with nothing. But virtually all those who met him, whatever they thought of him, commented on the extraordinary force of his personality, charm, authority, sense of destiny, self-assurance—in a word, charisma. So when he chose to be crowned emperor of the French on 2 December 1804, he placed the imperial crown on his own head.

Setting the pattern for later leaders, he insisted on a direct, personal relationship with his soldiers and his subjects, unmediated by parliamentary institutions and franked only by plebiscites. To his faithful servant Pierre-Louis Roederer he observed that a constitution should be 'short, and . . .'—he hesitated. 'Clear?' suggested Roederer. 'No, short and *obscure*', replied Napoleon.[113] From the start, his lucid appreciation of the power of personal myth in the cultivation of public opinion led him to found his own newspaper in Italy to propagate the right image not just to his army but also to the home front.[114] For good or ill, his amazing roller-coaster ride shattered old Europe, demonstrating in the process all the explosive force—and all the implosive risks—of a regime based solely on charisma.

This dangerous new world ushered in by Napoleon had as profound an effect on culture as it did on state and society. Of all the arts, music was best placed to take advantage of the promotion of charisma as a legitimator. Stendhal's equation of Rossini with Napoleon was not fanciful but a prophetic insight. Had Stendhal lived in the late twentieth century and witnessed the incomparably greater impact exerted by Elvis Presley or John Lennon, he would have had every reason to feel vindicated.

In the immediate aftermath of the Napoleonic episode, the musician who traced out the shape of things to come was the violinist Niccolò Paganini. The bare bones of his career can be recounted quickly. Born at Genoa in 1782, he was middle-aged before he made an impact outside Italy. His reputation blazed briefly between 1828 and 1834 before ill health forced him into semi-retirement. He died in 1840. But in those few years of touring he took Europe by storm, his stupendous skill as a violinist giving new meaning to the word *virtuoso*. He also earned a colossal fortune in a very short space of time. Just before returning to Italy in 1834 as a burnt-out case, he told a German journalist that he had given 162 concerts in the space of twelve months, earning 42,000 francs at one of them (in London).[115]

Not only audiences but musicians, intellectuals and critics fell at his feet. His first performance in Paris was attended by Auber, Delacroix, Donizetti, Halévy, Heine, Liszt, Musset, Rossini and George Sand. After his

Niccolò Paganini by J. A. D. Ingres (1819).

first performance in London in 1831, the critic of *The Times* wrote: 'He is not only the finest player that has ever existed on that instrument, but he forms a class by himself'.[116] In Vienna, where by the 1830s normally anything or anyone Italian was treated with disdain by intellectuals, a critic wrote: 'With each new achievement the conviction deepens that he is the greatest instrumentalist the world of music has ever known'.[117]

No voice was raised in dissent: Paganini's technical skill was phenomenal. But there was much more to it than that. He attracted—and carefully cultivated—an aura of mystery, danger, even diabolism. That his career had taken off so late was thought to be especially suggestive. A rumour circulated that he had perfected his technique while serving twenty years in prison for murdering his mistress—indeed, that his G string was made from a section of her intestine.[118] Others went further: no one could play so well without supernatural assistance, so Paganini must have captured the Devil in his sound box or made a Faustian pact with the Devil, sacrificing his soul in return for matchless skill. It was further alleged that he never allowed anyone to see him without footwear, lest his cloven hoof should become visible. In Vienna, some members of the audience claimed to have seen the Devil directing his bow, thus allowing him to play at superhuman speed.[119] A French musical periodical exclaimed in 1831: '[Paganini is] Satan on stage . . . Fall to the knees of Satan and worship him.'[120]

Paganini by Ferdinand-Victor-Eugène Delacroix (1831).

Paganini himself was well aware of his special gifts, even before he began his triumphal progress through the capitals of Europe. In 1818 he wrote: 'There emanates from my playing a certain magic which I can't describe to you.'[121] If his admirers did not use the actual word 'charisma', this was what they had in mind when they struggled to articulate their response. No less a figure than Goethe observed: 'The demonic is that which cannot be explained in a cerebral and a rational manner. It is not peculiar to my nature but I am subject to its spell. Napoleon possessed the quality to the highest degree. Among artists one encounters it more often with musicians than with painters. Paganini is imbued with it to a remarkable degree and it is through this that he produces such a great effect'.[122]

Other first-hand tributes are equally impossible to ignore: Schubert's comment after a concert was that he had 'heard an angel sing'; Berlioz (normally dismissive of his fellow musicians) called him 'a Titan among the giants'; Heine lauded him as 'the glory of his country'; and so on.[123] Although not the most prestigious in terms of the source, perhaps the most eloquent was the verse written on the score of Paganini's second violin concerto by one of the musicians who had performed it in Paris:

> In our present century nature wished
> To demonstrate her infinite power;
> To amaze the world she created two men:
> Bonaparte and Paganini![124]

A further indication of his fame was the fact that the three greatest living French artists—Ingres, Delacroix and David d'Angers—portrayed him in a drawing, a painting and a sculpture respectively.

Paganini was not above giving his natural talent a little assistance. To the technical repertoire of the musician he brought two characteristics that were eventually to become all-important: showmanship and sex appeal. To heighten tension, he perfected the art of the delayed entry to the concert platform, entering only when audience expectation had reached fever pitch. Of his numerous gimmicks, the most famous was to appear with three of the four violin strings dangling uselessly—and then to unleash a bravura piece on the sole survivor. He was also very careful to maintain his mystique by never allowing the music he played at his concerts to be published: he memorised his own contributions and took the orchestral parts away as soon as the performance was over.[125] The combination of much art and artifice was to create an image of great potency.

That sex appeal also played a part comes out clearly from contemporary accounts. If the public insisted more than ever before that its rulers and politicians should be models of chastity, they were more indulgent toward their cultural icons—and may even have been attracted by raffishness, as the immense popularity of Byron demonstrated. Certainly Paganini's rakish reputation did him no harm. His music, his lifestyle, his looks formed a complementary package. Although very different, the images presented by Ingres and Delacroix both show a man of very striking appearance—tall, elegant, slender to the point of emaciation, with strong features and luxuriant curly hair. As various fruitless attempts to arrest his syphilis took their toll, his oxymoronic beauty-ugliness began to slide toward the latter but, if anything, his appeal increased.

In *Florentine Nights* (1836) Heinrich Heine wrote as eloquent a word-picture of a Paganini concert as one can imagine short of an actual recording. It also captures perfectly the musician as charismatic hero:

> [After the intermission] Paganini again quietly set his violin to his chin, and with the first stroke of the bow, the wonderful transformation of tones began again. But now they were neither so startling in colour nor so marked. They issued calmly, majestically—moving, and swelling like organ chorales in a cathedral. Everything around him seemed to have expanded into colossal space, such as no bodily eye but only that of the spirit can grasp. A shining sphere hovered in the centre of this space, on which stood a man of giant stature and pride, playing the violin. Was that sphere the sun? I don't know. But in the features of the man I recognized Paganini, ideally beautiful, celestially transfigured, smiling, and at peace. His body was in the bloom of vigorous manhood, and a light-blue garment enclosed his noble limbs. The splendid locks of his black hair fell in waves about his shoulders; and as he stood there, firm and confident, a sublime divinity, and played the violin, it seemed as if all of creation were obeying his song. He was the human planet around whom the universe revolved, ringing out in measured raptures and beatific rhythms.[126]

Paganini blazed across the musical sky like a meteor, his burnt-out shell quickly falling back to earth. But long before he died in 1840, a far brighter and much more durable star had risen in the firmament. This was Franz Liszt, who was taken by his father from Vienna to Paris in 1823 at the age of twelve. Attending one of Paganini's concerts in 1832, he was completely bowled over: 'What a man, what a violin, what an artist! Heavens! What suffering, what misery, what tortures in those four strings! . . . As for his expression, his manner of phrasing—they are his very soul!' As he wrote to a friend afterward, so dwarfed did he feel when confronted by such a colossus that he sought to regain a sense of his own value by repeating Correggio's defiant remark when seeing Raphael's *St. Cecilia* at Bologna: 'I too am a painter!'[127]

That Liszt was as gifted a pianist as Paganini was a violinist was recognised by all who heard him. After his very first public concert, given at Vienna in March 1824, when he was still only twelve, the *Allgemeine Musikalische Zeitung* reported that some members of the audience had cried out 'A miracle!' while others suspected that some sort of trickery must be involved, until the piano was shifted to an oblique angle so that the audience could see that he really was playing himself.[128] The professionals were as impressed as the amateurs. In 1834 Mendelssohn came away from Erard's piano showroom in Paris shaking his head and proclaiming that he had just witnessed a miracle, for his fiendishly demanding new piano concerto had just been played by Liszt with great brilliance and without error, even though he had never set eyes on the score before.[129]

As with Paganini, flawless technique was only the start. Liszt also had the ability to inspire in his listeners the belief that he was superhuman, with the capacity to transport them to a level of aesthetic experience previously undreamt of. From the rich stock of contemporary testimony, the following will give some idea of the impact he made: 'When he appears, he will eclipse all others like a sun! Such a talent, or, rather, such powers, would make you believe in miracles!' (Caroline Boissier, 1832). 'When I first heard him I sat speechless for a quarter of an hour afterwards, in such a stupor of amazement had the man put me. Such execution, such limitless—truly limitless—execution no one else can possess. He plays sometimes so as to make your hair stand on end! He who has not heard Liszt can have no conception—literally no conception—of what his playing is' (Charles Hallé, 1837). 'I have never found any artist, except Paganini, to possess in so high a degree as Liszt this power of subjugating, elevating, and leading the public. We are overwhelmed by a flood of tones and feelings' (Robert Schumann, 1840). 'When Liszt entered the saloon, it was as if an electric shock passed through it . . . The whole of Liszt's exterior and movements reveal one of those persons we remark for their peculiarities alone; the Divine hand has placed a mark on them which makes them observable among thousands' (Hans Christian Andersen, 1840).[130]

The fame Liszt achieved was commensurate with his skill, and far greater than anything enjoyed by any previous musician. Wherever he went—and his tours took him all over Europe, from Galway to the Ukraine—crowned heads and their courtiers clamoured to meet him, flatter him and give him decorations. When he left Berlin in 1842, he rode in a carriage pulled by six white horses, accompanied by a procession of thirty other coaches and an honour guard of students, as King Frederick William IV and his queen waved goodbye from the royal palace. As the music critic Ludwig Rellstab put it, he left 'not *like* a king, but *as* a king'.[131] He was travelling on a passport issued by the Austrian authorities bearing the simple legend *Celebritate sua sat notus* (Sufficiently known by his fame).[132] Perhaps the climax—or rather *reductio ad absurdum*—was reached in 1845 when a rumour made the rounds that Liszt was going to marry the fifteen-year-old Queen Isabella II of Spain, who had created the title of duke of Pianozares for him.[133]

Liszt was everything that Paganini had been, but more so. He helped himself by promoting a much more sophisticated and cultured image. He sought escape from a relatively humble background—his father had been a clerk-musician employed by Prince Esterházy—not just by his art but also by his intellect. Highly intelligent and exceedingly well read, he cultivated the literary world of Paris, consorting with the likes of Balzac, Lamennais, Sainte-Beuve, Dumas, Heine, Victor Hugo and George Sand. When checking in to a hotel at Chamonix in 1836, he recorded in the register that his profession was musician-philosopher and that he was in transit from Doubt to Truth.[134]

The knowledge that he was the greatest pianist that had ever lived and that he could more than hold his own with even the cleverest people gave Liszt a legendary self-confidence. It was saved from any taint of arrogance by his equally legendary charm, generosity and approachability. He also endeared himself to the liberal bourgeoisie of Europe by his demonstrative indifference to social privilege. This began right at the top. In 1834, when they met at the Erard piano showrooms in Paris, King Louis Philippe reminded Liszt that he had once played for him when Louis Philippe was still duke of Orleans, adding that much had changed since then. Liszt replied curtly: 'Yes, Sire, but not for the better'.[135] More risky was the snub he delivered to the notoriously despotic Tsar Nicholas I in 1840 when the latter arrived late to his recital and started talking. Liszt immediately stopped playing and sat motionless with head bowed. When the tsar asked why the music did not continue, Liszt replied icily: 'Music herself should be silent when Nicholas speaks'.[136]

A man who was rude to kings and emperors was not likely to be impressed by aristocrats, who were indeed nonplussed by the 'self-sufficiency of his manners'.[137] In 1838 Heinrich Ehrlich, a pupil of another virtuoso,

A French caricature of Liszt with his famous—and phallic—
sword prominent.

Sigismond Thalberg, watched in amazement at a concert in Vienna as Liszt
'broke through all social barriers'. When he had finished his performance,
Liszt casually stepped down into the audience and conversed in French
with the members of the high nobility sitting in the front row 'as though he
were one of the family'. At the next concert, the nobility came to him: 'On the
platform, grouped closely around the artist, sat ladies of the highest aristocracy, with whom he chatted during the intervals'.[138] And not just chatted. As with Paganini, part and parcel of his charisma was his sex appeal.

An important part of his titanic image was his well-deserved reputation as a lady-killer, with a preference for ladies of the highest society. Among
his early conquests was the Countess Adèle Laprunarède, who later became the duchess de Fleury, and Countess Pauline Plater. When the latter
was asked to rank the three great pianists who had performed in her salon—Hiller, Chopin, and Liszt—she replied that Hiller would make the best
friend, Chopin the best husband, and Liszt the best lover. The relative merit
of their piano playing does not seem to have been her main concern.[139]

Liszt's most durable relationship was with Countess Marie d'Agoult,
scion of a rich German banking family and married into one of the oldest
families in France—her marriage contract with the count was witnessed by

A contemporary caricature of a Liszt concert at Berlin in 1842.

King Charles X. Nevertheless, she produced three illegitimate children with Liszt. One daughter, Blandine, married the French politician Émile Ollivier, who took France into the catastrophic war with Prussia in 1870, and another, Cosima, married first Hans von Bülow and then Richard Wagner.[140] 'A match made in heaven' was the well-publicised liaison Liszt enjoyed in the mid-1840s with Lola Montez (*née* Eliza Gilbert), the most notorious courtesan of her age, before she moved on to King Ludwig of Bavaria.

Between 1838 and 1846 Liszt appeared more than a thousand times in public across Europe, and everywhere he went he was received with rapture, especially by the female members of his audience. The *Oxford English Dictionary* records that the first use of 'Beatlemania' was in December 1963 when *The Times* defined it as a condition 'which finds expression in handbags, balloons and other articles bearing the likeness of the loved ones, or in the hysterical screaming of young girls whenever the Beatle Quartet performs in public'. 'Lisztomania' was invented by Heinrich Heine to identify a very similar phenomenon observed at Liszt's concerts: 'Frenzy unparalleled

Franz Liszt, lithograph by Josef Kriehuber (1846).

in the history of frenzy!' A specialist in women's diseases whom Heine consulted gave him a 'mysterious smile' and then talked at length about mass hysteria in a confined space when excited by a musical aphrodisiac.[141] Women wore his image on cameos and brooches, fought to collect the dregs of his coffee cup, tore his handkerchiefs and gloves to shreds, wore his cigar butts in diamond-encrusted lockets, turned his discarded piano wires into bracelets, and so on and so forth. A contemporary caricature of a Liszt concert at Berlin in 1842 shows the audience of excited women variously screaming, swooning, trying to storm the stage, observing him through binoculars (from the front row), and throwing flowers at him as he plays. Today only the nature of the missiles has changed.

Heine commented cynically that 'the whole enchantment is to be traced to the fact that no one in the world knows how to organise "successes" as well as Franz Liszt—or better, how to stage them. In that art, he is a genius'.[142] Certainly Liszt left nothing to chance. In particular, he had a very clear appreciation of the need to project the right visual image. He was lucky that, just as his career was beginning, a new and more efficient method of capturing and reproducing images was becoming available. This was lithography, invented by Alois Senefelder of Prague in 1798 and already well-established by the time the first lithograph of Liszt was produced in Vienna in 1823. Much better looking than Paganini, his strong features, luxuriant hair and dreamy expression lent themselves perfectly to the medium, as the numerous portraits produced by Josef Kriehuber demonstrate.[143] By the mid-1850s Liszt was also being photographed by the leading exponents of the new art, most notably by Franz Hanfstaengl of Munich. From that moment on, Liszt's career and life can be followed with a pictorial detail undreamt of by previous generations.

Advancing years did not diminish Liszt's capacity for exciting adoration. Seeing him in Munich in 1869, Judith Gautier (later the inamorata of
his son-in-law, Wagner) wrote: 'Was he a saint? They showed him such extraordinary veneration—the women above all! Hurrying towards him, they
virtually knelt down, kissed his hands and raised looks of ecstasy to his
face'. By this time, Liszt was in minor orders and was known as the Abbé
Liszt, but when Judith Gautier asked whether this made a difference, she
was told by a mutual friend: 'On the contrary, it excites them all the more,
having the attraction of the forbidden fruit!'[144]

What might Liszt's reputation be today if the necessary technology
had existed to record his performances? As it is, we have to rely on the impressions of contemporaries. Although these were as numerous as they
were enthusiastic, his achievement as a performer had to die with him. As
a composer, he is held in high regard—indeed, his reputation benefited
from a significant revival in the late twentieth century—but Liszt could not
be said to stand in the very first rank. Arguably his greatest achievement
was to complete the transition of musician from servant to master. This
was very well put by his biographer, Alan Walker, when he wrote:
'Beethoven, by dint of his unique genius and his uncompromising nature,
had forced the Viennese aristocracy at least to regard him as their equal.
But it was left to Liszt to foster the view that an artist is a superior being,
because divinely gifted, and the rest of mankind, of whatever social class,
owed him respect and even homage'.[145]

With Liszt the triumph of music seemed to reach insurmountable
heights. But, as is often the way, reaching the summit only served to reveal
an even higher peak in the distance. For there was a limit to what Liszt
could achieve. Although the impact he made on those who met him, saw
him perform or listened to his music was often profound, public life was
left largely untouched.

Richard Wagner and the Apotheosis of the Musician

That extra dimension was left to his even more imperious son-in-law, Richard Wagner. On 12 August 1876 the German Emperor William I and many
other princes travelled to the small Franconian town of Bayreuth to attend

the first performance of Wagner's four-part music-drama *The Ring of the Nibelung*, for which Wagner had composed the music, written the words, recruited the orchestra, singers and technicians, raised the money and built the theatre. In his retrospective account of the festival, Wagner wrote with justifiable pride: 'It seemed true indeed that never had an artist been thus honoured; for though it was not unknown for an artist to be summoned before an emperor and princes, no one could recall that an emperor and princes had ever come to him'.[146] Also present was the emperor of Brazil who, when he checked in at his hotel, wrote in the register under 'name': 'Pedro', and under 'profession': 'emperor'. Ludwig II, king of Bavaria, left after the dress rehearsals, to escape the crowds he detested so much (and to avoid his elderly Prussian uncle, whom he detested even more), but he wrote to Wagner: 'You are a god-man, the true artist by God's grace who has brought the sacred fire from heaven to earth to cleanse, sanctify and redeem it!'[147]

Among the composers attending were Bruckner, Tchaikovsky, Saint-Saëns, Vincent d'Indy, and Grieg.[148] According to a French musical periodical, eighteen journalists from France attended the opening, along with eighteen from England, fourteen from the United States, twenty from Berlin and thirteen from Vienna.[149] As the emperor himself observed to Wagner, the festival could be regarded as a 'national affair', although his comment was based on a fundamental misunderstanding of what Wagner was trying to achieve, as we shall see. In the short term, this imperial journey to the musician consummated the triumph of music. When he saw Wagner driving in an open landau to the railway station to greet his imperial guest, Sir George Henschel reflected on how things had changed since 1849 when Wagner had fled into exile pursued by the Saxon police: 'Truly a wonderful illustration of the all-conquering power of genius'.[150]

The imperial visit was celebrated in all manner of media. For example, a marketing card distributed with Liebig's Meat Extract showed Wagner receiving his imperial guest outside his theatre. This episode might be thought to represent the climax of the musician's elevation in the nineteenth century—less than a century had passed since Mozart had been literally booted out of the service of the archbishop of Salzburg. By the time Wagner died in 1883, he was already the unprotesting object of a cult, and the number of books and articles about him had reached five figures.[151] As for pictorial records, Wagner was drawn, painted, engraved,

On 12 August 1876, the German Emperor William I is driven through the streets of Bayreuth on his way from the railway station to Wagner's Festival Theatre.

etched, sculpted, silhouetted, lithographed and photographed on hundreds—thousands—of occasions.[152]

Wagner made greater claims for himself and his music than anyone ever before or since. He continues to be denounced and venerated with an intensity no other creative artist can inspire. One achievement not in doubt, however, was his positioning of music at the very centre of public life, from which it has never been dislodged. Many other forces were working in the same direction, but what dramatised music's arrival was Wagner's special belief in his own destiny and the paramount value of his art. Taking a long perspective, we can see that something of a ratchet effect had been at work, so that never again would the leading musician of the day have to eat with the servants.

But Wagner proved to be the last of his line. Such a combination of genius and personality has never recurred. So overpowering was his art that a reaction of corresponding magnitude could not be long delayed. Although at all levels Arnold Schoenberg can be seen as the great fount of modernism in music, his abandonment of tonality in 1908 and the development of the Second Viennese School were both symptom and cause of an ever-widening gulf between composers and public. As a growing num-

'Liebig's Meat-Extract. Wagner with Emperor William I in Bayreuth at the opening of the Festival Theatre 1876'. Standing behind Wagner are Franz Liszt and the conductor Hans Richter.

ber of composers journeyed on into ever more recondite realms, it began to look as though they were writing music mainly for one another. To pander to audiences who liked melody, harmony and rhythm came to seem like a sacrifice of integrity on the altar of commercial success. In 1997 Sir Harrison Birtwistle defended himself against charges of inaccessibility with the contemptuous remark: 'I can't be responsible for the audience: I'm not running a restaurant'.[153] So concert promoters and the audiences turned their backs on contemporary music in favour of the classics. This did not lead to a loss of status—on the contrary. But it did lead to a divorce of serious music from society at large.

The Triumph of the Musician in the Modern World

Although space does not permit every strand to be followed from Wagner's death in 1883 to the present day, the sustained rise in the status of musicians is not difficult to illustrate. The place once occupied by the composer as the mediator between music and society has been taken over, in the last century, by singers and conductors. Until the early nineteenth century, not just the word 'conductor' but the very concept of conducting was unknown. Any direction for the orchestra came from the *Kapellmeister* seated at the keyboard, who waved his hand, or from the first violinist, who waved his bow, and sometimes from both. For choral works they might be joined by a third person, who attempted to maintain communication between the two. They did little more than indicate the tempo, and could not have done much more, for they had only a single instrumental part in front of them, not the full score. As late as the 1820s, even Beethoven's symphonies were being played in Leipzig from just the parts.[154]

This began to change with the increase in the size of orchestras and the complexity of orchestral music during the first quarter of the nineteenth century. More or less simultaneously, around 1820 individual conductors began to use a baton and read from a full score; they also ceased playing an instrument while conducting. For the first seven years of its existence, the London Philharmonic Society, founded in 1813, listed in its programmes 'Leader Mr. X, Pianoforte Mr. Y', but with the second concert of 1820 the announcement changes to 'Leader, Mr. Spagnoletti; Conductor, Mr. Cramer'.[155] South of the Alps, where very little purely orchestral music was played and the relatively simple operatic scores made fewer demands on the players, the old order continued deep into the nineteenth century. At Naples in 1831 Hector Berlioz was irritated by the leader of the orchestra tapping continuously on his desk but was told that 'without it his musicians would sometimes have been hard put to it to play in time'. Berlioz commented: 'This was unanswerable', adding sourly 'and in any case one cannot expect orchestras of the quality of those of Berlin, Dresden or Paris in a country where instrumental music is almost unknown'.[156]

Progress elsewhere was rapid. In 1856 Berlioz himself wrote a short treatise on conducting with a baton in which he stressed that much more important than time-keeping was interpretation.[157] This development was then taken much further by Wagner, who can reasonably claim to have been the first star conductor.[158] By all accounts he was able to inspire his orchestras with his own vision of the work and also to make them play out of their skins. Anton Seidl wrote: 'As a conductor, technically and intellectually, Wagner can surely be given the highest place. He ruled the musicians completely with his gestures—yes, even sometimes with his eyes alone. He lifted them up into the fairy realms'.[159]

In transporting them there, Wagner provided powerful support for Carlyle's maxim that genius is an infinite capacity for taking pains. For his legendary performance of Beethoven's *Choral Symphony* in April 1848 Wagner insisted on twelve rehearsals of the double basses and cellos just for the recitative that begins the final movement.[160] Despite his modest stature (five foot five-and-a-half inches tall, which is a very good height to be), his charisma allowed him to dominate both players and audience.[161] The aura he gave to conductors was helped by the anecdotes that projected his image into the popular consciousness. In London, for example, he was criticised by the music critic of *The Times* for conducting the *Eroica* without a score, which was held to be disrespectful to Beethoven. So on the next occasion Wagner duly appeared on the podium with a score in front of him. This won the approval of his critics, until they discovered that it was *The Barber of Seville.*[162] His substantial treatise on the art of conducting in 1869 helped to perpetuate his achievement, as did the many young conductors who worked for him, notably Hans von Bülow, Hans Richter, Felix Mottl and Hermann Levi.

Conductors really came into their own in the twentieth century, as improved transportation and communication allowed them to travel the world and recordings brought their interpretations to a global audience. The glittering careers of Arturo Toscanini (1867–1957) or Wilhelm Furtwängler (1886–1954) exemplified the opportunities now available to interpreters as well as composers and performers. These opportunities have not just been musical and material; they have also had a strong social dimension. The comings and goings of the star conductors, their likes and dislikes, their relationships both marital and extramarital, continue to exercise the various media, from music critics to gossip columnists. Their batons have combined the command of a field marshal with the excitement of a phallic symbol.

The same sort of observations could be made about singers, and for the same sort of reasons. Of course stars have always existed. Sopranos and castrati especially commanded enormous salaries in the eighteenth century. In the nineteenth century, however, the ability to tour quickly, comfortably and cheaply allowed singers to take advantage of the ever-growing market for music and to become very rich and famous. Between September 1850 and June 1851 Jenny Lind, 'the Swedish Nightingale', gave ninety-five concerts in the United States and earned $176,675 net of all expenses. Along the way she was fêted as a queen.[163] As with conductors, the advent of recording increased singers' opportunities enormously. It also shifted the gender balance. The most famous singers of the nineteenth century had been mostly women—Giuditta Pasta, Adelaide Tosi, Adelina Patti, Maria Malibran, Jenny Lind, Teresa Stolz, to mention a few. The twentieth century produced many famous sopranos too, of course, but they were joined by male singers, especially tenors, beginning with Caruso, who recorded for the first time in 1902. In the 1990s the Three Tenors—Placido Domingo, Luciano Pavarotti and José Carreras—achieved colossal success with a series of stadium concerts for each of which each of them was reported to have been paid over a million dollars.[164]

In the United Kingdom, the sustained rise in the status of musicians can be followed in the formal recognition granted by the sovereign. Painters and architects were knighted freely in the days when the visual arts and architecture were the primary means of representing the power of the British throne: Anthony van Dyck in 1632, Christopher Wren in 1673, Peter Lely in 1679, Godfrey Kneller in 1692, John Vanbrugh in 1714, James Thornhill in 1720, Joshua Reynolds in 1768, William Chambers in 1770, and so on. Inigo Jones declined a knighthood in 1633. Some obvious talent was omitted from this list—Hogarth, Gainsborough, Blake, for example—but on the whole, deep into the nineteenth century, the surest way for a creative artist to acquire a title was to paint or build a work that would display the power of a royal patron for all to see.

Musicians got off to a very slow start in this competition. The first to be knighted was William Parsons in 1795, quickly followed by John Stevenson in 1795 and George Smart in 1811. Even those elevations were less impressive than they looked, for they were made not by the king (or prince regent) but by the lord lieutenants of Ireland. The first musician to be knighted by a reigning monarch was Henry Bishop in 1842.[165] In the second half of the century, the pace began to pick up. A simple list of names and dates is revealing: Michael Costa was knighted in 1869, William Sterndale Bennett in 1871, John Goss and Robert Prescott Stewart in 1872, George Grove, George Macfarren and Arthur Sullivan in 1883, John Stainer and Charles Hallé in 1888, Alexander Mackenzie in 1895, Frederick Bridge in 1897. Hubert Parry was knighted in 1898 and created baronet in 1902.

The pace was sustained during the first half of the twentieth century: Edward Elgar was knighted in 1904 and created a baronet in 1931, Henry Wood and Frederic Cowen were knighted in 1911, George Henschel in 1914, Thomas Beecham in 1916, William Hadow in 1918, Henry Walford Davies, Richard Terry and Dan Godfrey in 1922, Hamilton Harty in 1925, Edward German in 1928, Arthur Somervell in 1929, Granville Bantock in 1930, Donald Tovey in 1935, Arnold Bax and Adrian Boult in 1937, Malcolm Sargent in 1947, John Barbirolli in 1949, Arthur Bliss in 1950, and William Walton in 1951. Ralph Vaughan Williams (1872–1958) turned down several offers of knighthood. Ethel Smyth was appointed dame of the British Empire—the female equivalent of knighthood—in 1922. This does not pretend to be a complete list.

Nor has the knighting of musicians slackened in more recent times; on the contrary. Of the more prominent composers working in the United Kingdom during the second half of the twentieth century, Michael Tippett was knighted in 1966, Lennox Berkeley in 1974, Benjamin Britten was given a peerage in 1976, Peter Maxwell Davies was knighted in 1987, Harrison Birtwistle in 1988, Richard Rodney Bennett in 1998, Andrew Lloyd Webber was knighted in 1992 and given a peerage in 1997, Malcolm Arnold was knighted in 1993. Of the conductors operating today, the following are knights: David Willcocks (1977), Charles Mackerras (1979), Colin Davis (1980), Neville Marriner (1985), Roger Norrington (1977), Simon Rattle (1994), John Eliot Gardiner (1998), Andrew Davis (1999), Philip Ledger (1999), and Richard Armstrong (2004). To their number can be added music administrators such as John Tooley (1979) and Peter Jonas (2000), producers such as George Martin (1996) and even disc jockeys such as Jimmy Savile (1990).

Singers and instrumentalists also picked up momentum as the twentieth century progressed, as the following selection of elevations shows: Charles Santley (1911), Nellie Melba (1918), Harry Lauder (1919), Maggie Teyte (1958), Eva Turner (1962), Geraint Evans (1969), Joan Hammond (1974), Vera Lynn (1975), Janet Baker (1976), Peter Pears (1977), Joan Sutherland (1979), Kiri Te Kanawa (1982), Bob Geldof (1986), Gwyneth Jones (1986), Cliff Richard (1995), Josephine Barstow (1996), Felicity Lott (1996), Gillian Weir (1996), Paul McCartney (1997), Cleo Laine (1997), Elton John (1998), Shirley Bassey (1999), Thomas Allen (1999), Anne Evans (2000), Mick Jagger (2003), Willard White (2004), and Tom Jones (2006).

To the objection that Harry Lauder received his knighthood for his recruiting activities during the First World War and Jimmy Savile and Bob Geldof received theirs for raising money for charity, one can counter that these achievements were conditional on their fame as musicians. This last list reveals that recognition of singers has redressed an otherwise very lopsided gender balance, and also that since the 1990s popular music has begun to claim an increasing share.

In short, in the United Kingdom, the fast track to formal honour is through music. This could not have happened without the intervention of politicians, for the prime minister of the day draws up the honours list. A great deal can be learned about the nature of a regime simply by analysing the kind of people it chooses to recognise. A sure sign that the status of popular musicians was in the ascendant came when British politicians scrambled to hitch themselves to The Beatles' bandwagon as soon as they became an international phenomenon. Surprisingly, the Conservatives were quickest off the mark. Perhaps because he had been a journalist (and was later to be editor of the *Daily Telegraph*), Bill Deedes, a cabinet minister no less, sensed that The Beatles' triumphant tour of the United States in early 1964 marked a cultural watershed. He told the City of London Young Conservatives that The Beatles heralded 'a cultural movement among the young which may become part of the history of our time. For those with eyes to see it, something important and heartening is happening here'.[166]

Although vilified by the more reactionary members of his own party, Deedes's views were adopted by its leaders. Conservative parliamentary candidates were advised to mention The Beatles (favourably) as often as possible in their speeches, and the prime minister, Sir Alec Douglas-Home, hailed them as 'our best exports', making 'a useful contribution to the balance of payments'.[167] With a general election on the horizon, the leader of the opposition, Harold Wilson, moved decisively to prevent the Conservatives from turning The Beatles into their 'secret weapon', as he put it. When he learned that the group had been named Showbusiness Personalities of 1963 by the Variety Club of Great Britain, he approached the chairman of EMI, The Beatles' record company, to propose himself as the ideal person to make the award at a luncheon in March 1964.

It was probably of no concern to Wilson that The Beatles jostled and baited him, for the episode allowed him to position himself literally and symbolically as the politician most in touch with youth culture. This was

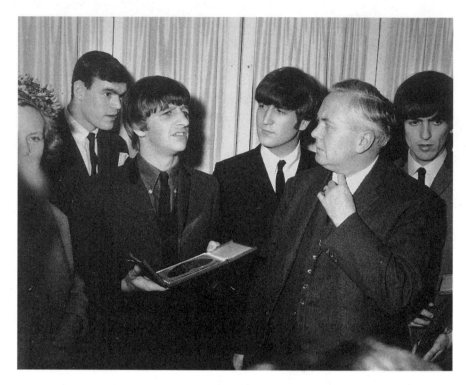

The leader of the opposition, Harold Wilson, is harassed by The Beatles after present-ing them with their awards at the Variety Club ceremony on 19 March 1964.

hardly a difficult task, given that the Tory prime minister he was trying to oust was Sir Alec Douglas-Home—an Old Etonian Scottish laird and, until he renounced his peerage, fourteenth earl of Home. After informing the Variety Club audience that this was not an occasion to make a partisan speech, Wilson of course did just that, trading on the happy coincidence that he was MP for a Liverpool constituency. We have no way to assess how much Wilson's seizure of this photo opportunity helped him win the gen-eral election in October 1964, although John Lennon reputedly claimed credit for the Labour victory. In any event, Wilson showed his gratitude the following year by making The Beatles Members of the Order of the British Empire (MBE). He continued the association throughout his term in office, for example by officiating at the reopening of the Cavern Club in Liverpool, a Beatles shrine, in July 1966.[168]

Wilson was the first British politician to woo popular musicians, but he was by no means the last. As the long Tory hegemony began to crumble in the mid-1990s, both sides turned to the musical world for support. It was symptomatic of the times that the prime minister, John Major, should look to the more senior end, giving knighthoods to Cliff Richard (born 1940) and Paul McCartney (born 1942), while Tony Blair targeted a much younger constituency.[169] An early sign of his strategy was the visit in 1995 by Damon Albarn of Blur to the Houses of Parliament at the invitation of the Labour Party. There he conferred with John Prescott, Alistair Campbell and Tony Blair on how the Labour Party's appeal to the young might be enhanced.[170]

Blair's credentials were much more impressive than Wilson's had been a generation earlier. This had less to do with age—Blair was forty-one in 1995, Wilson had been forty-eight in 1964—than with style. Blair did not wear three-piece suits, did not smoke a pipe and did not go on holiday in the Scilly Isles. Moreover, as Blair's publicists were keen to emphasise, he himself had been a rock musician while a student at Oxford, playing guitar and singing in a group called Ugly Rumours. One of his fellow musicians recalled: 'He had a kind of Mick Jagger-esque delivery. Quite high, not enormous volume. But it was coupled with this very entertaining act. He definitely modelled himself on Jagger. There was a lot of "Well alright!"'[171]

As with Wilson's victory over Douglas-Home in 1964, it is impossible to assess how much Blair was helped by his identification with youth culture in achieving his landslide victory in May 1997. He certainly went out of his way to continue the alliance, famously inviting Noel Gallagher (although not his more dangerous brother Liam) of Oasis to a party at Downing Street shortly after the election. Damon Albarn was also invited but declined: 'I left a message at the House of Commons saying, "Dear Tony, I've become a communist. Enjoy the schmooze, comrade. Love, Damon."'[172] Later in the year, Alan McGee, founder and owner of Creation Records, who had also been at the Downing Street party, was appointed by Blair to the Creative Industries Task Force and invited to dinner at Chequers. He wrote a revealing account of the evening: 'We didn't know what to expect. I was wearing a suit, Kate [his wife] was dressed up. When we drove up to the house, there were SWAT teams everywhere: guys crawling around on the grass, with guns. He [Blair] answered the door wearing jeans, with a pint in his hand. We went in, and that was when it got totally fucking psychedelic. Judi Dench was there, a guy from Psion computers, that author,

Tony Blair greets Noel Gallagher of Oasis at a reception at 10 Downing Street shortly after the general election of 1997.

John O'Farrell . . . and Jimmy Savile. I introduced him to Kate, and he started kind of sucking her fingers. It was all totally weird'.[173]

Predictably, this alliance between New Labour and Britpop was of short duration. The minister of culture, Chris Smith, began to have second thoughts, lamenting later that 'judging by our critics, we are a platoon of philistines that have had to boogie to Oasis'. He blamed this mistaken image on 'the famous photograph of the Prime Minister with Noel', adding ruefully 'I think that with hindsight, allowing an iconic image of that kind to become common currency was a mistake'.[174] But it was Smith, whose own tastes tended toward high culture, who proved to be out of step with the regime and was sacked in 2001. Blair continued to cultivate the popular music scene, never missing an opportunity to be photographed holding a guitar or to broadcast his musical enthusiasms (U2, The Foo Fighters, The Darkness) and letting it be known that he played his guitar every day. And it seemed to work. However hard the Tory leader David Cameron tried to keep up—attending rock concerts, advertising his enthusiasm for Radiohead, choosing a suitably cool selection of records on Desert Island Discs (Pink Floyd, Radiohead, R.E.M., The Smiths, The Killers)—Blair managed to stay one step ahead.

Indeed, rock artists came to him. In the course of an interview with Chris Martin of Coldplay in May 2005, the journalist Miranda Sawyer revealed that she was seeing the prime minister the next day. Martin seized her notebook and wrote him a letter:

> Dear Mr Blair, My name is Chris; I am the singer in a band called Coldplay. Please forgive the slightly ramshackle nature of my letter; I don't have any smart stationery . . . I think all the stuff you're doing this year in terms of trying to sort the whole place out is BRILLIANT. The Make Poverty History campaign that you're behind is not just a slogan, it's a real possibility, and myself and most of my friends feel like you're one of the only politicians on the world stage who gives a [last two words crossed out] actually wants to achieve it.

According to Sawyer's account, 'Then he wishes Blair good luck in the election, offers him some guitar lessons and signs off, leaving his mobile number. When I give the note to the Prime Minister the following day, he says: "Have you read this?" I say: "Of course." The day after that, Chris gets an official phone call; he doesn't tell me what was said, but I get the impression that it was more of a "So, can we rely on your support?" chat than a "How do you get your fingers round an augmented fifth?" one.'[175] Politicians would do well not to put their trust in rock musicians, most of whom subscribe to anarchic hedonism rather than a specific programme, as Chris Martin's subsequent utterances showed. In June 2006 he ended Coldplay's set at the Isle of Wight Festival with the exhortation: 'Don't vote Cameron . . . Don't vote for Blair either. Whatever you do don't vote for the Tories, never ever! Fuck Cameron it's all spin, bullshit!'[176]

From politicians seeking out the support of musicians, the next and final step was for musicians to enter the world of politics. Such a move had been anticipated by Wagner, but in the late twentieth century musicians became a major proactive force. The personification of this development has been Bob Geldof, who began quite modestly, in December 1984, with a single record entitled 'Do They Know It's Christmas?' to raise money for the Ethiopian famine victims. He demonstrated his formidable powers of persuasion by assembling forty-five of the most celebrated singers of the day (including Paul McCartney, Boy George, David Bowie, Phil Collins, Bono, George Michael and Sting). The result was both the fastest- and big-gest-selling single of all time in the United Kingdom.[177] Suitably encour-aged, Geldof moved on to organise the biggest ever concert in the world, Live Aid. On 13 July 1985 concerts were held simultaneously at Wembley Stadium in London, where 72,000 attended, and at JFK Stadium in Phila-delphia, where 90,000 attended. The event was watched on television in fifty countries by two billion people. Initial hopes that a million dollars would be raised were exceeded 150 times.[178]

In 2005 Geldof struck again, this time with the assistance of a number of other rock stars, most notably Bono of U2. On 2 July ten concerts known collectively as Live 8 were held across the world, from Japan to Philadel-phia, and were broadcast to a global audience via one hundred television stations and two thousand radio networks. It was claimed subsequently that 3.8 billion people—or more than half the population of the world—had tuned in to a concert at some point.[179] The organisers showed that they had learned from their mistakes, for this time the intention was not to raise money, which might well find its way into the wrong hands, but to bring pressure to bear on the G8 organisation of the world's most advanced coun-tries, whose leaders were meeting at Gleneagles in Scotland. As Geldof put it: 'We don't want your money, we want your voice'.

Among other methods employed to put pressure on the G8 summit, an Internet petition was launched (attracting in excess of 38 million signa-tures) and a march of 225,000 people on Edinburgh was organised. The re-sults were impressive: the chancellor of the exchequer, Gordon Brown, agreed to waive VAT on the British concert's proceeds, thus saving the or-ganisers around £500,000, and the G8 finance ministers agreed to cancel the debts of the eighteen poorest countries, to double their aid globally, half of which was to go to Africa, and to reform restrictive trade re-gimes.[180]

Geldof's compatriot Bono now behaves like the world leader he has undoubtedly become, visiting the pope (to whom he gave his shades in ex-change for a rosary), taking the U.S. Treasury Secretary Paul O'Neill on a fact-finding and opinion-changing tour of Africa and telling presidents and

Bono and Bob Geldof visit Tony Blair at 10 Downing Street, 22 May 2003.

prime ministers what to do. At Gleneagles he was able to persuade a reluctant Gerhard Schröder to fall into line by making him an offer he could not refuse: to endorse Schröder and his SPD party at every concert during U2's impending tour of Germany.[181] As Chancellor Schröder was facing a very difficult re-election campaign, he capitulated.

In 2003 Jacques Chirac admitted Bono to the Légion d'Honneur; in 2005 *Time* named him 'Person of the Year'; in January 2007 Blair made him an honorary knight 'in recognition of his services to the music industry and for his humanitarian work.'[182] When the Clinton Presidential Center and Park was opened at Little Rock, Arkansas, in November 2004, attending were President George W. Bush and three former presidents—George

Bush Sr., Jimmy Carter and Clinton himself. As the audience reaction showed, however, the real star of the occasion was Bono, who not only played and sang but made a speech in which he addressed each president individually and commented on their contributions to Africa.[183] As an illustration of the triumph of music in the modern world, this is hard to beat.

2
Purpose
'Music Is the Most Romantic of All the Arts'[1]

Louis XIV and the Assertion of Power

Why compose music? Why perform music? Why listen to music? The obvious answers are, respectively, money, money, and pleasure. They are not entirely wrong, but they are not entirely right either. Much depends on the period, for the historical context determines the mix of the various elements that constitute music-making.

A common but serious error is to suppose that music consists of notes on the staff, if it is written down; or sounds, if it is performed. Conceivably, a composer might write music without any intention of its ever being seen or heard by a third party—but such extreme isolation must be as rare as being stranded on a desert island. Virtually all western music consists of a three-way interaction between creators, performers and audiences. Moreover, each of the three is an active and crucial participant. The notes move from abstraction to form only when they are turned into sound by musicians and are perceived by listeners. When choosing notes for a score, the composer will have in mind what instruments can be used, what sort of space the work will be performed in and what sort of people might be coming to listen. Making music is a social process.[2]

In some important respects, the purpose of music has remained the same throughout its history. One constant has been redemption, transporting human beings closer to God by encouraging their spirits to soar to a sonic heaven. Music still performs that function for organised religions, although its transcendental embrace has now expanded to include almost everyone. Another constant function has been recreation and entertainment, albeit to audiences that have constantly grown in size and social inclusion. What was once the monopoly of prince or prelate is now the shared experience of all but the tone deaf.

But the greatest change has come in the *primary* purpose of music: from representing the power of the patron to expressing the feelings of the individual musician. The pivotal moment occurred in the decades around 1800. Until the emergence of an anonymous public as a major cultural player, the individual patron usually identified who would compose, what would be composed, for what instruments and for what audience. In the case of Monteverdi and Haydn, the dominant influence on much of the music they created was the duke of Mantua and Prince Esterházy, respectively. But the perfect example of patron-led—or rather patron-dictated—music was provided by Louis XIV's Versailles project.

In the course of his very long reign (1643–1715), the Sun King turned what was virtually a green-field site roughly ten miles from Paris into the biggest palace complex in all of Europe. Its purposes were various but related. Most fundamental was the need to distance the king from the over-mighty subjects who had caused so much mayhem during the past century, most recently during the civil wars of 1648–53. By creating a court culture of such opulence that only a royal purse was deep enough to sustain it, King Louis reduced even the grandest magnates to satellites. When he appeared in a coat encrusted with 14 million *livres*-worth of diamonds, for example, he was demonstrating to his courtiers that no private individual could compete with royal resources.[3] By providing the best in aristocratic entertainment—the best hunting, the best balls, the best opera, the best music, the best theatre, the best gambling and so on—he lured the top echelons of the French nobility out of the provinces to a place where he could keep an eye on them. And because he made clear that those staying away from court would also be cutting themselves off from royal patronage, there were few absentees.

The enormous cost of trying to keep up with one another made the courtiers dependent on royal largesse. In 1683 royal pensions were paid out to the tune of 1.4 million *livres*, a substantial sum representing about 1.2 percent of total government expenditure, but even so a cost-effective

Seconde Journée
Theatre fait dans la mesme allee, sur lequel la Comédie, et le Ballet de la Princesse d'Elide furent representez

Performance of *The Princess of Elis* within *The Pleasures of the Enchanted Isle,* an openair multi-media extravaganza staged at Versailles in honour of Louis XIV's mistress Louise de la Vallière over seven days in May 1664. Molière was in charge of the theatrical side, while Lully directed the music. Engraving by Israel Silvestre (1664).

investment in social harmony.[4] This was not one-way traffic, for both the monarch and the nobility gave and took, in what was less a gilded cage than a mutually beneficial space.[5] And if Versailles distanced the king from his peers, it also served to elevate him above the other crowned heads of Europe. By concentrating in one project all the best talent in all the various branches of the arts, Louis XIV laid claim to a cultural supremacy that would match his military invincibility. The architecture of Le Vau and Mansart, the painting of Lebrun, Mignard, Largilliere and Rigaud, the sculpture of Coysevox and Girardon, the gardens of Le Nôtre, the plays of Molière, Corneille and Racine, and the music of Lully, Lalande, Couperin, Marais and Charpentier were 'the continuation of war and diplomacy by other means'.[6] Even flowers were pressed into service, as Versailles and its satellite palaces were turned into a year-round floral feast for eye and nose.[7]

Those who could not travel to Versailles to experience its wonders at first hand could make their acquaintance through the numerous descriptions and illustrations that were published. In 1663 Louis instructed Israel Silvestre to engrave 'all his palaces, royal houses, the most beautiful views and aspects of his gardens, public assemblies, Carrousels and outskirts of cities'.[8] This commission initiated a series of magnificent volumes, them-selves art objects of high value, which broadcast French culture across the length and breadth of Europe. Also published were the word books of the various operatic performances, all of them praising the royal achieve-ments.[9] By 1682 Ménestrier could claim that the cultural hegemony of Italy was over—it was France that now set the standards in all the arts: 'It is the glory of France to have succeeded in establishing the rules for all the fine arts. During the past twenty years, scholarly dissertations have regulated drama, epic poetry, epigrams, eclogues, painting, music, architecture, her-aldry, mottoes, riddles, emblems, history and rhetoric. All branches of knowledge are now conducted in our language'.[10]

This culture can be described as representational, in the sense that it served to re-present the glory of the king by making it visible, tangible and audible. Its primary purpose was to say something about the patron, and to say it loudly. In this process, music was ubiquitous and omnipresent: it was played at the *lever*, the elaborate ceremony staged when the king got up in the morning; in chapel when he attended Mass; during meals, promenades and water excursions; at the departure for the hunt; at receptions and balls; at military exercises; during fireworks displays; at the opera; at the evening *appartements* when the king and his courtiers played at cards and billiards; and during the *coucher*, another elaborate ceremony staged when the king went to bed.[11] Musicians were even on hand to sound a fanfare at the cli-max of the hunt when the master of the hunt delivered the *coup de grâce* to the exhausted stag by slitting its throat with his hunting knife. When Louis' heir, his great-grandson Louis XV, went hunting for the first time, eighty horn players were in attendance (not to mention 900 dogs and 1,000 horses).[12]

Especially popular was dancing, not least because, by all accounts, Louis XIV was a superlative dancer who could hold his own with the pro-fessionals. The marquis de Dangeau recorded in his diary that in the six months between 10 September 1684 and 3 March 1685, no fewer than sev-enty royal entertainments involved dancing, including one grand ball, nine masquerades and fifty-eight *appartements*—in other words, an event every two or three days.[13] To provide the enormous amount of music needed, about 200 singers and instrumentalists were required, divided between the chapel, the chamber and the hunt. The musical establishment at Versailles was certainly the largest in Europe, and probably the best too.[14]

The most elaborate musical performances were initially the *ballets du cour*, lengthy and elaborate combinations of dance, music, verse and spectacular theatrical effects, all designed to sing the praises of the king. But they were too closely associated with their Italian origins to be suitable for a king of France. As the contemporary poet Pierre Perrin observed, it was unacceptable that a nation invincible in war should continue to be influenced by the cultures of inferior nations.[15] So a new genre—French lyric tragedy—was invented. Ironically, the man mainly responsible was a Florentine, Giovanni Battista Lulli, who in 1660 at the age of twenty-eight became 'composer of the king's chamber music' and the following year 'music master of the royal family'. Marrying the daughter of another senior figure of the royal musical establishment and adopting French nationality, the newly Gallicised Jean Baptiste Lully encouraged the king to turn his back on the previously dominant Italian school. The last Italian opera to be performed in France for sixty-seven years was Cavalli's *Ercole amante* in 1662. In 1666 Louis dismissed his Italian musicians.[16]

The invariable features of the lyric tragedies that streamed from Lully's fertile pen included a prologue devoted to singing the praises of Louis XIV, a five-act structure and subject matter drawn from classical mythology or (less often) medieval romance.[17] Eschewing the sweet melodies and brilliant singing of the Italian tradition, Lully made dramatic dialogue his prime concern. It was conducted mainly in the form of melodic recitative, interspersed with short lyrical passages for the expression of especially impassioned moments. These austere exchanges, which all too easily became monotonous in performance, were interrupted periodically by *divertissements* in the shape of choruses, ballets and magical stage effects.[18]

Great were the rewards for the musicians who rose to the top of the Versailles establishment. By the time Lully died in 1687 he was a very rich man, owning five substantial properties in Paris and leaving an estate valued in excess of 800,000 *livres.* Six years earlier he had bought the honorific office of *secrétaire du roi* for 63,000 *livres* and with it immediate hereditary nobility.[19] He was the only man in history to run the Paris Opéra at a profit.[20] Also indicative of his standing was his ability to use royal favour to escape from a potentially fatal scandal, when he was exposed as a member of a homosexual ring at court and accused of debauching the pages who served in his household.[21]

The price Lully and the other musicians had to pay for their privileges was total submission to the royal will. Louis XIV was very much a hands-on patron, personally deciding what should be played, when and where. Among other things, he supplied the subject matter for several of Lully's lyric tragedies (*Persée*, *Amadis*, *Roland* and *Armide*).[22] He also took a close interest in personnel matters, often attending the elaborate auditions and making the appointments. It was at his insistence, for example, that Michel-Richard Delalande was promoted.[23] Any decisions he did not make himself were delegated not to the composer but to the Royal Academy of Music he founded in 1669. There was no question of any originality or liberty in the creative process.[24]

The sophistication, self-confidence and glamour of Versailles combined with Louis' military victories to create a cultural model of irresistible attraction to the rest of Europe. Symbolic of its triumphant march was the accompanying linguistic victory. When Louis came to the throne in 1643, French was only one of several competing European languages. At a time when Latin still dominated academic discourse, either Spanish or Italian could have made as good if not a better claim to be the *lingua franca* of educated Europe. By 1700 the marquis de Dangeau could tell the Académie Française with majestic complacency that 'the wonders achieved by the King have made French as familiar to our neighbours as their own vernacular.'[25] In the world of power politics, the decisive revelation of French hegemony came in 1714, the year before Louis' death, when for the first time a Holy Roman emperor deigned to sign an international treaty (Rastatt) drafted in the French language rather than in Latin.[26]

Opera and the Representation of Social Status

Although Louis XIV did not invent representational culture—it was as old as civilisation itself—he did establish a model that most European sovereigns followed for the next century or so. But it was a model, not a template. They took the form but contributed their own content. In music, the lyric tragedy developed by Lully was just too French to have international appeal. Everywhere else in Europe the dominant genre was Italian *opera seria* (serious opera dealing with a heroic or tragic theme, as opposed to *opera buffa* or comic opera), better known to contemporaries as *dramma per musica*. Of all the musical genres, *opera seria* was the representational genre *par excellence*, for it was grand, formal, classical, elitist, hierarchical and ideally suited to the propagation of an absolutist political message.

Hundreds—probably thousands—of *opere serie* were written during the late seventeenth and eighteenth centuries, but the format was almost invariable. They began with an overture or sinfonia in three sections (fast, slow, fast), consisted almost entirely of *da capo* arias, with very few duets or ensembles, lasted for three to four hours, and ended with a rousing chorus to make explicit the opera's central message.[27] The libretto was usually based on a subject taken from classical antiquity, employed six characters—two pairs of lovers, a noble king and a treacherous general—and ended happily with the pairing-off of the lovers, the exposure of the villain and the celebration of the ruler.

This was very much 'singer's opera', with the main emphasis on the ability of the principals to demonstrate their mastery in the three styles of Italian singing—*cantabile, grazioso* and *bravura*. Especially in the third section of the *da capo* aria, the singer was not just permitted but encouraged to improvise, embellish and take risks to dazzle the audience with technical virtuosity.[28] This required a great deal of verbal repetition, which can seem wearisome if not absurd to modern ears but should not be allowed to obscure the importance of the text. Contemporary aesthetics held that the voice was the only true means of expression and that therefore the prime function of music was to intensify the meaning and expression embodied in the words.[29] The text should not be regarded as a 'libretto' in the nineteenth-century sense; it was a drama, and the genre was not called *dramma per musica* for nothing.[30] Members of the audience had every opportunity to verify the contemporary belief that the most important librettist, Pietro Metastasio, was a great poet in his own right, for the house lights were not dimmed and they could follow every word in the text they were handed at the door or had obtained in advance.

Music may have been central to these grand representational exercises, but it was also subordinate to their essentially social and political ob-

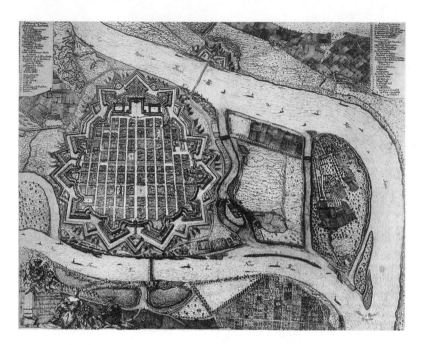

Town plan of Mannheim in the mid-eighteenth century.

jectives. At Mannheim between 1743 and 1777, the elector of the Palatinate, Karl Theodor, created one of the great musical centres of eighteenth-century Europe. Although he treated his musicians well by the standards of the day, giving them good wages, security and even pensions, the music they played was embedded in a wider ceremonial structure supporting the regime's legitimacy. Before a performance of an *opera seria*, the court assembled in the apartments of the electress in the west wing of the gigantic palace and then proceeded to the opera house to the sound of fanfares, much as if they were processing to attend Mass in the chapel.[31]

The town of Mannheim itself was a wholly artificial creation, built after 1720 at the confluence of the Neckar and the Rhine on a rectilinear grid. The novelist Wilhelm Heinse wrote to his friend Jacobi in 1780: 'With its magnificent palace, Mannheim is a really beautiful town, but it is built in such a way that it looks as though its inhabitants *ought* and *must* rather than *want* to live there. It has been made, it has not become. Just like any true residence, it has a despotic appearance.'[32] Charles Burney stated the same point rather differently when he visited the town in 1772: 'His [Karl Theodor's] passion for music and shews, seems as strong as that of the emperor Nero was formerly. It is, perhaps, upon such occasions as these that music becomes a vice, and hurtful to society; for that nation, of which half the subjects are stage-players, fiddlers, and soldiers, and the other half beggars, seems to be but ill-governed'.[33]

Part of Karl Theodor's motivation derived from personal preference, for he was a gifted flautist and competent cellist. There was always a strong recreational element in representational culture. Part of it stemmed from a desire to keep up with the Joneses, or rather the von Joneses. With the exception of Austria and Prussia, none of the princes of the Holy Roman Empire could hope to raise armies sufficiently large to give them an independent voice in European affairs. So they competed at a cultural level instead, seeking the reputation of having the best opera, the best orchestra, the best composer, the best theatre, the best academies, the best universities, the best hunting or whatever. This was good news for both the creative and the performing artists, because competition drove up salaries and improved conditions of service. Less appealing was the arbitrary nature of some of the choices made.

Karl Theodor had the Stamitzes, the Cannabichs, Richter and Holzbauer on his payroll but missed the opportunity to add Mozart. Frederick the Great more than doubled Johann Joachim Quantz's salary when he lured him to Prussia from the employment of the elector of Saxony in 1740, treating him with uncharacteristic solicitude. Indeed, there was a popular jest in circulation that Prussia was run by Mrs. Quantz's poodle, for Frederick deferred to Quantz, Quantz deferred to Mrs. Quantz and Mrs. Quantz deferred to her poodle.[34] Yet Frederick also employed Carl Philipp Emmanuel Bach, regarded in his day as *the* great Bach, but treated him shabbily as a mere keyboard player. Frederick knew what he liked—opera in a conservative Italian style, and music for the flute—and that was what his musicians had to like too.[35] Working conditions were no better further south. When the noble estates of Bohemia chose Mozart to compose the music for *La Clemenza di Tito* to mark the coronation of Leopold II in 1791, they did so only because Salieri was too busy.[36] Similar examples of what to twenty-first-century eyes seem to be crass errors of judgment could be multiplied *ad nauseam*.

Bach, Handel and the Worship of God

Music and musicians could flourish in the world of the courts, but theirs was always a subordinate and uncertain business. The same could be said of another, and equally important, kind of representation—religious music. So deeply embedded is the misleading notion that the eighteenth century was the Age of Reason that the importance of religious music has been underestimated. Even court composers spent much of their time writing masses, motets and oratorios, not least because sacred music was ranked first in the hierarchy of genres.[37] For most people in society at large, music meant religious music, but it was not confined to the congregational singing of responses or psalms. In France before 1789 more than four hundred churches employed a *maîtrise* of at least a dozen musicians performing sophisticated music.[38]

Even in the notoriously disputatious world of music scholarship, there is general agreement that no greater religious music has ever been written than that of Johann Sebastian Bach. Everything Bach wrote—and he was amazingly prolific in many different genres—he did for the glory of God, often writing at the beginning of a score 'J.J.'—*Jesu Juva* (Jesus, help me) and at the end 'Soli Deo Gloria' (To the Glory of God alone). In two extraordinary bursts of creativity, at Weimar in 1713–16 and Leipzig in 1723–29, he wrote about three hundred cantatas, of which two hundred have survived. To these should be added five passions (of which only two have survived) and three oratorios, not to mention his musical last will and testament, the B-minor Mass.

It is one of the great ironies of history that Bach's religious music should be so much more available and so much more esteemed in a secular age than at any other time. In 1727, when he wrote the *St. Matthew Passion* for its first performance on Good Friday, the entire population of Leipzig went to one of the city's churches at least once on Sundays to attend services that lasted several hours. Just how enthusiastic they were about this activity cannot of course be assessed; but without a doubt the community's values and world view were steeped in religion. Yet the *St. Matthew Passion* was performed only four times during Bach's lifetime, and then sank without a trace, not least because it had not been published. It was not revived until 1829, when Mendelssohn staged his famous so-called centenary performance.[39]

This neglect, both contemporary and posthumous, was all the more amazing in view of the stupendous quality of a work that also contained all the attributes associated with popular musical success—melody, rhythm and variety. Indeed, some criticism was voiced at the time that it was altogether too worldly: 'What will come of this? God save us, my children! It's just as if one were at an Opera Comedy' was the reported comment of one elderly lady in the congregation.[40] Today, when in Europe at least only a small and dwindling proportion of the population goes anywhere near a church, the *St. Matthew Passion* is universally regarded as one of the greatest achievements of European culture, is performed regularly across the globe and is available in scores of different recordings.[41]

A strong clue to this conundrum was provided by the success of a work by Bach's exact contemporary, Handel. *Messiah* was first performed in Neale's New Musick Hall in Dublin as a benefit for three local charities. The public rehearsals had already attracted enthusiastic press notices, which hailed the work as 'the finest Composition of Musick that ever was heard'. The premiere, on 13 April 1742, opened the rhetorical flood gates: 'Words are wanting to express the exquisite Delight it afforded to the admiring crouded Audience. The Sublime, the Grand, and the Tender, adapted to the most elevated, majestick and moving Words, conspired to transport and charm the ravished Heart and Ear'.[42] Such was the enthusiasm that two further performances were arranged, this time the proceeds going to Handel and Neale rather than charity.

Back in London, *Messiah* got off to a slow start, because of opposition to the performance of sacred music in theatres, but gradually became established as a permanent fixture in and outside London. From 1749, the year in which it was performed at Oxford to mark the opening of the Radcliffe Camera (built to house the Radcliffe Science Library), Handel always concluded his oratorio season with performances of the work. In 1750 it reached Salisbury, in 1755 Bath and Bristol, in 1757 the Three Choirs' Festival, in 1759 Cambridge, in 1760 Birmingham and Bury St. Edmunds, and so on. By the time Handel died in 1759, *Messiah* had been performed fifty-six times, all but twelve of them in secular venues. It has never been out of the repertory since. In 1763 a selection of extracts was published, followed in 1767 by the full score. Two performances were given in 1784 as part of the great Handel Commemoration organised to mark what was believed to be the centenary of his birth.[43]

The different fates of the *St. Matthew Passion* and *Messiah* had less to do with the quality of the respective scores than with the differences between Dublin-London and Leipzig. In the middle of the eighteenth century, the population of Dublin was at least three times the size of that of Leipzig, while London was more than twenty times as populous. So the public sphere in the two larger cities was correspondingly more extensive. They were also magnets for the nobility and gentry of Ireland and Great Britain respectively, whereas in Saxony the equivalent elites were attracted not to Leipzig but to the elector's court at Dresden. This greater depth and breadth of demand allowed Handel to become immensely rich and famous, and also influenced the kind of music he wrote. Bach composed for a captive audience of worshippers, whose primary purpose when they went to St. Thomas's Church on Good Friday 1727 was to attend a religious service, although many of them no doubt hoped to hear some good music into the bargain. Handel wrote for a voluntary audience of paying customers whose main concern when they went to Neale's New Musick Hall on 13 April 1742 was to attend a concert, although many of them no doubt also hoped to be edified spiritually.

Moreover, Bach was writing for a formidable musical establishment which he himself had built up and trained since he arrived in the city four years earlier. In the 1736 revised version, the *St. Matthew Passion* requires a double choir, each with its own orchestra and separately placed; a third choir of trebles with organ support; nine vocal and five instrumental soloists; and an orchestra of modest size. The music they are asked to sing and play is, to put it mildly, demanding. Handel was writing for singers and players he had recruited locally in Dublin since his arrival the previous December (with the exception of a star soprano he had brought with him). *Messiah* requires one choir, four solo singers and three instrumental soloists. The music they are asked to play, for all its wonderful quality, is within the range of a good amateur choral society. 'Turn up and sing *Messiah*' events are common, but opportunities to 'turn up and sing the *St. Matthew Passion*' are very rare if not nonexistent.

These contrasts also explain the very different endings of the two works. *Messiah* is divided into three parts, each of which concludes with a chorus. Because part two ends with perhaps the best-known chorus in all of sacred music, the 'Hallelujah Chorus', Handel's task of bringing the whole work to a close without a sense of anti-climax posed a real challenge. He met it by writing a chorus, 'Worthy Is the Lamb', that was almost twice as long, by adding brass and timpani to the orchestra, and by winding it all up with a musical *coup de théâtre*. With the chorus roaring out 'Amen' again and again, the trumpets blazing and the timpani thundering, a great climax builds until suddenly, at bar eighty-four, he calls for complete silence. After a pause of just a bar, the combined forces return *fortissimo* for three more bars to bring the work to a triumphant, deafening conclusion. It was, of course, a device designed to unleash a storm of applause, and in that it rarely fails to deliver, although the finale makes great demands on conductor, orchestra and singers.

How different is the conclusion to the *St. Matthew Passion.* Of course Bach writes a great chorus too, but he ends *diminuendo* on a resigned note, the final words being 'With profound contentment may your eyes find slumber' *(Höchst vergnügt schlummern da die Augen ein).* In part, at least, this is the difference between writing for a congregation and writing for an audience.

Concerts and the Public Sphere

These reflections are not intended to imply that Bach's work is superior or that his religious motivation was stronger. What it does suggest, however, is that an important step in the elevation of music and its creators was to divorce them from service to a third party. In the case of *opera seria,* that party was the prince; in the case of religious music, it was God. Although Handel appears to have been every bit as devout as Bach, his staging of oratorios in theatres for the paying public pointed the way to music's eventual emancipation from function. By the time he died in 1759, the formation of a musical public had progressed to the point that it was exercising a growing influence on the status of both music and musicians. The chief institutional expression was the public concert, which came into its own in the eighteenth century. In the authoritative verdict of one of the most influential critics of the nineteenth century, Eduard Hanslick, by 1800 the concert had become 'the main medium for music *per se*'.[44]

Music lovers had always got together to play and listen, but a concert defined as a musical performance that clearly distinguishes between performers and audience and that admits an anonymous public upon payment of an entrance fee was of relatively recent origin. The best candidate for first ever concert in Europe was held at John Banister's house in London in 1672, when members of the public were charged the considerable sum of one shilling and sixpence to listen to 'Musick performed by excellent Masters'.[45] Banister's success attracted other musician-entrepreneurs, and by the end of the century advertisements for public concerts were appearing regularly in the newspapers. The English were in the vanguard of commercialisation here, for concert advertisements did not appear in Paris's newspapers until 1725 or in Vienna's until 1780.[46]

London was the natural venue for the new genre, not only because of its size and wealth but also because of the relative liberality of its culture. Anyone possessing the necessary enterprise, capital and contacts could organise a concert by assembling an orchestra, hiring a hall and advertising a programme. If that seems self-evident, it should be contrasted with conditions in the only other metropolis of comparable size and wealth, Paris. The royal musician Anne-Danican Philidor had the bright idea of organising concerts during Lent, when theatres were obliged to close their doors, but first he had to secure the consent of Jean-Nicolas de Francine, who had inherited the monopoly of public musical presentation bestowed on his father-in-law, Lully, by Louis XIV. It cost Philidor 10,000 *livres* a year and a promise not to perform operatic music, or indeed any vocal music with texts in the French language.[47] Such was public demand, however, that his Concerts Spirituels, when launched in 1725, were a resounding and lasting success.

It is tempting to place the rise of the concert in the context of a socio-economic development that might be labelled 'the rise of the bourgeoisie'. In J. S. Bach's Leipzig, for example, the link between concerts and commerce is easy to see. By German standards, this was a cosmopolitan world, famously lauded by Goethe in *Faust* as 'Little Paris' and by Lessing as 'a place where one can see the whole world in microcosm'.[48] As a major entrepôt at the crossroads of central Europe, Leipzig enjoyed a new lease on life in the eighteenth century with the rapid expansion of Russian markets. Concerts began in the city in the 1680s, staged by an informal gathering of musicians known as a Collegium Musicum. When Georg Philipp Telemann came to the city in 1701 to study law at the university, he founded another,

The old Gewandhaus, Leipzig, painted by the multi-talented Felix Mendelssohn.

which survived his departure in 1705 and involved around sixty people.[49] This was the group run by Bach from 1729 until 1736.

In 1743 a more ambitious association calling itself the Grand Concert was founded by sixteen citizens, each promising to donate sixteen imperial talers annually to subsidise concerts.[50] The merchants who sat on the board responded to increased demand like good entrepreneurs by increasing the number of concerts during the three great trade fairs held in the city each year. In 1781 a splendid new concert hall was opened by a new association in the former clothiers' hall, whose German name, Gewandhaus, has given its name to a symphonic tradition that has lasted to the present day. At the first concert, an orchestra thirty-strong played a mixed programme of symphonies, chamber music, operatic arias and a choral work to an audience of five hundred.[51]

A similar pattern could be found in other commercial centres such as Frankfurt am Main, Hamburg and Lübeck. Yet almost everywhere, the lead was taken not by commoners but by nobles. Even in Leipzig the sixteen citizens who founded the Grand Concert series in 1743 included nobles as well as burghers. The professional musicians who first organised concerts in London were anxious to confine their clientele to high society, and their noble patrons determined what should be played and when. Writing in 1728 about the last quarter of the previous century, the first historian of London concert life, Roger North, recognised that 'nothing advanced musick more in this age than the patronage of the nobility, and men of fortunes, for they became encouragers of it by great liberallitys, and countenance to the professors'.[52] That did not change appreciably as the eighteenth century progressed: when the concert promoters announced in their advertisements that they were addressing 'the Nobility and Gentry', they meant what they said.[53]

Elsewhere, the aristocratic element was even more dominant. In the German musical world, the concerts of the self-governing Free Imperial Cities such as Hamburg and Frankfurt am Main were overshadowed by the princely capitals. Then as now, Frankfurt am Main was the financial capital of Germany, but it was also a by-word for cultural conservatism. No less a witness than the city's most famous son, Goethe, complained about the 'narrow and slow-moving' burgher culture which, as he told his mother after his move to princely Weimar, would have driven him mad if he had stayed any longer.[54] It was not from these cultural backwaters that musical innovation would come, nor even from relatively lively Leipzig. The development of instrumental music, and especially the symphony, owed far more to Mannheim (capital of the elector of the Palatinate), Eisenstadt (residence of Prince Esterházy), Salzburg (home of the archbishop), Berlin (capital of the king of Prussia) and Vienna (residence of the Holy Roman Emperor). In these residential cities, whose social and economic *raison d'être* was the presence of the court, the public consisted mainly of state employees, most of whom—like the patrons of Mozart's concerts in the 1780s—were nobles.[55]

The Secularisation of Society, the Sacralisation of Music

One very important service performed by the public concert was to make music respectable. Performances in church could not be anything else, of course, but in the secular world music had a decidedly raffish image. Female singers and dancers had a reputation for doubling as prostitutes that was well merited in many cases.[56] In France this association was established by the end of Louis XIV's reign. Jean de Tralage wrote in 1690 that in times gone by, most of the women performing at the opera had been married, but that nowadays almost all were 'protected' by some great noble. He concluded that the Academy of Music (the official title of the opera house in Paris) had become the Academy of Love.[57] When not required on stage, the girls visited male admirers in their boxes, and after the performance men milled around making *négociations de volupté*.[58] This steamy atmosphere naturally attracted full-time professional prostitutes to the theatre, who monopolised the most prominent seats in the balcony to advertise their charms.[59]

That kind of impropriety was completely absent from the concert room. In her novel *Evelina* of 1778, Fanny Burney's heroine wrote to her clergyman friend: 'About eight o'clock we went to the Pantheon. I was extremely struck with the beauty of the building, which greatly surpassed whatever I could have expected or imagined. Yet, it has more the appearance of a chapel, than of a place of diversion; and, though I was quite charmed

La Petite Loge by Jean-Michel Moreau (1783). A procuress presents her girl
to two aristocrats in a box at the Opéra.

with the magnificence of the room, I felt that I could not be as gay and
thoughtless there as at Ranelagh [a pleasure garden], for there is something
in it which rather inspires awe and solemnity, than mirth and pleasure'.[60]

This development was greatly assisted by the popularity of oratorios,
which became a permanent feature of concert programmes across Europe.
Their importance lay not just in the respectability they brought to the event
but also to the change in attitude they inculcated in concert-goers. Perhaps
because the early performances were so closely connected to taverns, audi-

ences continued to behave in a relaxed fashion long after they had moved to proper music rooms, arriving late, moving around during the concert, chatting with their neighbours, and so on. An oratorio that proclaimed religious truths had to be approached in a quite different frame of mind. As an observer of the Handel Commemoration of 1784 recorded, when George III led the audience in standing for the 'Hallelujah Chorus', it was a demonstration of 'national assent to the fundamental truths of religion'.[61]

Also linking the sacred to the secular were the music festivals that developed in the course of the eighteenth century. The very first seems to have been the annual service in St. Paul's Cathedral in London for the Corporation of the Sons of the Clergy, a charitable organisation founded for the benefit of needy clergy and their dependants. When first held in 1655, it was just a service of thanksgiving, followed by a banquet, but gradually the musical element became dominant, with Purcell's *Te Deum* and *Jubilate* performed regularly.[62] These two works were also the staple fare of the festivals organised jointly by the cathedrals of Gloucester, Worcester and Hereford, beginning in 1713 and eventually becoming known as the Three Choirs Festival.

Although religious in location and charitable in purpose, these festivals—and others founded across England in the decades that followed—were more like concerts than divine worship, especially as they also included purely orchestral works. As the American musicologist William Weber has neatly put it: 'The musical festival . . . was a ritual that was *in* the church but not *of* the church'.[63] The same applied to the continental equivalents that began after 1800, the first at Frankenhausen in Thuringia in 1810.[64] Although slow off the mark, the Germans took to the festivals with relish, as they mushroomed across the country in the 1820s and 1830s. Indeed, Edward Dent held them responsible for the 'semi-religious attitude to music' that developed there with such earnestness in the nineteenth century.[65]

The Romantic Revolution

Opera in eighteenth-century France (or anywhere else in Europe for that matter) was central to polite society, being variously described as 'a place where everyone goes' (Voltaire in 1732) and 'the dominant passion of good society' (Diderot in 1762). Of those who criticised the immorality of this operatic world, none was more outspoken, radical or influential than Jean-Jacques Rousseau. In his autobiographical *Confessions*, completed in 1770 and published posthumously in 1782, he vilified the Paris Opéra as 'that centre of vice'.[66] Rousseau had good reason to be hostile, for in 1753 the publication of his *Letter on French Music* had unleashed a campaign against him so vituperative that even a less sensitive soul would have been wounded. Baron Grimm and the marquis d'Argenson reported separately that Rousseau had been hanged and burned in effigy by the Opéra's orchestra, jostled and kicked when he visited the theatre and denied entry even when his own work was being performed.[67] This episode—known collectively as the 'squabble over the bouffons' *(querelle des bouffons)*—also revealed a great deal about music as a source of national pride.[68]

Rousseau's views on music had a special authority because he was a musician himself. As a young man, he recalled, 'I was so entirely absorbed in music that I was in no state to think of anything else'.[69] For long periods he earned his living as a music copyist, he devised a new system of musical notation, he wrote many of the articles on musical topics for Diderot and D'Alembert's *Encyclopédie* and he composed one of the most popular French operas of the eighteenth century, *Le Devin du Village* (1752), which stayed in the repertory for the next fifty years. Yet his most important service to music was to make a crucial contribution to the great Romantic revolution that shook European culture to its foundations in the late eighteenth and early nineteenth centuries.

Of the various candidates for the initial date of this eruption, the best is July 1749, for that was the month when Rousseau had his conversion experience. Walking from Paris to Vincennes to visit his friend Diderot in prison, he was reading the *Mercure de France* when his eye lighted on an advertisement for a competition for the best essay on the question: 'Has the progress of the sciences and arts done more to corrupt morals or improve them?' For Rousseau, this was not a rhetorical question: 'The moment I read this I beheld another universe and became another man'.[70] The scales now fallen from his eyes, he could see that civilisation was nothing less than a gigantic swindle, perpetrated by the great, the rich and the powerful to keep oppressed humanity in a state of servitude: 'The Sciences, Letters and Arts . . . spread garlands of flowers over the iron chains with which they are laden'.[71] In uncovering the mechanical laws of the universe, the natural scientists had only opened up new ways of exploiting it. Indeed, every branch of their vile calling was rooted in a vice: astronomy in superstition, geometry in avarice, physics in idle curiosity, and all of them in human pride.[72] Their desire to subject the world is a desire to have luxury, and luxury is the most corrupting of all vices, both for individuals and for states.[73]

Rousseau now turned against his *philosophe* friends with a vengeance. Against reason, he advanced passion; against logic, intuition; against the universal, the particular; against doubt, faith; against civilisation, nature. Above all, he advanced introspection as the only authentic source of inspiration. The only previous autobiographies to bear comparison—St. Augustine's *Confessions* and St. Teresa's *Life of Herself*—were intended to promote the greater glory of God. Although in his own way deeply religious, Rousseau was interested only in a greater understanding of himself.

With a characteristic lack of modesty, he asserted right at the start the uniqueness of what he was doing: 'I have resolved on an enterprise which has no precedent, and which, once complete, will have no imitator'.[74] What he wrote had value, he believed, because it came from inside: 'The true object of my confessions is to reveal my inner thoughts exactly in all the situations of my life. It is the history of my soul'.[75] The founding father of enlightened rationality, Descartes, had advanced as his central axiom the need 'to lead the mind away from the senses'. Rousseau proposed just the opposite. The problem with Madame de Warens, one of his lovers, he observed, was that she listened to her reason, which gave her bad advice, rather than to her heart, which would have given her good counsel.[76]

Rousseau knew that he was different, and he gloried in the fact: 'I may be no better, but at least I am different', he wrote in the opening paragraph of *The Confessions*. Especially after his epiphany on the road to Vincennes, he cultivated that difference, dressing simply, eating frugally, placing himself deliberately outside the *beau monde* of his former friends. Invited to the palace of Fontainebleau to attend the premiere of *Le Devin du Village*, he took good care to dress 'in my usual careless style, with a rough beard and an ill-combed wig'. When the duc d'Aumont invited him to meet Louis XV, giving a broad hint that a pension would be granted, Rousseau left the court, 'thus freeing myself from the dependence it would have imposed upon me'.[77] The style was the man. His craggy integrity, contempt for material success, disregard for social convention and glorification of his outsider persona all combined to make Rousseau a role model for future bohemians.

Nowhere did Rousseau have a bigger impact than in the German-speaking world. If reviews of his *Discourse on the Arts and the Sciences* were mainly hostile, they were also numerous and detailed.[78] Together with his literary successes, most notably *La Nouvelle Héloïse* of 1760, which was *the* international best-seller of the eighteenth century, the *Discourse* paved the way for the *Sturm und Drang* (Storm and Stress) of the 1770s. During its short life, this angry-young-man movement led by Goethe and Herder flared with such dazzling intensity as to incinerate the old consensus about aesthetic standards. Subjectivism, emotional excess, spontaneity, violence, even a kind of anarchism were no longer deprecated but welcomed and encouraged. Responding to Goethe's epistolary novel *The Sufferings of Young Werther* (1774), the journalist Christian Daniel Schubart told his readers: 'Here I sit, my heart melting, my breast pounding, my eyes weeping tears of ecstatic pain, and do I need to tell you, dear reader, that I have been reading *The Sufferings of Young Werther* by my beloved Goethe? Or should I rather say that I have been devouring it?'[79]

By this time, it had become fashionable for stiff upper lips to tremble not just in response to lachrymose novels like *La Nouvelle Héloïse* and *Werther* but to all cultural media. In 1780 one of the first professional art critics, Johann Georg Meusel, lamented that until relatively recently the excessive rationalism of the philosophers had been very damaging to the arts. The accumulation of too much knowledge of the physical world, he argued, had led to arid desiccation: 'We are thinking more, but we are feeling less, and our ceaseless striving for omniscience has only resulted in coldness'.[80] What was needed was more feeling and fewer rules. As Herder's mentor, Johann Georg Hamann, put it in two memorable epigrams, 'Passion alone gives hands, feet and wings to abstractions and hypotheses; gives spirit, life and voice to images and symbols' and 'Rules are vestal virgins; unless they are violated, there can be no issue'.[81]

In tipping the balance away from cold reason, instrumental music had a special part to play. C. P. E. Bach, for example, argued that music was the language of feeling, the mirror of one's emotional life; its primary task was 'to transport the heart into soft emotion' and thus promote virtue.[82]

Music alone could go straight to the listener's feelings. Even a visual image required some sort of intellectual mediation before its effect was experienced. That was why E. T. A. Hoffmann could refer to music, in his analysis of Beethoven's instrumental music, as 'the most Romantic of all the arts, one might almost say the only one that is genuinely Romantic'.[83]

This had always been the case, of course. What was new was the greater emphasis placed on sound and originality at the expense of form and tradition. By 1800 many composers had shifted from a mimetic to an expressive aesthetic—from an aesthetic that viewed art in relation to nature to an aesthetic that viewed art in relation to the artist.[84] To employ the helpful metaphor devised by M. H. Abrams, art had changed from mirror to lamp, no longer reflecting the natural world outside but shining into the mind and heart of the creator.[85] If a work of art is to have value, then it must come from inside the artist, it must be individual, personal, original, spontaneous and authentic. As Wordsworth wrote in the preface to his *Lyrical Ballads*: 'Poetry is the spontaneous overflow of powerful feelings', a conviction shared by Shelley ('Poetry in a general sense may be defined to be "the expression of the imagination"'); Byron ('I can never get people to understand that poetry is the expression of excited passion'); Novalis ('Poetry is representation of the spirit, of the inner world in its totality'); and Tieck ('Not these plants, not these mountains, do I wish to copy, but my spirit, my mood, which governs me just at this moment').[86]

The idea that art should be essentially expressive interacted with the related and contemporary cult of the genius. Hitherto, the word 'genius' had meant the essence of something, as for example in 'the genius of the British constitution' (Adam Smith). In the course of the eighteenth century, however, it came to be applied to the creative artist, as in: 'What, for the most part, mean we by Genius, but the Power of accomplishing great things without the means generally reputed necessary to that end? A Genius differs from a good Understanding, as a Magician from a good Architect . . . Hence Genius has ever been supposed to partake of something Divine'.[87] Those words were written in 1759 by Edward Young in *Conjectures on Original Composition*. He contrasted the diligent scholar working within an established tradition with the Promethean hero bursting through the carapace of the past: 'Rules, like Crutches, are a needful Aid to the Lame, tho' an Impediment to the Strong. A Homer casts them away'.[88] Significantly, Young was much less influential in his native England than in Germany, where his ideas were taken up by Hamann, Herder and the *Sturm und Drang* writers and pushed further.[89]

By the end of the century, the creative genius was being hailed as the highest type of human, replacing such earlier ideal types as sage, saint, *uomo universale* or even military hero. Moreover, 'genius' ceased to be an attribute and became the whole person: to possess genius was to have an exceptional talent, but to *be* a genius was to be superhuman.[90] An early indication that music would become the ideal medium for the genius was provided by Christian Daniel Schubart, himself a notable musician and brilliant keyboard player, who wrote in 1784 in an essay 'On the Musical Genius': 'Musical genius is rooted in the heart and receives its impressions through the ear . . . All musical geniuses are self-taught, for the fire that animates them carries them away irresistibly to seek their own flight path'.[91]

One final ingredient was needed before the musical superman could emerge. This was sacralisation, the process by which culture lost its representational and recreational function and became an activity to be worshipped in its own right. Once again, it was during the middle decades of the eighteenth century that this crucial development began. At its heart was its apparent opposite: secularisation. As traditional forms of religion went into retreat, a growing number of intellectuals began to look elsewhere for metaphysical and spiritual sustenance. Gradually, they promoted art from being an instrument for the glory of God to being the godhead itself.

The most influential single exponent was Johann Joachim Winckelmann (1717–68), a Prussian by birth who spent most of his adult life in Rome. Thanks to his literary gifts—in particular his ability to imbue penetrating analysis with emotional excitement—and to his knack for being in the right place at the right time, Winckelmann's ideas had a colossal impact. Looking back on his youth, Goethe (born in 1749) recalled 'the general, unconditional veneration' that Winckelmann excited among his generation: 'All the periodicals were unanimous in promoting his fame, travellers visiting him returned instructed and enraptured, and his opinions were spread throughout the world of scholarship and society at large'.[92] Indeed Goethe gave the title *Winckelmann and His Century* to a collection of essays on the art history of the eighteenth century he published in 1805. Winckelmann's works were quickly translated into the major European

Apollo Belvedere, Vatican.

languages, ensuring that his influence was as international as his ideas. By marrying Pietist introspection to sensualist paganism, he created an aesthetic religion. His account of the *Apollo Belvedere,* displayed in the Vatican, is more than an appreciation of a statue; it is a religious exercise, because for him the statue does not represent God, it *is* a god.[93]

For German intellectuals dissatisfied with Christianity but equally averse to what they saw as the superficial materialism of the English empiricists and French philosophes, beauty was an attractive substitute for holiness. The definitive version was delivered in the mid-1790s by Friedrich Schiller in two classic treatises, *On the Aesthetic Education of Man* and *Naive and Sentimental Poetry.* He argued that most humans were impervious to rational argument and could be affected only through their feelings. So the seeds of rational perception will wither where they fall unless the soil has been prepared by the emotions and imagination: 'The way to the head must be opened through the heart'. At a time when all Europe was in danger of being overwhelmed by revolutionary change, only through culture could humankind achieve liberty without license: 'If man is ever to solve the problem of politics in practice, he will have to approach it through the problem of the aesthetic, because it is only through Beauty that man makes his way to freedom' was Schiller's conclusion.[94] This might have a quaint, if not sinister, resonance for Anglophone ears, but it proved to be hugely and enduringly influential in German-speaking Europe.

Beethoven as Hero and Genius

In short, by 1800 developments in literature, the visual arts and philosophy had created a new kind of aesthetic ideal that can be called Romantic. Its chief characteristics were emotionalism, introspection, self-expression, originality, the cult of genius and sacralisation. Surprisingly, up until then the role played by music in the Romantic movement had been modest, partly because most musicians were still locked in a representational patronage structure and partly because they were not accustomed to articulating the wider significance of their art. Not one of the major composers of the eighteenth century, with the exception of Rameau, could be described as an intellectual. All this was about to change. To understand why, we return to Beethoven's funeral.

The oration composed by Franz Grillparzer and declaimed at the cemetery gates by Heinrich Anschütz, the leading classical actor of his day, was remarkable for many reasons, not the least being the total absence of God. Art was invoked as Beethoven's deity:

> The harp that is hushed! Let me call him so! For he was an artist, and all that was his, was his through art alone. The thorns of life

had wounded him deeply, and as the castaway clings to the
shore, so did he seek refuge in thine arms, O thou glorious sister
and peer of the Good and the True, thou balm of wounded
hearts, heaven-born Art! To thee he clung fast, and even when
the portal was closed where through thou hadst entered in and
spoken to him, when his deaf ear had blinded his vision for thy
features, still did he ever carry thine image within his heart, and
when he died it still reposed on his breast. He was an artist—
and who shall arise to stand beside him?[95]

Needless to say, because his own recorded utterances were inconsistent, not to say confused, Beethoven's views on religion have been endlessly debated, especially by parties anxious to claim him as their own. The best guess is that he was not an orthodox Catholic or indeed a Christian but that he did believe in a personal and beneficent god manifested primarily in a pantheist way through nature. Significantly, Beethoven venerated Schiller from an early age and clearly knew his work intimately, quoting passages from Schiller's plays in his correspondence.[96] He first considered a musical setting of his 'Ode to Joy' while still in Bonn in the early 1790s. The Bonn professor Fischenich wrote to Schiller's wife in January 1793 about his friend Beethoven: 'He proposes to compose Schiller's *Freude,* strophe by strophe. I expect something perfect, since he is wholly devoted to the great and sublime.'[97] Beethoven's own version of Schiller's aesthetic religion was the pithy observation: 'Only art and scholarship give us intimations and hopes of a higher life.'[98]

Beethoven both personified and advanced Romanticism. In music he was the true mould-breaker, establishing the model of the composer as the angry, unhappy, original, uncompromising genius, standing above ordinary mortals and with a direct line to the Almighty. Already during his lifetime a flood of anecdotes was in print, projecting, in the words of Paul Johnson, 'the composite picture of the archetype martyr to art, the new kind of secular saint who was taking over from the old Christian calendars as a focus of public veneration.'[99] Characteristic was the will he wrote in 1802 at the age of twenty-eight, leaving everything to his two brothers. This was not a legal document but an impassioned *cri de cœur* against the cruel stroke of fate that was depriving him of his hearing. Only his art, he wrote, and the need to express everything that was inside him had restrained him from taking

Title page of Beethoven's Third Symphony, *Eroica,* with the dedication 'intitolata Bonaparte' scratched out.

his own life. He ended with the anguished plea: 'Oh Providence, vouchsafe at least one single day to me—When, oh when, oh Divine Godhead—shall I once feel it in the Temple of Nature and among mankind. Never? No, that would be too hard'.[100] Discovered among his papers after his death and promptly published, this 'Heiligenstadt Testament' became one of the seminal documents of Romanticism.

Also in Heiligenstadt—a small spa a few miles from Vienna—Beethoven began the composition of his third symphony, the *Eroica,* the following year. It was performed in private for Prince Lobkowitz at his Vienna palace in the summer of 1804 and for the first time in public in January 1805. Twice as long as any symphony by Haydn or Mozart and sounding utterly different, this Symphony No. 3 in E-flat Major was recognised at once by friend and foe alike as an undoubted 'work of genius', as Haydn's first biographer Georg August Griesinger informed the music publishers

Breitkopf and Härtel.[101] A good impression of the consternation it aroused was conveyed by the review in the *Allgemeine Musikalische Zeitung* of Leipzig, the leading musical periodical of the day: 'This long, extremely difficult composition is actually a very long drawn-out, daring and wild fantasy. There is no lack of striking and beautiful passages in which one must recognise the energetic and talented spirit of their creator; but very often it seems to lose itself in anarchy'.[102] Beethoven had called the symphony 'Bonaparte', which he wrote on the title page, but learning in 1804 that his hero had declared himself emperor, he scratched the name out with such passion that his pen went through the paper.[103]

Problems with the Public

For all succeeding generations of musicians, Beethoven was the great original. Liszt wrote: 'For us musicians, Beethoven's work is like the pillar of cloud and fire which guided the Israelites through the desert—a pillar of cloud to guide us by day, a pillar of fire to guide us by night, "so that we may progress both day and night"'.[104] It was also Liszt's experience of how his hero was treated by posterity that encouraged him to further the sacralisation of music. For as Beethoven moved on into ever more adventurous realms, he began to leave many of his listeners behind. Even the distinguished critic Ludwig Rellstab found the late quartets mystifying, writing that opus 127 'contains only the ruins of the youthful beauty and manly nobility of his genius, often buried deep under arid rubble'.[105]

Many of those professing to be enraptured by Beethoven's music appear to have been more attracted by his name and reputation. At a recital in Paris, Liszt changed the order in the programme but without announcing what he had done, so that when he reached the item advertised as being by Beethoven he actually played a piece by the little-known Johann Peter Pixis, and vice versa. Unable to spot the difference, the audience received the 'Beethoven' with rapture and the 'Pixis' with indifference. The one exception was Berlioz, whose contempt for Parisian philistinism was thus confirmed.[106] Liszt also recorded that as a child prodigy he had played a piece he had composed himself, only to be told patronisingly that 'it's not half-bad for a child'. Later, he played it again, saying it was by the minor composer Carl Czerny, and no one listened. Later still he played it a third time, now claiming it was by Beethoven—and everyone said it was wonderful.[107]

By no coincidence, it was during just this period that creative musicians began the long process of alienation from public taste. Back in the early eighteenth century, when public concerts in London were getting going, all kinds of nonmusical attractions had been inserted into the programme to bring in the customers, such as dancing, juggling, and circus acts. On occasions members of the audience were invited on stage to try their hands at any instruments that took their fancy.[108] Although such gimmicks were no longer needed once concert-going became established, as the market for music expanded rapidly in the early 1800s these sideline entertainments staged a revival. The impresarios who took over the running of concerts in the major European cities thought they knew what the public wanted, and that was first and foremost *variety*. Rightly or wrongly, they did not believe that their customers could sit still long enough to listen to a whole symphony, so they inserted operatic arias or even dance tunes between the movements.

When Schubert's last complete symphony, No. 9 in C Major (known as the Great), was eventually performed, arias from Donizetti's *Lucia di Lammermoor* were interpolated to 'enliven' the proceedings.[109] At the Promenade Concerts at the Royal Adelaide Gallery in the Strand, selections from the latest Meyerbeer opera were accompanied by 'the real Scotch Quadrilles, introducing the Highland pipes . . . followed by the performances of the Infant Thalia, Experiments with the Colossal Burning Lens and the new Oxyhydrogen Microscope, Popular Lectures, and The Laughing Gas every Tuesday, Thursday and Saturday evenings'.[110] Conductors began to play to the audience, the best example of showmanship being Louis Jullien, who dominated the London concert scene in the 1840s and 1850s and on special occasions launched a performance by having himself shot out of a trap-door, baton in hand.[111]

This commercialisation led to a growing bifurcation between musicians who composed and performed for a mass public and those who composed and performed for themselves, always hoping of course that connoisseurs would add popularity and material reward to the integrity they prized so highly. For these latter composers, the new mass audience was composed of 'philistines'—a pejorative term used to deride unsophisticated, unintellectual, money-grubbing *bourgeois*. According to the Grimm brothers' dictionary, 'philistine' was first used in this sense in Jena follow-ing a brawl between town and gown that resulted in the death of a student. At his funeral the parson preached a sermon on the text 'The Philistines be upon thee, Samson' (Judges 16:9).[112]

Looking back at his student days in Göttingen in 1820, Heine wrote in 'The Journey to the Harz': 'In general the inhabitants of Göttingen can be divided into students, professors, philistines and cattle, although these four groups are not sharply divided from each other. The cattle are the most important'. The complaint that music had become popular, commercial, vulgar, and superficial was a favourite topic of the musical periodicals that mushroomed during the period.[113] The distinguished French critic Joseph d'Ortigue, who wrote the first biography of his friend Berlioz, satirised the philistine *bourgeoise* as a lady from the fashionable Chaussée d'Antin who gives her daughter piano and music lessons in the same sort of spirit that she gives her son a coat and herself a cashmere jacket, because she regards music simply 'as an item of fashion and vanity'.[114] The most distinguished musical statement of this hostility to the middle class was surely Robert Schumann's *Carnaval*, composed in 1834, whose last of twenty-one pieces is entitled 'The March of the League of David against the Philistines'.

For the time being, musicians and public could maintain some sort of contact because enough of the latter showed appreciation of the former to hold out the hope that more might follow. Nevertheless, the growing feel-ing that the public at large was suffering from 'cultural retardation' encour-aged further sacralisation, to place music on an altar high enough to be out of reach of the grubby hands of consumers.[115] This operation was helped by the fact that many musicians—Berlioz, Schumann, Mendelssohn, Liszt, Wagner and innumerable lesser lights—also turned their hand to journal-ism, both to improve their earnings and to propagate their message. Prob-ably the most influential and certainly the most eloquent was Liszt, whose belief in the redemptive power of music was matched by his Catholic piety. In a remarkable series of articles entitled 'On the Situation of Artists and Their Social Condition', published in installments in the *Gazette musicale de Paris* in 1835, he launched a passionate critique of modern civilisation.

Its degeneration, he argued, was due to the separation of religion, politics, art and the natural sciences into separate activities. Only when they could be reunited under the aegis of the arts, especially music, could man's alienation be resolved. Alas, he continued, the dominant characteristic of musicians in modern times was their subordinate status: they *should* count for everything, but in reality they counted for nothing. They had only themselves to blame, because most of them were characterised by a lack of faith in their art, by egocentricity, and by squalid commercialism. It was high time they all got together to realise that they had a 'great religious and social MISSION'.[116] In a further article two years later, he likened the artist to a priest, for both bore the mark of predestination—neither could resist their vocation. Even when he lived in society, the true artist's life was interiorised, and not even the most powerful of human emotions—vanity, ambition, greed, jealousy, love—could break through the magic fence surrounding the sanctuary that was his creative centre.[117]

Wagner and Bayreuth

The sacralisation of music reached its climax with Wagner. Liszt's gifts to Wagner were manifold: material (gifts and 'loans'); artistic (Liszt's production of *Lohengrin* at Weimar in 1850 began Wagner's conquest of the German operatic world); musical (however reluctant Wagner was to admit it); and also intellectual (even if underestimated by most Wagner scholars). Wagner even seduced Liszt's daughter, Cosima, away from her husband, Hans von Bülow, an act that strained Liszt's legendary good humour. Although Wagner rarely acknowledged the work of other musicians, especially if they were still alive, he made an exception for Liszt.

At the dinner held on 18 August 1876 to mark the end of the first Bayreuth Festival, at which *The Ring of the Nibelung* had been performed in its entirety for the first time, Wagner rose to pay special tribute to Liszt: 'For everything that I am and have achieved, I have one person to thank, without whom not a single note of mine would have been known; a dear friend who, when I was banned from Germany, with matchless devotion and self-denial drew me into the light, and was the first to recognise me. To this dear friend belongs the highest honour. It is my sublime friend and master, Franz Liszt!'[118] Liszt returned the compliment with interest, writing at various times that Wagner was the equal of Beethoven and Dante.[119]

Wagner took Romanticism to new and insurmountable heights.

Surely the best illustration of Romantic inspiration is his account in *My Life* of how he began the composition of *The Rhinegold*, the first part of *The Ring*. On the afternoon of 5 September 1853, while travelling in Italy, Wagner was lying on a sofa in his hotel room in La Spezia. He was suffering from diarrhoea, insomnia and the after-effects of the sea sickness he had suffered on the steamboat that brought him there from Genoa. Not for the first or last time, he was also feeling lonely, homesick, neglected and generally depressed. Try as he would, he could not get to sleep, and instead he

> sank into a kind of somnambulistic state, in which I suddenly had the feeling of being immersed in rapidly flowing water. Its rushing soon resolved itself for me into the musical sound of the chord of E flat major, resounding in persistent broken chords; these in turn transformed themselves into melodic figurations of increasing motion, yet the E flat major triad never changed, and seemed by its continuance to impart infinite significance to the element in which I was sinking. I awoke in sudden terror from this trance, feeling as though the waves were crashing high above my head. I recognised at once that the orchestral prelude to *Das Rheingold*, long dormant within me but up to that moment inchoate, had at last been revealed; and I also saw immediately precisely how it was with me: the vital flood would come from within me, and not from without.[120]

'From within me, and not from without'—there could hardly be a more concise definition of the essence of the Romantic project, unless it is Hegel's pithy formulation, 'absolute inwardness'. Only when the shackles of the world of appearances were loosened and access gained to the subconscious—only then could the creative springs flow. Wagner loved the 'wonder world of the night' and the dreams it brought, putting into the mouths of Tristan and Isolde a paean of praise to 'endless night, sweet night! Glorious, exalted, night of love!' and their hatred for 'deceitful day, our worst enemy'.[121] And he liked to work himself into a passion of introspection before he could create. When composing *Tannhäuser*, he told the Berlin critic Karl Gaillard: 'Before starting to write a verse or even to outline a scene, I must feel intoxicated by the musical aroma [*Duft*] of my subject, all the tones, all the characteristic motives are in my head'.[122] To aid the process, he needed to be surrounded by—and indeed to be wearing—luxurious fabrics and strong perfumes, a fetish with an unmistakable erotic component.

Appropriately, it was at Bayreuth that Wagner paid tribute to his friend and (by then) father-in-law, Liszt. For Bayreuth represented the climax of sacralisation that Liszt had done so much to encourage. Although Wagner did not settle on Bayreuth as the location for his festival theatre until 1871, the essential features of his undertaking had been worked out twenty years earlier in the so-called Zürich reform writings written in his Swiss exile after the failure of the Dresden insurrection of 1849. In *Art and Revolution* (1849) he argued that only the total work of art, incorporating dance, music, drama and poetry, could redeem humankind from the abyss into which it had sunk:

> The theatre is the most comprehensive, the most influential of all artistic institutions, and before human beings can freely practise their noblest activity, which is art, how can they hope to be free and independent in other, lower directions? . . . Eternally youthful art, always able to refresh itself from the noblest spirits of its time, is better equipped than a senile religion that has lost its hold on the public, than an incapable government, to steer the turbulent currents of social movements past the wild cliffs and treacherous shallows towards their great and noble goal—the goal of true humanity.[123]

The work in question was of course *The Ring of the Nibelung*, whose composition he had begun in the revolutionary year 1848. But it could not be performed in any existing theatre, where either the representational pomp of the prince or the squalid commercialism of the impresario held sway. He wrote to Hans von Bülow in 1861: 'A single look at the present-day theatre has shown me once again that there is only one thing which will enable my art to take root and not to vanish, totally misunderstood, into thin air. I need a theatre such as I alone can build.' At first he proposed to locate it in one of the large German cities, probably Berlin, but he soon thought better of it, for he did not wish a 'clash with an existing theatre of any great size nor a confrontation with the usual theatre-going public of a large city and its habits', as he put it in the preface to the libretto of *The Ring*, published in 1863.[124]

An early photograph of the Festival Theatre at Bayreuth taken from the town.

Bayreuth was chosen eventually because it was the right size, housed no competitor (although it did have a magnificent eighteenth-century opera house whose large stage had first drawn Wagner's attention to the town), was Protestant, was in northern Franconia (far away from detested Munich but still in Bavaria and thus within the realms of Ludwig II, on whose financial support the whole project depended) and, last but not least, was accessible by railway.[125] Not everything Wagner had intended was accomplished at Bayreuth, but one aim he certainly did fulfill. Going there was (and is) not in any sense like 'going to the opera'. Right from its inception, the event was intended to be a festival—he referred to *The Ring* as a 'stage festival play' as early as 1851. The Festival Theatre (Festspielhaus) stands outside the town on a green hill—'without a city wall'—and the audience that makes its way there consists of pilgrims seeking redemption, not opera-goers seeking entertainment.

Although such stupendous works do not lend themselves easily to paraphrase, it can be said that *The Ring* delivers a fundamental critique of the modern world and shows how humankind can come to terms with it.

At the heart of Wagner's analysis was the clash between love and power. Drawing on his deep reading of both the ancient Greeks and the Young Hegelians (especially Ludwig Feuerbach), he demonstrated the corrosive self-destructiveness of men seeking power, whether it was Alberich formally renouncing love in order to seize the Rhinegold or Wotan ripping a branch from the world-ash tree to fashion the spear on which he inscribed the contracts that underpinned his authority.[126] *The Ring* suggests at least four possible solutions: revolution, symbolised by the sword that is first wielded by Siegmund, then smashed by Wotan but remade by Siegfried; sexual revolution, symbolised by the incestuous union of Siegmund and Sieglinde that produced Siegfried; 'the eternally feminine', personified by Brünnhilde's self-immolation that takes the ring back to the Rhinemaidens; and renunciation of the will, first accepted by Wotan and then taken to a higher level by Parsifal in the eponymous opera that formed the fifth part of *The Ring* and was first performed at Bayreuth in 1882.

With *Parsifal*, the sacralisation of culture reached its pinnacle. Wagner called it a 'Festival Play for the dedication of a Stage' (*Bühnenweihfestspiel*). Although the word 'Christ' never appears, Christian references and symbols are important throughout, and the work ends with Parsifal administering Communion to the knights of the Grail. Although not a Christian work, *Parsifal* is certainly religious. Following Wagner's death six months after its first performance, Liszt told a Hungarian friend, Count Géza Zichy: 'We have suffered a heavy loss. Wagner is dead—relatively dead, for such men never quite die. He enjoyed a splendid, glorious sunset. His last work was a prayer. In his heart he had dedicated *Parsifal* to the everlasting God. Wagner could not pray liturgically, and so in this way he created his own prayer. What a beautiful life, and what a magnificent death! Fully lived out, fully expressed, fully recognised: we have no right to complain!'[127]

This is a real insight, but it does not go quite far enough, for in *Parsifal* Wagner was doing much more than praying. As his correspondence with King Ludwig showed, he was seeking nothing less than the regeneration of humankind.[128] Members of an audience who experienced a music drama together would experience the 'the truth of a work of art'. Through aesthetics, social integration could be achieved by creating a general ethical consensus. In other words, Wagner was claiming for art the function previously exercised by religion and arrogated in modern times by politics

The summit of the sacralisation of music: Paul von Joukowsky's sketch of the closing moments of the first performance of *Parsifal* at Bayreuth in 1882.

or economics. The Christian religion, although inadequate and in its organised form positively harmful, could help through its large stock of liturgical symbols and rituals and its central idea of the suffering saviour. Through *Parsifal* Wagner sought to show why there was so much suffering in the world and how it could be overcome only by the negation of the self. Unlike Siegfried, the hero of *The Ring*, Parsifal has the capacity to learn from experience and to realise that he must redeem himself before he can redeem others. That is why the work ends with the words 'Redemption to the redeemer'.[129]

As the emphasis on the negation of the will indicates, the dominant philosophical influence on *Parsifal* was Arthur Schopenhauer (1788–1860). When Wagner first read *The World as Will and Representation* in 1854, the libretto of *The Ring* was already complete. By the time he wrote the first draft of *Parsifal* in 1857 he had immersed himself in Schopenhauer's philosophy with characteristic single-mindedness. It is some measure of Wagner's intellectualism that he read Schopenhauer's *magnum opus*—two volumes, over a thousand pages—four times in twelve months. As the philosopher Bryan Magee has justly observed: 'There has rarely been so productive a relationship between one great mind and another when the two were in different fields'.[130] All of Wagner's last music dramas—*Tristan and Isolde*, *The Mastersingers of Nuremberg* and *Parsifal*—are imbued with Schopenhauer. There was no self-delusion in Wagner's claim that Schopenhauer had helped him to articulate intuitions he had held long and deeply but without understanding.

On his first reading, Wagner was especially taken with Schopenhauer's aesthetics, 'particularly his surprising and significant conception of music'.[131] As well he might have been, for Schopenhauer was the first philosopher not just to recognise the value of music but to see it as so superior to other art forms as to constitute an aesthetic category all by itself.[132] No less a figure than Friedrich Nietzsche summed up what Wagner took from Schopenhauer in this regard, namely, the claim that music represents 'the triumphant culmination of all art, not concerned like the others with images of the phenomenal world but, rather, speaking the language of the will directly from the deep source of Being, its most quintessential manifestation'.[133]

The first performance of *The Ring* in 1876 had been only a qualified success artistically and an unequivocal disaster financially, as Wagner ruefully recognised. *Parsifal*, however, was a triumph in all respects. Immediately after the first performance, Liszt wrote: 'The general feeling was that there is nothing that can be said about this miraculous work. Silence is surely the only possible response to so deeply moving a work; the solemn beat of its pendulum is from the sublime to the most sublime'.[134] Gustav Mahler wrote to his friend Friedrich Löhr: 'When I left the Festival Theatre, incapable of speech, I knew that the greatest, most painful thing had happened to me, and that I should have it with me in all its sanctity for the rest of my life'.[135]

Although *Parsifal* had its detractors, most famously Nietzsche ('the alliance of beauty and disease') and Igor Stravinsky ('At the end of a quarter of an hour I could bear no more'), the success of Wagner's sacralised art-religion was immediate, colossal, international and enduring. In 1891 the French writer Romain Rolland wrote to his mother that *Parsifal* was 'the fifth Gospel or rather the first, the greatest of them all . . . everything in it is simple and sublime, from beginning to end, and the poet is the equal of the composer. It is illuminated through and through by a divine compassion, an infinite mercy, a purified suffering. That is truly no longer theatre, that is no longer art, that is religion and like God Himself'.[136]

The Invention of Classical Music

During the course of Wagner's life (1813–1883) the world changed more rapidly and radically than ever before in human history. Very few, if any, of those changes proved to be reversible: the modernising process is a ratchet, not a cycle. And so it was in music. For all the inevitable reaction against the kind of cultural project that Wagner stood for, there could never be a return to the representational scene of a century earlier. Future musicians working in the classical tradition would accept as axiomatic the need to create music that was sincere, expressive, spontaneous, individual and, above all, original. The most pejorative adjective in a modern music critic's arsenal is 'derivative'. Even when being playful in deliberate contrast to the solemn Germans, composers have remained essentially serious. Any idea that one might write incidental music to be played as aural wallpaper while elites dined, played cards or watched fireworks is anathema. Yet Mozart had not thought it beneath him to write dozens of dances, cassations, divertimentos, serenades and nocturnes and to do so with great care.

This period also marked a major shift in the way music was regarded. Instead of writing something recognised as ephemeral, to be played once or twice and then discarded, composers aspired to create works that would become a permanent part of the classical repertoire. One indication of this fundamental change was the sharp reduction in the amount of music created by an individual composer. Antonio Vivaldi (1678–1741) wrote around five hundred concertos; Mozart (1756–91) wrote about fifty; Beethoven (1770–1827) wrote eight. Haydn (1732–1809) wrote 104 symphonies; Mozart wrote forty-one; Beethoven wrote nine; Brahms (1833–97) made his first sketches for a symphony in 1855 but did not complete it until 1876.[137] The delay appears to have stemmed from his sense of being overshadowed by Beethoven. As he wrote to Hermann Levi: 'You can have no conception how it feels to someone like myself always to hear the tread of a giant like this at one's back'.[138] He cannot have been pleased to learn that Hans von Bülow had referred to his creation as 'Beethoven's Tenth' (although to my ears it sounds more like 'Schumann's Fifth').

As music was sacralised and placed on an altar, so were its creators elevated to become high priests of this secularised religion. As early as 1802 Haydn had referred to himself as 'a not wholly unworthy priest of this sacred art'.[139] By the middle of the nineteenth century, the use of quasi-religious language to describe the musician's calling was common—for example, when an English periodical referred to Mendelssohn and Spohr as 'high priests of art who wield the sceptre by right of intellectual power' or when Prince Schwarzenberg praised Liszt as 'a true prince of music, a genuine *grand seigneur* . . . a priest of art'.[140]

The objects of their veneration responded by becoming much more self-conscious than their predecessors. If getting much beyond the bare bones of Johann Sebastian Bach's life has been difficult, we know too much about his fellow Saxon Richard Wagner for his own good. He left a dozen fat volumes of theoretical writings and commentaries on his own works, an autobiography of more than 300,000 words, and at least 12,000 letters, many of them very long. His second wife, Cosima, kept a diary from 1 January 1869 until Wagner's death fourteen years later, in which she recorded on a daily basis everything of importance he did and said. As usual, Wagner is an extreme case, but he personified a trend. Every nineteenth-century composer of significance left a body of correspondence, and many wrote autobiographies or kept diaries too—for example Spohr, Weber, Berlioz, Liszt, Schumann and Moscheles. Thanks to the explosive increase in the periodical press, any musician who attained even limited contemporary fame could also count on being the subject of reports, reminiscences and obituaries. Lithography and then photography broadcast their visages far and wide.

Part and parcel of this process was the establishment of a body of works generally regarded as being of 'classical' status. Not by accident, this occurred first in England, where the unique size and commercialism of the capital's public sphere led to an early separation of music from its representational function. The absence of a powerful court also helped, as did the precocious development of public concerts and festivals.[141]

One sign of a change in attitude to the music of the past was the foundation of the Academy of Ancient Music in 1726, a group of professional musicians dedicated to reviving the sacred music and madrigals of the previous two centuries. More influential was the Concert of Ancient Music founded in 1776 at the instigation of the earl of Sandwich to promote the performance of works at least twenty years old. It was dominated by peers and landed gentry and patronised by the king, and its success provided further evidence that the development of public concerts did not represent the victory of the middle class.[142] In promoting the interests of music by dead composers, the founders were helped by the enduring popularity of Handel, whose commemoration they organised in 1784. In German-speaking Europe a similar function was performed a generation or so later by Haydn, Mozart and Beethoven.

By 1900 the major axioms of 'art music' were all in place. Despite all the vagaries of modernism and postmodernism, an expressive aesthetic emphasizing originality, sincerity and authenticity has remained at center stage. Even those who appeared to turn their backs most resolutely did not wander very far. A good example was Stravinsky. The Romantic legacy was such a heavy burden that he even found himself 'alienated from Beethoven for many years'.[143] *Parsifal* at Bayreuth in 1912 was, for him, 'revolting . . . ridiculous . . . unseemly and sacrilegious'. In his autobiography, he tried to deny music any expressive element: 'Music is, by its very nature, essentially powerless to *express* anything at all, whether a feeling, an attitude of mind, a psychological mood, a phenomenon of nature, etc. . . . *Expression* has never been an inherent property of music'.[144]

Yet every note of his own wonderfully original and expressive music belied his theoretical self-effacement. Indeed, he had already given the game away earlier in his autobiography when he stressed the need for a solid technical grounding: 'No matter what the subject may be, there is only one course for the beginner; he must at first accept a discipline imposed from without, but only as the means of obtaining freedom for, and strengthening himself in his own method of expression'.[145] Moreover, the inability of his audiences to respond to his later work drove him back inside himself: 'Unfortunately, perfect communion [with the public] is rare, and the more the personality of the author is revealed, the rarer that communion becomes. The more he eliminates all that is extraneous, all that is not his own, or "in him," the greater is his risk of conflicting with the expectations of the bulk of the public, who always receive a shock when confronted by something to which they are not accustomed'.[146]

Jazz and Romanticism

All the various threads of music's expressive nature and sacral purpose cannot be followed here to the present day. But two genres outside the classical tradition illustrate this growing power. From the time it emerged toward the end of the nineteenth century, jazz fit very well with the Romantic aesthetic, for it was nothing if not spontaneous, improvisatory and individual. Its African-American origins also made it the potential ally of liberation movements. During much of the twentieth century, however, for all of jazz's ability to express the suffering and aspirations of an oppressed community, the genre was very much part of the entertainment industry. Even its greatest exponents—Louis Armstrong or Duke Ellington—worked within a social and cultural structure underpinned by a sense of hierarchy and deference. It was not until the consensus (or perhaps hegemony would be a better word) that characterised American culture during the Second World War began to break up after 1945 that jazz musicians became more ambitious, both in theory and in practice.

One example must suffice, but it is a good one, in all senses. In December 1964 John Coltrane recorded in a single evening session an album he called *A Love Supreme* with a quartet consisting of himself playing tenor saxophone, Wynton Kelly at the piano, Elvin Jones on drums and Jimmy Garrison on bass. When released early the following year, with a suitably serious cover, the album was accompanied by liner notes written by Coltrane himself. They began: 'All Praise To God To Whom All Praise is Due. Let us pursue Him in the righteous path. Yes, it is true; "seek and Ye shall find". Only through him can we know the most wondrous bequeathal'. He went on to explain that he offered his music as 'an attempt to say "THANK YOU GOD"' for rescuing him from the slough of despond into which addiction to heroin, alcohol and nicotine had previously cast him. The conversion experience had actually occurred some seven years earlier, but as with Bunyan's Christian, Coltrane's journey from the City of Destruction to the Celestial City had not been straightforward.

The liner notes also contained a poem entitled 'A Love Supreme', which thanks God for breathing gently through the human race and ends with heartfelt gratitude.[147] Coltrane placed this poem on his music stand to inspire the improvisations that formed 'Psalm', the fourth and final part of the suite (the others being 'Acknowledgement', 'Resolution' and 'Pursuance'). Apart from these words, nothing had been written down, for Coltrane had been fumbling intuitively for the sounds he sought. Earlier in 1964 he had told the critic Nat Hentoff that 'I'm still primarily looking into certain sounds, certain scales. Not that I'm sure of what I'm looking for, except that it will be something that hasn't been played before. I don't know what it is. I know I'll have that feeling when I get it.'[148]

The birth of a son gave him the necessary inspiration. His second wife, Alice, recorded that Coltrane locked himself away in an upstairs room, alone with only his saxophone for company. When he emerged, 'It was like Moses coming down from the mountain, it was so beautiful. He walked down and there was that joy, that peace in his face, tranquillity. So I said: "Tell me everything, we didn't see you really for four or five days". He said, "This is the first time that I have received all of the music for what I want to record, in a suite. This is the first time I have everything, everything ready"'.[149]

Every Romantic artist, no matter what the medium, would have had sympathy with Coltrane's account of his aspirations:

> My goal is to live the truly religious life and express it in my music. If you live it, when you play there's no problem because the music is just part of the whole thing. To be a musician is really something. It goes very, very deep. My music is the spiritual expression of what I am—my faith, my knowledge, my being . . . When you begin to see the possibilities of music, you desire to do something really good for people, to help humanity free itself from its hang-ups. I think music can make the world better and, if I'm qualified, I want to do it. I'd like to point out to people the divine in a musical language that transcends words. I want to speak to their souls.[150]

John Coltrane in 1964. This image would adorn the
cover of his *A Love Supreme* album.

Also quintessentially Romantic was his comment to the earnest French interviewer who asked him whether it was possible to improvise when employing Schoenberg's twelve-tone system: 'Damn the rules, it's the feeling
that counts'.[151]

How offensive Stravinsky would have found all this is not hard to
imagine. Its seriousness, portentousness even, does indeed invite a disdainful curl of the lip. Yet, just as even a few bars of Wagner's music can efface
the memory of even his most ponderous theorising, so can Coltrane's
amazing music confound the most cynical. In just thirty-two minutes and
fifty seconds of sustained inspiration, Coltrane and his three colleagues
created one of the great musical masterpieces of the twentieth century.
Moreover, despite the demands *A Love Supreme* places on the listeners, it
struck an immediate, powerful and enduring chord with the public. By the
end of the decade, the album had sold more than half-a-million copies and
continues to be heard with undimmed enthusiasm.[152]

Coltrane's own religious views were as imprecise as they were deeply

felt. He belonged to no church and subscribed to no creed, expressing belief in all gods. It was just his ability to combine deep introspection with a
transcendental vision that allowed his music to have such a powerful and
enduring appeal. Coltrane's achievement provided further evidence, if it
were needed, of the validity of Wagner's assertion that music 'is better
equipped than a senile religion that has lost its hold on the public' to satisfy
the spiritual aspirations of a secularised society. The response *A Love Supreme* evoked from Bono of U2 illustrates this perfectly:

> I was at the top of the Grand Hotel in Chicago [on tour in 1987]
> listening to *A Love Supreme* and learning the lesson of a life-
> time. Earlier I had been watching televangelists remake God in
> their own image: tiny, petty, and greedy. Religion has become
> the enemy of God. I was thinking: religion was what happened
> when God, like Elvis, has left the building. I knew from my
> earliest memories that the world was winding in a direction
> away from love and I too was caught in its drag. There is so
> much wickedness in this world but beauty is our consolation
> prize: the beauty of John Coltrane's reedy voice, its whisper, its
> knowingness, its sly sexuality, its praise of creation. And so Col-
> trane began to make sense to me. I left the music on repeat and
> I stayed awake listening to a man facing God with the gift of
> his music.[153]

Mutatis mutandis, the same could be said about *Parsifal.*

Rock and Romanticism

After *A Love Supreme,* Coltrane became ever more experimental. He continued to inspire the avant-garde, but he left much of his public behind.
Three months after he died from liver cancer in July 1967, the front page of
Down Beat proclaimed 'Jazz as we know it is dead'.[154] Yet just when jazz was
falling away as a vehicle for musical sacralisation, another genre was beginning to develop similar aspirations. This was rock music, just moving out
of Tin Pan Alley into much more demanding territory. Although rock 'n'

roll had led a social and cultural revolution in the 1950s, by the early 1960s it was dominated by managers, impresarios and record companies with no ambitions beyond making as much money as quickly as possible. The raw energy of its early days had made way for a blander, less challenging style. In 1956 Elvis Presley was singing 'Heartbreak Hotel' as if he meant it; by 1962 he was crooning 'Good Luck Charm' to a smooth Nashville accompaniment; and by 1965 he was turning out wholesome pap like 'If Everyday Was Like Christmas'.

The eruption of The Beatles during the winter of 1962–63 did not really change much. The trite lyrics of their first successes—'Love Me Do', 'Please Please Me', 'From Me to You', 'She Loves You' and so on—were still firmly anchored in the June-moon-spoon tradition of the trials and tribulations of young love. Much more adventurous were the groups that resisted the sort of sanitisation that The Beatles' manager, Brian Epstein, imposed on his charges—identical haircuts, uniforms, public relations—in favour of staying loyal to the African-American blues tradition that had originally inspired them. John Mayall's Bluesbreakers, The Animals, The Yardbirds and The Rolling Stones kept their music rough, ready and rooted. When The Rolling Stones' manager bought them three-piece suits, they wore them once for a television performance and once for a photo shoot, and then threw them away.[155] In one of the great ironies of twentieth-century musical history, it was English blues groups who created a mass market for African-American musicians in their own country by making palatable to the white American record-buying public standards such as 'The House of the Rising Sun' (The Animals) and 'I Just Wanna Make Love to You' (The Rolling Stones). For The Animals, this was a case of carrying coals to Newcastle *from* Newcastle—their hometown.

For all their commercial success, these blues-inspired groups managed to maintain at least the image of independence and integrity, using their music to do more than court popular success and material gain. As the better of them gained confidence, they moved away from slavish imitation to find their own voices. A comparison between Robert Johnson's iconic recording of 'Crossroads' in 1936 and the performance by Cream (Eric Clapton, Ginger Baker, Jack Bruce) at the Albert Hall in May 2005 shows how differently the same material can be interpreted. Arguably the greatest living master of the electric guitar, Clapton personified the Romantic aesthetic: 'The classic Clapton pose—back to the crowd, head

A sixties icon is defiled.

bowed over his instrument, alone with the agony of the blues—suggests a supplicant communing with something inward: a muse or a demon . . . his entire career can be seen as a search for a form in which he could express the staple blues emotions—fear, loneliness, anger and humour—in a personally valid way'.[156] Clapton's struggles with drug addiction, loss of faith, unrequited love, alcoholism and bereavement, which could be charted through songs such as 'Layla' (1970) and 'No Tears in Heaven' (1991), only served to confirm his quasi-divine status. Since the mid-1960s his innumerable fans have called him simply 'God'.[157] Neither his excesses nor his single-minded pursuit of his own vision has prevented Clapton from accumulating a vast fortune, reliably estimated to be in excess of £100 million.[158]

Just as Clapton and the other bluesmen were carving out their own expressive medium in the mid-1960s, a rather different but equally potent contribution to the sacralisation of popular music was being made by Bob Dylan. His great service was to show how poetry, music and performance could be combined to form a work of art that totaled more than the sum of its parts. His immensely influential protest songs of the early 1960s evolved into something more durable when he moved away from overt politics to expressing a less topical but more personal and introspective vision. They also reached a much larger audience in 1965 when he adopted an electric guitar and added a full rock backing group. For every one of his folk following who shouted 'Judas!' or 'Traitor!' when he appeared with his new band (which included three members of the Paul Butterfield Blues Band from Chicago), thousands more were brought to their feet by his fusion of memorable lyrics and a driving rock beat. Not to mention his charisma.

Forty years on, Dylan continues to tour and to record, personifying the enduring ability of music to reach untold millions, and not just to entertain but also to stimulate, elevate, perhaps even to redeem them. His work, like John Coltrane's, has been spiritual if not religious, and his aesthetic has been essentially Romantic. In his autobiographical *Chronicles*, published in 2004, he wrote: 'I can't say when it occurred to me to write my own songs . . . Sometimes you just want to do things your way, want to see for yourself what lies behind the misty curtain . . . You want to say something about strange things that have happened to you, strange things you have seen. You have to know and understand something and then go past the vernacular'.[159]

Not the least of his achievements has been to inspire popular musicians to become their own songwriter. Groups that simply play their own versions of the creations of others have come to be known contemptuously as cover bands. This crucial difference distinguished pop (ephemeral, hedonistic, superficial) from rock (expressive, committed, deep, at least in the eyes of its exponents). Dylan played a major part in raising popular music's sights from a horizon bound by profit to infinite transcendental heights. As he said in 1986: 'Tin Pan Alley is gone. I put an end to it. People can record their own songs now. They're almost expected to do it'.[160]

In going electric, Dylan was returning to his roots, for he had started out as a teenager obsessed with rock 'n' roll, had moved on to the blues and thence to folk. But perhaps he was also encouraged by the success of The

Beatles, whom he met in New York in August 1964 during their second tour of the United States. In the history of popular music, this encounter at the Hotel Delmonico on Park Avenue has acquired mythic status, for it marked The Beatles' first acquaintance with marijuana. Until then, the only drugs they had used were amphetamines (speed). Whether it was the joints Dylan rolled for them or the force of his personality, the result was an epiphany: 'I discovered the meaning of life that evening', recorded Paul McCartney, adding, 'Till then we'd been sort of hard Scotch and Coke men. It sort of changed that evening'.

That the nature of The Beatles' music changed abruptly is not in doubt. In the words of James Miller, 'Up till then, rock and roll had been primarily a music of revelry, a medium for lifting people up and helping them dance their blues away. Under the combined influences of marijuana and Bob Dylan's unkempt persona, The Beatles would turn it into something else again: a music of introspective self-absorption, a medium fit for communicating autobiographical intimacies, political discontents, spiritual elevation, inviting an audience, not to dance, but to listen—quietly, attentively, thoughtfully'.[161] Marijuana was not the only substance that took The Beatles off in this direction, of course. In the following year while making their feature-length film *Help!* they discovered LSD and took to it with enthusiasm.[162] The results could be heard on their albums *Rubber Soul* (1965), *Revolver* (1966) and especially *Sergeant Pepper's Lonely Hearts Club Band* (1967), generally agreed to be the most influential single recording of the second half of the twentieth century. The Yeah! Yeah! Yeah! days of the early sixties were but a dim memory.

By the time The Beatles split up in 1970, the ratchet effect had moved up several cogs. Ten years later, after John Lennon was murdered in New York City, the cult surrounding him would take the sacralisation of music one step further. Karl Marx's famous dictum that 'Religion is the opium of the people' would need to be rewritten: by the 1980s, it could be said that 'Music is the religion of the people'.[163]

3
Places and Spaces
From Palace to Stadium

Churches and Opera Houses

The most important Baroque church in Vienna is the Karlskirche—the Charles Church—designed by Johann Bernhard Fischer von Erlach (1656–1723). It was commissioned by the Emperor Charles VI (reigned 1711–40) in fulfillment of a vow made in 1713 to build a church dedicated to St. Charles Borromeo if the city was spared the plague then threatening the region. Following the saint's successful intercession with the Almighty, planning began in 1715, the external structure was completed in 1725 and the finished building was consecrated in 1737.[1] Its location outside Vienna's great fortifications proclaimed the emperor's confidence that the threat from the Ottoman Turks, who had besieged the city as recently as 1683, was now over once and for all.

Fischer von Erlach placed at the centre a pillared portico surmounted by a tall drum and dome and flanked on either side by giant triumphal columns and towers. It was not just a happy coincidence that both the emperor and the object of his votive offering should share the same Christian name. Although the bas-reliefs on the columns depict the achievements of the saint, the whole ensemble is also an architectural affirmation of the symbiosis of the Holy Roman Emperor and the Roman Catholic Church and their joint Roman inheritance.[2] It was 'the summa of ecclesiastical art in union with dynastic symbolism'.[3]

The iconographical scheme of both exterior and interior was carefully planned by Carl Gustav Heraeus, the imperial inspector of medals and antiquities. That this was the church of Emperor Charles as well as Saint Charles was made clear by a bronze plaque symbolically placed on the foundation stone, bearing the legend *Carolus VI. Imperator Fortitudine et Constantia immotus* (Emperor Charles VI, steadfast in courage and perseverance).[4] For the stone-laying ceremony, Johann Joseph Fux—imperial director of music *(Kapellmeister)*—wrote his *Missa San Carlo,* a coincidence that reveals a lot about the relationship between space and music in early modern Europe.[5] Although music was immensely important for the Baroque, it was only one part of an experience that appealed to all the senses. When the Karlskirche was completed, the ear listened to Fux's counterpoint, the eye soared aloft to the immense oval dome where Johann Michael Rottmayr's fresco depicted the intercession and virtues of St. Charles Borromeo, while the nose was stimulated by incense and the mind contemplated the transcendental verities. Perhaps not every worshipper responded with identical fervour to each part, but the subordination of the parts to a total work of art dedicated to God and emperor was clear. No art for art's sake was to be found in the Karlskirche, or any other Baroque building for that matter. Nor was it to be found in the church of St. Thomas in Leipzig when Bach's *St. Matthew Passion* was being performed.

The same could be said of secular music. In 1716 Fux composed the music for *Angelica vincitrice di Alcina* (Angelica triumphs over Alcina), an opera with a libretto written by Pietro Pariati that had been commissioned by Charles VI to celebrate the birth of an (alas, short-lived) heir. The scope of the self-congratulation was extended to embrace the victory over Louis XIV's France, sealed two years earlier by the Peace of Rastadt, and more generally to proclaim the glory of the House of Habsburg.[6] Significantly, this great multimedia exercise in representation was never intended to be anything more than a *pièce d'occasion* and was staged just four times. Its temporary quality did not inhibit the extravagance of the production, however.

Designed by Giuseppe Galli-Bibiena, the enormous and elaborate sets were built across the ornamental fish pond in the gardens of the Favorita, an imperial palace outside Vienna. Among those attending the first night was Lady Mary Wortley Montagu, *en route* to the British Embassy at Constantinople, who reported to her friend Alexander Pope that 'the theatre is so large that 'tis hard to carry the eye to the end of it'. The story that it had cost £30,000 to stage was easy to believe, she added, for 'nothing of the kind ever was more magnificent'. Unfortunately, a sudden thunderstorm dispersed the audience 'in such confusion that I was almost squeezed to death'—only the emperor and his immediate entourage had covered seating.[7] Needless to say, the performance was carefully captured visually, engraved, reproduced and sent around Europe to advertise to those unlucky enough not to have been present just what unsurpassable magnificence they had missed.

By the early eighteenth century, grand but ephemeral multimedia extravaganzas of this kind were making way for equally expensive but more durable operatic presentations in permanent theatres, and *opera seria* had emerged as the representational genre *par excellence*. When Frederick Augustus, king of Poland and elector of Saxony, wished to announce his promotion to the top table of European rulers after the marriage of his son and heir to a Habsburg in 1719, he built the biggest opera house north of the Alps.[8] The opera chosen to inaugurate it was *Teofane* with music by Antonio Lotti, the leading Venetian composer brought to Dresden expressly for the occasion, and a libretto by the Saxon court poet Stefano Benedetto Pallavicino. The brightest star of the all-star cast was the greatest castrato of the day, Francesco Bernardi, better known as Senesino. Among the audience of princes and nobles from all over the empire, room was found for at least two men capable of appreciating the music—Handel and Georg Philipp Telemann. The political message of *Teofane* was conveyed through analogy, for it dealt with the marriage of the great Saxon Emperor Otto II to Theophanu, daughter of the Byzantine emperor. Just in case anyone missed the point, for the closing scene the stage was transformed into the temple of Hymen in which Germania paid homage to the union of Austria and Saxony.[9]

Perhaps the most helpful contemporary illustration of an *opera seria* in progress was Pietro Domenico Olivero's painting of a performance of Francesco Feo's *Arsace* in the Royal Theatre at Turin in 1740. Among other points of interest, it reveals the splendour of the costumes and the sets, the boxes arranged primarily to allow their occupants to view one another rather than the stage, a waiter bringing drinks to the stall seats during the performance, some members of the audience reading the libretto, others turning their back to the stage and chatting with friends in the row behind, the size of the orchestra (thirty-two players, including two keyboard play-ers but no separate conductor) and the prominently displayed coat of arms of the House of Savoy.[10]

What it does not show is the magnificence of the royal box, placed on the central axis and rising through three ranks of boxes, expressly designed to distance the king spatially from the rest of his subjects. Its location at the apex of the horseshoe shape meant that he was the only spectator able to view the stage from the optimum vantage point. Surviving opera houses of the period, the most notable being the Cuvilliès Theatre in Munich and the margrave of Bayreuth's Opera House at Bayreuth, still provide an architec-tural reminder of the personal nature of representational display. The latter also sported two *Trompettenlogen*—boxes on either side of the stage from which trumpeters sounded a fanfare to announce the arrival of the mar-grave.[11]

Visiting Naples in the late 1830s, the countess of Blessington left an excellent description of the royal box at the San Carlo: 'The royal box is in the centre of the house, and forms a very striking and ornamental object. It projects considerably, is supported on gilded palm trees, and is surmounted by a large crown; from which descends, on each side, a mass of drapery, ap-parently of metal painted and gilt, to resemble cloth of gold, which is held up by figures of Fame. The interior is cased by panels of looking-glass; and fitted up with crimson velvet, trimmed with bullion fringe.'[12] In some houses, the boxes flanking the stage were also reserved for the prince, in case he wanted to get closer to the action. At Dresden on gala occasions, the king sat in the right-hand stage box and the queen in the left, while other members of the royal family sat in the stalls directly in front of the orchestra. At ordinary performances, the boxes of the first level were re-served for the highest court dignitaries, ambassadors and foreign visitors; the second level for other members of the court, for higher ranking offi-cials, army officers and foreigners; while the gallery was assigned to com-moners.[13]

From Stockholm to Naples, opera houses were built for the greater glory of the reigning sovereign. Never before or since have so many rulers devoted so much time and money to the promotion of operatic music. Many of them were only second- or third-rank players in the European states system; indeed, it almost seemed that the splendour of the house stood in inverse ratio to the power of its builder. The margrave of Bayreuth

The Teatro Regio at Turin in 1740 during a performance of *Arsace*,
music by Francesco Feo and libretto by Antonio Salvi, painted by
Pietro Domenico Olivero.

was of modest importance even within the confines of the Holy Roman
Empire, but he left behind a superb opera house with a stage big enough to
catch the eye of Richard Wagner when looking for a suitable venue for *The
Ring of the Nibelung.*

The biggest opera house in Europe was the San Carlo at Naples, finished in 1737. The lavishness of its productions became legendary. A production of Domenico Sarri's *Ezio* in 1741 featured on stage eight horses,
four camels, an unspecified number of lions, sixty-four extras dressed as
Romans, sixteen freed slaves dressed in multicoloured silk, six slaves
dressed as soldiers of Attila the Hun, a stage band of eight, thirty-seven
swordsmen representing the Roman people, twelve swordsmen playing the

Bayreuth: the margrave's box in the Margrave's Opera House, by Giuseppe and
Carlo Galli Bibiena, 1744–48.

soldiers of the emperor, twelve Praetorian guards and fourteen pages and maids attending the principal singers.[14] Yet in the following year, 1742, Charles IV was humiliated when a British naval squadron dropped anchor close inshore and gave him half-an-hour to withdraw unconditionally from the war he was currently fighting on the side of Spain, on pain of seeing his capital reduced to rubble. He duly obliged. The king of England had no opera house.

As the great royal boxes proclaimed, the opera house was a space dedicated first and foremost to advertising the majesty of the sovereign. This was a priority expressed most obviously by its location within the fabric of the royal palace (Versailles, Munich, Mannheim, for example) or immediately adjoining it, allowing the royal party to access their box via a private passage (as in Turin and Naples). A secondary but closely related service was to reinforce the social hierarchy. As an extension of the court, the opera house replicated its nice distinctions of rank and elaborate etiquette. So the design of the house was determined by the need not to see the stage and hear the music but to see and be seen by other members of the audience. Its function was not aesthetic but social.

In the hall of the Palais Royal at Paris where Lully's *tragédies lyriques* were staged, the partitions between the boxes were not angled towards the stage but towards the boxes opposite. Despite having the worst view, the most favoured were the six stage boxes, because they placed the occupants in full view of the entire audience, and so were reserved for princes of the blood royal.[15] This form of spatial stratification long outlived the eighteenth century. At Turin in 1820 Lady Morgan found that the queen (of Sardinia) took a keen interest in how the seating was distributed: 'Her list decides the number of quarterings requisite to occupy the *aristocratici* rows of the first and second circles, and determines the point of *roture*, which banishes to the higher tiers the *piccoli nobili*.'[16]

When the sovereign was present, deferential silence was the order of the day, to the extent that applause was permitted only when the royal hands first gave the lead. This was the king's house, and admission was by invitation only. When *Cleofide*, an *opera seria* by the Saxon court composer Johann Adolf Hasse, was performed for the first time in Dresden on 17 August 1731, the audience consisted only of King Frederick Augustus and a few specially invited courtiers. Not until a month later did the rest of high society have the opportunity to see it.[17] One of the finest opera houses in

Haydn directs a performance at the opera house at Esterháza.

Europe was entirely private, namely that at Esterháza, the remote country seat of Prince Nicholas Esterházy, Joseph Haydn's patron. Both in terms of quantity and quality, Esterháza rivalled the greatest houses in Europe. In the course of the 1780s, Haydn staged 880 performances there, including three new works of his own and twenty by other composers.[18] The utter dependence of this space on one man's will was starkly revealed when Prince Nicholas died in September 1791. His heir promptly dismissed the opera company and demoted Esterháza to its original function as a hunting lodge. In 1824 a visitor reported that the opera house was being used for storing hay.

Esterháza was exceptionally personal, in that when the owner was absent the opera house promptly fell dark. Elsewhere, opera houses continued to operate as meeting places for the court. Especially in aristocratic republics like Venice, or where the ruler was represented by a viceroy, as at

Interior of La Scala, Milan, showing the six tiers of boxes.

Milan, the nobles set the tone by turning their boxes into homes away from home, fitting them out with furniture, paintings and the means of refreshment. Curtains could be drawn across the front to ensure complete privacy for whatever was going on inside.[19] Especially in Italy, the opera house was first and foremost a social centre, to which the elites of the city went virtually every night. As they might hear the same work dozens of times in the course of a season, the amount of attention they paid to the stage was fitful. They broke off from card playing, receiving visitors or chatting only when a star singer appeared or a favourite aria was reached.

A contemptuous Louis Spohr reported from Milan in 1816: 'During the powerful overture, several very expressive accompanied recitatives, and all the *pièces d'ensemble,* the audience made so much noise that one could scarcely hear the music. In most of the boxes, the occupants played at cards, and all over the house, people conversed aloud. Nothing more insufferable can be imagined for a stranger who is desirous to listen with attention, than this vile noise . . . I can imagine no task more ungrateful than to write for such a public, and one is surprised that good composers will submit to it'.[20]

Although the boxes were allocated strictly according to rank, most opera houses were simply too big to be solely an aristocratic preserve. If they were to perform their representational role, they had to be as splendid as possible, but so enormous was the cost of erection, maintenance and production that it had to be spread among the population at large. La Scala, San Carlo and Dresden, for example, could seat audiences of over two thousand people, so commoners had to be admitted to the upper tiers of boxes. According to Lady Morgan, La Scala was 'the evening home of almost all ranks, the recreation of the tradesman and the exchange of the merchant'. It was also a centre of political discussion, for 'there alone, amidst the openest publicity, can privacy find an asylum against the intrusion of espionage'.[21]

As this comment suggests, upwardly mobile members of the middle classes were just as keen on display as their social superiors. The grandest French opera house of the eighteenth century was built not at Versailles but at Bordeaux, the great commercial centre whose overseas trade had increased more than twenty times since 1715. The Grand Théâtre that opened in 1780 was special because as much space was devoted to the foyer and the staircase as to the auditorium. They were there to allow members of Bordeaux high society the opportunity to parade before one another in all their finery—to see and be seen. As the architect Victor Louis grasped, in an opera house the audience is as important a performer as the singers on stage. In an opera house built for a king, the royal box is the chief architectural feature, but in a public opera house built for a great commercial city such as Bordeaux, the foyer, staircase and other public rooms dominate.[22]

Concerts in Pubs and Palaces

The Grand Théâtre also included a room for public concerts, very much a phenomenon of the eighteenth century. For a long time, patrons of inns had been able to hear good music as an incidental accompaniment to eating and drinking. Samuel Pepys, for example, wrote in his diary on 27 September 1665: 'We to the Kings-head, the great Musique-house, the first time I was ever there and had a good breakfast'.[23] What was probably the first proper public concert, organised by John Banister in London in 1672, cannot have been a very grand affair, as it was held in his own home. Nor did the elevation of music to the primary purpose of the occasion mean that eating, drinking and smoking were abandoned. On the contrary, according to Roger North, Banister's concert room 'was rounded with seats and small tables, alehouse fashion. One shilling was the price, and call for what you pleased'.[24] This close association between the performance of music and the consumption of comestibles was long-lasting: for example, the Collegium Musicum that J. S. Bach directed at Leipzig after 1727 met in Zimmermann's or Richter's coffee house.[25]

At the aristocratic end of the social scale, orchestral concerts were performed in spaces whose size and splendour proclaimed their place in the representational culture epitomised by *opera seria*. A particularly good example was furnished by the court at Mannheim, variously described by contemporaries as 'the musical Athens of the German-speaking world' (Christian Daniel Schubart), 'the paradise of composers' (Friedrich Heinrich Jacobi) and 'that famous court, whose rays, like those of the sun, illumine the whole of Germany, nay even the whole of Europe' (Leopold Mozart).[26] Here the elector of the Palatinate, Karl Theodor, assembled the best orchestra in Europe, including in its ranks, among others, Franz Xaver Richter, Ignaz Holzbauer, Christian Cannabich and Johann Stamitz. Out of a total of thirty-five composers in the 1761 catalogue of a French music publisher, twenty symphonies were written by Mannheim musicians.[27] No wonder that Charles Burney reported in 1772 that 'there are more solo players and good composers in this, than perhaps in any other orchestra in Europe; it is an army of generals, equally fit to plan a battle, as to fight it'.[28] Mozart's comment five years later was: 'The orchestra is excellent, and very strong'.[29]

Although Karl Theodor was unusually accommodating in allowing the general public to attend both his opera house and his concerts, whose music was being played by whose musicians was never in doubt. Indeed, no better spatial illustration of the proprietorial nature of court music in the period can be found than the Mannheim concert hall, for it was not a dedicated music room at all but the Knights' Hall (Rittersaal), which served

The Rittersaal in the Electoral Palace at Mannheim (1730), which also served as the main concert hall.

other representational purposes such as receptions, balls and banquets. Symbolically, it had no autonomous external structure, being embedded in the enormous palace. And for all his love of music, the elector habitually treated performances as background. This was revealed by a noble visitor, Gottfried von Rotenstein, who in 1785 published a helpful account of a visit to a concert in the Rittersaal: 'After six o'clock the court entered, the elector and electress, the dowager electress of Bavaria, and the ladies-in-waiting and cavaliers. Then the music began, and at the same time everyone began to play cards . . . The elector stood up every now and then and went from table to table with a cheerful laugh'.[30]

This was not at all unusual. Louis Spohr recorded in his autobiography that at the court of Brunswick, silence prevailed during concerts only when the duke was actually present. In his absence, the orchestra was under orders to play quietly, to avoid disturbing the card parties. Indeed, a thick carpet was placed underneath the musicians' desks to deaden the

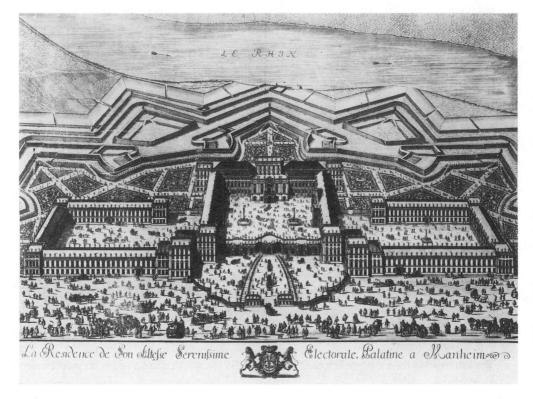

The Electoral Palace at Mannheim. The Rittersaal is located on the first floor of the central pavilion.

sound.[31] But Spohr also revealed that with a new century, attitudes were changing. When told by a lackey that the duchess wanted him to play more quietly, he actually increased the volume. On another occasion, when playing for the king of Württemberg, he insisted that all card playing had to stop during his performance. And so it did (but it resumed as soon as he had finished).[32]

Concert Halls and the Sacralisation of Music

Whether providing Muzak for card-playing courtiers, an agreeable background for drinking and eating in pubs and coffee houses, or even accompaniment for divine worship, music's role was subordinate to other social concerns until the mid-eighteenth century. If it was ever to emerge as an activity valued in its own right, music had to carve out its own dedicated space. The very first is generally agreed to have been the Holywell Music Room in Oxford, built in 1748 for the Musical Society, which previously had held concerts in the hall of Christ Church or the King's Head Tavern.[33] This building, however, was too modest in size and too provincial in location to set a trend. More influential was the concert hall in the Hanover Square Rooms in London, the first such space to be purpose-built in the capital. Opened in 1775, it was owned by Giovanni Gallini, a Swiss-Italian dancing-master who styled himself Sir John Gallini (a papal title) and left the colossal fortune of £150,000 when he died in 1805. Here, J. C. Bach and C. F. Abel organised their highly successful series of subscription concerts in the 1770s and Salomon mounted the legendary Haydn concerts in the 1790s.[34] On the continent, the Gewandhaus at Leipzig led the way in 1781.

These early concert halls, with their public performances, gave architectural expression to the growing and powerful sacralisation of music. The spatial arrangement of the Hanover Square Rooms, for example, resembled a church, with the audience seated as if it were a congregation, the orchestra positioned in a chancel-like space on a raised dais fenced off by a rail, and an organ taking the place of the altar. The interior of the Gewandhaus is very similar. All these early concert rooms were relatively austere, both inside and outside, their decorations reflecting the limited resources of the builders. Not until the state took a hand could music and musicians find a dwelling place of splendour commensurate with their rapidly inflating self-image.

A first step in this direction had been taken by Frederick the Great of Prussia. Immediately on coming to the throne in 1740, he commissioned a grand new opera house from his favourite architect, Georg Wenzeslaus von Knobelsdorff. Although war with Austria was raging, the work was driven on with such purpose that the first performance—of Carl Heinrich Graun's *Cesare e Cleopatra*—was staged in December 1742. Frederick treated his opera house very much as if it were his private possession, as a cultural expression of his absolute monarchy. On opening night, which was attended by all senior military personnel in the capital by royal command, the officers stood in ranks in the pit, behind two lines of chairs reserved for the king and his entourage.[35] When the king entered the building, a military band of trumpeters and drummers played a fanfare.[36] This military

The Hanover Square Rooms in 1843.

motif proved to be persistent: where else but in Prussia could one find a sovereign ordering an opera house to be filled with soldiers before a performance, as a cheap (if malodorous) form of central heating?[37] And where else but in Prussia could one find soldiers being drafted to bulk out the audience when attendances fell?[38]

Characteristically, Frederick chose to sit not in the royal box but on a seat immediately in front of the orchestra pit, so that he could keep a sharp eye on both the stage and the musical director's score.[39] A graphic eye-witness account of what this could involve for the performers was provided by the English musical historian Charles Burney, who visited Berlin in 1772: 'The king always stands behind the *maestro di capella,* in sight of the score, which he frequently looks at, and indeed performs the part of director-general here, as much as of generalissimo in the field . . . In the opera house, as in the field, his majesty is such a rigid disciplinarian, that if a mistake is made in a single movement or evolution, he immediately marks, and rebukes the offender'.[40]

Frederick the Great's opera house on Unter den Linden, designed by Georg Wenzeslaus von Knobelsdorff. Behind it is the Catholic church of St. Hedwig, proclaiming Frederick's attachment to religious toleration; to the right is the royal library.

So far, so conventional. But—as in many other things—Frederick's musical conservatism was also forward-looking. His new opera house was not built as part of the royal palace but was located on Unter den Linden in the form of an autonomous classical temple, the first free-standing opera house in Europe.[41] The inscription above the portico proclaimed *Fridericus Rex Apollini et Musis*—Dedicated by King Frederick to Apollo and the Muses. The rules of conduct for the audience, enforced by armed guards, demanded silence during the performance.[42] Frederick reviled Christianity as a tissue of pernicious fictions and turned instead to the arts to satisfy his need for transcendental experience. His aestheticism was hugely influential, especially in Protestant Germany, where he became a role model for those who found inherited religious forms inadequate.

Unlike most patrons of representational art, he was an active creator. As a political theorist, historian, poet, dramatist, composer and flautist, he would deserve a niche in any cultural history of the eighteenth century, even if he had not been also king of Prussia.[43] Whatever one might think about his regime or its impact on the subsequent course of German history, no one can read his works or listen to his music without realising that he possessed extraordinary gifts. Although he did not call it such, the importance he attached to *Bildung*—individual self-cultivation—placed him squarely in the progressive mainstream of German culture. A man who took Lucretius' *De Rerum natura* into battle and whiled away the intervals in the negotiations leading to the Peace of Hubertusburg by reading Rousseau's *Émile* was a man who gave high priority to the intellect.[44] We have no reason to doubt the sincerity of his numerous declarations of faith, such as: 'Since my childhood I have loved the arts, literature and the sciences, and if I can contribute to their propagation, I dedicate myself with all the zeal at my disposal, because there can be no true happiness in this world without them.'[45]

Frederick's free-standing temple dedicated to art was an architectural expression of the sacralisation process. As the eighteenth century wore on, visual evidence of an epochal shift in the way all the arts were viewed—both literally and metaphorically—began to accumulate. In one country after another, rulers began to open their collections to the public. In Berlin itself, Friedrich Nicolai published a guidebook for visitors which, among other things, told them how to gain access to the royal collections, stating that 'everyone is allowed to view these rarities'. By adding the injunction that 'it is to be understood that what is customary and conventional in other places will also be enforced here', he also revealed that this was now commonplace.[46] So the modern museum evolved. The objects on display were divorced from their original representational context and were presented for worship in their own right.

A particularly good illustration of this was provided by Friedrich Schiller in 1785 when he put the following words into the mouth of a fictional Danish tourist who had just been to see the galleries of the elector Karl Theodor of the Palatinate at Mannheim:

> Today I had an inexpressibly pleasant surprise, which has enlarged my whole heart. I feel nobler and better. I have come from the Hall of Antiquities . . . Every native and foreigner has the unlimited freedom to enjoy these treasures from antiquity because the clever and patriotic Elector has brought them from Italy, not to add to his glory by possessing one more rarity nor,

like many other princes, to provide the casual traveller with something to admire. He made this sacrifice for *art* itself, and a grateful art will forever praise his name.[47]

Schiller's friend Goethe was even more explicit about the sacralising function of museums when he recalled the impression made on him by a visit to the elector of Saxony's collection at Dresden: 'This sanctuary . . . imparted a unique feeling of solemnity which much resembled the sensation with which one enters a church, as the adornments of so many temples, the objects of so much adoration, seemed to be displayed here only for art's sacred ends'.[48] The first free-standing museum in Europe was the Museum Fridericianum in Kassel, constructed between 1769 and 1779 to contain the collections and library of the landgrave Frederick II.

Temples for Music

That the British would have been in the vanguard of this development might have been expected, given the size of their public sphere, the depth of their material resources and their parliamentary constitution. But ironically, it was just these apparently progressive traits that inhibited the construction of temples to art in London. The National Gallery did not acquire its own building in Trafalgar Square until 1831. The British Museum had been in existence for nearly a century when its collections were finally moved to its own dedicated site in the 1850s. The contrast with contemporary developments on the continent, especially with impoverished, autocratic Prussia, was striking. Whereas in the latter the government could make the transition from royal to state patronage, untroubled by public scrutiny, in Great Britain Parliament kept expenditure on a tight rein.[49]

Reinforced by a common hostility to the French Revolution and a common sense of triumph over the French in 1815, the union between the British state and society was so secure as to need no extra cultural cement. In most continental countries, the story was different. There, a sustained crisis of legitimation encouraged a search for fresh ways to bind the educated middle classes (the *Bildungsbürgertum*) to the state. One promising way to promote a sense of common purpose without actually sharing po-

The National Theatre on the Gendarmenmarkt, Berlin, designed by Carl Gotthard Langhans and opened in 1801.

litical power was through cultural projects. The expansion of the Louvre in Paris under Napoleon and the creation of the National Art Gallery (Rijks-museum) in Amsterdam in 1800, the Royal Museum of Painting and Sculpture (the Prado) in Madrid in 1819, and the Royal Museum in Berlin (Das Alte Museum) in 1822 were all part of the same exercise in political and social control.

A good example was provided by the history of the theatre on the Gendarmenmarkt in Berlin. The first was erected in 1774 on the orders of Frederick the Great to accommodate a French-language troupe. It went dark four years later with the outbreak of the War of the Bavarian Succession. On 12 September 1786, the day after Frederick's burial, his successor, Frederick William II, made a grand programmatic gesture by ordering the reopening of what had been known as the French Comedy House as a National Theatre for the performance of works in the German language.[50] In

The Schauspielhaus on the Gendarmenmarkt in Berlin, designed by Karl Friedrich Schinkel and opened in 1821. The wing to the left of the entrance portico housed a concert hall.

1801 it was replaced by a much larger building on the same site, designed by Carl Gotthard Langhans, with a seating capacity of two thousand. Although primarily designed for spoken drama, the space was also used for operas in German and for subscription concerts.[51]

After the National Theatre burned down in 1817, the site was incorporated into the major rebuilding of Berlin currently being pursued under the direction of Karl Friedrich Schinkel, the greatest architect of his age. The result was the Schauspielhaus (Play House), one of the most splendid of all European theatres. Here, the sacralisation of the arts, and music in particular, was made explicit, especially in the concert hall located in the west wing. It was approached through a vestibule that resembled an antechapel adorned with busts of the great composers of the past, a strategy that was repeated in the hall itself. In this sacred place, music was to be listened to with reverence, so that its redemptive purpose could be realised. But both place and purpose were open to all, irrespective of rank. The democratic implications of sacralised art were brought out in Schinkel's design for the auditorium of the theatre, which abandoned the traditional

The concert hall in the Schauspielhaus. It was destroyed by bombing in the Second World War and was not restored.

horseshoe in favour of a semicircle. This architectural gesture widened the proscenium arch and made the stage—and the action that took place on it—the focal point, not the royal box.[52] Although some boxes were provided, the interior of the Schauspielhaus is more like a cinema than an opera house of the traditional kind.

In the very first year of its opening, the Schauspielhaus was the site for an episode which revealed that cultural spaces can have political implications. This was the world premiere of *Der Freischütz*, a Romantic opera with music by Carl Maria von Weber, director of music to the king of Saxony. The performance was destined to be a huge success for the simple but good reason that one great melody followed another. The opera immediately became an international hit and has remained in the repertoire ever since. In Berlin in 1821, however, supplementary forces were at work. The very setting of the opera—Bohemia in the aftermath of the Thirty Years War—had a resonance for anyone living in Germany at the end of the Napoleonic wars. Although there is no overt political message, a populist message is conveyed by the fact that most of the characters are simple country people, and the music they sing is steeped in a folk idiom.

More specifically political was the location of the production. Aesthetically, the new Schauspielhaus was greatly superior to Knobelsdorff's Court Theatre just round the corner on Unter den Linden. Yet in the pecking order of the royal Prussian stages, the Schauspielhaus's German-language repertoire ranked below the Italian fare offered at the Court. Just two years earlier, King Frederick William III had advertised his continuing attachment to traditional grand opera by hiring at considerable expense Gasparo Spontini, whose work he had come to know and like when in Paris for the victory celebrations in 1814. Italian by birth, Spontini had made a successful career as the favoured composer of Napoleon's first wife, the Empress Josephine. Spontini's arrival in Prussia in 1820 was celebrated by two hugely extravagant productions of his most famous works, *La Vestale* and *Fernando Cortez.* So the unprecedented jubilation that greeted Weber's *Der Freischütz* the following year was also an assertion of national and popular values against the foreign representational culture of the Court Theatre.[53] All accounts agree that this opera was acclaimed with a frenzy of enthusiasm hitherto unknown, at least on the German stage.[54]

For the time being, the king of Prussia and his subjects could agree to disagree about musical taste, although a warning signal had been hoisted. Continuing coexistence if not harmony was promoted by the well-founded belief that, for all its defects, Prussia was a *Kulturstaat,* a state in which culture was cherished and promoted. In the same year that *Der Freischütz* was staged, Frederick William gave a building plot just off Unter den Linden to the Sing-Akademie (Singing Academy), a choral society first formed in 1791 by Carl Friedrich Christian Fasch. Its early history provides compelling evidence of the growing sacralisation of music. After Fasch's death in 1800, a commemorative bust by no less a sculptor than Gottfried

Schadow was put on display, and Carl Friedrich Zelter took the occasion as an opportunity to discuss the academy's purpose. Fasch's great achievement, he extolled, had been to serve as 'a worthy priest of the muse', using his choir to close the gap between art and people and to demonstrate that music was not something incidental but a central part of a national project. He had understood that only a heart could affect a heart and that it was the sublime mission of 'divine music' to purify the heart and lead it to inner self-awareness. Not just the individual but all society would be influenced, for 'music embraces the wounded heart with soothing hands and pours on it a balm that both heals and strengthens'.[55]

By this time the Singing Academy's choir numbered around two hundred and had caught the approving eye of the authorities. In 1802 the minister Count Friedrich von Hardenberg became its patron, and in 1809 a government-funded chair of music was established with Zelter as its first incumbent. He responded by organising a performance of Handel's *Dettingen Te Deum* to mark Frederick William III's return to Berlin at the end of the year after a long exile in the wake of the 1806 defeats. The Singing Academy was also to the fore during the War of Liberation of 1813 against the French, among other things organising charity concerts to raise funds for the Lützow Freikorps.[56] In 1812 Schinkel designed a new concert space for the academy that combined both secular and religious sacralisation in the shape of a barrel-vaulted hall dominated by a gigantic fresco celebrating St. Cecilia, the patron saint of music. Unfortunately, the academy was never able to raise the necessary funds and so had to make do with a more modest—but very elegant—structure designed by Theodor Ottmer. It still survives, as the Maxim Gorki Theatre, as indeed does the Singing Academy.

The Sing-Academie can serve as an exemplar of the initiatives that peppered Europe with dedicated concert halls in the course of the nineteenth century. In some places, private ingenuity was decisive, for example in the addition of a music hall to the assembly rooms in Edinburgh in 1843. In others, so ambitious was the scale that state or municipal assistance was required, for example for the sumptuous new Gewandhaus ('Clothiers' Hall') in Leipzig, completed in 1884, which inspired a local newspaper to boast that such a large and magnificent temple of the muses was only to be found in a true 'city of the world'. The first-night audience, it reported, was entranced by the luxury, splendour, comfort and all the modern conveniences—including electric lighting—that distinguished not just the main concert hall but also the huge foyer, staircase and refreshment rooms through which Leipzig's great and good could promenade in their finery during the intervals.[57] It also included a smaller hall for chamber music, built as a replica of the previous Gewandhaus hall, as if to emphasise how much progress the city had made during the past century.

Throughout Europe, rulers sought to come to terms with the post-Revolutionary world by forging a new alliance with their educated classes. But this was not the only motive at work, and it would be misleading to exaggerate the functional nature of their grand building projects. No doubt also involved was an element of old-fashioned representation—self-indulgence, even—combined with cultural competition among peers. All motives were on display in Munich, where Ludwig I (reigned 1825–48) transformed his capital from a provincial backwater into a metropolis in the space of a generation. It became 'the Florence of the nineteenth century'.[58] Among Ludwig's projects was the Odeon, a new concert hall designed by Leo von Klenze, which opened in 1828. The three ceiling frescoes proclaimed its programme: *Apollo among the Muses, or Art in the Highest Sphere of Culture; Apollo among the Shepherds, or Art as the Means of Educating Unspoilt Natures;* and *Apollo and Midas, or Art Confronted by Degeneracy [Afterkunst] and Stupidity.*[59]

Limping along behind the Hohenzollerns and the Wittelsbachs came the Habsburgs, slow to get the point, as usual. Only after the revolutions of 1848–49, the failure of neo-absolutism in the 1850s and the political and military disasters in Italy in 1859–60 did they finally initiate something similar. But then the Habsburgs made up for lost time with a project for Vienna's reconstruction that bears comparison with Baron Haussmann's contemporary rebuilding of Paris. This was the Ringstrasse project—the removal of the gigantic, and now useless, fortifications that surrounded the old city. In their place came a ring of boulevards, flanked by great public buildings proclaiming the new alliance between the dynasty and the liberal middle classes. Moving counter-clockwise from north to west to south, one passes the University, the Town Hall, the Burg Theatre, the Natural History Museum, the Art History Museum, the Academy of Art, the Opera House, the Artists' House, and the Music Association (Musikverein).

The Musikverein was built between 1866 and 1869 to designs by Theophil von Hansen, who was also responsible for the Parliament Build-

The original appearance of the main hall of the Musikverein in Vienna, designed by Theophil Hansen, completed 1869. Later an organ was installed at the far end, and the caryatids supporting the gallery were moved back to the side walls.

ing and the Academy of Arts. It provided new premises for the Imperial and Royal Society of Friends of Music in Vienna, originally founded in 1812. As the title suggested, this had always been a semi-official body, for its founder, Josef Sonnleithner, had been a civil servant, it was granted an imperial charter and its first patron was the Cardinal-Archduke Rudolph, brother of the Emperor Francis I and friend of Beethoven. Among other things, the society organised concerts, published a musical journal, created a musical library for public use, awarded scholarships to aspiring musicians and established a Conservatoire.[60] Always at the heart of Viennese musical life, it was one of the principal beneficiaries of the Ringstrasse project, receiving a prime site opposite the Karlskirche.

In this temple of music Hansen created an enormous concert hall approximately twenty metres wide, eighteen metres high and fifty metres long, capable of housing no fewer than five hundred performers and two thousand listeners. Smaller but no less magnificent was the hall intended for chamber music. Both outside and inside, a plethora of sculptures and insignia referred both to the musical gods of the past and the members of the Habsburg dynasty.[61] Among the patrons whose donations made construction possible were the Emperor Francis Joseph and the Empress Elizabeth, five archdukes and a virtual roll-call of the great aristocratic families of the Austro-Hungarian Empire (Batthyány, Kinsky, Liechtenstein, Schönborn, Schwarzenberg, Lobkowitz and so on).[62]

Two Ways of Elevating Music—Bayreuth and Paris

Of all the great buildings devoted to music and erected in the nineteenth century, it was the festival theatre that Wagner created at Bayreuth which encapsulated the spatial developments that helped to elevate musicians and sacralise music. Wagner's personal contribution to its design was just as emphatic and original as the attention he gave to every other aspect of the project. In the preface to the text of *The Ring of the Nibelung*, published in 1863, he stated that the actual structure should be 'as simple as possible, perhaps just of wood, and with no other consideration in mind but the suitability of its interior for the artistic purpose'. What the latter required, among other things, was an amphitheatrical shape and a concealed orchestra.[63]

He was lucky enough to number among his friends one of the greatest of contemporary architects, Gottfried Semper, who had also fled from Dresden after the failure of the insurrection in 1849. Semper turned Wagner's ideas into a practical design, although always acknowledging who was in charge. When sending Wagner a set of sketches in 1865, Semper was careful to stress that he was seeking reassurance that the 'specifications match your intentions and ideas entirely'. Wagner insisted that the exterior should be as simple as possible, and across a preliminary drawing of the facade he scrawled: 'Get rid of the ornaments' *(Die Ornamente fort!)*. In a letter to the mayor of Bayreuth he wrote that the building 'should be no more solid than is necessary to prevent it from collapsing. Therefore economise here [on the exterior], economise—no ornamentation . . . Stage machinery and scenery, and everything that relates to the ideal inner work of

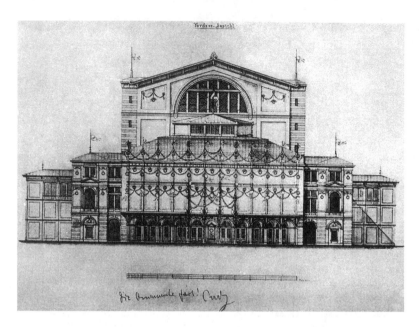

Architect's sketch for the exterior of the Festival Theatre at Bayreuth. Wagner has written across the bottom: 'Get rid of the ornaments!'

art—*perfect* in every way. *No* economies here; everything as though de-signed to last a long time, nothing provisional.'[64]

When the theatre eventually opened in August 1876, it was indeed truly revolutionary. There was no ornamental facade, no foyer, no staircase, and no public rooms, just an auditorium, an enormous stage and a massive fly-tower to expedite scene changes. The seating was organised as an am-phitheatre, giving every member of the audience a clear sight-line to the stage. There were no boxes, only two galleries of loges along the back wall. The orchestra was completely invisible to the audience, being sunk below the stage. A double proscenium arch enhanced the illusion of the stage's great depth and created what Wagner called a 'mystic abyss' between the audience and the drama.[65]

The use of gas lighting allowed the house to be darkened completely when the performance began. The conventional opening ritual of the con-ductor threading his way through the orchestra to the podium, turning and bowing to the audience, indicating to his musicians that they should stand to acknowledge the applause too, before eventually raising his baton to start proceedings was completely absent. At Bayreuth (then and now) the

Cross-section of the Paris Opéra House designed by Charles Garnier, showing that as much space was devoted to the public rooms and staircase as to the auditorium and stage.

house lights go down, the audience falls silent—and out of the darkness comes the music. Writing about the first performance of *Parsifal* in 1882, the conductor Felix Weingartner recorded: 'The auditorium grows completely dark. A breathless hush falls. Like a voice from another world the first expansive theme of the prelude begins. This impression is unlike anything else, and is ineradicable'.[66]

The originality and sacral nature of a performance in the Bayreuth auditorium are thrown into sharp relief when the space is compared with another opera house built almost simultaneously—the Paris Opéra designed by Charles Garnier and completed in 1875. Although not opened until after his regime had collapsed, this was very much an imperial project of Napoleon III, who had decided that one of the *grands points de vue* with which his reconstructed Paris was to be embellished should end with a grand new opera house.[67] As the very detailed instructions to the architect made clear, every aspect of opera-going was to be given its special space: alighting from a carriage under cover, passing ceremoniously through a mirror-lined vestibule, *avant-foyer* and foyer to the great staircase, ascending the staircase to a palatial grand foyer, where the visitor could see and be seen by other members of high society, and progressing to a box in the auditorium. As the ground plan reveals, far greater resources were devoted to these representational rooms than to the musical space (the seating capacity of 1,800 was only slightly larger than that of Bayreuth). All these rep-

View of the Paris Opéra House.

resentational spaces made for a colossal edifice 155 metres long and 100 metres wide at its widest point (the facade is 70 metres wide) and 60 metres high.[68]

Although the auditorium of what has become known as the Palais Garnier is imposing enough, including as it does the gigantic crystal chandelier that plays such a dramatic role in *The Phantom of the Opera*, contemporaries had no doubt that the staircase dominated the building. This was quite deliberate. Garnier wrote that the coming and going of members of the audience was a central part of the operatic experience, so 'huge and conveniently located staircases' were an essential part of a modern opera house.[69] The poet Théophile Gautier pointed out that Garnier's staircase was itself a theatre—he compared it to a painting by Veronese in which the people are simultaneously spectators and spectacle, a perfectly designed space to display 'that marvel of modern civilisation that is called "leaving the opera", that is to say a cascade of diamonds, pearls, feathers, flowers, bare shoulders, satin, velvet, silks, gauzes, lace, pouring down the steps of

Grand staircase of the Paris Opéra House.

La Danse Bachique by Gustave Boulanger, one of the murals in the Foyer de la Danse of the Paris Opéra House.

white marble, sparkling in the bright lights, and all framed by a fairy-tale architecture'.[70] Gautier defined the opera house itself as 'a radiant centre, a sort of secular cathedral of civilisation in which art, wealth and elegance can celebrate their finest festivals'.[71]

As these comments reveal, the primary purpose of the Paris Opéra was not aesthetic but social. So the first-night programme of 15 January 1875, to which high society from across Europe was invited (including the lord mayor of London), was an agreeable pot-pourri of easy listening extracts from the period's favourite operas—'a thing of shreds and patches', *The Musical Times* observed disdainfully.[72] Jealousy may well have played a part, but foreign visitors in particular professed to be horrified by the sumptuous opulence of 'this strange, stupendous, Babylonish, Ninevritish temple of modern pleasure', as another English periodical put it. This was *The Musical Standard*, whose correspondent worked himself into a frenzy of denunciation: 'utterly over-charged, over-done, over-elaborated in every sense . . . absolute deficiency of anything approaching to good taste . . . hard, coarse, brutal, licentious paganism . . .', and so on.[73]

Special offence was caused by the Foyer de la Danse—'simply shocking, sickening in its voluptuousness'—understandably perhaps, because this was a room in which members of the *corps de ballet* could be approached during the interval and assignations made. The murals, especially those representing *La Danse bachique* and *La Danse amoureuse*, were suitably erotic.[74] In short, no greater contrast could be imagined between Garnier's carnal riot of hedonism and the austere redemptive solemnity of Bayreuth. Perhaps the only thing the two houses have in common is a very large fly-tower. Not the least difference was the fact that the Paris Opéra cost seventy times as much as Bayreuth.[75]

The Democratisation of Musical Space

It might be thought that Garnier's structure was traditional, whereas Bayreuth pointed the way to the future.[76] Certainly the Paris Opéra was a much more exclusive space in social terms. Those sitting in the cheaper seats were not even allowed to enter through the grand entrance or to process up the staircase but were obliged to use side doors and were kept at a safe distance from their superiors. The original plan called for an immense Pavillon de l'Empereur reserved for the exclusive use of Napoleon III, complete with a closed entrance into which the imperial carriage could drive, with plenty of space for bodyguards.[77]

Yet, is it so clear that this sort of opera house had seen its day? The opera houses built across the world in the late nineteenth century—Buenos Aires (1857), St. Petersburg (1860), Vienna (1869), Prague (1881), Budapest (1884), Manaus (1896), Rio de Janeiro (1909), São Paulo (1911)—look a lot more like Paris than Bayreuth.[78] They were designed primarily to allow fashionable society to meet in agreeable surroundings and patronise an elitist art form that enhanced their sense of cultural distinction. Any sense of being engaged in a revolutionary or redemptive exercise in the Wagnerian sense was absent. This ossification was assisted by the simultaneous contraction of the operatic repertoire. By the middle of the twentieth century the repertoire had shrunk to a core of just 120 works, virtually all by dead composers.[79] No less than the royal patrons of the past, the paying public knew what it liked, and insisted on having it. During the twenty-two years he was in charge of the Metropolitan Opera in New York—the richest company in the richest city in the world—Rudolf Bing staged just three brand-new works and was quite candid about his role: 'We are similar to a museum: my function is to present old masterpieces in modern frames'.[80]

Not that Bayreuth is as different as it at first appears. Although Wagner's original intention had been to offer free admission, his idealism quickly foundered on finance. As soon as he had to rely on debenture-holders and the paying public, not to mention King Ludwig II, to keep his project afloat, his audience began to look like that for any other opera house, just rather more discriminating and hardy. This paradox was well put by George Bernard Shaw in *The Perfect Wagnerite* when he pointed out that all the praise heaped on the first festival in 1876 'had no other effect upon Wagner than to open his eyes to the fact that the Bayreuth experiment, as an attempt to evade the ordinary social and commercial conditions of theatrical enterprise, was a failure ... nothing can be further off the mark than to chatter about Bayreuth as if it had succeeded in escaping from the conditions of our modern civilisation any more than the Grand Opera in Paris or London'.[81] Bayreuth became a populist space populated by elites.

So Wagner's grand scheme for opening up musical culture to the

The concert hall in the Paris Conservatoire.

common people—the *Volk*—proved to be a *cul de sac*. A more promising venue than the opera house (or rather festival theatre in the case of Bayreuth) was the concert hall. Yet, as we have seen, most of the concerts of the eighteenth century were dominated by the upper reaches of society. This exclusivity proved to be tenacious. In Paris, for example, the best concerts were held at the Conservatoire, one of the few positive cultural creations of the French Revolution. In its acoustically excellent concert hall could be heard an orchestra including some of the best instrumentalists in Europe, who also benefited from the rare advantage of adequate rehearsal time. The outstanding achievement of the orchestra and its long-serving conductor, François-Antoine Habeneck, was to demonstrate the full force of Beethoven's symphonies. In the thirty years following Beethoven's death in 1827, his symphonies were performed 280 times, compared with 58 performances of Haydn's symphonies and 37 of Mozart's.[82] Among the many to be bowled over was the young Wagner, for whom a performance of Beethoven's Ninth Symphony was 'so perfect and so moving that the conception of this marvellous work . . . suddenly stood before me bright as day and as palpable to my touch . . . a stream of inexhaustible melody, gripping the heart with ineluctable force'.[83]

The Conservatoire concerts became famous across the length and breadth of the musical world, setting new standards not just for the music that was performed but also for the way it was received, for this was 'a sanctuary where writers, painters and all serious artists come together', as the critic Joseph Ortigue put it. Here the sacralisation of music reached a new pitch of intensity. Hermione Quinet wrote in her memoirs about the period before 1848: 'I often forget that the Conservatoire is not a church, that the hundred musicians in the Société des Concerts live scattered throughout the twenty arrondissements of Paris and not in a seminary, that they are not a college of priests gathered before us to perform a holy service each Sunday'.[84] Unfortunately, the congregation was strictly limited by the seating capacity of the auditorium, which barely reached a thousand. Wagner was able to gain admission only through the kindness of Maestro Habeneck.

Demand exceeded supply to such an extent that the subscription concerts were sold out months in advance. In 1830 an irate Parisian music lover complained to the *Revue Musicale* that in the previous December he had tried to subscribe for the following year's concerts, only to be told that all tickets had been sold. So he applied again for tickets for the year after that and got the same reply. In short, he concluded, a place on the subscription list had become a sort of heirloom, to be kept within the family and passed on from one generation to the next.[85] All that was left to him were the concerts in the rue de la Harpe mounted by the ominously named Société des Amateurs, at which anyone could turn up with an instrument and play. The results were predictably 'grisly'.[86]

The same sort of social contraction occurred in Great Britain, where Haydn's last visit in 1794–95 had marked both the climax of London's public concert life and the beginning of its decline.[87] The founding of the Philharmonic Society in 1813 by a group of professional musicians was a rare flash of light in an otherwise sombre scene. Although it helped to make London the kind of city that musicians such as Weber, Spohr and Mendelssohn wanted to visit, the concerts were handicapped by the lack of rehearsal time and the absence of a conductor and were confined by the high price of admission—one guinea—to the upper middle class.[88] The kind of aristocrats who had sponsored Haydn in the 1790s preferred to retreat to their drawing rooms, where private concerts and recitals were safe from the pollution of the general public. What had once been the flagship of classical concerts—The Concert of Ancient Music—declined, becoming merely 'the hobby of a very few old lords', as *The Musical World* lamented in 1839.[89]

What flourished instead were the unashamedly popular concerts directed at the middle-brow taste of the middle classes and organised by entrepreneurs with the sole intention of making money. The most flamboyant of them was Louis Jullien (1812–60), who moved to London from his native France in 1838. Seven years later, *The Musical World* posed the question, 'Who can anatomise the career of Monsieur Jullien?' He had arrived 'without a penny and without a prospect', but now 'a more prosperous man than Monsieur Jullien does not inhabit London'. The secret of his success was simple: it was his ability to read the signs of the times and, in particular, to harness the power of the press to his cause: 'Everyone tells you that Jullien does not know a note of music—but what then?—he can twang the chord, which moves the popular heart by its vibration—and manages to derive twenty times more profit from his ignorance than most other artists from their erudition'.[90]

Contemporary accounts agreed that, as a conductor, Jullien possessed extraordinary charisma. In January 1845, for example, the music critic of *The Manchester Times* rhapsodised about 'THE JOY WHICH HE FELT he communicated with the talismanic influence of his wand, throughout the vast hall, which was the scene of universal radiance and pleasure'.[91] He was not the last charismatic leader to spot that the larger the crowd, the easier it was to arouse to a frenzy of enthusiasm. The venues of his Concerts Monstres were capacious enough to allow cheap tickets (two shillings and sixpence if bought in advance), huge orchestras and vast crowds—the Surrey Zoological Garden, for example, where an audience of ten thousand was entertained by an orchestra numbering three hundred.[92]

By the end of the 1840s he was staging concerts with an orchestra of four hundred, three separate military bands and three separate choirs. *The Musical World* commented: 'Jullien is the very colossus of public concerts. His conceptions are universal—his speculations gigantic. The age seems made for Jullien, and Jullien for the age. He is the very henchman of the times, and marches in the rear of occasion . . . This is an age of exaggeration and extravagance—a used-up age—an age that requires strong stimulants to keep excitement alive'.[93] Among other gimmicks, he introduced rifle shots and fireworks to liven up extracts from Meyerbeer's dreary *Les Huguenots*.[94]

Yet his flashy showmanship was accompanied by much serious music too. When he conducted Beethoven, Jullien first demonstratively donned white gloves in readiness for the large jewel-encrusted baton ceremoniously carried into the hall on a velvet cushion by a liveried servant.[95] But he did conduct Beethoven. Moreover, sometimes his orchestra performed a Beethoven symphony in its entirety, which was by no means standard practice even in the smartest concert series. His technique was to mix novelties, dance music and 'easy listening' with more demanding items. As *The Musical World* acknowledged, Jullien could educate his audiences while persuading them that they were really being entertained.

One concert in 1849, for example, was divided into three parts, the first consisting of Felicien David's *The Desert*, depicting a journey across the desert by a caravan, using music and verse; the second comprised Mendelssohn's A Minor Symphony (the *Scottish Symphony*) and Bach's Prelude and Fugue in A Minor; and the third a mixture of popular vocal and instrumental items, including 'God Save the Queen'.[96] The performance of the national anthem on these occasions was very much a response to popular demand. In the autumn of 1848, as revolutions raged across the continent, his concert at the Drury Lane Theatre inspired a massive royalist demonstration:

Though the performance of 'God Save the Queen' be altogether indescribable, we must endeavour to give some faint idea of the impression it produced upon the public. Let the reader imagine a regular grand orchestra of one hundred performers; let him then fancy the addition of four military bands, with their side drums and other thundering appurtenances; let him then conceive the further addition of two hundred choristers, the whole roaring and bawling out *fortissimo*, through their voices and instruments, the very spirit of loyalty in the National Anthem, and even then he cannot have the most remote idea of the effect produced by Jullien's arrangement of 'God Save the Queen'. After the performance, an encore was the inevitable result, and by degrees the audience seemed to be worked into a state of frenzy that defies description.[97]

A third encore followed, the audience now divided into those calling for 'God Save the Queen' and those preferring 'Rule Britannia'. Similar concerts staged in large halls, or even in the open air, and aimed at middle-class and lower middle-class audiences could be found all over Europe during the mid-nineteenth century.[98] A comparison of the 1826–27 and 1845–46 seasons revealed that the number of concerts increased by three times in London and five times in Paris.[99]

From 1861 until 1884 Jules Étienne Pasdeloup organised a series of Concerts Populaires de Musique Classique at the Cirque Napoléon (now known as the Cirque d'Hiver) in Paris, where the size of the hall—with a capacity of over five thousand—meant that he could charge as little as fifty centimes for admission and thus attract even working-class customers. Yet he pitched the level of his programmes appreciably higher than that of his compatriot Jullien in London. Especially commendable was his favouring of contemporary composers, including Berlioz, Schumann, Tchaikovsky, Grieg, Bizet, Rubinstein, Gounod, Saint-Saëns and Massenet.[100]

But most impressive of all was his championing of Wagner, even after the Franco-Prussian War had made the work of any German controversial. In 1876 the mere sight of additional instrumentalists taking the stage in preparation for a performance of 'Siegfried's Funeral March' was enough to unleash a storm of protest, although there was also a counter-demonstration from the Wagnerians present.[101] The reaction of Jules Ruelle, covering the event for *L'Art Musical*, was surprise that music 'so empty, so feeble, so insignificant' could arouse either aversion or enthusiasm.[102] Although competition and failing health forced Pasdeloup to terminate his concerts in 1884, by that time they had been copied across France: in Toulouse, Nantes, Bordeaux, Lyon, and Marseille.[103]

Big spaces meant big orchestras, big audiences, low prices and social diversity. By 1861, five thousand people were attending concerts in Paris every week.[104] In England, large audiences were now being attracted in the provinces. In Manchester, the orchestral concerts organised by Charles Hallé (*né* Carl Halle in Hagen, Westphalia) after 1858 reached a long way down the social ladder, at least according to *The Musical World*, which reported in January 1860 that 'Mr Charles Hallé's Manchester concerts are becoming the vogue with all classes, from the rich merchant and manufacturer to the middle-class tradesmen and bourgeois . . . to the respectable and thrifty, albeit humbler artisans'.[105] In 1896 Hallé's son claimed that working-class people also attended, 'standing packed together in great discomfort . . . listening for hours, and evidently with much appreciation'.[106]

The democratic implications of cheap public concerts were too obvious to be missed. This could be a source of dismay, as it was to the Parisian critic who lamented that during the musical season, with no fewer than two concerts a day and often as many as eight, everything had become completely commercialised and vulgarised.[107] Those of a more egalitarian stamp gloried in the opening up of what had been an elitist genre. A newspaper correspondent in Frankfurt am Main in 1856 took a visiting pianist to task for reserving the front row at his concert for members of the nobility, asserting: 'In our free city we are not accustomed to this kind of thing. In a public concert hall all classes are equal because they have all paid the price of admission, and only latecomers can be sent to the back'.[108]

Meanwhile, another prime space for the performance of music—the dance hall—had been following a similar trajectory. Of course ordinary people have always danced—in pubs, at patronal festivals, at weddings, and so on. But dancing as a regular, organised activity is much more recent. The court of Louis XIV at Versailles was the source of many of the characteristics of modern dance and ballet, and the notation of 330 dances performed at that venue have survived.[109] The formal balls especially were strictly regimented affairs, serving more to demonstrate the hierarchical structure of the court and the social disciplining of its members than to allow rhythmic intercourse.[110] Only a small proportion of those attending actually danced; the great majority were spectators. As a contemporary recorded: 'First one must know that no one is admitted to the circle except princes and princesses of the blood, then the dukes and peers and the duchesses, and after these the other lords and ladies of the court, each according to rank'.[111]

Dance as a reflection of the social hierarchy continued through the eighteenth century and into the next. A perfect musical illustration was provided by Mozart in the ballroom scene at the end of Act Two of *Don Giovanni,* when three different bands play three different dances for three different social groups: a minuet for the nobles, a contredanse for the bourgeoisie and a rustic dance for the peasants.[112] The commercialisation of dancing, which developed more or less simultaneously with that of concerts, did little to break down the barriers. At the Assembly Rooms in Bath, for example, the proceedings were led off by the highest-ranking couple attending. Neither there nor at its many equivalents in the capital were 'sons of commerce' admitted.[113] At the rooms opened in 1816 at Cheltenham—a byword for gentility then as now—the rules stated firmly that 'no clerk, hired or otherwise, in this town or neighbourhood; no person concerned in retail trade, no theatrical or other public performers by profession be admitted'.[114] Such people could dance too, but they had to go to a secondary or even tertiary level of assembly rooms and dance halls until they found their correct level.

One change that did occur, however, was the growing standardisation of dances. By the end of the nineteenth century it would have been anachronistic for a composer to assign different dances to different social groups. Everyone was now doing the same steps, though in different spaces. The two most popular dances were the quadrille, a dance of five figures for sets of four couples, and of course the waltz. When first introduced at the beginning of the nineteenth century, the waltz, which had no set configuration and allowed close physical contact between couples, provoked a moral panic. It was described as 'choreographic rape', and even so notorious a roué as Byron was moved to condemn it.[115] In 1816 in a poem entitled 'The Waltz; an Apostrophic Hymn' he wrote:

> But ye—who never felt a single thought
> For what our morals are to be, or ought;
> Who wisely wish to view the charms you reap,
> Say—would you make those beauties quite so cheap?
> Hot from the hands promiscuously applied,
> Round the slight waist, or down the glowing side,
> Where were the rapture then to clasp the form
> From this lewd grasp and lawless contact warm?[116]

Probably assisted rather than obstructed by this kind of finger-wagging, the waltz took Europe by storm. In its birthplace, Vienna, it reached large numbers of people and produced music of very high quality. The complex of dance halls known collectively as Zum Sperlbauer in the Leopoldstadt district of the city could accommodate several thousand people, and the first two masters of the waltz, Josef Lanner and Johann Strauss, began their careers there, sharing a desk as violinists. Their different vocational paths neatly advertised the waltz's universal appeal: in 1829 Lanner became director of imperial court balls, while Strauss negotiated an exclusive contract and huge fee with the Sperl.[117] Lanner enjoyed the prestige of a court position, but Strauss made the money, commanding a stable of approximately two hundred players whom he sent out to dance halls across Vienna.

Even with allowances for a journalist's instinctive hyperbole, Heinrich Laube's account of a Strauss dance-cum-concert in the 1830s illustrates well the impact of his music:

> Under illuminated trees and in open arcades people are seated at innumerable tables, eating, drinking, laughing, and listening. In their midst is the orchestra from which come the new waltzes ... that stir the blood like the bite of a tarantula. In the midst of the garden on the orchestra platform stands the modern hero of Austria, *le Napoléon autrichien*, the musical director Johann Strauss. The Strauss waltzes are to the Viennese what the Napoleonic victories were to the French ... All eyes were turned to him; it was a moment of worship ... The power wielded by the black-haired musician is potentially very dangerous; it is his especial good fortune that no censorship can be exercised over waltz music and the thoughts and emotions it arouses ... I do not know what other things besides music Strauss may understand, but I do know that he is a man who could do a great deal of harm if he were to play Rousseau's ideas on his violin. In one single evening the Viennese would subscribe to the entire *Contrat social.*[118]

When Strauss travelled to England in 1838, not only did he play at Queen Victoria's pre-coronation ball, he also made £200 a night, a fabulous sum by the standards of the day.[119] His son, Johann Strauss II, became even more popular, thanks to waltzes such as 'The Blue Danube' and operettas such as *Die Fledermaus.* A poll conducted across Europe in 1890 revealed that the second Strauss—the 'Waltz King'—was the third most admired European, after Queen Victoria and Bismarck.[120]

Places and Spaces for the Masses

Without a doubt, the dramatic increase in the market for music in the course of the nineteenth century fed into, and off of, a proliferation in the places and spaces for its performance, both concert halls and dance halls. Yet the great mass of the population continued to be excluded. Very few manual labourers could be found dancing the quadrille or the waltz, and although some did gain admission to large public concerts of the kind staged at the Crystal Palace or the Cirque Napoléon, working-class men and women were very much occasional interlopers in an essentially bourgeois space. But the rapid progress of industrialisation during the boom years of the 1840s, 1850s and 1860s increased both the overall size of the working class and the disposable income of many of its members. However patchy and fitful, a trend towards shorter working hours and more leisure was also discernible during this period.

The music hall was created specifically for this new group of consumers. Although singing in pubs was as old as time, toward the middle of the nineteenth century music-making in these establishments became both more ubiquitous and more ambitious. An 1849 report for *The Morning Chronicle* investigating 'Labour and the Poor' discovered that thirty-two public houses in Liverpool offered musical entertainment: 'The attention of the stranger who walks through the streets of Liverpool can scarcely fail to be directed to the great number of placards which invite the public to cheap or free concert rooms. Of all shapes, size and colours to attract the eye, they cover the walls of the town, and compete with one another in the inducements which they offer to the public to favour with its patronage the houses which they advertise.'[121]

In the course of the next decade, these informal and often semi-professional venues developed into the full-blown music halls that would dominate popular urban entertainment for the next generation or so. The best qualified candidate for the title of first in the field was Charles Morton (1819–1904), who in 1852 demolished the skittle alley of his pub The Old Canterbury Arms in Lambeth and erected a music hall in its place. He sold his customers a sixpenny ticket to enter, redeemable against drinks bought from the bar.[122] So successful was he, especially after he opened a hall 'up west' in Oxford Street, that many other entrepreneurs moved in. By the mid-1860s London had thirty large halls with an average seating capacity of 1,500, along with 200–300 smaller halls.[123] The provincial response was almost simultaneous, as great 'palaces of varieties' mushroomed in the industrial cities of the north. A sure sign that the institution had arrived was the founding of a specialist agency by Ambrose Maynard in 1858, the publication of a dedicated trade journal—*The Magnet* in 1866—and the creation of trade associations for both promoters and performers in 1860 and 1865 respectively.[124]

The musical fare on offer was various, ranging from opera extracts, through drawingroom ballads, folk songs and traditional patriotic fare, to parodies, burlesques, patter-songs, sentimental ballads and comic ditties (often smutty). What they all had in common was melody. The music hall was not a place for harmony or counterpoint. Patrons wanted a good rousing tune, something they could tap their toes to and whistle on the way home. And they felt no inhibitions about letting the performers know what they thought. The successful songwriter Felix McGlennon observed cynically: 'It is not the kid-gloved critics in the stalls, the eminent literary men, who do the trick for you, but the people in the pit and gallery, who are not afraid to shout their approval or disapproval. And they like simple pathos or homely humour—something to do with wife and mother-in-law, and so on. The main thing is catchiness. *I would sacrifice everything—rhyme, reason, sense and sentiment to catchiness. There is, let me tell you, a very great art in making rubbish acceptable*'.[125] Among the catchy songs that proved durable were 'The Man Who Broke the Bank at Monte Carlo', 'Burlington Bertie', 'Lily of Laguna', 'Daddy Wouldn't Buy Me a Bow-Wow', 'Roamin' in the Gloamin'', 'I Love a Lassie', 'My Old Dutch', 'Down at the Old Bull and Bush', 'My Old Man', 'Oh! Mr Porter!' and 'Pack up Your Troubles', all of which could (and can still) be hummed after a single hearing.[126]

It was not just the working class that liked a good tune. Among the hundreds of thousands who flocked to the music halls at the end of the nineteenth century were plenty from the middle classes and also a good number of upper-class 'slummers'. They occupied the more expensive seats in the stalls and dress circle. Most of the poor were still excluded by the minimum admission price of sixpence. But in London, where the price could go as low as two pence, the music hall was within reach of anyone who had a job. The philanthropist H. Lee J. Jones observed: 'I think quite two thirds of the poor of Liverpool never go near music halls; at any rate, by no means as a rule. Their almost sole "music hall" is the Italian organ [-grinder]'.[127] To fill this yawning gap at the very bottom of the pile, Jones organised what became known as 'court and alley' concerts, involving just a platform and piano, taken right in among the tenements by a horse and cart to perform sacred and comic songs, Scottish and Irish medleys (depending on the ethnic mix) and instrumental solos.[128]

As the nineteenth century drew to a close, in the United Kingdom the stratification of musical consumption appeared to be complete. The 'upper ten thousand' displayed themselves to best advantage at the opera; the middle classes favoured orchestral concerts and the better seats of the better music halls; the working class made do with the galleries of music halls, brass bands, cooperative choirs and itinerant German bands. A similar pattern could be found in any of the industrialising countries of Europe. But before the century was over, a new invention erupted on the musical scene to burst the social barriers and standardise, homogenise and internationalise musical experience. This was cinema, whose beginning is usually dated to 28 December 1895, when Auguste Marie Lumière and his brother Louis Nicholas showed a moving picture to a paying audience at the Salon Indien of the Grand Café on the Boulevard des Capucines in Paris. The film, which showed a group of mostly female workers leaving the Lumière factory in Lyon, lasted just forty-five seconds.

After a slow start, cinema carried all before it as the preferred medium of entertainment for all classes. In 1906 Paris had ten cinemas, but just two years later the city counted eighty-seven. By 1920 thousands of screens could be found in every country.[129] Rather than becoming a threat to the growing hegemony of music, film was in reality an opportunity. Not for the first or last time, music showed its wonderfully protean nature by turning the new technology to its advantage. That very first performance in the Salon Indien included piano accompaniment. At the first demonstration of the new invention in London, which took place the following February at the Polytechnic on Regent Street, a harmonium was brought from the chapel.[130]

All films shown in cinemas before 1927 were silent and required musical accompaniment to provide atmosphere and mask the whirring of the projector. In the small picture houses—often a village hall hired for the oc-

A Mighty Wurlitzer theatre organ.

casion—a single pianist had to suffice; but the great picture palaces boasted a theatre organ such as the Mighty Wurlitzer or even a complete orchestra. Or indeed both: the sumptuously decorated Strand Cinema in Manhattan, with a seating capacity of 3,300, boasted a thirty-three-piece orchestra and a massive Wurlitzer organ.[131] The opportunity was seized by Max Winkler, a clerk in the music publishing house of Carl Fischer in New York. He invented the simple but brilliant device of the music cue sheet, which told the musician in the cinema pit exactly what music to play exactly when during the movie, to create maximum effect.

To sell the idea to the Universal Film Company, he drew up a cue sheet for an imaginary film, *The Magic Valley:*

> Cue 1. Opening—play Minuet No. 2 in G by Beethoven for ninety seconds until title on screen "Follow me, Dear".
> Cue 2. Play—Dramatic Andante by Vely for two minutes and ten seconds. Note: play softly during the scene where mother enters. Play Cue No. 2 until scene of hero leaving the room.
> Cue 3. Play—Love Theme by Lorenz—for one minute and twenty seconds. Note: play soft and slow during conversations until title on screen "There they go".
> Cue 4. Play—Stampeded by Simon for fifty-five seconds. Note: play fast and decrease or increase speed of gallop in accordance with action on the screen.[132]

After forming his own company, Winkler assembled a team of hack composers to turn out appropriate short snippets of music for all the various situations the silent films showed, from car chases to love scenes. He also plundered the classics, as he explained in his autobiography *A Penny from Heaven*, published in 1951: 'We turned to crime. We began to dismember the great masters. We murdered the works of Beethoven, Mozart, Grieg, J. S. Bach, Verdi, Bizet, and Wagner—everything that wasn't protected by copyright from our pilfering. Today I look in shame and awe at the printed copies of these mutilated masterpieces. I hope this belated confession will grant me forgiveness for what I have done.'[133] One can only wonder how Wagner, for example, might have reacted to finding 'The Ride of the Valkyrie' being boomed out by a theatre organ to accompany the arrival of the cavalry in the last reel of a western. He and his colleagues might have reflected, however, that in this way their music was reaching an enormously greater audience than ever before.

The notoriously hypersensitive Wagner would have been more upset to find himself sharing a score assembled from extracts of various composers. This was what D. W. Griffith and Joseph Carl Briel did for *The Birth of a Nation* in 1915. Beethoven, Wagner would have accepted; Liszt, he might just have stomached; but Verdi and Tchaikovsky would have provoked a seismic reaction, and as for 'Dixie' and 'The Star-Spangled Banner', the imagination fails. By this time, however, film music was emerging as an art form in his own right. Edmund Meisel's score for Sergei Eisenstein's *The Battleship Potemkin* (1925) was an early indication of what could be done when marrying image with sound. Other composers to write scores for important silent films were Arthur Honegger (*La Roue,* 1922), Darius Milhaud (*L'Inhumaine,* 1924) and Dimitri Shostakovitch (*The New Babylon,* 1929).[134]

The coming of 'talkies' after 1927 certainly caused problems for the music industry. Poor Max Winkler found himself with seventy tons of printed music that nobody wanted. Even the paper mill that took it off his hands at fifteen cents a hundredweight went bankrupt before he could cash the cheque.[135] Yet, despite teething problems, musicians and their music were coming of age in a whole new world. Whether it was Marlene Dietrich singing 'Falling in Love Again' in *The Blue Angel* (1930) or Fred Astaire and Ginger Rogers singing and dancing in *Flying Down to Rio* (1933) or Busby Berkeley choreographing *42nd Street* (1933) or Bing Crosby crooning his way through *Blue of the Night* (1933), music had acquired an immensely potent new medium. In 1938 around 80 million Americans, or 65 percent of the population, were going to the cinema every week.[136] Not all of the movies they saw were musicals—although many of the most popular were—but all of them included music in some way.

And so it has continued. Some of the most ambitious high-budget films around the turn of the twenty-first century—*Star Wars, Titanic, The Lord of the Rings,* for example—are more dependent on their scores than any movies that came before. The places in which this music is played could hardly be more ubiquitous or the spaces more democratic. There is hardly a town in the developed world without a cinema, and every cinema is designed to allow everyone to see the screen. The lights are dimmed almost to the point of darkness, thus allowing members of the audience a wholly personal and intimate relationship with events and people on the screen— or, if attending as a couple, with each other.[137]

The same sort of couples were also getting close to each other on the dance floor. In his 1904 *History of Dancing,* Sir Reginald St. Johnston wrote: 'I cannot now find even among the rural population any traces of what might be called a national dance . . . the country-folk dance the waltz, polka and lancers just as the upper classes—albeit, generally, with more abandon and fun.'[138] All those dances are still being danced today, but are categorised

An advertisement for the Hammersmith Palais de Danse from
the 1920s.

as 'old time'. Their relegation from present to past was quite sudden. Seven
years after St. Johnston's observation, the arrival of the tango from South
America, swiftly followed by ragtime from the United States, revolutionised
the dance floor.

A succession of short-lived dances—the Bunny Hug, Grizzly Bear,
Turkey Trot (later known as one-step), Crab Step, Kangaroo Dip, Horse
Trot—announced a style of dancing that was much less staid and inhibited
than even the waltz, and also—crucially—much easier to learn. They also
called for a different kind of music. Out went the string-dominated orchestras and in came bands with brass sections, saxophones and percussion.
These groups were also very much louder, easily able to fill the largest hall

with rousing sound. So, first across the United States and then across the rest of the world, great commercial dance halls were opened, the terpsichorean equivalents of the cinema, with low admission prices and huge audiences.

In England the leader in all senses was undoubtedly the Hammersmith Palais de Danse, established in 1919. It both reflected and encouraged a craze for dancing that penetrated society at every level. In February 1922 the *Daily Mail* reported: 'Some hundreds of dance schools have reduced the shortage of dancing men. For every man who danced two years ago, eight or nine dance now. Freak steps . . . have gone out, and easy straightforward steps are the rule'.[139] By the end of the decade, just about every town of any size in the country had a dance hall.[140] The social barriers had not fallen, of course. When the upper and middle classes wanted to dance, they went to a hotel or a restaurant rather than a 'palais', but they were all now dancing the same sort of steps to the same sort of music, and every urban dweller with an income could gain access to dancing and dance music.

With the creation of very large buildings for concerts, film and dancing, the provision of musical places and spaces for the general public might seem to be nearing completion. Yet in the twentieth century a remarkable—and paradoxical—bifurcation occurred, one whose spatial implications cannot be ignored. Even though the darkened cinema promoted a special relationship between the individual moviegoer and the actors on the screen, going to the movies was also a communal experience. The arrival of television after 1940 confined that communal experience to the family, although—as we shall see—it did not reduce the amount of music being played. The next step in the contraction of the audience was the development of the transistor in the 1950s, which allowed the first genuinely portable radios to be manufactured. Although the first transistor radios were expensive, mass production soon brought the unit cost tumbling down, within reach of even the shallowest pocket. Today in Europe and the United States one can buy a radio for less than the hourly minimum wage.[141]

The invention of the cassette by Philips in 1963 and the Walkman by Sony in 1979 allowed the individual to create a sound world that was completely personal and isolated. Among other things, the Walkman and its successors such as the iPod have put an end to any chance that people

The Beatles at Shea Stadium, 15 August 1965.

might converse with strangers on public transport. It is now rare to enter a train or subway carriage in the West in which the majority of passengers are *not* sporting earphones.

At the same time, public spaces for music were also heading in exactly the opposite direction — to the gigantic and impersonal. The concert given by The Beatles on 15 August 1965 in Shea Stadium, New York, before a crowd of 55,600 was, by most people's estimation, the first true stadium concert. It was to be the first of a large number, as both promoters and musicians discovered that huge sums of money could be made literally overnight. Although difficult to describe and impossible to quantify, a special quality about tens of thousands of people crowding together made these audiences much greater than the sum of their parts.

The Shea Stadium concert was a one-off, but as the cost of providing better sound systems and giant screens escalated, so did the pressure for multi-concert tours. For their Forty Licks Tour of 2002–03, The Rolling Stones employed three hundred specialists, including accountants, an immigration lawyer and a pastry chef. Over a hundred workers were needed simply to transport the equipment in thirty-eight trucks.[142] The Rolling Stones were encouraged by the knowledge that between 1989 and 2002 they had earned in excess of £650 million from touring.[143] That figure seems rather less incredible when one learns that they can charge up to £225 a seat at Las Vegas, or attract more than a million people to a single concert at Copacabana beach in Rio de Janeiro (as they did in February 2006) and gross $2 million a night.[144] For the Bigger Bang tour of 2006, tickets sold for $4,000 a pair on eBay.[145] Although generally recognised as the most profitable rock band in history, The Rolling Stones are by no means alone in generating such sums of money from monster concerts. Robbie Williams sold 400,000 tickets for three openair concerts at Knebworth House in 2004, which helped to raise his earning for the year to £26 million.[146]

In just three centuries we have gone from Fux's *Missa San Carlo* in the Karlskirche in Vienna to 'Angels' (the name of Robbie Williams' biggest hit to date) at Knebworth. The religious terminology these two musical illustrations have in common is more than coincidence. Sticking with our earlier conclusion that music is the religion of the people, we can go further now and state that the stadiums and arenas used for rock concerts are the cathedrals of the modern age. What made that possible was a complex web of interacting technological innovations that changed every art, but music most of all, and it is to technology that we must now turn.

4
Technology
From Stradivarius to Stratocaster

Musical Gas and Other Inventions

In 1837 one of the many French periodicals devoted to music published a satirical article entitled 'Musical Gas'[1] It reported that a brilliant English chemist called Pumpernikle, who had sensibly emigrated to Paris, had made a discovery that would revolutionise the world's leisure time. In an earlier experiment, he had shown already how the sound of a piano could be transmitted from one building to another across a distance of forty metres. Now he had gone one step further by discovering how to carbonise sound waves and thus create musical gas.

The original sounds were conveyed via a bell-shaped receiver through tubes to a furnace, where they were condensed and reduced to a substance rather like coal. Using a technique similar to that employed in manufacturing hydrogen, this 'acoustic carbon' was then reduced to gas, which could be stored in tanks underground. From there it could be piped to subscribers, who needed only to turn on a tap at the appointed hour and out would come a concert. In the future, Parisians returning home at night might well hear odd notes, melodic groans and even bursts of harmony escaping from the network of pipes below the streets. The distilling process would weed out false notes and botched passages, and this detritus could be turned into musical cakes and sold to suburban dance halls at modest cost—a useful byproduct.

Parisians making their way through city streets in the twenty-first century do not have to rely on escaping gas to hear music. An almost infinite variety is available to them, conveyed through automobile radios or the headphones of a personal stereo weighing just a few ounces. Those who prefer silence are likely to be interrupted constantly by blasts of amplified music from bars, cafés, clubs and passing cars. These experiences encapsulate the salient characteristics of music today: accessibility, portability, diversity and, above all, ubiquity. For the tone deaf, the modern world is a torture chamber—an unremitting blast furnace of meaningless noise.

Even those who enjoy music find its constant presence irritating, whether it is the buzzing from neighbouring earphones on public transport, the Muzak in lifts, restaurants and shopping malls, or the 'easy listening' that has to be endured when a telephone message puts the caller on hold. These are just a few of the horrors that give music a bad name. Not even the satirist who welcomed the arrival of 'musical gas' could have imagined this degree of saturation. It has been the result of a sustained technological revolution. All the arts have been affected, but music has changed the most.

When the many threads of this amazing transformation are pulled apart, it is hard to identify one as primal. All were necessary, none was sufficient. This interactive process can be exemplified by the development of keyboard instruments. When the eighteenth century began, church music was dominated by the organ and secular music by the harpsichord. The power and range of the former made it ideal for the cavernous spaces of European cathedrals and churches, although its size and expense anchored it to the building for which it was constructed.

The harpsichord had flourished for the previous two centuries, because its portability and incisive tone suited the polyphonic music of the period. But because it creates sound by plucking the strings, the harpsichord is restricted dynamically, being unable to move from soft to loud and back again. Another keyboard instrument of the time, the clavichord, which strikes rather than plucks the strings, was able to manage dynamic nuance, but the price it paid for its delicacy was a corresponding softness of sound that disqualified it from large ensembles and concert halls. Though

Bartolomeo Cristofori pointing to a diagram of his new hammer mechanism; and one of only three surviving pianos made by him.

a significant body of music was composed specifically for this instrument, clavichords were used mostly for composition, practice, and recitals in intimate settings.

The advance of opera and the move away from polyphony during the late seventeenth century intensified the need for an instrument that would be more expressive—one that would combine the power of the harpsichord with the dynamic range of the clavichord. The man of the hour was Bartolomeo Cristofori, a Paduan by birth who was employed by Ferdinando III de' Medici as an instrument maker. An inventory compiled in 1700 noted the presence in the ducal collection of 'a harpsichord by Bartolomeo Cristofori of a new invention, which plays piano and forte, with two sets of unison strings . . . with jacks with red cloth, which damp the strings, and hammers producing the piano and forte.'[2] It was this crucial ability to vary the dynamics that made what became known as the fortepiano ('loudsoft') so attractive to performers. In the early nineteenth century, by which time being first in the field had become a matter of national pride, French and German candidates were advanced as rivals for the honour, but Cristofori's claims have been established beyond reasonable doubt.[3]

Many decades would pass before before Cristofori's invention established itself as the keyboard of choice. In the early days, its popularity was restricted by a lack of volume. For all its revolutionary action, the lightness of the stringing and hammers meant that its sonic impact could not compete with that of the harpsichord. There is even evidence that some disappointed customers had their Cristofori instruments converted into harpsichords.[4] Before long, however, manufacturers elsewhere began to improve on the original. To the fore here was the Saxon Gottfried Silbermann (1683–1753). His early creations met with a mixed reception from his friend Johann Sebastian Bach, who admired the tone but found the high register feeble and the mechanism too heavy. Johann Friedrich Agricola recorded that Silbermann was both offended and stimulated by this criticism and sought to correct the defects.[5]

He appears to have succeeded, for several of his later creations—perhaps as many as fifteen—were purchased by Frederick the Great of Prussia. According to Bach's first biographer, Johann Nikolaus Forkel, when he visited Frederick at Potsdam on 1 May 1747, 'the King gave up his concert for the evening and invited Bach . . . to try his fortepianos, made by Silbermann, which stood in several rooms of the Palace. The musicians went with him from room to room, and Bach was invited to try them and to play un-premeditated compositions'.[6]

The harpsichord proved tenacious. Indeed, it has been argued that the great days of the harpsichord began *after* 1750.[7] Even so, the balance of power was beginning to shift. It can be traced in a number of ways, most agreeably through the keyboard sonatas of Joseph Haydn. Although he did not acquire his own fortepiano until 1788, he had the use of one owned by his patron, Prince Esterházy, from 1773 and was beginning to write works that would suit both harpsichord and piano. His six sonatas published by Artaria in 1780, for example, are listed as being 'for the harpsichord or the fortepiano'.[8] By the middle of the decade, the dynamic marks make clear that Haydn was writing exclusively for the latter.[9]

In 1790 he wrote to his close friend Anna Maria von Genzinger: 'What a pity that Your Grace does not own a Fortepiano by Schanz, because everything can be expressed better on it. I believe Your Grace should pass on your harpsichord, which is still in very good condition, to Miss Peperle, and buy a new Fortepiano for yourself'.[10] Haydn had been encouraged to make the change to piano compositions by the knowledge that there was a market for what he wrote—and what he wrote encouraged that market to grow larger. This kind of self-sustaining process was destined to continue until the twentieth century, when the easy availability of recordings began to erode the demand for sheet music.

The popularity of the piano concertos written by Johann Christian Bach for the London concerts he organised with Carl Friedrich Abel in the 1760s marked an important step forward. According to Charles Burney, 'After the arrival of John Chr. Bach in this country, and the establishment of his concert[s] . . . all the harpsichord makers tried their mechanical powers at piano-fortes'.[11] He has also been credited with performing the first public piano solo, in 1768.[12] But perhaps the clearest sign that the piano had come of age was provided by Mozart. Both his early career as a travelling prodigy, which began when he was just six years old, and his concerts in Vienna in the 1780s demonstrated the capability of the instrument in as irrefutable a manner as could be imagined. His eighteen piano sonatas, thirty-six sonatas for violin and piano (in which the piano plays an equal role), twelve piano trios and, above all, the twenty-seven piano concertos propelled the pianist to the front rank of instrumentalists. In 1774 Voltaire had dismissed the fortepiano as 'the instrument of a boilermaker when compared with a harpsichord'; by the end of the century only the violinist enjoyed equal stature with the pianist.[13]

Part and parcel of this development was the response of manufacturers. In London, Paris, Vienna and many towns of the Holy Roman Empire, one entrepreneur after another seized the opportunities presented by a rapidly expanding market. They were helped by a simultaneous improvement in communications that allowed both information and people to be exchanged more rapidly than at any time since the fall of the Roman Empire. Representative was the career of Johann Christoph Zumpe, who was born at Fürth near Nuremberg in 1726, trained as a cabinet maker there and then set out for London to seek his fortune. After working for the Swiss-born harpsichord maker Burkat Shudi for a number of years, he set up his own shop. Soon he found a niche market, making a 'square' fortepiano that was compact enough to fit into a middle-class living room and, at sixteen guineas (£16.80), inexpensive enough to be within the reach of a middle-class pocket (though Zumpe also counted the admirably frugal Queen Charlotte among his customers).

The rapid success of the square piano was helped along by endorsements from leading lights of the musical world such as Charles Burney and Johann Christian Bach. By 1782 Zumpe had made a fortune large enough to allow him to withdraw from business and enjoy life as a rentier (a gentleman of leisure living from investment income).[14] His example was soon imitated in one European centre after another, not to mention the American colonies, where Thomas Jefferson was so impressed by the Zumpe square piano he saw in 1771 that he wrote hurriedly to his agent in London to change his original order for a clavichord.[15]

Zumpe's most successful follower was John Broadwood, a Scot who took the high road to London in 1761. He also learned his trade while working with Burkat Shudi, whose daughter he married before becoming a partner in the firm in 1770. This venture proved to be more durable than Zumpe's, for the Broadwood firm is still in existence today. Its letterhead and website proclaim that it has supplied pianos to the kings and queens of England in unbroken succession since 1727.[16] The first John Broadwood was lucky to set up in business at a time when demand was expanding faster than the industry's capacity. By the 1790s the company was making around four hundred square pianos and one hundred grands each year.[17]

Significantly, after 1793 no more harpsichords were manufactured by Broadwood.

Also indicative of the future was John Broadwood's constant search to improve the power, tone and range of his instruments. Cristofori's forte-piano had been small and delicate, with a range of just four octaves; by 1800 a Broadwood grand piano was much larger, stronger and louder and covered five and a half octaves.[18] In improving the various mechanisms, the enterprising Broadwood also sought advice from scientists such as Tiberius Cavallo, a Neapolitan by birth who had settled in London in 1771 and had published a number of scientific treatises. Among other things, this consultation resulted in a divided bridge to overcome the problems previously experienced in the transition from iron strings (for high notes) to brass strings (for low notes) so that the tenor octave was now much richer and more sonorous.[19]

Important in determining a manufacturer's success was the response from professional performers. In October 1777 Mozart wrote to his father from Augsburg that he now much preferred the pianos manufactured locally by Johann Andreas Stein, chiefly because of the excellence of the escapement mechanism: 'When I strike hard, I can keep my finger on the note or raise it, but the sound ceases the moment I have produced it'. He also recorded Stein's own explanation of his search for perfection: 'If I were not myself such a passionate lover of music and had not myself some slight skill on the clavier [keyboard], I should certainly long ago have lost patience with my work. But I do like an instrument which never lets the player down and which is durable'.[20]

Enterprising manufacturers were quick to advertise any endorsements received from famous pianists. In 1818 Thomas Broadwood, the founder's son, achieved a public relations coup when he made a well-publicised donation of a six-octave grand piano to Beethoven.[21] The recipient was delighted: 'It is a wonderful present, and it has a beautiful tone', he told Ludwig Rellstab.[22] Beethoven composed his next major work, the Piano Sonata in B-flat, op. 106, the *Hammerklavier*, on this instrument. When the touring piano virtuosi—Weber, Moscheles, Kalkbrenner, Field, Thalberg, Liszt—took the instrument to ever wider audiences, they also acted as travelling salesmen. Chopin gave very few public concerts, but it was well known—and well publicised—that his instrument of choice was a

Pleyel.[23] The multi-talented Muzio Clementi managed to combine all functions, being simultaneously composer, pianist, teacher, publisher and manufacturer.

Although John Broadwood and Sons was the biggest piano company in the world by this time, many other manufacturers throughout Europe were engaged in improving the instrument. The Viennese came relatively late to the piano but then took it up with enthusiasm. A key figure was Leopold Koželuch (also spelt Kotzeluch and Koželuh), who was almost as versatile as Clementi, lacking only the latter's manufacturing capacity. In 1796 a periodical recorded of him: 'The monotony and muddled sound of the harpsichord could not accommodate the clarity, the delicacy, the light and shade he demanded in music; he therefore took no students who did not want to understand the fortepiano'.[24] Thanks to the advocacy of teachers like Koželuch, a market for pianos positively exploded in Vienna during the last two decades of the eighteenth century, and the number of makers grew proportionally. They came from as far afield as Prussia, Württemberg and Frankfurt am Main, lured by the employment opportunities offered by the largest German-speaking city in Europe. By 1830 there were eighty manufacturers of pianos in the three Vienna suburbs of Landstrasse, Laimgrube and Wieden alone, and only a handful of them were born in Vienna.[25]

Pianos for the Middle Classes

In less than a century the piano had advanced from invention to acceptance to dominance. Its expressiveness both satisfied and encouraged the demand for music that appealed to the emotions. As the Romantic revolution gathered pace, the piano's fortunes rose, reaching a climax with Franz Liszt, certainly its most charismatic and very likely its greatest ever exponent. Liszt made the most of the improved instruments provided for him by the Erard company. He was the first pianist to play entirely from memory; the first to place the piano at a right angle to his audience so that he would be more visible (indeed, he liked to have two pianos on stage so that he could change places periodically and thus display his profile from the other side); the first to play with an open lid, reflecting the sound across the auditorium; and the first to devote a whole concert to a single instrument—

indeed, he invented the term 'recital', introducing it for the first time for a concert in London in 1840.[26]

Liszt also gave the definitive statement of the piano's capacity:

> In my opinion, the piano must take pride of place in the hierarchy of instruments. It owes its importance to the harmonic power which it alone possesses . . . Within the scope of its seven octaves it embraces the complete range of the orchestra, and the ten fingers of a performer suffice to reproduce all the harmonies produced by a hundred orchestral players playing together. Through its mediation, works can be broadcast that otherwise would remain unknown, due to the difficulties of assembling a full orchestra.[27]

Liszt proceeded to prove the accuracy of this claim by writing a large number of piano arrangements for music by (among others) Beethoven, Berlioz, Schubert, Rossini and Verdi. His amazing versions of Wagner's operas are masterpieces in their own right, incontrovertibly proving the expressive power of his instrument. As Dieter Hildebrandt drily observed: 'Try playing the Venusberg music [from Wagner's *Tannhäuser*] on the harpsichord!'[28]

Yet one did not have to be a genius to play the piano tolerably. A learner could extract agreeable sounds on day one, unlike an aspiring violinist, who would still be inflicting pain on the neighbourhood many months—indeed years—after taking up the instrument. There were also social benefits. A square or (later) an upright piano added tone to a living room without dominating it. And the cost was not excessive. In 1780 a basic Broadwood could be had for twenty guineas (£21) plus a guinea for packing and delivery. A generation later, economies of scale had brought the cost down to £18, carriage paid. This represented a substantial net reduction when inflation is taken into account.[29] Once the basics had been mastered, a pianist could entertain family and friends with dance music or transcriptions of arias from the latest opera. According to Volkmar Braunbehrens, 'a booming market for sheet music' arose in Vienna as early as the 1780s.[30] In the ten years following the first performance of Verdi's *I Lombardi* in 1843, no fewer than 245 arrangements of its arias were published, including the complete opera arranged for piano 'in the easy style'.[31]

This development gathered pace as the nineteenth century progressed and the European economy expanded. There were downs as well as ups, notably the prolonged recession that followed the end of the Napoleonic Wars, but the secular trend was positive. Wars were fewer, shorter and less murderous—in proportion to the population, *seven times* fewer Europeans died in battle than during the eighteenth century. Everywhere, the population was growing, more than doubling in the course of the century. Towns were becoming cities and cities metropolises. Railways and steamships made travel easier, faster, cheaper and more comfortable. A combination of division of labour and technological innovation brought a massive surge in industrial productivity. Although unevenly divided, more wealth was being generated than at any time in the history of humankind.

Of the many beneficiaries of this transformation, collectively the most striking were the middle classes. The academic controversies surrounding the nature of the category need not delay us here. Contemporaries could certainly see which way the social wind was blowing. Representative of a host of comments was the celebrated remark by the Scottish lawyer, journalist, reformer, politician and eventual peer, Henry Brougham: 'By the People, I mean the middle-classes, the wealth and intelligence of the country, the glory of the British name'.[32] Those words were uttered in 1831, a year before the enactment of the Great Reform Bill, in part due to Brougham's advocacy. The expansion of the franchise in the United Kingdom to embrace a significant portion of the middle classes symbolised their relentless march to political power. Half a century later, virtually every European country had followed suit, with the significant exception of Russia. Whether this represented a social revolution with cultural and political consequences or a cultural revolution with social and political consequences, the result was a massive expansion of the public sphere. At its heart was a corresponding elevation of music as a middle-class activity, greatly encouraged by the further technological advances. And its representative medium was the piano.

The first time a piano was played in public was on 6 March 1763 at Vienna, when Johann Baptist Schmid played a concerto 'on his new instrument called piano and forte'.[33] Seventy years later every family in Vienna owned a piano, and whole apartment blocks could be heard practising simultaneously.[34] In 1845 the violinist, composer and critic Henri Blanchard reported from Paris that not a palace, shop, family gathering or ball could be found where the piano was not heard.[35] This kind of hyperbole is as revealing as the hard facts it obscures. Despite the exaggeration, plenty of statistical evidence supports the impression that pianos were ubiquitous. For example, writing in 1830, the Belgian-born Paris-based musicologist François-Joseph Fétis estimated that around 6,000 pianos were being manufactured each year in Paris (compared with 130 in 1790 and 1,000 in 1800).[36] The Paris-based piano manufacturing firm founded in 1807 by the Austrian Ignaz Joseph Pleyel was still employing just twenty workers in 1825, but ten years later the payroll had expanded to 250. By the 1860s the plant was turning out around a thousand pianos a month.[37]

By that time, the Germans were beginning to establish a dominant position in the mass production of musical instruments. Eight thousand workers were engaged in the industry in 1860, a figure that doubled by 1875 and tripled by 1882. In the 1880s the total production of pianos in Germany was between 60,000 and 70,000 units a year, three times that of France. The all-time peak of more than 100,000 was reached just before the outbreak of the First World War.[38] This success was a microcosm of Germany's domination of the so-called second industrial revolution based on high technology (as opposed to the first heavy-metal phase when coal and iron had predominated). Taking advantage of the best technological education system in the world, German piano manufacturers applied the latest technology. They also showed that they knew how to make the most of it, building up a network of multilingual commercial agents around the globe.[39] Even so, although its claim to be 'the workshop of the world' was looking dated, it was the United Kingdom that produced the most impressive figures: by 1911 it has been estimated that there were between two million and four million pianos in the country, or one for every ten to twenty inhabitants.[40]

The same sort of phenomenon could be illustrated through literature. In the first year of the nineteenth century, the novelist Henri Beyle, better known as Stendhal, wrote to his sister Pauline in Grenoble urging her not to neglect the piano, for 'in this country, it is absolutely essential that a young lady should know her music, otherwise she passes as totally uneducated.'[41] Eighty years later his view was confirmed in the century's most notorious novel, Émile Zola's *Nana,* when Bordenave, the owner of the theatre in which Nana makes her début, observed of his current mistress, Simone Cabiroche, 'She was an educated girl who played the piano and spoke English'.[42] Standards were no different across the Channel. On the first page of Elizabeth Gaskell's *North and South* (1855), the unassuming heroine, Margaret, is told by her rich cousin, Edith, that the problem of keeping a piano in tune on the island of Corfu, where she was obliged to live with her soldier-husband, was 'one of the most formidable that could befall her in her married life'. When Margaret later reveals that her family had had to sell their own instrument, Edith retorts: 'I wonder how you can exist without one. It almost seems to me a necessary of life'.[43]

The satirical tone of Mrs. Gaskell's treatment was made more explicit in the musical press. In 1860 the French composer and musical journalist Oscar Commettant published an article in his periodical *L'Art musical* entitled 'On the Influence of the Piano on Family-Life' in which he poked fun at the ubiquity of piano playing. Among other things, he recounted an anecdote about a Parisian seeking an apartment: he did not mind where it was, what floor it was on, or whether it faced north, south, east or west. His only requirement was that it should be out of earshot of a piano. He was told that such a sanctuary no longer existed.

Commettant also recorded the following conversation between two men-about-town:

> Oh! My dear chap, what a delightful person Miss Clarisse
> Filandor is!
> I know her: eighteen years old, a blonde and pretty.
> Yes, with blue eyes and dark eye-lashes.
> And she has a dowry of 200,000 francs.
> Exactly, and what is more, she is the sole heir of a rich uncle who is
> terminally ill.
> But her crowning glory is that *she doesn't play the piano.*
> I was just going to say that. So she is not a woman like any other, this
> one—she is an angel sent from heaven![44]

Commettant then added that he himself, however, regarded the piano as being very beneficial, for it kept the family together and 'brought the orchestra into the home'. Instead of going out to the pub (or worse) after

An intimate moment *At the Piano,* by Albert Gustaf Aristides Edelfelt (1884).

supper, fathers now stayed at home to be entertained by their piano-playing wives and children. Musical treats had replaced alcohol, as another French musical periodical revealed in 'Scenes from the Bourgeoisie's Craze for Music':

> MADAME GODET (TO OCTAVIE AT THE PIANO): Where is your father?
>
> OCTAVIE: He has just gone out.
>
> MADAME GODET: Do you know where he has gone?
>
> OCTAVIE: He has gone to the music shop for his sweeties.[45]

Other commentators were more critical, variously blaming the piano for the collapse of chamber music, for being a 'tyrannical usurper' that reduced a musical instrument to a piece of furniture, for encouraging immorality by allowing couples to sit in very close proximity while playing music for four hands, for inducing parents to overtax their children, including stretching their fingers, and so on.[46] Above all, it was accused of levelling and vulgarising musical taste. 'More' meant 'worse', complained the critics, pointing to the decline of serious genres such as the sonata in favour of trivia such as polonaises, écossaises, anglaises and waltzes. One of the most successful piano teachers of the nineteenth century was Antoine-Joseph Marmontel, whose pupils included Isaac Albéniz, Claude Debussy and Vincent d'Indy, but that did not prevent him from condemning his chosen instrument as 'ce grand vulgarisateur de la musique' (this great vulgarizer of music).[47]

Marmontel delivered that verdict in 1885, by which time the piano had become virtually the modern instrument we know today. Since 1800 it had been transformed: as the musicologist Jeremy Montagu has observed, 'Beethoven's piano was as different in tone from Brahms's as it was from Bach's harpsichord'.[48] Among the many changes introduced during the course of the century, the most important were the double escapement mechanism invented by the Erard brothers in 1822, which allowed the same note to be repeated very quickly; the construction of iron frames from 1825, which allowed greater tension on the strings and thus greater volume; overstringing, introduced after 1835, which also helped to increase string tension; and the expansion of the range to encompass seven octaves plus a minor third, which has remained the norm (although Bösendorf manufactures an instrument with eight full octaves).[49] Sigismond Thalberg wrote of the double escapement: 'By its ingenuity, the mechanism surpasses anything of its kind that has been made or tried. It permits the performer to communicate to the strings everything that the most skilful and most delicate hand can express'.[50]

Inevitably, the opportunities presented by bigger, louder, stronger, more agile instruments were seized by composers. The interaction between instrument and music can be seen, for example, in the changes Liszt made in 1837 to his *Études en formes de 12 exercices*, first composed in 1826. Robert Schumann was so struck by the differences between the two versions that he wrote a piece exploring the implications.[51] These changes should be called innovations, not improvements, for the latter word carries with it a normative implication. No doubt Liszt preferred to play an instrument that could fill a hall with sound, that displayed his fabled technique in all its glory and did not fall apart when pounded by 'this Attila of the piano' (as François Danjou dubbed him in 1845).[52] Yet, as the early music movement in Europe and the United States would make clear in the twentieth century, it is equally legitimate—and many would argue, more legitimate—to prefer to hear the keyboard sonatas of Haydn played on the clavichord, harpsichord, or small fortepiano for which they were written than on a modern grand piano.

In *The Rational and Social Foundations of Music*, published posthumously in 1921, the year after his death, Max Weber observed that 'it is the peculiar nature of the piano to be a middle-class home instrument'.[53] Although invented in Italy, he went on, it had been developed in northern Europe, where the climate kept people indoors for much of the year. Perhaps more persuasive than this meteorological argument was the relative weakness of the bourgeoisie in the south. That the piano was the middle-class instrument *par excellence*, however, can certainly be accepted. It suited the middle-class pocket, the middle-class living room and middle-class taste. With characteristic irony, Heinrich Heine expressed his sympathy for this bourgeois burden: 'The reigning bourgeoisie must suffer for its sins not just the old classical tragedies and the trilogies that are not classic, for the heavenly powers have blessed it with an even more ghastly delight, namely that inescapable pianoforte that one hears tinkling in every house, in every company, day and night'.[54]

Just as the piano's development was reaching completion in the late nineteenth century, the first signs could be seen of a technological revolution that would eventually democratise music by making it available to the rest of society too. Although not always in step, culture, society and politics were marching in the same direction. But before we move from the piano to the mechanical and electronic reproduction of music, a few words need to be said about the development of other musical instruments. Many very large books have been published on this topic—a 700-page volume on the instruments employed by J. S. Bach alone, for example—so concision is at a premium.[55] In broad brush strokes, it can be said that a long period of gradual development in the eighteenth century was followed by very rapid change during the second and third quarters of the nineteenth. As in the case of the piano, the chicken cannot be separated from the egg when it comes to causation. Did the change in the nature of music inspire the invention of musical instruments, or was it the other way around? Did the new instruments encourage the use of larger spaces, or did larger spaces require innovations in instruments? Was necessity the mother of invention, or did invention create the need? In any event, technical, social and spatial forces combined to make music ever more popular and ubiquitous.

Valves, Keys and Saxophones

In the decades around 1700, several new instruments were created—the oboe, bassoon, clarinet, French horn and cello, for example, while others fell out of use, among them the shawm, flute douce (a kind of recorder), the dulcian, lute, theorbe, and the Pandor-zither.[56] Also on the downward path were the various viols (bass viol, viola da gamba, lyra viol and so on), although their popularity as continuo instruments kept some of them going until the middle of the eighteenth century.

In some cases, the innovations represented an accelerated evolution more than a brand new creation: the oboe grew out of the shawm and the bassoon from the dulcian, for example. In other cases, musicians exploited instruments originally created for a practical purpose. The French horn, for example, was invented for the immensely lavish hunts staged for Louis XIV and his court. It developed from the little hunting horn still used by English fox hunters into the large-belled, long-coiled instrument that quickly found its way into instrumental ensembles.[57] Also adding to the sonority of the orchestra was the trombone, long in existence but so closely associated with church music as to be overlooked by most secular composers. Toward the end of the eighteenth century, however, there were signs of a belated discovery of its potential—by Gluck in *Alceste* or by Mozart in *Don Giovanni*, for example.[58]

Other old instruments were so tinkered with by succeeding generations of manufacturers and practitioners as to become virtually new creations. The flute of 1800 no more resembled the flute of 1700 than the flute of 1700 resembled that of 1600. The introduction of keys in the 1750s made the flute both easier to play and more versatile. Significantly, a strong commercial impetus was behind the development of what had become a consumer item, as Richard Potter showed in 1785 when he became the first flute manufacturer to protect his product by patent. To encourage sales, a tutorial manual was published, entitled *A Description of Potter's New Invented Patent German Flute, with a Complete Scale or Gamut Explaining the Use of All the Additional Keys.*[59]

Instrumental changes were accompanied by a growing specialisation on the part of players. In the past, trumpeters and drummers had usually been borrowed from the ruler's military band, and the horn players from the hunting establishment. With the ever-accelerating move toward symphonic music, wind players 'abandoned their communistic life in the orchestra and became individualists' (Adam Carse).[60] As the various wind instruments became more numerous and prominent, the orchestra had to be rebalanced. For the moderate-sized forces of the early and middle decades of the eighteenth century, this was not a serious problem. A typical Haydn symphony of the 1770s, for example, was scored for two oboes, two horns, three first and three second violins, one viola, one cello, one double bass, and continuo (bassoon and harpsichord). But when he—and other composers—began to write more elaborate symphonies for public concerts in public spaces, a strengthening of the string section became necessary.[61]

Another approach to the problem of orchestral imbalance was to adapt string instruments to make them more assertive. For the all-important violin, this meant increasing the tension of the string to produce a louder and more penetrating sound. One result was that the pitch of most orchestras rose by a semitone (half step) during the second half of the eighteenth century. The additional strain on the instrument imposed by this innovation was accommodated by improving the joint between the body and neck, lengthening the neck and canting it backwards, raising the bridge, strengthening the tail piece, and increasing the thickness of the soundpost and bass bar inside the body. Probably of equal importance was the simultaneous transformation of the bow to allow a fiercer attack and a fuller sound.[62]

By 1800 the violin was 'a dominant force in Western musical culture', according to Simon McVeigh).[63] The last stage in its modernisation came in 1820, when Louis Spohr invented the chin rest, which released the left hand to range freely up and down the fingerboard without having to worry about supporting the instrument.[64] The way was now open for the violin not only to dominate the orchestra but also to provide a medium for virtuosi such as Paganini.

No matter what instrument they played, the success of the travelling virtuosi demonstrated the extent to which music penetrated the public sphere during the early nineteenth century. The proliferation of musical periodicals was further evidence, as was the repeated assertion by those who wrote for them that music had now permeated every class of society. Usually, this claim was not advanced as cause for self-congratulation but more as a lament for the pollution of the sacred art by grubby plebeian hands. A hundred years earlier, social commentators had been struck (and made fretful) by the craze for reading; now it was the craze for music that caught their eye and ear.

Two examples must suffice. From Vienna it was reported in 1824 that for a long time now 'an incredible amount of music is being performed both in public and private' and that whenever it might be thought that musicomania had reached an unsurpassable peak, it just kept on growing.[65] The same observation was made by a French periodical but was applied to the whole continent. It even conceded that in England—'hitherto so very backward in musical matters'—a household could hardly be found that did not boast a musical instrument and an amateur able to play it tolerably well.[66] In short, music had become a commodity.

One of the most influential instrument manufacturers to take advantage of this commercial potential was the Bavarian Theobald Boehm (1794–1881), who combined in one person four very valuable attributes: the practical skills of a master craftsman (he had trained as a goldsmith); outstanding musical ability (he was first flautist in the royal orchestra in Munich for years and was regarded by many as the finest German flautist of his day); international experience (he toured widely in the 1820s and made a point of investigating the flutes he encountered on the road); and a scientific approach (he consulted acoustical experts at the University of Munich).[67] Between 1831 and 1847 Boehm developed a flute with large holes placed in the acoustically correct positions and of the acoustically correct size. To overcome the physical problems thus created, he devised a system of ring-keys linked by rod axles which allowed the player to open and close fourteen tone holes.[68] Although the need to adopt new fingering inhibited acceptance, so great were the advantages offered by the Boehm system in terms of dexterity and tonal accuracy that eventually it carried all before it. Moreover, its system could be translated into similar improvements for most of the other woodwinds, directly so in the case of the clarinet.[69]

Of the many new instruments to make their appearance, the one with the most glittering future was the saxophone, patented in France by the Belgian Adolphe Sax in 1846. Only twenty-eight years old when he moved to Paris in 1842, Sax was already famous in musical circles for the creation of a greatly improved bass clarinet. Welcoming his arrival, Berlioz wrote in an article in the *Journal des débats:* 'He is a man of penetrating mind; lucid, tenacious, with a perseverance against all trials, and great skill . . . He is at the same time a calculator, acoustician, and as necessary also a smelter, turner and engraver. He can think and act. He invents and accomplishes'.[70] In other words, he was very like his fellow-inventor Boehm. Sax's greatest creation looked like no other instrument and sounded like no other instrument, although in essence it was a metal clarinet with a wide bore, a clarinet mouthpiece and a single reed. One enthusiast has claimed it to be 'the most flexible and expressive of musical instruments, exceeded, perhaps, only by the human voice'.[71]

Like the voice, saxophones came in several different shapes and sizes, from soprano through alto and tenor to baritone. Its great advantages were (and are) its range, volume and robustness, all of which made it ideally suited for the military music it was created to play. Despite occasional use by Debussy and Bizet, the saxophone did not come into its own as a high-art instrument until the twentieth century, when it was adopted by jazz musicians—and even then some time after jazz had emerged as an autonomous genre.[72] Adolphe Sax's posthumous importance rivalled that of Boehm, but in his own lifetime he careered from one financial crisis to another, never able to benefit financially from his creations, thanks largely to the vicious campaign against him organised by native Parisian manufacturers. His most appropriate tribute was written by his fellow Belgian expatriate François Fétis: 'All other instruments have come under notable modifications through time and migration. And last, all have been perfected by slow progress. The saxophone, on the other hand, was born yesterday. It is the fruit of a single conception, and from its first day it has been the same instrument it will be in the future'.[73]

Though the saxophone was relatively easy to manufacture and play,

The saxophones of Adolphe Sax: soprano (in front), alto, tenor and baritone.

its impact turned out to be long delayed, largely because of changes in brass instruments. As anyone who has had the misfortune to be drafted into a military band of bugles will know, although it is easy to extract a sound from a mouthpiece attached to a coil of brass ending in a bell shape, making that sound euphonious is a different matter. Producing notes on a bugle depends entirely on the player's embouchure, that is to say, the coordination of lip, muscle, jaw and teeth when blowing.

Around 1760, a horn player in the orchestra at Dresden, Anton Joseph Hampel, discovered that inserting his fist into the bell of his instrument allowed him to increase the range. This technique of 'hand stopping' quickly spread. Also common was the introduction of additional lengths of pipe—'crooks'—into the instrument, to alter the fundamental note and thus the key in which the instrument could be played. Although ingenious, neither of these techniques was ideal. Hand stopping also muted the instrument, while the insertion of a crook took time and ran the risk of faulty intonation when cold metal was added to warm. The horn player in Mozart's *Don Giovanni* is kept busy with thirty-five crook changes, whereas in the first movement of the *Eroica*, Beethoven has to give him a good rest to change crook in readiness to play a few notes in the key of F instead of E flat.[74]

The solution was first demonstrated in Berlin in 1814 by Heinrich David Stölzel, who added two tubular valves to a horn, thus enabling him to alter the length of piping (and thus the sound) without resorting to fist or crook. That began a twenty-five-year period of experimentation and improvement across Europe and America, which ended in 1839 when Etienne François Périnet of Paris patented 'a medium-diameter, medium-stroke, cylindrical piston valve'.[75] So obvious was the value of this invention that it encountered none of the resistance that held up acceptance of the Boehm system. Valves were soon added to all brass instruments, including the trombone. And new instruments were invented, the most important being the tuba, patented by the Prussian bandmaster Wilhelm Wieprecht and the instrument maker J. G. Moritz in 1835. At the same time, the physical properties of brass instruments were improved, thanks to new metallurgical discoveries that produced better brass, and improvements in manufacturing techniques that produced better springs, better machined tolerance of components, better soldering and electroplating.[76] Writing in 1851, Fétis observed that during the past half-century, and at an ever accelerating pace, the balance of power in the orchestra had shifted away from strings to wind instruments.[77]

Composers responded accordingly. The exhilarating prelude to Act Three of *Lohengrin* could have been composed only for valved horns, not to mention the contribution from the tuba. Yet the most profound impact of the changes in brass instruments was more social than musical. Valves made them easier to learn and play, and the application of mass production techniques brought their price tumbling to within range of working men and women, especially those with access to the new marketing device of hire purchase (also called rent-to-own). For once, the overworked adjective 'revolutionary' can be used with confidence: as the musicologist Trevor Herbert has argued, the explosive growth of brass bands in the second half

Visual evidence of the advance of brass bands in England: The Besses o' Th' Barn Band in 1860 . . .

of the nineteenth century represented 'one of the most remarkable socio-logical shifts in the history of music'. He goes on:

> Almost anyone who, in say 1820, possessed a sophisticated skill on an art-music instrument and did not make a living at it was, virtually by definition, an aristocrat or a member of the wealthy bourgeoisie. Yet within a single generation, such skills were commonplace among amateur brass band players across Europe and America. It was a moment of vast importance; it led to changes in the idiom of many brass instruments, and it was one of the ways in which sophisticated music making can genuinely be said to have contributed to social emancipation.[78]

Now working people were making music in ways other than singing. No one will ever know just how many were involved, but the total certainly ran into hundreds of thousands. *Wright and Round's Amateur Band Teachers Guide* estimated in 1889 that there were 40,000 amateur wind bands in Britain.[79] Many were linked to work places, such as the Black Dyke Mills Band or the Holmes Tannery Band; some took their names from their com-

. . . and in 1903. Immediately behind the bass drum is the Crystal Palace 1,000 Guinea Trophy.

munity, such as the quaintly named Besses o'Th' Barn Band from a manufacturing town between Bury and Manchester; others had an ulterior purpose, such as the Salvation Army bands or the Brampton Total Abstinence Band (disbanded by its patron, Lady Carlisle, after the members celebrated victory in a competition by filling and refilling the trophy with beer until they finally dropped and broke it).[80]

All of these bands were bound together in a sense of common pursuit by competitions. The first to be organised, at Burton Constable near Hull in 1845, was a small affair, but before long the great national contests were attracting 70,000 to 80,000 participants and listeners.[81] The repertoire was eclectic, to put it mildly, ranging from simple hymn tunes to highly sophisticated arrangements of music originally written for operas or symphonies. An account of the test piece prescribed for the Crystal Palace championship in 1907 gives a good impression of the demands made on the bands:

> This year [it] consisted of an ingenious interweaving of extracts from the works of Schumann, presenting many points of difficulty and no mean standard of appeal. A piece comprising frag-

ments from the *Hermann and Dorothea Overture,* the Fifth study for the pedal piano, the songs *Widmung* and *Talisman,* the A minor concerto, the *'Fest'* overture and the overture to *Genoveva*—even if these have suffered a certain violence in extract—must still be regarded as claiming a larger culture than goes to the general conception of popular musical interest in England.[82]

The ubiquity and popularity of Salvation Army bands brought more religious music to the streets and squares of Great Britain than ever before. Inside churches and chapels the same phenomenon occurred, thanks to the enormous increase in the number of organs. When the Commonwealth ended in 1660, puritan austerity had banished virtually all organs from places of worship. Their return was slow and hesitant, with the result that in 1800 more than 90 percent of English parish churches still had no organ.[83] But then an intense and sustained revival began, led on one side of the liturgical spectrum by Methodists and Evangelicals and on the other by Catholics, both Anglo- and Roman. In the course of the nineteenth century, more music was composed and sung and, moreover, was sung much better, by bigger choirs, in the great cathedrals than ever before.[84]

By 1900 the great majority of places of worship, both Anglican and nonconformist, could boast some form of instrument to lead and accompany the congregation. This was a movement with many origins but it was undoubtedly assisted by the simultaneous technological developments that made organs less cumbersome and cheaper. In particular, various versions of the so-called free reed organ, first manufactured in France by Gabriel-Joseph Grenié in 1810, proved popular, because it was easier to keep in tune, did not require pipes to resonate and could be played *piano* and *forte.*[85] A later version patented by another French manufacturer, Alexandre-François Debain, in 1842 gave its name to a whole family of small reed organs—Harmonium.

In 1847 Debain was only one of forty organ manufacturers in France producing more and more instruments. Their number had increased by another third as of 1860, but their collective production had tripled.[86] Well might François Danjou claim in 1845 that the organ is 'the king of musical instruments, the sacred orchestra, the instrument *par excellence*' and that *'it is spreading with remarkable speed'* (his italics). Within a few years, he predicted, most village churches in France would have an organ.[87] The Germans proved to be even more enthusiastic organ builders. The Ludwigsburg firm of E. F. Walcker exported huge numbers of organs all over the world and is still going strong, in the ownership of the same family.[88] One good indication of the spread of the instrument was the creation in 1851 of a dedicated journal, *Neues deutsches Orgel-Magazin*.[89]

Recording

By the end of the nineteenth century, technology had taken music to parts it had not reached in the past, into middle-class parlours and onto working-class bandstands. In the 1890s, just as the cinema was opening up even wider avenues for music's incursion into leisure time, the marketplace saw the arrival of an invention with equal if not greater revolutionary potential. This new marvel was recorded sound. On 12 August 1877 the American inventor Thomas Edison first recorded his voice on a cylinder made of tin foil. When he patented his 'phonograph' the following year, he predicted ten possible uses, the first being as an office tool to take dictation. The 'reproduction of music' was number four.[90] Edison then appeared to lose interest, going back to work on the electric light bulb, and left the development of his new machine to others. By the time he returned to the fray in 1888, he had been overtaken by Emil Berliner, a German immigrant who in 1887 took out a patent for a mechanism he called the 'gramophone', which played flat discs rather than cylinders. During the first public demonstration, at the Franklin Institute in Philadelphia, Berliner predicted that his invention would eventually play a central role in domestic leisure.[91]

But progress was slow, as Edison, Berliner and a host of other inventors struggled to turn a bright idea into a commercial proposition. Whether flat or cylindrical, early records could run for only around two minutes, they were fragile and expensive and they soon wore out. Duplication was a special problem. Until Berliner discovered a way of creating a master from which copies could be made, each record had to be created individually. So an orchestra was obliged to play the same piece again and again before a maximum of ten recording instruments.[92] In fact, 'orchestra' is a misnomer, as a very limited number of a very limited range of instruments could be

The Stroh violin.

used. As all sound generated had to find its way down a large horn, the recording process put a premium on instruments that were both loud and directional. So brass did well, woodwinds were acceptable but pianos were virtually inaudible. To overcome the special problems posed by the violin, Augustus Stroh gave it the necessary volume and direction by replacing the sound box with a flexible membrane to which a large metal horn was attached, mounted to one side of the bridge.

A good reason for the thin sound of early orchestral recordings is this paucity of musicians, for a typical band might consist of a flute, two clarinets, two cornets, two trombones, two Stroh violins, a viola and a bassoon playing the cello part.[93] The lower-register stringed instruments could not be picked up at all, so tubas were usually substituted. When Arthur Nikisch made the first complete recording of Beethoven's Fifth Symphony with the Berlin Philharmonic in 1914, he was confined to six violins and two violas, no double basses or timpani and no pianissimos or fortes.[94] To maintain some sort of a balance of forces, the brass players were obliged to sit with their backs to the recorder, taking their cue from the conductor with the help of mirrors.[95] Singers had to move backwards and forwards as the dynamics of the piece required, for too much volume would cause the needle to jump from the surface.

These and other problems prevented economies of scale, with the result that both gramophones and the records played on them were expensive. Edison's Electric Motor Phonograph of 1893 cost $190 and the standard model of the Disc Phonograph of 1913 was $200, reflecting his intention that they should appeal to 'people of cultured and elegant tastes'.[96] In England, a single disc cost between ten shillings (50p) and a pound, although the complete eight-record set of Nikisch's recording of Beethoven's Fifth could be had for just £2. If that sounds like a bargain, remember that the average weekly wage was a mere £1 6s 8d (£1.33).[97]

Yet the recording industry flourished mightily in the two decades before the First World War. When listening today to Tennyson croaking out 'The Charge of the Light Brigade' (he had been recorded on an Edison machine in 1890) or Alessandro Moreschi, 'the last castrato', doing his best with 'Ave Maria' in a recording of 1904, we would do well to remember that those who bought the originals in pristine condition not only heard a much more convincing sound but were also free from the condescension that today's excellent digital technology has bred. To early twentieth-century ears, the gramophone record was a sensational revelation, allowing people to hear music and musicians hitherto confined to a tiny elite. And even that elite had its horizons broadened: when Artur Schnabel was studying the piano in Vienna in the 1890s, he confessed that not only had he never heard a Mozart piano concerto, he had never even heard *of* them.[98]

Of course the manufacturers used every marketing ploy at their command to promote a 'discourse of verisimilitude' (in the words of Colin Symes), advertising the soprano Geraldine Farr in 1915, for example, by proclaiming: 'Both are Farrar: The Victor Record of Farrar's voice is just as truly Farrar as Farrar herself. The same singularly beautiful voice, with all the personal charm and individuality of the artist'.[99] The singers played their part, of course. When the sixty-two-year-old Adelina Patti was coaxed out of retirement in 1905 to make recordings for The Gramophone Company, she was induced to endorse the results as follows: 'The gramophone of today, I find, is such an improved instrument for recording the human voice that my hitherto objection to allow the thousands who cannot hear me sing personally to listen to the reproduction of my voice through the instrumentality of your gramophone is now quite removed, and the records you have lately made for me I think are natural reproductions of my voice'.[100] Patti probably knew just what fabulous financial prospects recording was opening up for singers.

The industry reached a major milestone in 1902 when Fred Gaisberg of The Gramophone Company persuaded Enrico Caruso to record ten arias. His voice was perfect for the gramophone, turning its defects into assets—'the answer to a recording man's dream' was Gaisberg's verdict.[101] With the huge commercial and critical success of these recordings, the gramophone's arrival in the cultural mainstream was at last recognised. The founding editor of *The Gramophone* magazine, Compton Mackenzie, wrote in 1924 that Caruso had made the gramophone what it had become: 'He impressed his personality through the medium of his recorded voice on kings and peasants'.[102] The compliment was returned with interest: by 1914 Caruso was earning £20,000 a year from world sales of his records, a colossal sum in the currency of the day, which may even have increased tenfold after 1918.[103] Tenors were especially favoured by the new medium, as the comparable successes of Beniamino Gigli and John McCormack demonstrated, but baritones and basses (Peter Dawson, Fyodor Chaliapin) and sopranos (Nellie Melba, Luisa Tetrazzini) also flourished.

The next technological breakthrough came in 1924, when verisimilitude was given a massive boost by the appearance of electrical recording. Made possible by work on wireless telegraphy for military purposes during the First World War, it was introduced to counter the growing competition from radio. This was one change where 'improvement' could be quantified. An acoustic recording ranged between 164 vibrations per second at the bottom and 2,088 at the top (that is, from E below middle C to three octaves above middle C), while in the concert hall the range was much wider: from 20 cycles to 20,000. The use of microphones and amplifiers extended the frequency range of recordings by two-and-a-half octaves, to 100–5,000 cycles.[104] Now pianos, proper violins and all the other orphans of the acoustical era could make their long-delayed entry.

After an initial period of hesitation that invariably follows the arrival of new technology, the record-buying public responded with enthusiasm. Not only did they want new recordings, they also wanted new versions of music they already owned. Production in the United Kingdom soared from 22 million records in 1924 to over 70 million in 1930. *Gramophone Review* commented in 1928: 'The gramophone is one of the greatest treasures of the modern home. The time is fast passing when the average man can profess to be beyond the spell of music'.[105]

Half a century had now passed since the invention of the phonograph/gramophone, and the long-term consequences for musicians were becoming clearer. For those working in the classical tradition, the greatest beneficiaries were conductors, singers and virtuoso instrumentalists. Those artists who were lucky, charismatic and enterprising enough to compete effectively could find fame and fortunes matched only by their very greatest predecessors. When the sensitive Hans von Bülow heard the playback of a recording he had made at Edison's laboratory in 1888, he fainted. As he died soon afterward, posterity has had to take or leave contemporary reports of his supreme qualities as pianist and conductor. Although Arturo Toscanini was born just thirty-seven years after von Bülow, his place in the pantheon is secure, thanks to the scores of recordings he made.

For composers, the gramophone proved to be a mixed blessing. Many of them gave it a warm welcome: Tchaikovsky, for example, hailed it as 'the most surprising, the most beautiful, and the most interesting among all inventions that have turned up in the nineteenth century', while the more laconic Debussy believed that it would confer on music 'une totale et minutieuse immortalité'.[106] What they could not see so easily was that, in the short term, recording would accelerate a trend toward the ossification of a classical canon. The record producers now decided what should be recorded and by whom; however intelligent and cultured many of these entrepreneurs may have been, commercial considerations were decisive. So if the choice were between, say, Beethoven's *Choral Symphony* and, say, Arnold Schoenberg's *Pierrot Lunaire*, projected sales figures made the decision. By 1923, even before electrical recording, all of Beethoven's symphonies were available on record.[107] Schoenberg's masterpiece had to wait until 1940 for its first recording (conducted by the composer), twenty-eight years after it was written.

For a while, the two worlds of mechanized music and live performance co-existed comfortably. In 1913 Trinity College of Music conducted examinations for 28,000 students, most of them girls learning the piano. Since its foundation in 1872 to improve the quality of church music, the college had examined around half a million, despite confining its constituency to Anglican males during its early stages.[108] In the years around 1914, production and ownership of pianos reached a peak, and in 1919 the song 'That Old Fashioned Mother of Mine' sold more than three million copies of sheet music in the United Kingdom. In 1924 the value of the musical instruments trade exceeded £5,000,000.[109]

Yet for many of those who made their living from music, the spread of recording caused much pain. For every person who found employment in the new industry, many more found themselves on the scrap heap. Just as the division of labour and assembly-line production had made craftsmen redundant, so the mechanisation of music reduced the need for traditional musical skills. The combination of cinema, radio and records inexorably turned the music-playing public into a music-consuming public. After a last golden age in the 1920s, the Great Depression brought a crash from which music teachers, musical instrument manufacturers and professional musicians took a very long time to recover. As Cyril Ehrlich observed, this was not due to a short-term collapse in purchasing power on the part of the public but a long-term decline in demand. Why buy and learn how to play a piano when a gramophone offered a superior musical performance for much less money? During the 1930s and 1940s the number of professional musicians fell from 26,000 to 15,000 and music teachers from 21,000 to 11,000.[110]

Many tears can be shed for these casualties, but this is a book about the triumph of music, not about the triumph of musicians (and certainly not musicians working in the classical tradition). Recording made it possible for music that had been composed years, centuries, millennia ago to be disinterred and broadcast throughout the world. The classical canon expanded to such an extent that the concept itself dissolved. This was well put by the American cultural pundit Jacques Barzun, when he wrote in 1954:

> This mechanical civilisation of ours has performed a miracle for which I cannot be too grateful: it has, by mechanical means, brought back to life the whole repertory of Western music—not to speak of acquainting us with the music of the East. Formerly, a fashion would bury the whole musical past except for a few dozen works arbitrarily selected . . . [Today] neglected or lesser composers come into their own and keep their place. In short the whole literature of one of the arts has sprung into being—it is like the Renaissance rediscovering the ancient world of the classics and holding them fast by means of the printing press. It marks an epoch in Western intellectual history.[111]

Although Barzun does not cite him, he would have found authoritative confirmation for his claim in the confession by Rachmaninov that he had not known that Schubert had written any piano sonatas untill the BBC started to broadcast recordings of them. As Noel Malcolm has observed: 'This was a cultural revolution as significant in its own way as the effects of Gutenberg's invention in the 15th century'.[112]

Moreover, just as one group of music's practitioners was sliding into inexorable decline, another was thrusting its way to the front. Until the advent of recording, music could be stored only through musical notation or through human memory, passed from one generation to the next in purely oral form as folk music. The latter may well be the 'archive of the people', as Herder put it, but that archive changed radically over the course of time as people added their own flourishes or misremembered earlier versions. What recording did was to take forms of music that were performance-based—not notation-based—and give them permanency and then broadcast them all over the world.

The greatest beneficiary was jazz, coincidentally emerging as an autonomous musical form just as recording was beginning. Nothing survives by Buddy Bolden, the New Orleans bandleader usually credited with being the first jazzman (although, like everything else in jazz history, this is contested). But we have plenty of music by a band that included Bolden's next-door neighbour, Larry Shields, a member of the Original Dixieland Jazz Band, the first group to record jazz. 'Livery Stable Blues' and 'Dixie Jass Band One Step' were released on 26 February 1917 by the Victor Talking Machine Company.[113] Although the band had made an impact through live performances in Chicago and New York, it was through records that this group enjoyed a dazzling if brief international career, including a spell in London. At least a dozen CDs of various selections of its recordings, including a complete collection, are available today. The claim of the leader, Nick La Rocca, that the band had 'invented jazz' was manifestly absurd, but the recordings were certainly the first to advertise the commercial potential of the new genre.

Historians usually downplay the contribution of the Original Dixieland Jazz Band to the development of jazz, partly because its members did not conform to the dominant version of jazz's origins as the music of the black ghetto. All five members of the band came from New Orleans, which ticks one box, but all five were white, which definitely does not. Indeed, they were at some pains to deny any black influence: 'The coloureds only play plantation music' was the verdict of Tom Browne, the band's trombonist.[114] Nor has their penchant for playing in smart suits at restaurants and night clubs commended them to historians. A more substantive handicap was the modest quality of the music they played. Even making allowances for the state of acoustic recording at the time, their version of Dixieland seems limited in every sense.

The first jazz musician to demonstrate the importance of recording was Louis Armstrong, whose *Hot Five* and *Hot Seven* recordings of 1925–29 included many undeniable masterpieces that still sound as fresh as the day they were played. Without those recordings, the superlative, peerless cornet playing on 'West End Blues' or 'Potato Head Blues' (the only two contenders for the title of 'the greatest jazz record ever made', in the view of Eric Hobsbawm) would have been lost forever.[115] Ironically, the value of these recordings is underlined by Peter Ecklund's transcription of Armstrong's solo on the latter track.[116] A competent trumpeter might well play the notes, yet still utterly fail to reproduce the original sound. This was the verdict of Humphrey Lyttelton, who wrote in his autobiography: 'A transcription of a trumpet solo by Louis Armstrong, however detailed, cannot convey any idea of the actual performance on record. And no orchestral trumpeter, reading it off, could bring it to life, because so much of its quality lies in the originator's personal tone and sense of timing.'[117] Indeed, as anyone who has listened to even a small amount of Armstrong's playing will confirm, the tone he produced was so original that hearing only a bar or so reveals his identity. The same could be said of all the greatest jazz musicians.

Radio and Television

The first regular radio broadcast—regular in the sense that it was announced in advance—took place on 2 November 1920 when station KDKA went on the air in Pittsburgh. So easy was it to obtain a license in the early days, and so modest was the capital outlay in setting up the primitive equipment, that by the beginning of 1923 more than 500 radio stations operated in the United States. From the start, of all the aural arts (drama, poetry, even comedy), music was the main beneficiary of radio, for it was the cheapest, the easiest and by far the most popular form of entertainment. In

Donald Sassoon's succinct formulation: 'The radio was, substantially, a music box to which news and other items were added.'[118]

Unlike the gramophone record, radio established an immediate, direct, even intimate relationship between performer and audience. Even those musicians who had enjoyed success through recordings were overwhelmed by the popular response to radio. At the end of 1921 Vincent Lopez and his band broadcast a performance from the Grill of the Hotel Pennsylvania in New York. Cleverly, he did his own announcing, introducing himself with the words 'Hello, everybody: Lopez speaking'. In a memoir he related that within an hour

> telephone calls had soaked up every table reservation for the following evening and the calls kept coming in that night and all next day . . . What's more, the entire hotel was sold out by mid-afternoon . . . The mail response to our next broadcast was simply unbelievable. At the microphone . . . I blurted out an offer of a photograph to anyone who'd write us. The next day's mail filled ten big clothes hampers . . . I couldn't possibly take care of it and apologized on the air, but offered an autographed photo to people who telephoned their requests to Hotel Pennsylvania. The incoming calls so jammed the hotel switchboard the next two days that people calling for room reservations grew tired of getting a busy signal.[119]

In 1923, 550,000 radio sets were sold in the United States; two years later, 2 million. In 1928 a survey conducted by *Radio Retailing* on behalf of the Federal Radio Commission revealed that around 12 million sets catered to as many as 40 million listeners.[120]

Across the Atlantic, the hand of the state was heavier and innovation was correspondingly delayed. The first European radio station—the British Broadcasting Corporation—began transmission on 14 November 1922, and just 35,000 licenses were issued that year. But by the eve of the Second World War, around three quarters of all British households had a set, which meant a total potential audience of 34 million.[121] Similar developments occurred across Europe, albeit on a west-east and north-south gradient reflecting descending levels of income. Although state direction brought more varied and less populist programming, music took the lion's share of air time everywhere. Even in Great Britain, where the grim puritan Sir John (later Lord) Reith was in charge, plenty of room was found for dance music, first broadcast as early as 1923. In 1928 a resident BBC dance orchestra was formed under the direction of Jack Payne.[122] By 1939 the BBC was the largest employer of musicians in the country, retaining 400 orchestral players on regular contracts and offering several thousand more occasional engagements.[123] In the mid-1930s, music broadcasts amounted to 69 percent of the BBC's total output.[124]

The BBC's control of what the British public should or should not listen to was eroded in the late 1930s by the establishment on the continent of commercial radio stations such as Radio Luxembourg and Radio Normandie, which were unashamedly designed to give their audiences what they wanted to hear. Reith may well have complained in 1935 about 'the monstrous stuff that Luxembourg is putting out', but in the same year at least 60 percent of British listeners were tuning in to continental commercial stations, representing an audience of around 16 million. As an exultant *Advertisers' Weekly* claimed: 'A Sunday's sponsored broadcasting from Luxembourg, Normandie and Lyons often contains more stars than the BBC broadcast in a whole week. Take dance bands alone. Every Sunday you can hear Billy Cotton, Ambrose, Marius B. Winter, Debroy Somers, Geraldo, Billy Reid, Billy Bissett, Sidney Lipton, Jack Payne, Lew Stone. Beat that, BBC!'[125] In 1938 there was even an experiment with a pirate ship broadcasting from international waters. That, along with the continental commercial stations, was killed off when war broke out the following year. Now, instead of the *Kraft Cheese Show* with Billy Cotton and His Band or the *Feenamint Laxatives Show* with George Formby and his little ukulele, it was *Germany Calling* with Lord Haw-Haw, the collaborator hanged as a traitor in 1946.

In its initial stages, radio was a threat to the record industry, because it provided much better quality reproduction at a lower cost. But once electrical recording was introduced, the two media proved to be mutually supportive. Records provided cheap and easy music for broadcasters, while radio provided publicity for performers (and record companies) who made the records. As Christopher Stone, who was the BBC's first disc jockey, put it in 1933: 'Experience has shown that the judicious broadcasting of gramophone records is a direct stimulus to the sale of records.'[126] Symbolising

A gramophone is used for broadcasting by station KWCR in Cedar Rapids in the mid-1920s.

this symbiosis was a piece of furniture called the radiogram, which combined a gramophone, radio, and speakers in one wooden cabinet; it first appeared in 1929.[127]

The star who best personified the alliance of records and radio was Bing Crosby (1904–77). He developed a technique of using the microphone not so much to amplify his voice as to make it seem more intimate, so that his legion of fans could believe he was singing for each one of them individually.[128] In the course of his long career he sold in excess of 300 million records, including Irving Berlin's 'White Christmas' of 1942, which quickly became the best-selling single of all time and can still be heard in shopping malls around the globe every December (or earlier).[129] As enterprising as he was multi-talented, Crosby added a third string to his bow by becoming a movie star in sixty-one films. After first singing 'White Christmas' on his radio show in December 1941—just as Pearl Harbor was being attacked by the Japanese and the United States was committing itself to a long, demanding world war—Crosby gave this nostalgic tune a massive boost when he performed it on screen the following year in the film *Holiday Inn.*[130]

Music on records, on the radio and in the movies was joined shortly by music on television. Broadcasts began in several countries before 1939, but the medium became a major force after the war ended. In 1947 only 14,000 sets had been sold in the United States, but 4 million were in use by 1950, a figure that grew rapidly until the entire country was engulfed by the end of the next decade.[131] From the start, music was favoured by television programmers for the same reasons that had applied to radio. Classical music did particularly well. Not only was it an important part of television's civilising mission, in the style of Lord Reith, but it was also viewed by the commercial stations as a cost-effective way of making the new medium respectable.

Even for experienced concert-goers, the ability to see soloists and conductors in close-up provided an exciting new dimension. NBC's transmissions of Toscanini's famous concerts with the New York Philharmonic in 1948 proved revelatory. The music critic of *The New York Times*, Howard Taubman, wrote that 'the music welled out of him with a force that he seemingly could not brook, and one could see him humming, chanting and almost roaring . . . Watching him on television gave you the illusion that a new medium had been found for your comprehension of the music'.[132] The broad mass of the listening public was probably less entranced by, if not resentful of, the networks' attempts to force feed them high culture. A reviewer for *Musical America* reported on a televised production of *Carmen* in 1952: 'The relentlessness of the camera in exposing corpulence and other less attractive physical features of some of the performers aroused hilarity among the more unsophisticated viewers, of whom there were, perforce, very many'.[133]

For those unsophisticated viewers, television provided more than ample fare in the shape of endless light-entertainment programmes featuring sweet bands and sweet singers playing and crooning standards. In this respect it mattered little whether the paymaster was the state or the advertising executives. Both knew which audience mattered most—middle-aged, middle-class wage earners. Personifying this middle-brow culture was Lawrence Welk, whose show was first televised locally from Los Angeles in 1951. When it was networked nationally in 1955, its sponsor (Dodge Motor Company) wanted to spice it up with a comedian and a line of dancing girls. Welk vetoed the proposal on the grounds that the innovations would create 'an unhealthy atmosphere' and 'the mothers who watch our show are just not going to like it'.[134] He had his way and was proved right: over the next three decades, until his retirement in 1982, his orchestra's melodious if undemanding medleys helped to make him the second richest man in Hollywood (after Bob Hope).[135]

Television shows dedicated to music were just the tip of the iceberg. Musical sound suffused the new medium from the start, and programmes without it have been very few and far between. Whether in the form of advertising jingles (I have never eaten Vitalite but remember very well the advertisement of 1983 based on Desmond Dekker's 'The Israelites'); call signs (David Dundas reputedly earned a fortune from the four notes which identifies Channel 4); signature tunes (*Coronation Street, East Enders* and so on are unthinkable without them); atmospheric intensification (there were lengthy passages in a recent production of *Jane Eyre* in which the action was sustained entirely by music); or whatever, music is never far away.

As every parent knows, music on children's television is particularly obtrusive. One example must suffice: children wishing to watch the video of *Yoko! Jakamoko! Toto!* will first have to sit through no fewer than ten trailers for other television programmes, each of which features a different style of music: *The Rubadubbers* (bubblegum); *Bob the Builder* (rock 'n' roll—indeed the song was a number one hit in the UK in 2000); *Angelina Ballerina* (cod Tchaikovsky); *Bob the Builder* again; *Barney* (marching music); *Pingu* (music hall); *Oswald* (rural idyll); *Kipper* (mainstream jazz); *Percy the Park Keeper* (brass band nostalgia); *The Magic Key* (a juvenile version of *S Club Seven*); and *Yoko! Jakamoko! Toto!* itself (world music, complete with Andean flutes).

A brash Australian programme called *Hi Five*, televised every morning in the UK on Channel 5 from 6:50 until 7:20, has so much music (mostly in the style of Abba) as to be virtually through-composed, combining singing, dancing, costumes and acting to create a Wagnerian *Gesamtkunstwerk* (although there are perhaps a few more jokes). And if the music provided by *Hi Five*'s Charli [sic], Kellie, Kathleen, Nathan and Tim proves too subtle for the children, one can always turn to *The Wiggles*, another Australian group (Greg, Murray, Jeff and Anthony) who supply a non-stop rock 'n' roll fest of surpassing directness.[136]

The Electrification of Youth Culture

By the 1950s, in other words, technology had ensured that the developed world was suffused with music. An individual might well prefer silence—although it was becoming increasingly difficult to find—but that was a choice. A community without access to recorded sound or radio was a community living in a premodern world. Yet a revolution was about to erupt which would make everything that had gone before seem Lilliputian. Although technology was at its heart, the fundamental force that was to transform the world's culture in the space of a generation was social. To be more precise, it was demographic. The postwar world was a world in which the population was getting younger and the young were getting richer.[137] Moreover, these newly affluent teenagers spent the lion's share of their money on leisure. The sensitive antennae of business people soon began to twitch. As early as 1947 an article in *Business Week* discussed how best to tap the youth market, commenting: 'Nobody's sure of the best way to do it, but there's a growing agreement that it's worth doing.'[138] In 1957 *Newsweek*, in an article entitled 'The Dreamy Teen-Age Market: "It's neat to spend"', estimated that 17 million teenaged Americans had a disposable income of $9 billion.[139]

The richest, most precocious, most leisured and most liberated teenagers were to be found in America, and that is where the jukebox (a coin-operated machine for playing records) emerged. Mechanical devices for the reproduction of music had existed since time out of mind. Although now forgotten, in the late nineteenth century a flood of instruments came to market, most of them manufactured in Saxony—the Symphonion, the Polyphon, the Ariston, the Mignon, and the Orchestrion, among others. At the top end they were sophisticated and powerful, none more so than the behemoth constructed by Imhof and Mukle for the Jockey Club of New York, which was 10.5 meters wide and 5.34 meters high.[140] They were all made obsolete overnight when the first jukebox, manufactured by AMI of Grand Rapids, arrived on the scene in 1927. Its electrical amplification offered better tone, more volume and greater choice. Progress was then rapid. In the course of the 1930s the three main companies involved—Mills, Seeburg and Wurlitzer—turned out increasingly powerful and colourful machines.

Significantly, the early machines were not known as jukeboxes but

Wurlitzer Music Jukebox.

were called by their manufacturers autophones, audiophones, automatic phonographs, coin-operated phonographs, and the like. These names were aimed at the same sort of customers targeted by gramophone manufacturers, who from the start had been at pains to depict their imagined consumers in publicity material as white, middle-aged and middle-class. Representative was a pre-1914 advertisement for His Master's Voice which showed a group of upper-class English people—the men in white tie and tails, the women in ball gowns—listening to a gramophone designed to resemble a piece of antique furniture. Two generations later, the Automatic Musical Instruments manufacturers were presenting their customers in just the same way.[141] They were allowed out of evening dress, but the men were wearing ties and suits and the women hats and suits—even when they were sitting in a diner.

Perhaps such an eminently respectable market did exist. However, the people who really turned the jukebox into a potent musical force were the labouring blacks of the southern United States. Even if they could afford a radio set, they were very unlikely to find their own music being broadcast by the predominantly white programmers. But in their own jook houses or jook joints—public places for drinking and dancing, often with a brothel attached—they could install what records they wished in what came to be known as jukeboxes. Through the jukeboxes of black America, Wynonie Harris's 'Good Rockin' Tonight', recorded on 28 December 1947, heralded 'a new era in American popular culture'.[142]

As radio stations found their audiences deserting them for the new medium, many responded by abandoning the bland middle-of-the-road fare offered by the national networks in favour of more local or specialist niches. By the late 1940s, local stations catering to the black population and featuring 'race records' made by black musicians were reaching a rapidly expanding market. By 1952, 93 percent of black households in Memphis owned a radio and 30 percent owned two.[143] This audience was imperfectly segregated, for whereas black musicians might be kept off white radio, white listeners could not be prevented from listening to black radio. Nor could white local radio stations be prevented from responding to market opportunities. The most important was WLAC of Nashville, which used its powerful 50,000-watt transmitter to send black music as far north as Canada and as far south as the Caribbean.

One of the early deejays (from 'd.j.' standing for disc jockey), William 'Hoss' Allen, wrote of his senior colleague, Gene Nobles: '[He] was the first guy anywhere to play black music on a power station. And he got into it quite by accident. One night in 1946, some black GIs who had come back to Nashville to attend Fisk University on the GI Bill showed up at the station. They brought some black records and asked him to play them, which he did, just for kicks. And there was a response. The station started getting

Advertisement for His Master's Voice (pre-1914).

mail from all over the South. This led, in late '46, to a black music show with some black sponsors.'[144]

Technology then intervened on three further occasions to complete the revolution. The first was the invention of a new kind of gramophone record manufactured from vinyl rather than shellac, which greatly reduced surface noise and, more importantly, allowed discs with much smaller grooves to be played at a lower speed (33⅓ revolutions per minute as opposed to 78) and thus to contain much more music. The LP album (LP stood for long-playing) was first demonstrated in June 1948 by Edward Wallerstein of Columbia Records in two highly effective ways: visually, by

An advertisement from the early 1950s. The jukebox is a
Wurlitzer model 1015, the biggest-selling model of all time.

contrasting an eight-foot pile of 78s with a collection of LPs that contained
the same amount of music but was only fifteen inches high; and aurally,
by playing a symphony recorded on 78s, which had to be changed every
four minutes, followed by an uninterrupted performance of the same work
on an LP.[145]

In the early days, the genres to benefit most from the appearance of
the LP were classical and light classical music, but popular music also got a
tremendous boost when the 'battle of the speeds' broke out. In 1949 RCA
Victor responded to the 33⅓ revolutions per minute with a seven-inch vinyl disc revolving 45 times per minute. Although the record's compact size
limited the amount of music to just one tune per side, the format turned

This depiction of German teenagers in 1960 provides a more convincing image of the jukebox's clients than the Wurlitzer advertisements.

out to be ideally suited to popular music, especially jukeboxes. So a truce was declared, with all companies using the twelve-inch LP for albums and the seven-inch EP (Extended Play, also known as the 45) for singles. Hardware manufacturers closed the circle by developing a record player that could handle both formats—plus the old 78s into the bargain.

In the short term, the most striking result was a massive increase in the amount of classical music available. By 1954, in which year the American record-buying public spent $70 million on recordings of classical music, there were twenty-one different versions of Beethoven's *Eroica* symphony available and five unabridged versions of Bach's *St. Matthew Passion.* At the end of the year, sales of Toscanini's recording of Beethoven's *Choral Symphony,* issued two years earlier, totalled 148,993. As Roland Gelatt, writing at the time, observed: twenty years earlier Toscanini would have done well to have sold 500 copies, while forty years earlier not one recording of the work was available.[146] In quantitative terms, however, the future lay with popular music. The marriage of the jukebox and 45 rpm vinyl records greatly enhanced both quality and choice (jukeboxes could now offer more than a hundred selections). By the mid-1950s there were more than half-a-million jukeboxes in the United States, consuming around 74 million discs a year.[147] The world in which jukeboxes could be advertised as a medium for the middle class had disappeared—if indeed it had ever existed.

Jukeboxes in diners, clubs and cafes got teenagers out of the house and away from the ghastly good taste of their parents, who decided what the family heard or watched in the evenings. The next step in their technological liberation came with the transistor radio. This was a long drawn-out process, beginning in 1939 when an American scientist working at Bell Laboratories discovered the PN junction, which turned out to be the first step toward a form of amplification consuming less power and less space than the clunky valves previously in use. In late 1954 the first radio using transistors went on sale, and in 1957 the hugely successful Sony TR-63 appeared and transformed the market.

Portable tube-driven radios in the past had been cumbersome beasts, expensive to buy and run. Both the price and the size of the new invention allowed it to fit the shallowest pocket. From being a piece of furniture, the radio became a personal accessory to be carried anywhere and everywhere.[148] That this proliferation should occur as the rock 'n' roll revolution was getting under way was not entirely coincidental. Originally, manufacturers thought the best use of the transistor would be to make hearing aids smaller. But the burgeoning opportunities that opened up with the music market explosion in the 1950s and 1960s provided the incentive for the transistor's application to mass media. Reciprocally, the ready access to programming offered by the transistor radio encouraged music stations to proliferate. All kinds of shows benefited, of course, but music benefited most. A survey by the Radio Information Centre in 1983 of the top ten and top 100 radio markets in the United States showed clearly music's domination of the airwaves.[149]

Although spoiled for choice when it came to radio stations, at least in the United States, music listeners had one more river to cross before reaching the promised land. The waves were parted by Philips' development of the music cassette in the 1960s and the subsequent introduction of the Sony Walkman in 1979. Now individual consumers were completely in control of what music they listened to, so much so indeed that the musical

The top ten and top 100 radio markets in the United States in 1983.

Market	Top 10 (%)	Top 100 (%)
Rock	17.0	16.5
Adult Contemporary	13.9	16.9
Album-Oriented Rock	7.2	9.1
Classical	2.8	1.7
Urban Contemporary	4.1	2.5
Black/Rhythm and Blues	8.2	7.1
Country	6.2	11.2
All News	7.1	4.1
Spanish	4.0	2.7
Nostalgia	6.2	6.9
Talk	9.4	6.9
Religious	1.4	1.7
Golden Oldies	2.0	1.6
Jazz	0.8	0.0 [*sic*]
Soft Contemporary	1.3	1.4
Easy Listening	8.4	9.7

Radio Information Centre

experience had become self-contained. Only a tinny buzzing from the headphones (no less irritating for being faint) was audible to the rest of the world.[150] Since the introduction of the cassette player, the hardware has become more sophisticated and ubiquitous, but nothing essential has changed. By spring 2007, iPods and MP3 players offered enough memory to allow an average-sized record collection to be stored and carried around in one's pocket. In April of that year Apple celebrated the sale of the 100 millionth iPod, having sold 10.5 million since January alone.[151] By the last quarter of 2007, nearly half the world's population owned a mobile phone, most of which incorporated a music player.[152]

Listening to music in this manner is so different from attending a live performance that many musicologists and cultural theorists have thrown up their hands in horror. Representative is the following comment by Michael Chanan: 'A mutation of musical communication has occurred in which live performance has become a mere adjunct to most people's musical experience, which now comes to them overwhelmingly through loudspeakers or even earphones . . . Music has become literally disembodied, and the whole musical experience has been thrown into a chronic state of flux. And in these circumstances, in which ubiquitous mechanical reproduction pushes music into the realms of noise pollution, it often seems that musical values must inevitably become relative.[153] When were musical values anything other than relative? one might well ask. Much of the avant-garde music about which Chanan writes with such enthusiasm might also be classified as 'noise pollution', although not of course John Cage's '4'33"', which consists of four minutes and thirty-three seconds of silence.

Listening to noise can now take place while watching that noise being performed. Although watching and listening had always been possible with television, in the early days TV programmers favoured the same kind of bland middle-of-the-road easy listening that had dominated radio. Their conservatism proved more restrictive because, even in the United States, there were many fewer TV stations than radio stations, and the dominance of the national television networks was much greater. Occasionally popular music erupted onto the scene, notably the legendary appearances on the Ed Sullivan Show by Elvis Presley in 1956 (when he reached 82.6 percent of America's television audience) and The Beatles in 1964 (when they were watched by 73 million people, at that time the largest audience in the history of television or indeed in the history of the world).[154]

In Great Britain, a commercial channel (ITV) was added to the BBC's offerings in 1955, but it made no difference to the kind of music available. Two years later, however, the government minister responsible for allocating air time decided to abolish what was known as 'the toddler's truce'— the compulsory pause in transmission between the hours of six and seven in the evening to allow parents to put their small children to bed. Caught up short, the BBC had to scramble for programmes to fill the vacant hour. On weekdays they resorted to a cosy magazine called *Tonight,* aimed at adults returning from work, but on Saturdays they gave a younger audience a pop music programme named after the time it began—*The Six-Five Special.* ITV soon responded with the sharper and more teenage-oriented *Oh Boy!* (named after the Buddy Holly hit of 1957).[155] Neither of these half-hearted excursions into the alien territory of youth culture lasted long. More durable were the *Juke Box Jury* (BBC 1959–67), *Thank Your Lucky Stars* (ITV 1961–66), *Ready, Steady, Go* (ITV 1963–66), *Top of the Pops* (BBC 1964–2006) and *The Old Grey Whistle Test* (BBC2 1971–87). They all paled by comparison with their American equivalents, most notably *American Bandstand,* which began transmission in 1952.

Of quite a different order was the appearance of MTV (Music TeleVision), which began transmitting in the United States on 1 August 1981 with the oxymoronic introduction 'Ladies and Gentlemen, rock 'n' roll!'[156] Its formula was as simple as it was effective: nonstop 24/7/365 music videos. With conscious irony, the first video to be screened was *Video Killed the Radio Star* by The Buggles.[157] Of course it did nothing of the kind, as radio deejays still command daily audiences of millions. But MTV had certainly found a winning formula. The music video demonstrated once again music's uncanny ability to absorb, adapt and exploit a new medium. Pop and rock were the most obvious beneficiaries, for the moving images diverted attention from tediously repetitive music, gave spurious significance to trite lyrics and compensated for the less than crystalline diction of many singers. In the hands of a skillful director, a video could become more than the sum of its parts and achieve classical status—Queen's *Bohemian Rhapsody* (1975 and arguably the first true music video), Michael Jackson's *Thriller* (1983), Madonna's *Like a Prayer* (1989), Britney Spears' *Baby One More Time* (1999) or Missy Elliott's *Lose Control* (2003) being only a few in a great gallery of videos that are still being played.

For MTV, the marriage between the aural and visual media was made in heaven, for it joined fans who wanted to see as well as hear their heroes with record companies that wanted to publicise their products. As the facilitator of the union, MTV benefited from both parties. The effect on the recording industry was immediate: 'Rock video is the silver bullet that knocked the doldrums out of the record industry' was the comment of one grateful executive in 1983.[158] Helped by the rapid expansion of cable and satellite television, by 2005 MTV had become the most widely distributed television network in the world, reaching 400 million homes in 167 countries in twenty-two different languages.[159] Cleverly, MTV did not try simply to export the American version but adapted the basic format to local tastes as they set up satellites around the world—MTV Europe (1987), MTV Latin America (1993), MTV Mandarin (1995), MTV India (1996), MTV Australia (1997), MTV Russia (1998), MTV Japan (2001), and so on.

Although there have been imitators, the main threat to MTV has come from the inflexibility of the format. If the video currently being played does not appeal, viewers have no alternative but to press the mute button or switch off, for it cannot be fast-forwarded. As the manager of a rival,

Channel U, launched in 2003 just to transmit 'urban music', especially hip-hop, claimed: 'Music is everywhere now and there are niche operators opening up almost every day. MTV is in my view, too generic and there's just too much crammed into too little a space'.[160] MTV's response has been to diversify into dedicated channels—VH1 (aimed at a slightly older audience), MTV Dance, MTV Base, MTV Hits and MTV Classic.

The cumulative effect of jukeboxes, vinyl records, transistor radios, music cassettes, the Walkman, iPods, and all the other electronic devices has been to dissolve the traditional boundaries between listening to music and everyday life. Carrying the trend one step further, on 9 January 2007 Steve Jobs, CEO of Apple, announced the launch of iPhone, a device that downloads, stores and plays music and music videos, as well as dealing with phone calls and emails. For a certain kind of intellectual who knows just what the masses ought to like, this suffusion process has been a deeply depressing experience. Theodor Adorno gave the lead here in 1936, with his vitriolic attacks on popular music, especially jazz, which he dismissed as (among other things) 'mechanical soullessness', 'licentious decadence', 'pseudo-democratic', 'sado-masochistic', 'banal', 'depraved' and 'neurotic weakness'.[161] But along with the apparent self-isolation and even narcissism induced by technological change, these new ways to disseminate music were also a strong emancipatory force. For if technology made solo listening possible, it also was responsible for collective musical experiences.

At the heart of both was electronic amplification—tiny in the case of the Walkman, gargantuan in the case of stadium concerts. The 70,000 watts generated by the sound equipment of Led Zeppelin, the kings of stadium rock in the 1970s, seemed phenomenal at the time, but today the great banks of loudspeakers installed by touring sound companies can handle up to 400,000 watts.[162] Some idea of the complexity of the equipment required can be gained from John Vasey's practical guide to anyone thinking of organising a concert tour by a rock group. The audio requirements alone comprise a long list.

> Front of House (FOH) Speakers
> 16 x Meyer MSL4
> 4 x Meyer 650P sub-bass
> 6 x Meyer MSL2
> 4 x Meyer UPA-2C

FOH Consoles

    1 x Yamaha PM 4000–44 Mono and eight stereo channels

    1 x Yamaha PM 4000 or 3000 32 channels

FOH FX

    2 x Yamaha SPX 990

FOH Inserts

    10 x DBX 160X compressors

    4 x Drawmer DS 2012 gates

    1 x Klark Technic DN725 stereo delay line

FOH Drive

    5 x Meyer CP-10 parametric EQ (equalizer)

    1 x Klark Technic DN 360

    1 x Klark Technic DN 60 analyzer

    4 x stereo input delay units

FOH Playback

    1 x compact disc (CD) player

    1 x digital audiotape (DAT) player

    2 x Akai DR4 VR hard disc recorders with COP (change over) box.[163]

Several more pages follow, detailing further requirements grouped under Monitors, Microphones, Video, Audio Extras and Lighting Requirements. No wonder that the stages built for The Rolling Stones' Bigger Bang tour in 2006 had to be strong enough to carry 300 tons of equipment, including 443 lights, a video screen measuring fifty feet square, and 470 'pieces of pyrotechnics', the whole complex linked by 36 miles of cable and two generators big enough to power an entire community.[164] The financial rewards, as we have seen, were of corresponding dimensions.

Somewhere in between the Walkman and the stadium came the discotheque. Dancing to the gramophone was as old as the instrument itself, but in the 1960s the quality of sound reproduction and amplification reached the point where a new *kind* of communal musical activity became possible. The ubiquity of the discotheque suggests that it satisfies the entertainment requirements of a large swathe of the human race. By 1976 there were 10,000 discotheques in the United States alone.[165] From the end-of-term disco parties organised at primary schools to the studied decadence of Studio 54 in New York (memorably parodied as Studio 69 in

A discotheque on Ibiza, the clubbing capital of Europe.

Mike Myers' film *Goldmember*) to the streets lined with discotheques on the Spanish island of Ibiza—billed as 'the clubbing capital of Europe'— rhythmic motion in close proximity to others has conquered all parts of the world with access to electricity. The combination of alcohol, drugs, sex, fashion, dancing and, above all, ear-splitting incessant music made the discotheque the representative location of hedonism for the youth culture of the late twentieth century. If the music derived directly from it—disco— had a short (if immensely profitable) life in the 1970s, dance music more loosely defined has never gone away. Indeed, assisted by technology (the 12-inch single, the double turntable, the drum machine and so on), the discotheque deejay emerged as a creative artist in his own right. The gulf between a disc jockey of the old school such as Alan 'Fluff' Freeman (1927–2006) and Fatboy Slim (real name Norman Cook) is too great to allow them to be classified under the same heading.

Fatboy Slim's creations stand in a long tradition of synthetic music. It was first made possible when tape recorders were developed by the Germans before and during the Second World War. Captured by the Americans, these machines were soon put to good commercial use. Among the early patrons was Bing Crosby, who was looking for a way to record his radio programmes in advance so that all the risks of live performances could be eliminated.[166] Also to the fore was the guitarist Les Paul, who in 1948 introduced a fourth recording head to allow tracks to be added to existing material, a practice that came to be known as multi-tracking.[167] Further advances transformed the studio technician from being essentially a passive recorder of a musician's performance into an active creator of the final product.[168] Instead of turning up with a complete album well rehearsed and ready to record, bands in the 1960s and later spent days, weeks, even months in the studio experimenting with combinations of recorded sounds.

Not the least original aspect of The Beatles' *Sergeant Pepper's Lonely Hearts Club Band* of 1966 was the time it took to record—129 days.[169] So the key figure was not the leader of the band but the producer. Glyn John, who produced *Desperado* for The Eagles in 1973, claimed: 'So, when everyone's gone home, you take what you recorded and completely change it.'[170] Rather less brutal was the observation by Brian Eno, one of the most imaginative and successful of British record producers, who could play no instrument when he joined Roxy Music as 'technical consultant' but quickly turned himself into a master of the synthesizer: 'The technologies we now use have tended to make creative jobs do-able by many different people: new technologies have the tendency to replace skills with judgment—it's not what you *can* do that counts, but what you *choose* to do, and this invites everyone to start crossing boundaries'[171]

The very name of Eno's chosen instrument exemplifies its artificial, manufactured character. Invented by Robert Moog in 1964, 'the synthesizer is the only innovation that can stand alongside the electric guitar as a great new instrument of the age of electricity', as his biographers reasonably claimed.[172] At its heart were two discoveries: that the pitch of an oscillator can be varied by raising or lowering the voltage, and that an electrical instrument can be created by putting together a number of discrete modules (oscillators, amplifiers, envelope generators and filters).[173] So began a continuing process of innovation that has put the synthesizer in every recording studio.

Although its first popular success was Wendy Carlos' *Switched-On Bach*—the first classical album ever to sell more than half-a-million copies—the introduction in 1970 of a Minimoog, a portable version that could be played from a built-in keyboard, expanded its empire to embrace most rock and pop groups.[174] What appealed so much to musicians unconstrained by classical scores was the synthesizer's flexibility, its range limited only by the user's imagination. Moog himself recalled the impression his invention made when he went to Columbia Studios in New York to set it up for Simon and Garfunkel, who were recording their album *Bookends:* 'One sound I distinctly remember was a plucked string, like a bass sound. Then it would slide down—it was something you could not do on an acoustic bass or an electric bass. A couple of session musicians came through. One guy was carrying a bass and he stops and he listens, and listens. He turned white as a sheet'.[175]

The Triumph of Technology

But if the sophistication of studio resources concentrated the creative process in hands of producers such as Eno, other technological changes have been working in the opposite direction. Once again the Janus face of technological innovation has been revealed. On the one hand, gramophones, radio and television have helped to convert the active player into a passive listener. On the other hand, since the 1950s there has been a rapid and sustained increase in the number of people making music for themselves on their own terms. Central to this development has been the electric guitar.

Adding a pickup to an acoustic instrument was first tried in the 1930s but with mixed results, for the greater volume came at the cost of distortion and feedback: 'A mishandled amplified acoustic guitar could suddenly start howling like a supercharged coyote', as John Rockwell put it.[176] In the hands of very skillful performers such as Eddie Durham and Charlie Christian, it could sound wonderful—as the recordings of Christian with the Benny Goodman Sextet demonstrate—but they were few and far between. The solution was an instrument with a solid body, which allowed the pickup to amplify only the string and not the ambient vibrations. Of the various contenders for first in the field, the best case can be made for The Log, created by Les Paul in 1941.[177]

Eleven years passed, however, before Paul could persuade the Gibson

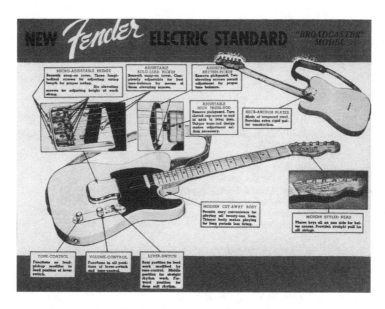

Advertisement for a Fender Broadcaster of 1951. The name was soon changed to Telecaster.

Guitar Corporation to bring a greatly improved version to market. By that time, he had been overtaken by another pioneer, Leo Fender. After many years of experimentation, Fender had developed a solid-body guitar that was effective, simple, robust, easy to manufacture and, above all, easy to play. As he explained: 'On an acoustic electric guitar you have a string fastened to a diaphragm top, and that top does not have one specific frequency. If you play a note the top will respond to it and also to a lot of adjoining notes, producing distortion, particularly at higher levels of amplification. A solid-body doesn't have that, you're dealing with just a single note at a time'.[178] Fender was the electronic equivalent of Theobald Boehm, being both a musician (although his preferred instrument was the saxophone) and a craftsman (he owned a radio repair shop in Fullerton, California). He also knew all about amplifiers. And that was the secret of his success—instead of taking the guitar as his starting point, he began with amplification.

Fender was also careful to have his prototypes tested by musicians, so that he could adapt shape, size and weight based on their comments. The result was an instrument first marketed in 1950 called the Broadcaster, a

Teenage heaven: a seventeen-year-old Jeff Beck plays with The Deltones at Downgate Hall in Tonbridge in 1961. The guitarists are all playing Fenders.

name that soon had to be changed to Telecaster when a drum manufacturer complained about a coincidence of names. In 1954 the Telecaster was joined by the Stratocaster, an improved model with three pickups and a tremolo arm for vibrato effects. It became the best-selling guitar of all time, truly deserving the adjective 'iconic'. So perfect was the first model that it has barely changed since. Its fiftieth anniversary was celebrated with a concert at the Wembley Arena, where its continuing supremacy was demonstrated by devotees such as Hank Marvin, Jeff Beck and Brian May.[179]

Not the least attractive feature of the Stratocaster was its appearance, the twin horns making it immediately recognisable. When Phil Manzanera passed an audition to join Roxy Music in 1972, he found that he had to change his guitar, and not for musical reasons: 'I had a Gibson 335, and Bryan Ferry and [Brian] Eno said, "No, it doesn't look any good!" What was needed was a white Stratocaster, so I had to borrow a hundred quid from a bank—can you believe this?—to buy a white Strat so I could join Roxy. It's on the cover of the first album. It shows the power of an icon: they sussed that my jazzy-looking 335 just wasn't acceptable as an image'.[180] Manzanera became a convert, and now speaks of the Stratocaster in hushed tones: 'It has definite moods, the top pick-up is very dark and it shades down to a much lighter, treblier sound on the bottom pick-up. So you can easily adjust to the mood of an individual song. And the older models do sound better—they almost play themselves. It's a bit like a Stradivarius—early Fenders are like cream, the tone is so beautiful.'[181] If the comparison sounds fanciful, confirmation may be found in the fact that one of Eric Clapton's Stratocasters, known as Blackie, was sold at auction in 2004 for $959,000.[182]

Almost as important as the Telecaster or the Stratocaster was Fender's invention of the solid-body electric bass guitar in 1953. With the six-stringed rhythm and lead instruments now so much louder, an amplified bass was essential. The Fender Precision Bass, as it was (and still is) called, filled the need and did much more besides, making possible the driving bass beat that in all senses has been at the root of rock music ever since. The path was now clear for the four-piece rock group—lead, rhythm and bass guitars plus drums—to conquer the world.

Quite rightly, Fender has been called 'the Henry Ford of the electric guitar'. Because his instruments could be mass-produced, economies of scale brought them within the reach of most aspiring musicians. And because his instruments were easy to play, a mass market opened up for producers as well as consumers of music. Anyone aspiring to emulate the popular music of the swing era needed a high degree of musical training and very expensive instruments. In the post-Fender era, a group could be assembled for little money and less expertise: three chords and they were in business. By 2007, an electric guitar and amplifier could be bought for less than £200. Of the great hordes of aspirants, very few ever find their way into the recording studio, let alone the charts, but so great are the material rewards and so glamorous is the lifestyle awaiting those who succeed that there has never been a shortage of people trying. They helped to make Leo Fender a very rich man, selling his business to CBS in 1965 for the then colossal sum of $13 million.[183]

In technological terms, the 1954 Stratocaster is very old indeed, but the power of technological advance to help music is undiminished even today. On 17 October 2005, for example, a group from Sheffield called Arctic Monkeys released a single entitled 'I Bet You Look Good on the Dance-floor'. It went straight to number one in the charts and was included on their first album *Whatever People Say I Am, That's What I'm Not*, released in January 2006, which sold more than 120,000 copies on the first day and 363,000 copies (all that were available) in the first week.[184] Such a phenomenon is not uncommon in the world of popular music. What made this episode special was the way the Arctic Monkeys made their music and found an audience. When they were ready to record, they did not go to an established multinational such as EMI or Warner but to a small independent company called Domino, founded as a one-man, one-woman enterprise in a South London flat in 1993. Next, they studiously avoided the usual route of demonstration disc, manager and record company, in favour of the Internet. They made their first music downloads available for free and encouraged their fans to exchange tracks. Whatever they may have forgone in royalties they made up many times over by creating a very large and loyal following who flocked to their concerts.[185]

An even more enterprising use of the Internet was made by Sandi Thom, who had tried in vain for several years to establish herself as a singer by conventional means. In February 2006 she launched a new series of concerts entitled Twenty One Nights from Tooting, the difference being that the venue was her basement flat in the South London borough of that name. She had no audience, and the medium was a webcam hooked up to the Internet. What then happened is much disputed. Claims that the number of hits on her site rose rapidly from 643 on 24 February to 86,325 on 4 March and then onwards and upwards to 150,000, 200,000 and so on have been dismissed by some as a clever publicity stunt. Certainly, the press reports generated as much interest as the performances themselves, and very likely her art was enhanced by artifice.

What is statistically verifiable, however, is that her next record, 'I Wish I Was A Punk Rocker (With Flowers in My Hair)', went quickly to number one, as did her first album, *Smile . . . It Confuses People*. Equally undoubted has been the importance of her ability to cut out all the middlemen and connect directly with her fans. The director of the company that established her webcast commented: 'What is really interesting is that the audience has been moving from country to country. You can see it in the viewing stats. It started in the UK, then it went Stateside, then it started trickling into Europe, Scandinavia, and the largest audience at the moment

Sandi Thom broadcasts to the world from her Tooting basement.

is now in Italy. It's been talked about on the blogs and word has spread all over the internet. It's turned into the ultimate virtual marketing campaign.'[186]

At the same time that Sandi Thom was building her audience from Tooting, at the other end of the world in South Korea a twenty-three-year-old self-taught guitarist called Jeong-hyun Ling alias Funtwo was using YouTube to demonstrate his amazing virtuosity by playing a rock version of Johann Pachelbel's *Canon*.[187] YouTube began in late 2005, quickly became the third or fourth most popular website in the world and was sold to Google for $1.7 billion in November 2006.[188]

In just 170 years we have come a long way since *Le Ménestrel* first dreamed of musical gas. Every time that the death of the music industry is announced, music wriggles around the apparent blockage and resumes its inexorable progress. Internet downloads, once thought to signal the end of recording companies, turned out to be another route to Eldorado. Looking back on 2006, which saw sales of singles increase by 40 percent, Peter Jamieson, chairman of the British Phonographic Association, said: 'Just a couple of years ago, some commentators predicted the death of the single.

We are now looking at a market which has doubled in three years, thanks to downloads'.[189] The appearance of the iPhone and other similar devices can only accelerate the trend. Fortunately, historians are not expected to make predictions. But what can be said, with a confidence based on the knowledge of what has happened during the past two or three centuries, is that, whatever technological advances are made in the future, the art form most likely to benefit is music.

5
Liberation
Nation, People, Sex

National Pride and Prejudice

On 5 December 1757, at Leuthen in Silesia, Frederick the Great and his army of 33,000 Prussians inflicted a crushing defeat on an Austrian army twice the size. With three volunteer battalions, Frederick pursued his enemy to Lissa on the road to Breslau, where a brief skirmish ensued. Hearing the gunfire, the main Prussian army came up in support. What then followed was well described in one of Thomas Carlyle's sonorous passages:

> Thick darkness; silence; tramp, tramp: a Prussian grenadier broke out, with solemn tenor voice again, into Church-Music; a known Church-Hymn, of the homely Te Deum kind; in which five-and-twenty thousand other voices, and all the regimental bands, soon join:

> > Now thank we all our God,
> > With heart and hands and voices,
> > Who wondrous things has done,
> > In whom this world rejoices.

The Leuthen Chorale by Arthur Kampf (1887). Frederick the Great can be seen standing in the distance on the left.

And thus they advance; melodious, far-sounding, through the hollow Night, once more in a highly remarkable manner. A pious people, of right Teutsch stock though stout; and except perhaps for Oliver Cromwell's handful of Ironsides, probably the most perfect soldiers ever seen hitherto.[1]

They had gone into battle that morning singing Lutheran hymns and, now that it was over, they gave thanks to the Almighty also in the way they knew best. Prussian historians liked to add that the hymn was offered less as thanks to God than as a tribute to their charismatic warrior-king. It was probably both. One can only wonder what the object of their veneration felt when he heard his soldiers singing. He certainly would have experienced no urge to join in. He himself famously despised Christianity as 'an old metaphysical fiction, stuffed with fables, contradictions and absurdities . . . spawned in the fevered imagination of the Orientals'.[2] Nor was the chorale itself to his taste. He knew what he liked, and that was *opera seria* sung by Italians.

Yet this culture clash could not prevent 'Nun danket alle Gott' from being forever associated with this triumphalist effusion. Indeed, it became known as 'the Leuthen chorale' and was commemorated in word and image throughout the next century. When the Napoleonic empire fell, the chorale was sung on innumerable occasions across Germany.[3] It was sung again after victories over the French at Gravelotte and Sedan in 1870 and after the proclamation of the German empire in the Hall of Mirrors at Versailles on 18 January the following year.[4] Then it turned out to be a musical Nemesis, as it followed the new state's hubristic headlong charge into war, defeat, democracy and dictatorship. It was sung lustily by the enormous crowd outside the royal palace in Berlin on 1 August 1914 when the outbreak of war was announced.[5] It was sung with equal enthusiasm on 21 March 1933 in the Garrison Church at Potsdam, when Hitler and Hindenburg laid wreaths on the tombs of Frederick William I and his son Frederick the Great as part of the great Day of Potsdam that inaugurated the Third Reich.[6] No more than Frederick the Great did Hitler really believe that it was God who should be thanked.

The association between music and the martial arts of a self-chosen people is a very long one. One of the earliest was the attack on Jericho mounted by Joshua and the Israelites when conquering Canaan. After a seven-day assault on the eardrums of the defenders by seven priests bearing seven trumpets of rams' horns, the city fell without resistance:

> So the people shouted when the priests blew with the trumpets: and it came to pass, when the people heard the sound of the trumpet, and the people shouted with a great shout, that the wall fell down flat, so that the people went up into the city, every man straight before him, and they took the city. And they utterly destroyed all that was in the city, both man and woman, young and old, and ox, and sheep, and ass, with the edge of the sword. (Joshua 6:20–21)

It was not always as easy as that, of course. But even when the Almighty made his anointed suffer casualties before victory, a musical invocation was believed to be effective. It was also good for the morale of the fighting men. After smiting the Scots hip and thigh at the battle of Dunbar on 3 September 1650, Oliver Cromwell prepared his cavalry for the slaughter of the fugitives by leading the singing of Psalm 117: 'O give Ye praise unto the Lord, all nations that be'.[7]

The Protestants had their psalms and hymns, while the Catholics responded with Te Deums.[8] In the eighteenth century, as the venom began to drain from confessional conflict, the texts of battle anthems took on a more secular flavour. Although God's support was still invoked by all sides, it was the nation that emerged as the prime legitimator of armed struggle. For all his sophistication and intelligence, in this regard Frederick the Great was increasingly out of step with his subjects. He found his own source of authority in the state, whose first servant he famously proclaimed himself to be, but not in the nation. Although well aware of national differences, his personal identity was cosmopolitan and non-German. While still the crown prince, he had written to Voltaire that Germany could never expect to develop a vernacular culture of any value. He conceded that the Germans had some virtues—they did not lack intellect, they had ample good sense (being rather like the English in this regard), they were industrious and even profound. On the other hand, they were also ponderous, long-winded, and boring.

The main problem, he believed, was linguistic: because Germany was divided into an infinity of territories, it would never be possible to reach agreement on which of the regional dialects would become the standard form.[9] This aversion to the German language became a recurrent theme of both his public works and private correspondence, as in 'If we still retain some vestige of our ancient republican liberty, it consists of the worthless opportunity to murder at our leisure a language that is coarse and still virtually barbaric'.[10] He confirmed his own prejudice by using a form of German that was crude, misspelt and ungrammatical.[11] His own preferred language was, of course, French.

This Francophilia (which has been much misunderstood and exaggerated) did not extend to music. French music, he asserted, was 'childish', adding, 'Only the Italians can sing and only the Germans can compose'.[12] This meant *opera seria* in the Italian style but written by composers such as Johann Adolf Hasse and Carl Heinrich Graun, whose German origin meant, in Frederick's view, that they could add emotional depth and harmonic complexity to the Italian flair for melody. But their compositions had to be sung by Italians. When told about a wonderful German soprano called Gertrude Mara (née Schmeling), Frederick is said to have snorted: 'A

German singer? I should as soon expect to receive pleasure from the neighing of my horse'.[13] Another version of the same story had him refusing even to hear her, on the grounds that she would have an 'accent tudesque,' and adding: 'I'd rather have the arias of my operas neighed by a horse than have a German prima donna'.[14] In fact 'howled by a dog' would have been a more appropriate metaphor, because La Mara recorded that when eventually she got her audition she found Frederick sitting on a sofa with General Tauentzien and three Italian greyhounds who at once started howling—as they always did when catching sight of a woman.[15]

Frederick's musical taste had ossified early. By the 1770s he was of the opinion that the music being created by the younger generation was 'mere noise, bludgeoning our ears rather than caressing them'. Haydn's music he dismissed as 'a shindy that flays the ears'; of Mozart he appears to have been unaware.[16] He went out of his way to offend contemporary German composers, telling his *Kapellmeister,* Johann Friedrich Reichardt, that 'he is not to compose an opera, because he doesn't know how to do it and does it all wrong', adding the insulting suggestion that he should change his name to Ricardetto or Ricciardini. By his own account, Reichardt replied: 'Your Majesty! I am proud to be a Prussian and do not wish to italianise my German name'.[17]

As this suggests, Reichardt felt he had a dual allegiance: he was a Prussian in terms of his political loyalties but a German by culture, in the same way that today many people feel themselves to be Welsh without wishing to establish an independent Welsh state. In other words, there is more than one kind of nationalism. Recognising the possibility of this duality is more important than it might sound, for there is a large and influential group of historians who believe that nationalism is essentially a modern phenomenon, to be dated from the French Revolution at the earliest. In their view, a true nationalist must always seek to make the cultural and political boundaries of the community coincide. The small print of historiographical disputes of this kind need not detain us, although, as Noël Malcolm observed, this 'modernist' argument is 'essentially circular: first it defines the nation in terms that only fit 19th- and 20th-century political conditions, and then it demonstrates that nations were constructed in the 19th and 20th centuries'.[18]

The history of music demonstrates that nationalism was a potent force long before 1789. Indeed, the 'nation' was one of two master nouns of political discourse in the eighteenth century. The other was the state, an abstract, bloodless concept that appealed mostly to rulers and their bureaucrats, leaving the bulk of the population unenthusiastic about—if not downright hostile to—its claims. The nation, on the other hand, proved to be a concept brimful with motivating force, for it triggered both positive and negative responses in a self-generating dialectical progression. For every virtue a nationalist ascribed to his own national group, there was a corresponding vice to be denigrated in the 'other' against which national identity was defined. And of course this was a two-way process, because the nationalist believed that the other both failed to give credit where it was due and refused to recognise its own shortcomings. This mutually exacerbating process can be called 'the dialectic of nationalism'.[19]

For most national groups, France served as the 'other', for during the long reign of Louis XIV (1643–1715) France had established an extraordinary degree of cultural hegemony, which it asserted with strident triumphalism. Nor was this self-confidence confined to the monarch. French musicians were fond of propagating the old saw that 'Spain sobs, Italy wails, Germany bellows, Flanders howls, only France sings'. Saint-Evrémond, who repeated it in 1684, added that the Italians had a low opinion of French opera, a prejudice that was heartily reciprocated.[20] Francesco Cavalli did his best to adapt his style to suit French tastes in his opera *Ercole amante* (Hercules in Love) in 1662, but it was no good. With one solitary exception, this was the last Italian opera to be presented in France for sixty-seven years.[21]

As the eighteenth century began, the pre-eminence of French music appeared to its native supporters to be just as self-evident as Louis XIV's military domination. In 1704 (the year that the battle of Blenheim put an end to the latter), the luxuriantly named Jean-Laurent Le Cerf de la Viéville published a comparison of Italian and French music very much to the advantage of the latter. Its superiority had been consummated by the genius of Lully—'a man of peerless talent, a man whose equal one seeks in vain in any of the sixteen centuries that went before him'.[22] The uncomfortable fact that Jean-Baptiste Lully had been born Giovanni-Battista Lulli in Florence was dealt with by the assertion that he had assimilated himself completely to the music of his adopted country.[23]

Ten years later, this treatise was reprinted by Pierre Bourdelot and Pierre Bonnet as an appendage to a history of music celebrating French supremacy in much more strident terms. Their tactical acknowledgment that Italian music was not entirely without merit was followed by an assault on it as bizarre, capricious, contrary to all the rules, reliant on excessive ornamentation, febrile, meretricious and producing effects without causes. It was like a painted whore, whereas French music was 'a beautiful woman, whose simple, natural, spontaneous charms win the hearts of everyone she meets, who only has to appear to give pleasure and who never has anything to fear from the affected mannerisms of an eccentric coquette'.[24] Bourdelot and Bonnet would have given any suggestion that nationalism was a modern invention short shrift: in their view antipathy between Italian and French musicians dated back to Charlemagne. Every nation had its own character, they argued, deriving from its own peculiar tastes, customs, and pleasures, so why should the French want to sing and play like the Italians?[25]

At least French commentators were aware that music was being created in Italy. The same cannot be said for their awareness of German musicians. In the middle of the eighteenth century, it was still possible for the abbé Marc-Antoine Laugier to write a long review of the contemporary music scene in Europe without mentioning German music once. Well might he comment that 'national prejudice does sometimes blind us to the merits of the music of others', given that Laugier's book was published six years after the death of Johann Sebastian Bach.[26] If a Jesuit-educated Catholic abbé might be forgiven for overlooking one resolutely Protestant heretic, the sheer abundance of musical talent *outre-Rhin* makes the abbé's myopia far less excusable.

Although music had always benefited from the pluralism of the Holy Roman Empire, during the first half of the eighteenth century the coincidence of numerous distinguished composers began to create a cultural tradition of special power. A list of the more prominent composers born before 1750 would include Leopold I (1640–1705), Heinrich Biber (1644–1704), Johann Joseph Fux (1660–1741), Johann Pachelbel (1653–1706), Georg Philipp Telemann (1681–1767), Johann Sebastian Bach (1685–1750), Georg Friedrich Handel (1685–1759), Johann Joachim Quantz (1697–1773), Johann Adolf Hasse (1699–1783), Carl Heinrich Graun (1703–59), Franz Benda (1709–86), Ignaz Holzbauer (1711–83), Frederick the Great (1712–86), Carl Philipp Emmanuel Bach (1714–88), Johann Wenzel Anton Stamitz (1717–57), Johann Friedrich Agricola (1720–74), Georg Anton Benda (1722–95), Christian Cannabich (1731–98),

Joseph Haydn (1732–1809), Johann Christian Bach (1735–82), Michael Haydn (1737–1806), Carl Stamitz (1745–1801).

No wonder that in 1741 a periodical published in Brunswick entitled *Der musikalische Patriot* (The Musical Patriot) offered the following triumphant proclamation of the supremacy of German music:

> Must not the Italians, who previously were the tutors of the Germans, now envy Germany its estimable composers, and secretly seek to learn from them? Indeed, must not the high and mighty Parisians, who used to deride German talent as something provincial, now take lessons from Telemann of Hamburg? Indeed, I believe that we Germans can go on instructing foreigners in how music can be developed still further, in much the same way that our fellow-countrymen, notably Leibniz and Wolff, have demonstrated how the philosophical and mathematical sciences can be raised to a still greater pitch of perfection[27].

The dialectic of nationalism operated powerfully too, for this pride in German music was intensified both by disdain for French music and the knowledge that this attitude was reciprocated by the 'high and mighty Parisians'.

As the eighteenth century wore on, even the most nationalistic French music lovers had to sense that the ground was moving beneath their feet as the rapid expansion of publishing made so much more foreign music available. In the 1750s the issue became a matter of more than musical importance. For the *beau monde* of Paris, the Opéra was the central cultural institution, as passion for operatic music ran high.[28] The fictional nephew of Diderot's Rameau asks the chevalier de Turcaret: "'Do you like music?'. "Yes" is the reply, "worst luck, I am a subscriber at the Opéra". "It is the dominant passion of good society" observes Rameau's nephew. "It is certainly mine", agrees Turcaret.'[29] Going to Paris without visiting the Opéra, wrote the Russian tourist Nikolai Karamzin, was like going to Rome and not seeing the pope.[30] So when a storm erupted in 1752 over the arrival of Eustachio Bambini's *opera buffa* troupe, it could not be contained in the teacups of the salons.[31] In his *Confessions* Rousseau claimed that the pamphlet he wrote on this occasion, *Letters on French Music,* 'prevented a revolution'.[32] This is less absurd than it might seem.

The Querelle des bouffons, as the affair became known, lined up on the one side those who thought traditional French opera had had its day and on the other those who were prepared to defend the superiority of French music against all comers. Significantly, the loudest voices in the first party were both foreigners. The German Baron Grimm told his correspondents that what the French liked to call opera was 'a collection of minuets, gavottes, rigaudons, tambourins and contredanses, interspersed with some scenes of plainsong that seemed to come straight from the evening service'.[33] Much more inflammatory was Jean-Jacques Rousseau, citizen of Geneva, who with characteristic bluntness told the French in 1753 that they had no music worth mentioning:

> I think that I have shown that there is neither measure nor melody in French music, because the language is not capable of them; that French singing is a continual squalling, insupportable to an unprejudiced ear; that its harmony is crude and devoid of expression and suggests only the padding of a pupil; that French 'airs' are not airs; that French recitative is not recitative. From this I conclude that the French have no music and cannot have any; or that if they ever have, it will be so much the worse for them.[34]

The pamphlet caused a sensation, provoking a counter-attack of sustained intensity and volume. Rousseau himself recorded: 'A description of the incredible effect of this pamphlet would be worthy of the pen of Tacitus', adding that the Opéra orchestra's plan to assassinate him had been prevented only by an escort of musketeers thoughtfully provided by a military admirer.[35] From the presses flowed a stream of pamphlets defending the honour of French music, which was held to be in better taste, more noble, more profound, better balanced, more expressive, more harmonious, more lucid, more sincere, and at the same time more substantial and more subtle.[36] Italian music, by contrast, was dismissed as over-elaborate, tedious, meretricious, volatile, superficial, platitudinous, formulaic, frivolous, puerile, over-emotional, pandering to base instincts, and constantly searching for effect at the expense of substance—just to give a sample of the abuse hurled.[37] A favourite metaphor applied to Italian music was 'coquette', a flirtatious lady of easy virtue, playful and pleasing but essentially trivial and superficial, best taken, to mix the metaphor, as an *hors d'œuvre* before embarking on more solid French fare.[38]

Louis-Bertrand Castel repeated his own version of *solus Gallus cantat:* 'For more than 200 years now it has been said that "the Spanish bark, the Germans bellow, the English whistle, the Italians quaver and the French sing". Of all these attributes, only that of the French can apply to real music, for singing is music *per se.* How is it possible that we could have no music of our own today—we who had music at a time when no one else did, we who have the same music today as we did then? Indeed that proverb I have just quoted sometimes runs: "*only* the French sing"'.[39]

Eventually, of course, the affair fizzled out, but not before it had demonstrated how much importance was attached to having a national music better than that of any other nation. This was indeed 'a dispute between nation and nation', asserted one pamphleteer, and 'it is up to us, as true Frenchmen, as true patriots, as true subjects of the King, to make our voices heard'.[40] It also demonstrated a keen awareness of national character. Nations were different because their languages were different, argued one, so only Italians could compose in the true Italian style.[41] Although in theory this implied that national cultures were different but equal, the rise in temperature caused by the *Querelle des bouffons* ruled out pluralism. French music was not just different, it was superior. No French composer should even try to commit cultural treason by imitating the Italians, it was argued, for the 'dominant taste of the [Italian] nation and the natural inclination of its people' had almost always been 'the mortal enemies of true feelings and sound reason'.[42] More ominously for the old regime, the affair had indicated that a locus of loyalty was emerging separate from, and potentially hostile to, the monarch. This locus was the nation.

Rule Britannia? Aux Armes, Citoyens!

'Every girl should have a husband, preferably her own', observes a character in James Hadley Chase's novel *No Orchids for Miss Blandish* (1939).[43] In the course of the eighteenth and nineteenth centuries, every nation came to think that it ought to have a music, preferably its own—and its own literature and visual arts too, for that matter. But music could express national aspirations more directly than the other arts. A good example was provided by England—perhaps surprisingly, since it had long enjoyed the reputation of being 'the country without music'.[44]

Looking back at the eighteenth century from the vantage point of 1802, the premier German musical periodical, the *Allgemeine Musikalische Zeitung* of Leipzig, observed that no one could understand why a country so rich in poets and dramatists should be bereft of first-rank composers: 'The English have neither a sense of, nor a respect for, and even less love of music—all they have is the money to pay the foreign musicians who know how to flatter them'.[45] Three years later, a correspondent reported from London that music could indeed be heard in almost every prosperous household, but played only by women. The art was learned in the same sort of spirit as embroidery, he added, serving mainly to provide social distancing and to pass the time.[46]

Although this prejudice stemmed in part from nonmusical considerations, not the least of them being jealousy of British economic power, it was difficult to rebut. The tragic death of the immensely promising Thomas Linley in a boating accident in 1776 at the age of twenty-two may well have robbed England of its Mozart but, with the best will in the world, neither Thomas Arne nor John Marsh could be mentioned in the same breath as continental imports such as Handel or Haydn. The less blinkered English commentators recognised the deficiency. Writing in *The Spectator* in 1711, Joseph Addison railed against the 'monstrous Practice' of singing operas in Italian but also acknowledged that England was indeed a country without music: 'At present our notions of Musick are so very uncertain, that we do not know what it is we like, only, in general, we are transported with any thing that is not English; so if it be of a foreign Growth, let it be Italian, French or High-Dutch [German], it is the same thing. In short, our English Musick is quite rooted out, and nothing yet planted in its stead'.[47]

Only twenty years earlier, Henry Purcell—universally acknowledged as a composer of the first rank—had written the music for a music-drama that both celebrated and promoted English nationality. This was *King Arthur*, with a libretto by no less a poet than John Dryden, first performed in 1691, in the immediate aftermath of the Glorious Revolution that had deposed James II and brought William and Mary to the throne. Its very form announced a national flavour, for it contained much spoken dialogue, included two main characters who do not sing and also featured many special effects, all very much in the tradition of the masque that stretched back to the days of Good Queen Bess and beyond. *Opera seria* and *tragédie lyrique* did not suit English tastes because all of the words were set to music (through-composed). As the Huguenot refugee Peter Motteux observed: 'Experience hath taught us that our English genius will not rellish that perpetual singing . . . Our English Gentlemen, when their Ear is satisfy'd, are desirous to have their mind pleas'd, and Musick and Dancing industriously intermix'd with Comedy or Tragedy'.[48]

Also specifically English was the nature of the patronage. *King Arthur* was not commissioned by the king or even a group of nobles but was written for a commercial theatre—The Queen's Theatre in London's Dorset Garden, designed by Sir Christopher Wren and with a seating capacity of over a thousand—and was intended to turn a profit. English patriots found plenty to enjoy in the fantastic story of how the legendary King Arthur defeated both the forces of darkness and the invading Saxons, for despite its quasi-mystical setting, this was very much a tract for the times, as Dryden's text repeatedly looked forward to later history. After leading in 'Valiant *Britains,* Who shall by Sea and Land Repel our Foes', Honour invokes the patron saint, forecasts the Glorious Revolution and enlists the aid of the Almighty in support of his chosen people.[49]

The white magician Merlin prophesies that the day will come when English and Saxons will join to form one Anglo-Saxon nation, as he tells the defeated Oswald.[50] The 'common faith' he proclaims must refer to Protestantism, although ironically Dryden had converted to Catholicism in 1685, probably to ingratiate himself with James II ('Such purchases were no greate losse to the Church' was the diarist John Evelyn's withering comment).[51] The Anglo-Saxons could also look forward to the two other legs of the tripod that was to establish their unique happiness: liberty and prosperity. No lyric tragedy performed at Versailles celebrated the benefits of commerce so explicitly.

> Now the Victory's won,
> To the Plunder we run:
> We return to our Lasses like Fortunate Traders,
> Triumphant with Spoils of the Vanquish'd Invaders.[52]

Also decidedly at odds with the representational ethos of continental court culture was the populism and even social criticism of passages writ-

The Queen's Theatre, Dorset Garden, London,
designed by Sir Christopher Wren, where Purcell
and Dryden's *King Arthur* was first performed. This
contemporary print brings out well the urban
commercial setting.

ten for the chorus of rustics, especially in their attack on the tithe, a charge
on agricultural produce paid by all cultivators: 'We ha' cheated the Parson,
we'll cheat him agen; For why shou'd a Blockhead ha' One in Ten?'[53] These
same peasants, at the end of the work, noisily celebrate the special virtues
of Old England before Venus appears to deliver a more sophisticated eu-
logy, which includes the celebrated verse beginning 'Fairest Isle, all Isles
Excelling.'[54]

Endorsed by a royal visit, *King Arthur* was a success when first performed and was revived periodically in the eighteenth century.[55] By the
time its hybrid nature fell out of fashion, it had made an important contribution to the foundation myth that sustained English and British nationalism, demonstrating that true religion, prosperity and liberty had roots
more than a millennium deep. In one of his numerous prophecies, Merlin
acclaims Arthur as the first 'of three Christian Worthies'.[56] Although the
other two are not named, everyone in the audience would have known the
second to be King Alfred, the ninth-century king of the Anglo-Saxons who
burned the cakes and scorched the Danes. He would be the subject of another and even more successful masque first performed in 1740, with a libretto by James Thomson and David Mallet and music by Thomas Arne.

The plot of *King Alfred*, such as it is, follows the monarch's recovery from hunted fugitive to triumphant vanquisher of the Danish invaders. Its purpose, however, was plainly political, in two senses. Most obviously, being performed the year after war against Spain began and with an undeclared war against France under way, it was a call to arms. In Act II, scene 3, for example, a hermit inspires the hard-pressed Alfred by conjuring up spirits from the future, including such hammers of the French as Edward III and the Black Prince. The greatest hero of the future, however, is William III, for it was he who banished that two-headed monster superstition and absolutism (James II) and his crony 'vile Servility, that crouch'd and kiss'd the whip he trembled at'. The hermit sees the Glorious Revolution as the turning-point in English history:

> From this great hour
> Shall *Britain* date her rights and laws restor'd:
> And one high purpose rule her sovereign's heart;
> To scourge the pride of *France,* that foe profess'd
> To *England* and to Freedom.[57]

What gave *Alfred* its immense and enduring power was neither the music nor the text but the combination of the two in the closing chorus, which was to become perhaps the most emotive and most popular tune in all of English music. The words of the refrain alone will be sufficient reminder of the melody:

> Rule, Britannia, Britannia rule the waves;
> Britons never will be slaves.[58]

With impressive economy, the six four-line verses manage to cover all the main characteristics of eighteenth-century British nationalism: divine assistance ('When Britain first at heav'n's command, / Arose from out the azure main'); a unique capacity for liberty ('The nations, not so blest as thee, / Must, in their turns, to tyrants fall: / While thou shalt flourish great and free, / The dread and envy of them all'); defiant resistance to continental despotisms ('Thee haughty tyrants never shall tame'); a flourishing agriculture and commerce ('To thee belong the rural reign; / Thy cities shall with commerce shine'); global naval supremacy ('All thine shall be the subject main, / And every shore it circles thine'); cultural excellence ('The muses still with freedom found; / Shall to thy happy coast repair'); natural beauty ('Blest Isle! With matchless beauty crown'd'); and virile masculinity ('And manly hearts to guard the fair').

Less obvious to posterity but easily accessible at the time was *Alfred*'s domestic political agenda. A clue is provided by Alfred's son Edward, who sings immediately before 'Rule Britannia' an aria celebrating 'liberty, virtue and honour'. The topical meaning of those words was underlined by the location of the work's premiere. It was first performed at Cliveden, the home of Frederick Prince of Wales, eldest son of George II, from whom he was bitterly estranged.[59] It was a family row with an ideological flavour. Against a king alleged to prefer Hanover to Britain and who relied on the notoriously corrupt Sir Robert Walpole to manage Parliament by illicit means, Frederick presented himself as a selfless British patriot. As part of his campaign to advertise his national loyalty and influence public opinion, he installed busts of King Alfred and Edward the Black Prince in the garden of his London residence, Carlton House.[60]

In 1739 Prince Frederick visited one of his main supporters, Viscount Cobham, at his country seat at Stowe, where he found an enormous park and garden stuffed with horticultural semiotics. Among other things there was a Temple of British Worthies completed the previous year and containing the busts of eight great patriots of action (King Alfred, Edward the Black Prince, Queen Elizabeth I, King William III, Sir Walter Raleigh, Sir Francis Drake, John Hampden, and Sir John Barnard) and eight men of the arts (Alexander Pope, Sir Thomas Gresham, Inigo Jones, John Milton, William Shakespeare, John Locke, Sir Isaac Newton, and Sir Francis Bacon). They all had in common a dedication to liberty and virtue fundamentally at odds with the despotism and corruption deemed to prevail in contemporary Great Britain.[61]

In short, 'Rule Britannia' was an anthem of a political party as well as a battle hymn. Britons would never be enslaved by the superstitious Catholic despots of the continent—but neither would they fall prey to the corrupt Hanoverian would-be despot closer to home. Although the attack on the king was conveyed in heavily coded form, his servants had been less fortunate. Walpole was lampooned unmercifully, most notably in John Gay's *The Beggar's Opera* of 1728, a ballad-opera set in contemporary London. When Peachum listed among the thieves for whom he fenced '*Robin of Bagshot,* alias *Gorgon,* alias *Bluff Bob,* alias *Carbuncle,* alias *Bob Booty . . .*

he spends his Life among Women', everyone knew that he had the prime minister in mind.[62] Eventually, Walpole lost patience and pushed through Parliament the Licensing Act of 1737, which confined the production of plays in the capital to two 'patent theatres' and required all texts to be submitted for vetting by the lord chamberlain in advance of performance.

Yet if music could be used as a weapon to promote a domestic campaign of dissent, its main function remained the assertion of the nationalist cause. During the glory years of the mid-eighteenth century, when the bells announcing victories across the globe never seemed to stop ringing, one after another enduring piece of music was found. Hard on the heels of 'Rule Britannia' came 'God Save the King'. Although its origins remain controversial, the most authoritative view is that of Percy Scholes: namely, that the tune is traditional, that it was first written down by John Bull in 1619, that it was first published in 1744 and that it was first sung in public the following year after the defeat of the royal army by the Jacobites at Prestonpans on 21 September 1745.[63] So when it was sung at Drury Lane Theatre in an arrangement by none other than Thomas Arne, the occasion was not a triumphalist celebration but an invocation for divine assistance in turning back the Scottish rebels. Hence the sixth verse, which understandably is no longer sung:

> Lord grant that Marshal Wade
> May by thy mighty aid
> Victory bring.
> May he sedition hush,
> And like a torrent rush,
> Rebellious Scots to crush.
> God save the King!

Also out of fashion is a further verse added during the course of the rebellion:

> From France and Pretender
> Great Britain defend her,
> Foes let them fall;
> From foreign slavery,

> Priests and their knavery,
> And Popish Reverie,
> God save us all.

Victory over the Jacobites and the final securing of the Protestant Hanoverian succession sealed the anthem's national status. From then on, it
was sung in theatres and other public places whenever news of victories
arrived.

In 1746 'God Save the King' was joined by the ultimate triumphalist
song, 'See the Conquering Hero Come', which first appeared in Handel's
oratorio *Judas Maccabeus*, dedicated to the duke of Cumberland—the hero
of Culloden and the hammer of the Highlands.[64] During the Seven Years
War (1756–63) a run of naval victories inspired 'Heart of Oak', with words
by David Garrick and music by William Boyce. The oak tree was a favourite
metaphor for British qualities, being slow-growing but long-lasting, a perfect symbol of the marriage between the oak timbers of the British warship
and the stout hearts of those who sailed her:

> Come cheer up, my lads! 'tis to glory we steer,
> To add something more to this wonderful year [1759];
> To honour we call you, not press you like slaves,
> For who are so free as the sons of the waves?
> *Chorus*
> *Heart of oak are our ships, heart of oak are our men;*
> *We always are ready, steady, boys, steady!*
> *We'll fight and we'll conquer again and again.*[65]

These songs were certainly expressions of popular patriotism, but did they
do more? Did they also inspire the soldiers and sailors to fight with greater
enthusiasm? Some observers thought they did. Reviewing the Seven Years
War, the *London Magazine* claimed: 'Mr Garrick's *Heart of Oak* warmed
our seamen with the love of glory, made them look upon the French as beings utterly contemptible, and persuaded them that they were all volunteers
[*sic*], when perhaps half the crew of many ships had been pressed.'[66]

On the other side of the channel, the objects of British contempt sang
with equal relish. Especially during the glory days of Louis XIV's reign

(1643–1715), there were so many songs celebrating his latest triumphs as to constitute a musical history of his campaigns, as their self-explanatory titles reveal: 'On the Second Capture of Besançon during the Months of April and May 1674', 'The Capture of Mons', 'On the Battle of Steinkerque, Where Many Were Killed', and so on.[67] Some songs even criticised the conduct of the war. The duc de Luxembourg cannot have enjoyed hearing 'On Henry de Montmorency-Luxembourg Who Did Not Hurry Himself Enough to Help Philippsbourg in 1676', for example.[68] The most durable proved to be 'Marlborough Goes to War' (Marlbrough s'en va-t-en guerre), sung to the tune of 'For He's a Jolly Good Fellow', which gloried in the supposed death of the English general at the battle of Malplaquet in 1709. That in fact was a victory for the English, albeit of the Pyrrhic kind. Less memorable melodically but more convincing textually was 'The Battle of Fontenoy' of 1745, written to mark the greatest French feat of arms before the Revolution.[69]

On the evening after the battle, Louis XV made a triumphant progress from one regiment to the next, to be acclaimed as a great warrior-king. It was the high point of his reign—indeed, the high point of the Bourbon dynasty in the eighteenth century. From then on, events slid mostly downhill. The treaty of 1748 was a disappointment, and the next conflict—the Seven Years War—was a disaster. Even during the long period of peace that followed, France was regularly reminded of how low she had sunk in the world; these reminders included the first partition of Poland (1772), the peace of Teschen (1779) and the Russian annexation of the Crimea (1783), all of which were accomplished without French participation. Even the prestige gained from alliance with the American revolutionaries in their War of Independence soon faded when it became clear that Britain's economy had been strengthened, not weakened, by the loss of her colonies. The collapse of France as a great power was not an accident, most contemporaries concluded; rather, it was due to the misguided policies of Louis XV, especially the alliance concluded in 1756 with the Austrian Habsburgs. His death in 1774 brought no relief; on the contrary, in 1770 his grandson and successor, Louis XVI, had married Archduchess Marie Antoinette, daughter of Empress Maria Theresa. So there was never any prospect that monarch and nation might be united musically in a French equivalent of 'Rule Britannia'.

The old regime produced no national anthem because French kings failed to see the necessity of wrapping themselves in the flag. Indeed, the nation had no flag either, only the symbol of the Bourbon dynasty, the *fleur-de-lys*. Neither of the last two Bourbons ever wavered in their belief that their authority was both personal and absolute. As Louis XV told the recalcitrant Parlement of Paris in 1766, in a session aptly known as the *séance de la flagellation*: 'Sovereignty resides in my person alone . . . I alone have the right to legislate. This power is indivisible . . . Public order emanates exclusively from me, and the rights and the interests of the nation, which some have had the audacity to separate from the monarch, are necessarily united with mine and repose entirely in my hands'.[70] By this time, however, a growing number of his subjects had come to believe that a source of legitimate authority existed which was separate from and superior to the king, and that source was the nation. The Parlements were now claiming to be 'the tribunal of the nation', 'the council of the nation', 'the depositary of the national interest' and the 'inviolable temple of the nation's laws'.[71]

Neither Louis XV nor Louis XVI heard the clock ticking. With midnight about to chime, the latter was still ignoring or fumbling every golden opportunity to place himself at the head of the nation and make its cause his own. The decision was taken out of his hands on 17 June 1789 by the Third Estate, when its deputies (aided and abetted by a number of renegade clerics and nobles from the First and Second Estates, respectively) declared that they constituted the National Assembly of France. Thus they asserted the principle of national sovereignty, later to be enshrined in the Declaration of the Rights of Man and the Citizen as 'sovereignty resides exclusively in the nation' (Article III). Making a declaration of principle was one thing—making it stick was quite another. Even the slow-burning Louis XVI could now grasp that the point of no return had been reached. His will was finally broken not by the oratory of the deputies of the National Assembly sitting at Versailles but by the violence on the streets of Paris. And it was there that music had a part to play.

Paris enjoyed a long tradition of political songs performed on the streets of the capital, especially on the Pont au Change. Even when the heavy hand of the old regime's police was a constant threat, scurrilous songs could be heard about the alleged impotence of the king, the promiscuity of his queen and so on. In the summer of 1788, for example, one singer likened Marie Antoinette to Messalina, asserting that she was literally a bastard, the 'odious fruit' of Empress Maria Theresa's adulterous liai-

A fiddler-cum-singer on the Pont au Change.

son with the duc de Choiseul. The singer accused her of seeking to exterminate the French nation and called on the Almighty to send a thunderbolt to destroy 'this infamous and detested monster'.[72] When censorship was removed altogether, the floodgates opened. The rise and fall of political songs was charted by Constantin Pierre, who observed that the total of approximately 3,000 must be an underestimate, as many songs did not survive.

Songs were especially well-suited to the expression of simple messages. In the admittedly biased opinion of the revolutionary songwriter Thomas Rousseau: 'The people sing more than they read'.[73] And as most new songs simply added new words to old tunes, everyone with the ability to construct rhyming verses could become a songwriter. Because words that are sung are easier to remember, the song was also an ideal medium for broadcasting news, opinion and rumour from street to street, quarter to quarter, town to town and city to country.[74]

Although most songs were ephemeral, a handful caught the popular imagination. In the early days of the Revolution undoubtedly the biggest hit was 'Ça ira' ('It'll be OK'), first heard in Paris in the run-up to the great Federation Festival held on the Champs de Mars (today, the site of the Eiffel Tower) to celebrate the first anniversary of the fall of the Bastille. On 9 July 1790 the *Chronique de Paris* reported that every municipal authority in the city was raising an altar to the fatherland, that every inauguration ceremony was marked by music and that everyone was singing what it called *le carillon national,* 'Ça ira'.[75]

The first set of words, written by a prolific songwriter simply known as Ladré to a tune by Bécourt, violinist at the Théâtre du Vaudeville, was conciliatory: the nobility and clergy had seen the error of their ways, it was optimistically stated, and things would turn out all right, 'for the French are always victorious'.[76] But almost at once a much more aggressive version promised to get rid of nobles and priests altogether, as indicated by this ominous refrain:

> Ah! Ça ira, Ça ira, Ça ira,
> The aristocrats to the gallows!
> Ah! Ça ira, Ça ira, Ça ira,
> The aristocrats will be strung up.[77]

Sébastien Mercier, a leading Parisian journalist of the day, had a low opinion of the professional singers who gathered on the banks of the Seine to relieve passers-by of their hard-earned cash, but he knew a cultural force at work when he saw one. He commented that 'Ça ira' was 'not a poetic masterpiece, but gives a striking example of the power of music, and was constantly sung by the workers of the Champ de Mars and caused universal enthusiasm wherever performed'.[78] In April 1792, with war on the horizon, the *Chronique de Paris* asked rhetorically: who could doubt the power of music after seeing the effect of 'Ça ira' on the French, adding, 'There is nothing we may not hope from Frenchmen animated by this tune when they go into battle against the enemies of liberty'.[79]

The pro-revolutionary singers did not have it all their own way. Royalists also resorted to song to advance their own programme. This did not always have the desired result. On 1 October 1789 the Regiment of Flanders arrived at the palace of Versailles to reinforce the royal bodyguard. At a banquet held that evening to welcome the newcomers, the king and queen put in an appearance, together with the four-year-old dauphin. On the following morning, the radical Parisian press reported angrily that the affair had degenerated into a bacchanalia, in the course of which the revolutionary cockade had been trampled under foot by counter-revolutionary officers.

Especially offensive had been the music played: 'Soon the party . . . changed into a complete orgy. The wine, poured with a truly royal munificence, went to everyone's heads; the musicians played several pieces appropriate to exalting people's spirits still further, such as *Ô Richard, ô mon Roi, l'univers t'abandonne!* the perfidious allusion of which could not be lost upon any one at this moment'.[80] The song in question came from Grétry's immensely successful opera *Richard Cœur de Lion* of 1784, in which the ever-faithful Blondel sings that he will always be loyal to his royal master even though the rest of the world has abandoned him. This was to become the great royalist song of the Revolution. In the short term, however, it helped to raise Parisian opin-

The rise and fall of political songs during the French Revolution.

1789	116
1790	261
1791	308
1792	325
1793	590
1794	701
1795	137
1796	136
1797	147
1798	77
1799	90
1800	25

Constantin Pierre, *Les Hymnes et chansons de la Révolution* (Paris, 1904), p. 34.

ion above the boiling point. On 5 October a crowd consisting mainly of women marched from Paris to Versailles, tried but failed to lynch the Queen and then brought the royal family back to Paris as virtual captives.

Toiling in their wake also came the National Assembly. What had so far been a two-centre revolution was now concentrated in one spot, the city of Paris. The most important result of this relocation was that the legislators were now subject to all the influences of the capital, especially its vibrant, not to say violent, democratic political culture. Now meeting in the cavernous Manège—the former riding school of the Tuileries Palace, where the royal family resided—the National Assembly ceased to be a debating chamber in the style of the contemporary British Parliament or the American Congress and became a continuous political rally.[81]

The deputies were now under heavy pressure from the public, which occupied the galleries that ran around three of the walls, and also from the delegations that appeared on the floor of the house to present petitions and make their voices heard. To prove their patriotic credentials—and also to intimidate the deputies—these citizen-interlopers often burst into song. On 5 July 1793, for example, at a particularly tense time for the Revolution's fortunes, 'une multitude immense' appeared outside what was now called the National Convention demanding to be let in. Admitted in batches, they sang variously 'Hymn to Liberty', 'Ça ira' and the most potent revolutionary anthem of this or any other age, the 'Marseillaise'.

By this time it was officially known as just that—the 'Marseillaise'—but it had started out in life as 'Battle Hymn for the Army of the Rhine'. The events surrounding its creation are well known and as unchallenged as anything can be in the contentious world of revolutionary music. On 20 April 1792 the National Assembly declared war on the Habsburg monarchy. Five days later the news reached Strasbourg on the easternmost extremity of the country and therefore now right on the front-line. That evening a dinner was given by the mayor of the city, Philippe Frédéric de Dietrich, a wealthy iron manufacturer. The party included Marshal Luckner, commander of the Army of the Rhine; General Victor de Broglie, *ci-devant* prince; General Achille du Châtelet; General Armand d'Aiguillon, *ci-devant* duc; Lieutenant Colonel Jean-Baptiste Kléber; General Louis-Charles-Antoine Desaix, who was later to save Bonaparte's bacon at the battle of Marengo; and a thirty-two-year-old captain of engineers called Claude-Joseph Rouget de l'Isle.[82]

In the course of a discussion about the war, Dietrich lamented the lack of good battle hymns and called for something better than 'Ça ira' or 'Carmagnole'. A public competition was ruled out because it would take too long, so Dietrich turned to Rouget de l'Isle, who was known to be both a poet and a musician. Although, or perhaps because, he had drunk a great deal of wine, Rouget de l'Isle agreed. He returned to his lodgings in the rue de la Mésange and worked with such intensity that by the morning of 26 April he had both text and music ready for performance. The same company reassembled that evening to hear Mayor Dietrich give the work's first performance, accompanied by his niece Louise on the harpsichord.[83]

As hardly anyone living in the developed world has not heard the 'Marseillaise' in some form or another, little needs to be said to explain its immediate and enduring impact. So far as the words were concerned, their author wrote that once he had thought of the first ('Allons'), all the others fell into place without resistance. It seems likely that at least some of the phrases came from the contemporary political scene in Strasbourg. For example, the injunction of the chorus, 'Aux armes!' (To arms!), had appeared already in an address from the local Jacobin club published when the declaration of war became known.[84] The phrase 'enfants de la patrie', which immediately follows the opening 'Allons', was the name given to battalions of volunteers, including the one from Strasbourg commanded by Dietrich's son.[85] Rather more remotely, the notorious command to 'drench the soil with impure blood' first appeared in an anti-British pamphlet published during the Seven Years War.[86] As for the music, despite claims made for this or that predecessor, no one has been able to prove that Rouget de l'Isle did not compose it himself.[87]

The first public performance came on the Sunday after its composition, 29 April, when the band of the Strasbourg National Guard played it on the Place d'Armes as eight battalions of their comrades were reviewed prior to marching off to war. The intention of the performance was both to encourage the troops and to recruit more volunteers.[88] By that time, copies had already been sent to the capital, and among the recipients was Rouget de l'Isle's friend and mentor Grétry. It was from the south, however, that the real breakthrough came. How the song reached Marseille remains a mystery. What is known is that on 22 June the Jacobins of Marseille organised a banquet in honour of visitors from the Montpellier branch. During the sing-along that brought the evening to a close, a Jacobin called

Claude-Joseph Rouget de l'Isle Sings His 'Battle Hymn for the Army of the Rhine' at Strasbourg on the Evening of 26 April 1792. In fact, it was the mayor of Strasbourg, Dietrich, who sang it first. Although the most famous depiction, this painting by Isidore Pils dates from 1849.

Étienne François Mireur sang the 'Battle Hymn for the Army of the Rhine' with 'electrifying' effect. The Jacobins decided to begin and end each of their sessions with it, and it was also taken up by the local National Guard.

When 400-odd volunteers marched off to Paris on 28 June to lend some muscle to their fellow radicals in what was to become the terminal struggle with the monarchy, they too sang the 'Battle Hymn' before leaving. As they marched their way through France, they sang it again and again, and were still singing it when they reached Paris, where they lost no opportunity to advertise its wonderful ability to mobilise revolutionary ardour.[89] Arriving on 30 July, they were just in time to join the assault on the Tuileries Palace on 10 August. One of the assailants made his way to Marie Antoinette's bedroom, where he found his comrades-in-arms tearing the room apart and throwing anything portable out of the window. To distract them from destroying the royal harpsichord—an exquisite object beautifully decorated with pictures—he sat down at the keyboard and played what was now becoming known as the 'Marseillaise'. They all joined in and spared the instrument. What happened to the instrument after this performance is not known.[90]

It was symptomatic of the French Revolution's fatal capacity for self-laceration that the first achievement of the 'Marseillaise' was to excite attacks against fellow Frenchmen. However, the tune also fulfilled its original purpose of providing a battle hymn for the armies. It was badly needed. Predictions that the war against the German powers would be quick and easy had been confounded almost at once. When the French invaders of the Austrian Netherlands ran into the enemy, far from proving to be the invincible freedom fighters they fancied themselves, they turned around and ran away, murdering their own general into the bargain. By late summer of 1792 the Prussians began a slow, cautious but apparently irresistible invasion through Champagne, and on 20 September they were confronted at Valmy by a French army. After an inconclusive artillery exchange, the Prussian commander, the duke of Brunswick, ordered the retreat.

Just how much of a contribution to the morale of the revolutionary soldiers was made by their singing 'Ça ira' and the 'Marseillaise' cannot be assessed. But certainly contemporaries believed it was important. When General Kellermann asked the government in Paris for permission to have a Te Deum sung, he was told that 'the Te Deum of the Republic is our national anthem known as the "Marseillaise": that is the song most worthy to reach the ears of a free Frenchman!'[91] As Mona Ozouf has written, the tune was now inseparable from the Revolution, 'spontaneously chosen by a whole people who, in doing so, seemed rather to have created it than to have adopted it'.[92] Two months later, on 16 November 1792 at the battle of Jemappes in the Austrian Netherlands, the singing of the new national anthem by hard-pressed French soldiers was given credit for turning the tide on three separate occasions.

The most crucial came when General Dumouriez rallied his troops by shouting: 'Forwards, my children! There is Jemappes! There is the enemy! Use cold steel! Use the bayonet! That's the way to smash them, that's the way to win!' With that, he put his hat on the point of his sabre, waved it in the air and started singing the 'Marseillaise'.[93] The Austrians duly succumbed. Four months later they were back again, reinforced and taking the war more seriously. Again Dumouriez invoked vocal support: 'If the enemy crosses the Meuse, close ranks, fix bayonets, sing the "Marseillaise", and you will be victorious'.[94] On this occasion, alas, it was not enough: the revolutionary army was routed at Neerwinden on 18 March 1793 and Dumouriez defected to the enemy.

Still, he was not the only revolutionary commander to believe in the power of music. At Cambrai on 7 July 1793, the commanding general read out the new constitution to the massed ranks of the Army of the North, and then 'on the spot I began to sing the "Marseillaise"; I can think of nothing to compare with the rapidity with which the song could be heard on all sides, with an inspiring effect. All the songs, all the patriotic airs, then followed; and it was only after two hours of republican joy that the troops' enthusiasm gave way'.[95] Eyewitness accounts all agree: the French soldiers were always singing—in camp, on the march and in battle, assisted by the hundreds of thousands of revolutionary songbooks dispatched from Paris.[96] From all over the war zone came tributes such as 'without the "Marseillaise", I'll fight even if outnumbered two to one, but with the "Marseillaise" I'll accept odds of four to one'; 'the "Marseillaise" enlightens, inspires and cheers at the same time; it would be enough to subjugate the entire youth of Brabant'; 'send me a thousand men or a copy of the "Marseillaise"'; 'I have won a battle because the "Marseillaise" commanded with me'; 'the "Marseillaise" has been worth 100,000 extra soldiers'.[97] That last remark was made by Lazare Carnot, 'the organiser of victory' in 1794. Even more authoritative was the view of General Bonaparte, who in 1797 told the Paris Conservatoire that, as it was music that exerted most influence on the passions, the government should do everything possible to promote it. However, when he himself seized power in 1799, the revolutionary songs of the past were no longer in fashion.

The revolutionaries did not just sing on the battlefield. They sang in the streets, in pubs and clubs, in the National Convention, and at the innumerable revolutionary festivals. On 24 November 1793 the National Convention ordered that the 'Marseillaise' should be sung at all republican spectacles (and there were a great many of them), on the *décadi* (the day designated for rest at the end of the revolutionary ten-day week) and 'whenever the people require it'.[98] They sang it around the guillotine as the severed heads dropped into the basket, they even sang it as they *went* to the guillotine. On 31 October 1793, for example, a group of prominent Girondins, including Brissot, Gensonné and Vergniaud, sang the 'Marseillaise' lustily as a convoy of tumbrels took them to the Place de la Révolution (later renamed the Place de la Concorde), the place of execution.[99]

As this musical exchange suggests, the warring factions were locked in a deadly competition to present themselves as representing the popular will. Their inability to contemplate a pluralist regime in which honest disagreement could thrive created a Manichaean world in which absolute good struggled with absolute evil. So every revolutionary symbol, whether conceptual (liberty, equality and fraternity), visual (tricolour cockade, cap of liberty, liberty tree) or aural ('Ça ira', 'Marseillaise') was hotly contested. Far more dangerous than the Austrian, Prussian or British enemies outside France was the fifth column inside the country, many revolutionaries believed. Much more seditious than the declared opponents of the Revolution, such as Marie Antoinette, these false friends spouted the rhetoric of the Revolution while secretly plotting its downfall. If they were not eliminated, in this view, a counter-revolutionary Armageddon was inevitable.

The language of the 'Marseillaise' was perfectly suited to a political culture that combined a sense of absolute rectitude with violent paranoia. It is surely the most bloodthirsty national anthem ever written.

> Come all ye citizens and fellow-countrymen,
> The day of glory is at hand!
> See how the tyrant's standard is raised against us,
> See how the bloody flag's raised aloft,
> See how the bloody flag's raised aloft,
> Hear how in the countryside
> The fierce soldiers roar,
> They are coming into your very arms
> To slaughter your children and your womenfolk.

Every verse is followed by a chorus, whose last two lines demand:

> Let all our furrows flow
> With their so tainted blood.

Of the Revolution's enemies, the worst fate does not await the 'horde of slaves' preparing to invade. On the contrary, generosity is commended for 'these sad victims who unwillingly took up arms against us'. But the parricidal traitors *inside* France—'these blood-thirsty despots, these henchmen of Bouillé, all these merciless tigers, rending their mothers' breasts!'—would receive no mercy.[100] It is their impure blood that will be drenching French soil.

Ironically, the author of the 'Marseillaise' was not an extremist *sans-culotte* but a moderate constitutional royalist who was appalled by the subsequent radicalisation of the Revolution. Imprisoned during the Terror, he only narrowly escaped with his life. Of the others who attended the first performance of the 'Marseillaise' on 26 April 1792, Dietrich, Luckner and Broglie were all guillotined.[101]

When the terrorist regime of Robespierre ended on 27 July 1794, the pendulum swung abruptly toward the right. Once repression was lifted, at least for the time being, the polarising effect of the last two terrible years became apparent. With the Jacobin Terror discredited by its dysfunctional violence, there was a powerful reaction from the right. It found a voice with the song 'Le Réveil du peuple contre les terroristes' (The People Rise Up against the Terrorists), first sung in January 1795. Neither words nor music are especially memorable, but they were turned into a potent symbol of counter-terror, if not counter-revolution, by vigorous effort on the part of right-wing activists, especially the young men known collectively as the *jeunesse dorée* (gilded youth).[102]

A favourite tactic was to force actors and singers known to have been Jacobin supporters to interrupt their performances to sing the song.[103] On 11 July 1795 a crowd on the Place du Carrousel intercepted General Menou and a detachment of soldiers on their way to change the guard at the Louvre. The military band's attempt to play the 'Marseillaise' was halted by threats to destroy their instruments if they did not play 'Le Réveil du peuple' instead. After a long stand-off, during which Menou vainly sought advice from the National Convention (they told him to use his discretion), he took the better part of valour. 'Le Réveil du peuple' was played to tumultuous applause and shouts of 'Long live the nation! Long live General Menou! Down with the "Marseillaise"! Down with the Jacobins!'[104] This kind of counter-revolutionary demonstration came to an abrupt halt on 5 October 1795 when an attempted royalist *coup d'état* was crushed by General Bonaparte's 'whiff of grapeshot'. Before the end of the year, the new executive—the Directory—had banned the playing of 'Le Réveil du peuple' and ordered that at every theatrical performance either 'Ça ira' or the 'Marseillaise' should be sung by the assembled company.[105]

One final characteristic of the 'Marseillaise' needs to be noted, revealed by the sixth and last verse. This is usually sung slowly and softly, partly to set up a final *fortissimo* rendering of the chorus and partly to emphasize the especially solemn nature of the words:

> Sacred love of the fatherland,
> Lead and uphold our brave avengers.
> Liberty, beloved liberty,
> Fight alongside your defenders!
> Fight alongside your defenders!
> Beneath our flags, may victory
> Answer the call of your warlike cries,
> And may your dying enemies
> Witness your triumph and our glory!

This is one of the earliest examples of what was to become a very common phenomenon in the century that followed: the sacralisation of the nation. The Revolution had abandoned all the belief systems of the old regime, most notably monarchism and Catholicism, and needed to find an alternative source of legitimacy and loyalty. Of the possible candidates, 'state' was too abstract and 'people' too vague. 'Patrie' (fatherland) had better credentials and was certainly popular after 1789, but was rather too passive and elitist. It was 'nation' that became the dominant concept. After the Revolution broke out, everything was 'national', as in National Assembly, National Gendarmerie, National Guard, national education, national cockade, national flag. The universal rallying cry was 'Vive la nation!'[106]

Where the French led, the rest of Europe followed, albeit in many cases very slowly. The British had already taken several steps in the direction of sacralising the nation—by adopting a national flag, a national symbol (Britannia) and a national anthem. But in Great Britain two other powerful institutions commanded loyalty, namely, the king and the church. One of the secrets of George III's popular success was that he managed to align the monarchy and the church with the national interest to form a tripod of immense stability. The nation was sacralised in Great Britain too, but there it had to share the altar with its two more ancient partners.

In the more rootless and shifting political landscapes of the European continent, sacralisation of the nation more closely copied the French example. In the land of its birth, the revolutionary national anthem has had a chequered history. Ignored by Napoleon, the 'Marseillaise' was sung when the allies invaded France in 1814 and again during Napoleon's 'Hundred Days' of rule after his return from exile in Elba the following year. Proscribed once more by the returning Bourbons in 1815, it resurfaced whenever France experienced one of its periodic bouts of instability, most audibly during the July Revolution of 1830.

No less a person than Hector Berlioz left a graphic account of its undimmed power to move a crowd. Caught up in a mob of demonstrators in the Galerie Colbert, he formed an impromptu choir to sing the 'Marseillaise' from the first-floor balcony of a haberdasher's shop: 'Almost at once the seething mass at our feet grew quiet and a holy stillness fell upon them. It was like the silence in St. Peter's Square when the Pope gives his blessing, *urbi et orbi*, from the pontifical balcony'. However, the watching crowd remained silent when it came to the refrain until Berlioz shouted out: 'Confound you all—sing!' The result was shattering, as four to five thousand people in the confined space formed by the arcade let rip with 'Aux armes, citoyens!' Berlioz recorded: 'I literally sank to the floor, while our little band, aghast at the explosion it had provoked, stood dumbfounded, silent as birds after a thunderclap'.[107]

During the war scare of 1840, the anthem was heard once again on the streets of Paris, as enormous crowds gathered to demand that the government avenge the humiliation suffered at the hands of the British in the Middle East. On 28 July, King Louis Philippe and his government wisely stayed away from the ceremony inaugurating the column raised in memory of the victims of the street fighting of the July Revolution ten years earlier. Their absence did not prevent 80,000 National Guardsmen from marching on the Tuileries, singing the 'Marseillaise' as they went, punctuated with abuse of the British and the Prussians. Arriving at the royal palace, they obliged the king to appear on the balcony and the band to play the 'Marseillaise' once again.[108] The song's undiminished power to press emotive buttons was given visual form by the artist Nicolas Toussaint Charlet,

La Marseillaise by Nicolas Toussaint Charlet (1840).

whose lithograph entitled *La Marseillaise* showed a soldier sitting on the shoulders of a burly worker and tearing down a poster bearing the words 'Treaties of 1815', while another soldier points to the words 'Our old frontiers or death!' scrawled on the wall.[109]

Until the socialist Internationale became popular toward the end of the nineteenth century, the 'Marseillaise' was unrivalled as a revolutionary anthem. Wherever insurrection erupted, the summons 'Aux armes citoyens!' could be heard. The following example of this power commends itself because it stems from a notorious Francophobe. Richard Wagner spent the night of Saturday–Sunday, 5–6 May 1849, as a lookout from the top of the tower of the Church of the Cross (Kreuzkirche) on the Old Market in Dresden. His task was to keep an eye on the movements of the Prussian troops trying to suppress the rising that had begun three days earlier and to restore the control of the king of Saxony. Wagner whiled away the time discussing the relative merits of classical Greek and Christian views of the world 'to the accompaniment of Prussian bullets splattering against the tower walls'. Eventually, the Prussians stopped shooting and Wagner stopped talking. In his autobiography Wagner recorded:

> Sunday May 6th was one of the most beautiful days of that year; I was awakened by the song of a nightingale wafting up from the Schütze garden close beneath us; a sacred calm and tranquillity lay over the city and the broad expanse of its surroundings I could see from my vantage point: toward dawn a light fog settled on the outskirts: penetrating through it we suddenly heard, from the area of the Tharandt road, the music of the 'Marseillaise' clearly and distinctly; as the source of the sound came closer, the mists dispersed and the blood-red rising sun glittered upon the guns of a long column marching into the city. It was impossible to resist the impression of this unfolding sight . . . these were no fewer than several thousand well armed and organized men from the Erzgebirge, mostly miners, who had arrived to help in the defence of Dresden. Soon we saw them march into the old market square, outside the city hall and, after a jubilant greeting by the people, encamp there to rest after their march.[110]

Alas, the Prussians were not impressed. By Tuesday evening they had regained control of Dresden, and on Wednesday Wagner escaped from the city, together with the Russian anarchist Mikhail Bakunin. With the help of his friend Franz Liszt, he then fled to exile in Switzerland and did not return to Germany for eleven years.[111]

In the twentieth century, the 'Marseillaise' reached an audience greater than ever before, thanks to its appearance in a number of popular films. The most militant was *La Marseillaise* of 1938, produced, directed and scripted by Jean Renoir. Dedicated to the Popular Front, it presented a bottom-up account of the fall of the old regime, seen through the eyes of the men of Marseille who marched on Paris to destroy the monarchy, singing their song as they crossed France. Partly financed by the Communist trades union organisation, the CGT (Confédération Générale du Travail), the film was very much *parti pris*, but it did allow the supporters of the monarchy to sing 'Richard ô mon roi' as they prepared to die in defence of their king.[112]

Probably the most widely heard rendition of the 'Marseillaise' was sung in one of the most iconic films of the century, *Casablanca* (1942). In Rick's Café a group of carousing German officers sing 'The Watch on the Rhine' with raucous brutality. Victor Laszlo (played by Paul Henreid), the Czech resistance fighter who has escaped from a concentration camp, asks the band to retaliate by playing the 'Marseillaise'. Rick (Humphrey Bogart) nods his agreement, and soon the entire café is on its feet, drowning out the Germans. The French may have lost the war ignominiously, but their musical victory is complete.

Liberation in Italy

To the sound of the 'Marseillaise', the French Revolution had shaken the old regimes so hard that their teeth rattled loose, and in some cases fell out. The restoration imposed by the Congress of Vienna in 1815 did no more than stretch a thin veneer of traditional rhetoric across a deeply fractured continent. So intense was the legitimacy deficit that sooner or later fragmentation was inevitable. The biggest fissures were vertical, between one nation and another. By their own aggressive nationalism and ruthless exploitation of the countries they claimed to be liberating, the French revolutionaries gave an enormous boost to counter-nationalisms. On the other hand, the power, glamour and excitement of the French example caused a reaction of envy and even admiration fused with hatred—a witches' brew of ambivalence.

Nowhere did music have a more important role to play in this process than in Italy, for its culture was drenched in music: 'There is singing in the squares, in the streets and on the canals. Merchants sing as they sell their wares, labourers sing as they leave their work, gondoliers sing as they wait for their masters', claimed the Venetian librettist and dramatist Carlo Goldoni.[113] At the centre of social life stood the opera house, 'the focal symbolic building at the heart of all Italian cities', according to David Kimbell.[114] It often included not just a stage and auditorium but also cafés, restaurants, gambling casinos and public spaces where people could just meet and socialise. Many people went four or five times a week.[115] Nowhere else in Europe and at no other time in European history has so much opera been performed as in Italy between 1815 and 1860. In Milan there were six theatres in which opera was performed regularly; in Naples there were five plus one more occasional venue.[116]

Looking back from 1869, a contemporary observed: 'No one who did not live in Italy before 1848 can imagine what the opera house meant in those days. It was the only outlet for public life, and everyone took part. The success of a new opera was a capital event that stirred to its depths the town lucky enough to have witnessed it, and word of it ran all over Italy.'[117] Modern commentators have variously compared the role of opera in Italian society at that time to football and television today.[118] From the opera house, music spilled over into the public sphere, as the latest tune was played by barrel organs on the streets and military bands in parks, by pianos in the home and even organs in church. At a wedding on Lake Maggiore, Figaro's entrance aria from Rossini's *The Barber of Seville* was played at the elevation of the Host.[119]

In 1815 the peace-makers redrew the map of Italy with no concern whatsoever for the inhabitants. Theoretically, the south was ruled by the Bourbons of Naples and Sicily ('The Kingdom of the Two Sicilies'), the centre by the pope, the northwest by the king of Sardinia and the rest by the Austrian Habsburgs. In reality, the Austrians controlled the entire peninsula, as they demonstrated convincingly in 1820–21 by intervening to crush insurrections in Naples and Piedmont. Considering Italy to be a mere 'geographical expression' and opining that 'Italian affairs do not exist', the all-powerful Austrian chancellor Prince Metternich set out 'to extinguish the spirit of Italian unity and ideas about constitutions'.[120] Although highly intelligent, he failed to understand the power of Italian nationalism. General Heinrich Count von Bellegarde, who had led the Austrians to victory over the French in Italy in 1813–15, knew better, informing Metternich in 1815 that 'the men of spirit and letters are trying to write with a common purpose, which under an academic form hides the political aim of making Italy its own master, an idea which is disturbing even as a Utopia'.[121]

Bellegarde was referring to the written word, but the Italian patriots knew that music mattered too. Giuseppe Mazzini, the most influential of them all (with the possible exception of Garibaldi), assigned 'a sacred mission' to composers, telling them that 'the art which is entrusted to you is intimately connected with the progress of civilisation, and can be its spirit, its soul, its sacred perfume'.[122] The response came from musicians and audiences alike. In 1828 the German radical Heinrich Heine visited the main opera house in Milan, La Scala, where he overheard an Englishman telling an Italian that his Italian countrymen seemed 'to be dead to everything except music; this is the only thing able to excite you'. The Italian rejected the slur: 'Ah, Italy sits amid her ruins, dreaming elegiacally, and if sometimes, at the memory of some song, she awakens of a sudden and springs wildly up, this enthusiasm is not just for the song itself, but rather for old memories and emotions which the song awakened, which Italy carries in her heart, and which now pour out in a torrent—and that is the meaning of that mad uproar which you heard at La Scala'.[123]

His insight was confirmed by another foreign visitor of high intelligence, Stendhal, who additionally noted the dialectic of nationalism at work. On the one hand, the Italians viewed the music of the Germans (among whom they included the Austrians, significantly referring to them not as *Austriaci* but as *Tedeschi*) as academic, pedantic, boring, and devoid of the essence of music, which is melody. 'German music' (*musica tedesca*) was a term of abuse, short-hand for the inability to write properly for the human voice.[124] As they could not write tunes, the Germans resorted to excessive harmony and counterpoint.[125] Paisiello remarked that because the Germans were bad singers, they had to rely on harmony to make their musical effects, whereas the Italians were good singers and could rely on melody to accomplish everything they wanted.[126] According to Stendhal, even Mozart was regarded by Italians as 'a crude barbarian, a vandal poised for invasion across the sacred frontiers of classical art'.[127] This prejudice was part of a wider aversion: 'The Italians are constantly poking fun at the Germans; they think them stupid, and never tire of inventing comic anecdotes about them'.[128] On the other hand, this sense of cultural superiority was exacerbated by daily reminders of their political enslavement by German-speakers, a humiliation intensified by the knowledge that their masters had a very low opinion of Italy: 'The land of idlers, buffoons, spongers, thieves, bandits, dandies and eunuchs'.[129]

Ironically, the first major composer to personify the Italian cause was an admirer of German music. This was the charismatic Rossini. Far from thinking Mozart a 'barbarian', he paid him the following perceptive tribute: 'The Germans have always been at every time the greatest harmonists and the Italians the greatest melodists. But from the moment that the North produced a Mozart, we of the South were beaten on our own ground, because this man rises above both nations, uniting in himself all the charms of Italian melody and all the profundity of German harmony'.[130]

By uniting first Italy and then all Europe in unanimous admiration of his own music, Rossini gave his fellow countrymen a cultural icon to be paraded as evidence of their continuing domination of music. Edward Dent put it well, in his classic study of the rise of Romantic opera, when he wrote that before Rossini, Italian music was regional (Neapolitan or Venetian), but after him it was national.[131] By moving to Paris for long periods, amassing a vast fortune, retiring early and turning conservative, Rossini got out of step with the Italian nationalist movement. But not before he had given the world an example of what Stendhal called 'modern national idealism'. *The Italian Girl in Algiers* was written in 1813 when Rossini was only twenty-one and is still in the repertory. In Act Two Isabella sings to the Italian slaves she is trying to rescue:

> If the sacred words 'fatherland, duty
> And honour' speak to your heart
> Then learn from someone else
> How to show yourself to be a true Italian;
> . . .
> Think of your fatherland, and boldly
> Do your duty:
> Behold throughout Italy
> Examples of daring and valour
> Are reborn once more.

As the Italian nationalist movement became more militant, so did the music that accompanied it. On 25 July 1844 nine survivors of a failed invasion of Naples were marched to the place of execution outside the town of Cosenza. As they reached the valley, whose sides were thronged with a huge silent crowd, the defiant prisoners sang a chorus from Saverio Mercadante's opera *Donna Caritea:*

> Who dies for the fatherland
> Has lived long enough.
> The laurel crown
> Will never fade.
> Rather than languish
> Under tyranny,
> It is better to die
> In the flower of our years.[132]

Recited, these words would have been poignant; when sung, they had a galvanising effect. So powerfully did Mercadante convey the self-sacrificing sentiment that the chorus became an established part of the patriotic repertoire. During the siege of Venice five years later, a soldier having his shattered arm amputated sang it as an aural anaesthetic.[133]

After 1815, as indeed at any time in Italy in the past, the heavy pen of the censor hovered over every librettist, waiting for anything inflammatory. A popular evasive technique was to set the opera in a period or region so remote as to avoid any topical relevance, while at the same time allowing the audience to make the necessary connection. A good example in every sense was Vincenzo Bellini's *Norma*, first performed at La Scala in 1831 with the legendary Giuditta Pasta in the title role. Her opening aria, 'Casta diva', quickly became one of the most popular of all soprano arias. Although the plot is centred on the familiar eternal triangle—Norma loves Pollione but Pollione loves Adalgisa—the action takes place in Roman Gaul and pits the native druids against the occupation forces. No great adjustment was necessary to cast the latter as the Austrians and the former as the oppressed Italians, especially not when Norma is summoning the Gauls to throw off the foreign yoke with an impassioned appeal beginning 'Guerra! Guerra!' (War! War!).

As anyone will confirm who has heard a good operatic chorus give this all it's got, the effect is sensational.[134] For example, when the revolutionaries ejected the Bourbon troops from Sicily at the end of January 1848, a ceremony of thanksgiving was held in Palermo Cathedral at which tricolour flags were blessed to strains of 'Guerra! Guerra!' and were carried up the aisle to the high altar accompanied by a passage from *I Puritani.* The latter opera was also by Bellini, who was a local boy born at Catania. When he died in Paris in 1835 at the age of thirty-three, the public lamentation was intense and politically charged: 'The delicate Bellini became a battle-cry against the Bourbons, almost as if they had murdered him'.[135] Another fervent Italian patriot of Sicilian origin, Giuseppe La Farina, delivered an elegy in which he represented Bellini's works as both laments from a people oppressed by a ruthless power and a summons for unity.[136]

In the year of revolution, 1848, the power of Italian music was tried, tested and found wanting, though its ability to inspire enthusiasm was never in doubt. In February 1848 during a performance at Parma of *Orazi e Curiazi,* with music by Mercadante and words by Salvadore Cammarano, a riot broke out when the lines 'Let us swear to triumph for the fatherland or to die in the attempt' were sung, the audience spilling out onto the streets to demonstrate.[137] The duke of Parma fled into exile. Later that year, with the revolutions now truly under way, Cammarano wrote to the most popular Italian opera composer of the day, Giuseppe Verdi: 'If there burns in you as in me the desire to treat the most glorious epoch in Italian history, that of the Lombard League, nothing could be easier than to construct around the battle of Legnano the same dramatic framework as is offered by Méry's drama *La battaglia di Tolosa*'.[138] The episode to which Cammarano was referring—the battle of Legnano—did indeed have a topical resonance. In 1176 the united forces of the north Italian towns comprising the Lombard League inflicted a decisive defeat on one of the greatest of all the German emperors, Frederick I (Barbarossa), thus putting an end to his attempts to extend his control south of the Alps. As a national foundation myth, it had a great deal to recommend it—unity created out of diversity overcoming the detested northern barbarian invader.

Verdi was in a receptive mood when Cammarano's letter arrived. Very much a man of the left, he had moved in liberal and nationalist circles from the time he arrived in Milan in 1839 at the age of twenty-five. Among other indications of his political allegiance was his adoption of a beard in the style of Mazzini; he also named his first child Virginia after the heroine of Alfieri's republican drama of the same name.[139] Verdi's first major success was *Nabucco,* first performed at La Scala in 1842. Depicting the liberation of the children of Israel from their Babylonian captivity, it bristled with patriotic references, especially in the 'Chorus of the Hebrew Slaves' ('Va, pensiero, sull'ali dorati') which quickly established itself as one of the most popular of all operatic choruses. When Verdi was buried on 27 February 1901, it was sung at the cemetery by a choir 820-strong conducted by Toscanini.[140] It is still treated by Italians 'with that mixture of condescension and throaty awe that marks a truly national monument', as Roger Parker has put it.[141]

The continuing dispute among historians as to how aware contemporary audiences were of these topical references can never be resolved conclusively. That the censors allowed performances of *Nabucco* and other operas with lightly coded political messages does not prove that those messages did not exist and were not received by their intended targets. All it shows is that the relatively easy-going Austrians—who liked going to the opera themselves—concluded they had more to lose by banning a performance than permitting it. All they asked was that a measure of discretion was exercised. In 1847, for example, the Milan commissioner of police reprimanded the conductor Angelo Mariani after a performance of *Nabucco* 'for having given to Verdi's music an expression too evidently rebellious and hostile to the Imperial Government'.[142]

In 1848 all censorship was swept aside, so Verdi and his librettist, Cammarano, no longer had to dissemble. The result was *La Battaglia di Legnano*, which received its premiere at the Teatro Argentina at Rome on 27 January 1849. The political atmosphere could hardly have been more highly charged. The pope had fled the city at the end of the previous November, leaving an anarchic situation from which a republic emerged in fits and starts. Just six days before the first performance, elections had been held to establish a constitutional convention. Almost everywhere else in Italy, the counter-revolution appeared to have triumphed, so the opera was as much an act of political defiance as a cultural event. By all accounts, the reception was ecstatic from the opening lines: as contingents from all over northern Italy gather in Milan to resist the German invader, the chorus sings:

> Long live Italy! A sacred pact
> Knits all her sons together:
> At last it has made of so many
> A single people of heroes!—

Repeatedly interrupted by applause, the work took a very long time to perform, not least because *the entire last Act* was encored (not an accolade granted to many new operas today, it can safely be conjectured).

Cammarano's libretto, written in close consultation with Verdi, showed that all the lessons of the French Revolution on how to mobilise a crowd had been learned. It highlighted the atrocities of the enemy ('The women and children murdered by the evil foe'), the defence of native soil ('Let us drive these savage beasts back to their native Danubian valley'), a determination to end alien oppression and achieve national liberation ('We swear to put an end to Italy's wrongs, Let our cities be free and ours again'), a fanatical hatred of the enemy and a determination to conquer or die ('Such hatred suffused with blood seethes . . . Sooner than retreat, rather than accept defeat, We swear to fall dead in battle'). Less French was the invocation of the God of Battles to come to the assistance of his chosen people ('Oh, my God, make them like a wheel, And as the stubble before the wind'). Prominent throughout is the sacralisation of the nation, culminating in the death of the hero-martyr, but not before he has ensured victory for the Italians. He expires clutching the Italian flag with the words 'Italy is saved!'

Of course it would be naïve to suppose that Italy was unified by music. For all the enthusiasm generated by *La Battaglia di Legnano,* the Roman Republic did not last long. By the end of June 1849 French troops had restored the rule of Pope Pius IX. Yet at the very least it can be said that Italy was eventually united only because sufficient numbers of Italians were able to imagine a country created out of a common history and culture. This explains the difference between the history of Italy and the history of the Balkans. Without a common music, Italy might well have remained a 'geographical expression' but not a nation. The Italians who scribbled the graffito 'VERDI' on walls were making a double point—celebrating the composer as national icon and using his name as an acronym to link him to the only native ruler who might be able to eject the *Tedeschi*:

Vittorio
Emanuele
Re
D'
Italia

Eventually the day came for Vittorio Emanuele, king of Sardinia, to fulfill his mission. When his prime minister, Cavour, learned that the Austrians had taken the bait and declared war, he rushed to the window of his study and launched into Manrico's great aria from Verdi's *Il Trovatore:* 'Di quella pira' (From That Pyre).[143]

Deutschland, Deutschland, über Alles

North of the Alps, the 'barbarians' were also dreaming of national unity. To the fore in this exercise were musicians. If pride in German music went back deep into the eighteenth century, how much more was that the case after Haydn, Mozart, and Beethoven made their mark. In the first year of the nineteenth century, the leading music periodical of the day, the *Allgemeine Musikalische Zeitung* of Leipzig, acclaimed its special quality: profundity. While the French and Italians were content with the superficial delights provided by melody and rhythm, the Germans concentrated on harmony, for harmony is to music what logic is to philosophy, draughtsmanship to painting, and mathematics to architecture. And of course the greatest master of harmony and counterpoint of all time was Johann Sebastian Bach, 'the Homer of music'.[144]

Pride in German music and a corresponding tendency to disparage that of other nations were not confined to journalists. No less a person than Mozart, often paraded as a paragon of enlightened cosmopolitanism, displayed both. In Paris in the spring of 1778 he found that the taste of the French had improved somewhat since his last visit, because at least they could now bring themselves to listen to good music as well as bad, but 'to expect them to realise that their own music is bad or at least to notice the difference—Heaven preserve us! And their singing! Good Lord! Let me never hear a Frenchwoman singing Italian arias. I can forgive her if she screeches out her French trash, but not if she ruins good music! It's simply unbearable'. When it came to music, he concluded, 'The French are and always will be asses, and as they can do nothing themselves, they are obliged to have recourse to foreigners'. Rather more chilling was the vow he made when the prospect of a commission from 'these stupid Frenchmen' for an opera appeared: 'I tremble from head to foot with eagerness to teach the French more thoroughly to know, appreciate and fear the Germans'.[145]

Mozart's Francophobia became intense. He complained about the offhand way he was treated by the aristocrats who kept him waiting in a freezing room and then paid no attention when obliging him to play on a 'wretched, miserable pianoforte'. He complained about the rudeness shown by the 'detestably self-conceited' Parisians, adding, 'If this were a place where people had ears to hear, hearts to feel and some measure of understanding of and taste for music, these things would only make me laugh heartily; but, as it is (so far as music is concerned), I am surrounded by mere brute beasts'. In a particularly revealing passage in a letter to his father, he appealed to nation, God and family: 'I pray to God daily to give me grace to hold out here with fortitude and to do such honour to myself and to the whole German nation as will redound to His greater honour and glory; and that He will enable me to prosper and make a great deal of money, so that I may help you out of your present difficulties'.[146]

Mozart did not live to experience the military conquest of the German-speaking lands by the armies of the French Revolution and Napoleon. He would not have enjoyed the cultural imperialism that accompanied their political domination. The revolutionaries did not create German nationalism, but their strident assertion of French superiority in all departments certainly gave it a massive boost. For all their cosmopolitan principles, the French gave their Revolution and its military expansion such a pronounced national flavour that it could not help but arouse opposition based on a sense of separate—and opposing—nationality. Symptomatic of this sense of superiority was a disdainful attitude towards foreign languages: 'Italian suited to effeminate delights, German the organ of militarism and feudalism, Spanish the cant of the Inquisition, English once glorious and free, now the patter of despotism and the stock exchange'.[147]

This linguistic chauvinism of the French was accompanied by withering contempt for the character and culture of the foreigners they annexed or occupied. A disappointed French agent reported from western Germany in December 1792: 'The French are not liked here, as we flatter ourselves they are. Some individuals and some communities may wish for liberty, but the mass of the country, always reactionary and superstitious, regard those who govern them as privileged beings. They seem to like the yoke that degrades their spirit'.[148] As the burdens of military occupation intensified and with it German resistance, so did a mutually supportive sense of France's superiority and the inferiority of foreigners. As Robespierre told the National Convention with majestic condescension: 'The French appear to have advanced beyond the rest of the human race by two millennia; one is tempted to regarded them as a different species'.[149]

When Robespierre made that claim in May 1794, France was in the throes of the Terror, an episode that convinced most other Europeans that what really distinguished this 'different species' was barbarism. Two more decades of bloodletting did nothing to improve the French image. Indeed, the powerful German contribution to the eventual defeat of Napoleon in 1813–15 added military self-confidence to what was already a strongly developed sense of cultural superiority.

French domination of Germany collapsed to the sound of much triumphalist music. The best of it was written by Carl Maria von Weber, who—like many other composers of the period—found the patriotic verses of Theodor Körner particularly congenial. Their appeal had as much to do with the circumstances of the poet's death as with their literary quality. Körner had been killed in action as a member of the Lützow Freikorps, the most glamorous of the volunteer units raised to fight the French in the 'war of liberation' of 1813. In the year before his death he had written a series of patriotic poems, published posthumously as *Lyre and Sword* and probably the most popular single collection of the nineteenth century, being reprinted scores of times. Aided by Weber's musical setting, one of the poems—'Lützow's Wild, Audacious Pursuit'—achieved universal currency, being heard as far afield as China (or so Weber claimed).[150]

After 1815, and especially after the Karlsbad Decrees of 1819, the authorities in all the German states sought to stifle the expression of nationalist opinion. They made the understandable but egregious error of supposing that liberalism and nationalism were two sides of the same coin and were both equally subversive. Denied the opportunity to assert their cause through politics, German nationalists turned to culture. Once again the dialectic of nationalism manifested itself, now in even more virulent form. In the pole position as 'the other' was of course France, now regarded as the 'hereditary enemy' *(Erbfeind)*. Two examples from the mid-1830s will convey the flavour of Francophobe discourse.

An anonymous author in the *Museum der eleganten Welt*, after a long attack on the insufferable arrogance of the French and their constant

At the Advance Post by Georg Friedrich Kersting (1814). Kersting provides a war memorial for his three friends, all of whom were killed fighting the French in 1813. The poet Theodor Körner is sitting with his back resting against the oak tree. The colours of the Lützow Freikorps—black, red, gold—became a symbol of national liberation and eventually the colours of the German flag.

prating about the superiority of their music, offered the following typical metaphor: 'Even if one must concede that the French have talent, even a lot of talent, it is still the case that they will always remain French: impulsive, volatile, as effervescent as champagne—and just as liable to go flat, and with no real content beyond titillating charm'.[151] Another gastronomic metaphor was supplied at about the same time by Johannes Fesky in the prominent journal *Cäcilia*:

> French music, when it is trying to be serious, is a half-way house between German and Italian. Profound emotions are alien to it. It is neither cold, nor warm; its nature is really like that of a frog. It is incapable of depicting even the common emotions, hatred and love. It takes its form from the Italians without their elegance . . . It is rather like an agreeable conversation, which only swirls around superficial thought and feeling, which provides pleasant entertainment after a big dinner or intense intellectual exercise, and which aids the digestion.[152]

When abusing French culture, Germans frequently used the adjective *wälsch,* an untranslatable word that had the advantage of extending the field of fire to embrace the Italians too, for it denoted all Latin culture. For a long time, however, the Italians were very much a subsidiary target, for the good reason that they were deemed to present much less of a threat. Every now and again German journalists indulged their incorrigible masochism by reporting with gloomy relish insulting incidents and anecdotes prompted by Italian malice or ignorance: of the Roman aristocrat, for example, who asked a distinguished visiting musician in the service of the elector of the Palatinate whether his master owned a carriage; of the Neapolitan lady who observed, after meeting several rich and educated Germans, that 'Germany must be a big town'; of the Milanese music critic who gave Italy the credit for Mozart, Haydn and Gluck because they had Italian teachers; and so on.[153]

This sort of thing did not require a major response so long as Italian music was manifestly inferior and less popular. It was quite a different matter when the German music scene was conquered by Italian opera in the second decade of the nineteenth century. Just as Beethoven seemed to be setting the seal on German supremacy, the phenomenal success, as rapid as it was complete, of Bellini, Donizetti and above all Rossini provoked an acute crisis of confidence among the German intelligentsia. As in Italy, opera was not confined to a small elite. In every German town of any size, the opera house was both the social and cultural centre, embracing a substantial proportion of the population.[154]

Consequently, when the popularity of the Italians drove home-grown products from the stage, German intellectuals were outraged. In 1828, looking back on ten years and more of Italian domination, the Bavarian critic Franz Stoepel lamented: 'Must we Germans always succumb to foreign influence? No sooner do we free ourselves from the fetters of French literature than Italian composers bind us in chains which are even heavier, contest our national identity on our own soil, rob us of what is our own and tell us what we shall enjoy.'[155] The counter-attack was not confined to praising German music at the expense of Italian. Certainly great delight was taken in deriding the banal melodies and rum-ti-tum rhythms of 'ice-cream opera'. One of the better-natured parodies was provided by Carl Maria von Weber in his semi-autobiographical novel *Tonkünstlers Leben* (A Musician's Life), in which he imagined the instruments of the orchestra chatting among themselves, moaning at the prospect of being given another Beethoven symphony, which left them utterly exhausted, and pleading for an Italian opera instead, during which they could drop off to sleep every now and again.[156]

Other critics were less charitable. This is how a contributor to *Cäcilia* countered a claim from an Italian that his country had invented music:

> You say that Italian music is the mother of all music. That may well be. But a mother is usually a woman, consequently she is also subject to the fate of that sex, which, as is well known, increases in talent and beauty only to a certain age and then with every year becomes richer in wrinkles and poorer in spirit . . . The music which lives in Germany is of the male sex, has a serious nature, is somewhat imbued with Protestantism, and therefore likes to ask the question—why?—and, when creating, thinks more about what is right than about what is beautiful . . . for that reason, the German deserves the place of honour.[157]

Even less appealing was the familiar tendency to extend disapproval of Italian music to contempt for the Italian national character. A good example was supplied by the Prussian critic Adolph Bernhard Marx in his review of a magnificently successful new production of Rossini's *Konradino* at Berlin in 1827. Rossini has now triumphed over everyone, he reported; he has anchored half the world to his cause; he is the pride of his nation, the joy of the public—and the master of the lower depths of mindless sensuality. He should not be made to carry all the blame himself, Marx added, for all he was doing was to express the sins of his virtually stateless, dependent, intellectually subservient people, who had now succumbed utterly to selfishness and sensuality.[158]

This was a constant theme of German critics, as they found themselves having to trudge off to the opera houses again and again to watch another triumphant Rossini first night. One cannot help but wonder whether their toes tapped in spite of themselves. Three years earlier, in 1824, Marx had used a performance of *The Barber of Seville* to launch a general attack on Italy's musical culture. The Italians had no public life anymore, he wrote, they were hopelessly decadent, egoistic, looking only for entertainment and pleasure, even needing to have ballets between the acts of an opera to keep them diverted. They paid scant attention to what was happening on the stage anyway, concentrating most of their faint energies on gossiping, gambling, drinking chocolate and making love, breaking off only occasionally to cheer some banal little aria screeched out by the prima donna of the hour.[159]

Because the French and the Italians impinged most on German culture, they attracted most of the abuse and served most often as sounding boards for the identification of those special German virtues of seriousness and profundity. But with ever-increasing insistence after 1815, a new target hove into view in the shape of the British. Once welcomed as the providers of an alternative model to France, especially in the form of Shakespeare, the British were resented increasingly on account of their wealth. It is difficult to imagine a time when Germans felt obliged to rationalise their material poverty in relation to the British by touting their cultural superiority, but such was the case.

Once again, and not without reason, German intellectuals believed that the British either ignored or disparaged foreigners in general and Germans in particular. In 1775 the German poet Christian Schubart had angrily pointed out that, although the Hanoverians had long stretched out welcoming arms to George III, the proud Britons—who believed they constituted a superior species—would not allow their sovereign to travel among people they regarded as subhuman.[160] Very reasonably, the Germans fastened on Britain's lack of native music as a sure sign of its cultural poverty.[161] Why was such a prosperous country so bereft of cultural distinction? the Germans asked themselves repeatedly. It is because of their climate, argued an imaginative critic in 1839, and because they are mostly fair-skinned—and because they eat excellent legs of mutton, and, above all, because they can afford to buy other people's music. He concluded with a neat triple insult: 'The Germans invent music, the Italians vulgarise it, the French plagiarise it, and the English pay for it'.[162] This emphasis on British materialism and philistinism reappeared whenever British culture was being discussed.

A good example of the heavy-handed humour this inspired was a satirical letter purportedly written to the editor of the *Berliner Allgemeine Musikalische Zeitung* by an Englishman in January 1824:

> Dear Sir, I know nothing about music because, given our political and commercial constitution, I wouldn't know how to get started. But so that my fellow-countrymen are not deprived of the honour of participating in your publication, I enclose £600, so that you can send me over a batch of musicians to be naturalised. I also take this opportunity of informing you that I have established a prize-competition for the best invention of an orchestra driven by steam, so that our musicians can be retrained for service in the fleet and in the counting-houses.[163]

The Germans' strident insistence on the superiority of their culture may well have stemmed from a nagging anxiety that they were whistling in the dark. The political fragmentation, religious divisions and fierce particularism of the various regions combined to sustain doubts as to whether Germany was really a nation at all. The enduring popularity of Italian opera among the general public was particularly depressing for them. Reviewing Mozart's opera *The Abduction from the Seraglio* in 1784, Carl Friedrich Cramer lamented, 'We are and must remain un-German, and we shall never be anything more than the eternal imitators of other nations, the eternal targets of foreigners' reproach and ridicule'.[164] And yet only a few months previously he had extolled the special greatness of German music in an article on Joseph Haydn.[165] This schizophrenic attitude persisted so long as Germany remained disunited politically (and even thereafter). In the same article boasting of the profundity of German music, an anonymous contributor to the *Allgemeine Musikalische Zeitung* admitted that Germany was nothing more than an 'aggregate of peoples' with the result that there could be no national cultural identity such as was to be found in France or England.[166]

Those words were written in 1801. During the next half-century a growing number of Germans actively sought to define, express and assert a national identity. Their preferred vehicle was the voluntary associations that proliferated as part of the ever-expanding public sphere. Reporting on a choral festival held at Mainz in August 1835, *Cäcilia* exclaimed: 'Today we live in the age of associations!'[167] Given the heavy hand of reaction that weighed on the German states, not one of these was overtly political. But when the natural scientists, doctors, philologists, historians, linguists, ornithologists, or whoever, organised themselves into associations and held national conferences, they were making a political statement.[168] And the most vocal, in every sense, were the singing associations that mushroomed after 1815.

Although the state gave sometimes modest assistance by allowing them to use churches or other public buildings for their meetings, these vocal organizations were essentially the result of private initiative. They varied in size and ambition, ranging from groups of villagers gathering to sing folk songs to metropolitan societies boasting their own orchestra, premises and concerts. Typical of a middling-size enterprise was the association at Mannheim, formed in 1829 by the amalgamation of two previously informal groups of friends. In the course of the next decade, it grew ten times, to more than 400-strong, along the way creating a library of sheet music, supplying musical instruments, staging regular concerts and even founding a singing school for boys and girls.[169]

Before long, individual associations got together to organise regional festivals. The first was held in 1815 in the little town of Frankenhausen in the tiny principality of Schwarzburg-Rudolstadt. The insignificance of the venue did not deter the organisers from thinking big, for they appointed as their director Louis Spohr, one of the greatest names in the German musical world of the day and thought by many to be the equal of Beethoven. Their confidence was justified when 101 singers and 106 instrumentalists were attracted from right across Thuringia, encouraging the promotion of the festival as a regular event.[170] From the start, in other words, these festivals were not confined to one principality. Typical was the Swabian Festival of Song held at Biberach in July 1839, which brought together more than a thousand singers from thirty-four different associations in Bavaria and Württemberg.[171] As the railway network expanded rapidly during the 1840s to cover the whole country, it became easier to organise transregional and even national gatherings: and not just national, but also national*ist*. The festival held at Frankenhausen in 1815 was turned into a celebration of victory over the French with the performance of Spohr's *Germany Liberated* and Gottfried Weber's *Te Deum*.[172]

Once both nationalism and liberalism were bracketed as subversive after 1815, open calls for German unity were no longer permitted. That did not prevent the musical fires from burning, most spectacularly with a great conflagration unleashed by the so-called Rhine crisis of 1840. Seeking compensation for a diplomatic humiliation suffered at the hands of the British in the Middle East, the French engaged in some vigorous sabre-rattling closer to home, including demands for the west bank of the Rhine. For a generation, German public opinion had been so repressed that little was known about its current condition. When the curtain was pulled back in 1840, a seething mass of Francophobe nationalism was revealed.[173]

The most powerful hand at work belonged to Johann Nikolaus Becker, a junior court official, who on 18 September 1840 published in a Trier newspaper a poem entitled 'The German Rhine':

> They shall not ever have it,
> Our free and German Rhine,
> Though they like greedy crows
> Cry out: 'It's mine! It's mine!'

> They shall not ever have it,
> Our free and German Rhine,
> Until its flood has buried
> The limbs of our last man![174]

Even in the German original, this is unremarkable, but so excited was public opinion that it proved to be nothing less than a sensation when set to music. The composer Ferdinand Simon Gassner exclaimed at the beginning of 1841: '"They shall not have it!"—Where is the town or townlet, village or hamlet, in Germany where this famous song has not been sung?'[175] In March 1841 the *Allgemeine Musikalische Zeitung* supported its claim that Becker's song had proved a sensation by listing seventy-nine different settings.[176]

Concert audiences and festival goers everywhere demanded it be played. In Oldenburg in February 1841, for example, news that it was going to be included in the programme filled the concert hall to overflowing:

> At long last it was played and received with roars of applause and the unanimous demand for an encore. And when it was played again, something unprecedented happened—the whole audience joined in, as if guided by an invisible power . . . Becker's Rhine song has ignited a million German hearts like a flash of lightning. In the north and in the south, on the Rhine and on the Oder, the national flame of German patriotic emotion has blazed forth . . . Consciousness of the unity of the Germans has experienced a mighty reawakening. This little song has turned into a great demonstration against you, you French, so watch out, it has become a mighty avalanche that will bury you! . . . The song is more than a poem, it is a *deed,* a deed shared by all Germans.[177]

The avalanche was delayed for thirty years because the French backed down. Ironically, by that time Becker's Rhine song had been displaced by two other songs written at the same time: Max Schneckenburger's 'The Watch on the Rhine' and August Heinrich Hoffmann von Fallersleben's 'The Song of the Germans', better known as 'Deutschland, Deutschland über Alles'. The latter had the advantage of being sung to a tune by Haydn that had started out in life as the theme of the slow movement of his String Quartet in C Major, op. 76, no. 2 (*The Emperor*).[178]

For those with eyes to see and ears to hear, the Rhine crisis had revealed that nationalism was both immensely powerful and easily detachable from its apparent soulmate, liberalism. The episode in general, and Becker's song in particular, marked a decisive turn on the part of German liberals away from the French Enlightenment and its cosmopolitan values to a nationalist ideology that prioritised unity.[179]

That some inkling of this nationalist fervor was beginning to dawn on the bone-headed German princes was revealed by their attempt after 1840 to associate themselves with Becker's poem. Frederick William IV of Prussia gave him 1,000 talers and an annual pension of 300 talers, while Ludwig I of Bavaria sent a trophy.[180] But that was the limit. The continuing repression only strengthened the public's belief that music festivals were expressing an irresistible national spirit. In 1842, for example, Julius Becker observed that music had become the central 'animating spirit of social life' in both the private and the public realm. The mass participation in music festivals, he believed, held out the cheering prospect that the German national spirit would continue to grow.[181] Gassner agreed, proclaiming the great festival at Cologne of the previous year to have been 'a truly national festival': 'Because it is Germany herself that we hear calling to us. It is the spirit of Germany that stares out from Beethoven's symphonies'.[182] These coded appeals for liberty and unity were the most that the censors would allow.

Foreign observers, however, were under no restraints when it came to pointing out the political nature of the choral and musical associations. In 1841 a French visitor reported that every town in Germany had a singing association. Just how political they could become he had seen at Frankfurt am Main, where the grand banquet bringing the festival to a close was turned into a political demonstration, encouraged by the consumption of a great deal of alcohol. Toasts were drunk to liberty and German unity, tyrants were attacked in song, and Ernst Moritz Arndt's nationalist poem 'What Is the German's Fatherland?' which was set to music by Wilhelm Speyer was sung lustily and encored twice to shouts of 'Long Live Germany!':

> What is the German's Fatherland?
> Is it Prussian land? Is it Swabian land?
> Is it on the Rhine, where the vine blossoms?
> Is it on the Belt where the sea-birds call?
> Oh, no! no! no!
> His fatherland must be bigger.
>
> What is the German's Fatherland?
> Tell me it is the entire land!

As far as the German tongue is heard
And God in Heaven sings His songs,
That's where it must be!
That's what, good German, you must call your own!

All of Germany must it be!
Oh, God in Heaven make it so,
And give us proper German courage,
That we shall love it good and true.
That's what it must be!
All of Germany must it be![183]

After the revolutions of 1848 had come and gone, a German journalist confirmed that many of the singing associations of the 1840s had been covers for political agitation, especially in the notoriously radical Grand Duchy of Baden, where hardly a village existed without an association.[184]

As alienation from the establishment intensified during the 1840s, German voices became more strident. Singers numbering more than 2,300 from across the country gathered at Cologne in 1846, their journey hastened by free steamship and railway tickets distributed by wealthy sponsors. Their main self-appointed task was to sing patriotic songs affirming their 'sacred duty' to fight for the unity and welfare of the German fatherland.[185] Two years later, it looked very much as if they had achieved their goal, when revolutions broke out across the land, the hated Austrian chancellor Metternich fled into exile and liberal governments were appointed in one state after another. If a claim that the revolutionaries sang their way to victory would be absurd, it would be an equal mistake to underestimate the power of music. This was the one art form that could reach every part of the nation, and it was also the most difficult to control.

In a collection of songs published in 1848 the Baden radical Friedrich Hecker stated: 'The political song is the indestructible property of the individual. One learns a song for the first time, one sings it in the thunderous jubilation and excitement of the moment, but in the still hours, in which one reflects and daydreams, and during walks and hikes, the political song hums softly in the heart . . . a person becomes political.'[186] This observation should be linked to Benedict Anderson's insight that nations cannot exist until they are imagined. As only a very limited number of people ever meet

face-to-face, they must have some means to conceive of themselves as be-
longing to the same national community.[187] In that fundamental act of
imagination, music played a hugely important part.

From the Woods and Meadows of Bohemia

In 1875 the Czech composer Bedřich Smetana published the orchestral
score of his tone poem 'From the Woods and Meadows of Bohemia'. The
cover could not have been more bilingual—Czech on the left, German on
the right. The only words left untranslated were those of the composer and
the printer. Most of the page was taken up by an idyllic rural setting—
mountains, valleys and forests, as well as the woods and meadows of the
title. A man is seated in the foreground, sketching the glories of nature ar-
rayed before him—a scene that members of both linguistic groups could
share. However, all may not have been well in this garden of Eden, for
scowling at each other across the valley are two great fortresses on rocky
crags. The circumstances surrounding this choice of image are not known,
but there could not have been a better representation of the ambiguities of
Bohemian culture and politics.

Smetana himself was born in 1824 into a family of Czech origin that
spoke German. His father, František, almost certainly knew Czech but used
German to conduct his brewing business. So when the adolescent Bedřich
started keeping a diary, he wrote in German. Although an intensifying
sense of his nationality made him feel ashamed to use an alien language,
learning Czech proved to be a slow business. At the age of thirty-four he
could still write to his friend Ludevít Procházka: 'I would ask you to excuse
my mistakes both in spelling and grammar, of which you will certainly see
plenty, for up to the present I have not had the good fortune to perfect myself in our mother tongue. Educated from my youth in German, both at
school and in society, I took no care . . . and to my shame I must confess
that I cannot express myself adequately or write correctly in Czech . . . But
I am Czech, body and soul, and I am not ashamed to assure you, albeit imperfectly in my native tongue, for I am proud to show that my homeland
means more to me than anything else'.[188]

My homeland (*Ma Vlast*) was the title Smetana gave to his collection

The bilingual title page of Smetana's tone poem 'From the
Woods and Meadows of Bohemia' (1875).

of tone poems, of which 'From the Woods and Meadows of Bohemia' was
the fourth. No wonder that the whole work was an immediate, colossal and
enduring success, for it pressed every semiotic button: geographical (the
great rock Vyšehrad), natural (the river Vltava, Bohemia's woods and fields),
legendary (Šarka, the Amazon maiden), historical (Tábor, the Hussite strong-
hold), and prophetic (Blaník, the mountain where the Hussite warriors lie
sleeping, awaiting the call to rouse themselves and drive out the German
invaders). The first complete performance, on 5 November 1882, became a
great national demonstration, as an eyewitness eloquently recorded:

> Since the opening of the National Theatre there has never been
> such an exalted mood among any Czech assembly. The solemn

chords of *Vyšehrad* . . . raised us to such a degree of enthusiasm
that immediately after its moving conclusion the cry 'Smetana'
rang from the hundreds who were there. After *Vltava* (Moldau)
a hurricane of applause broke loose and his name resounded on
every side amidst cheers . . . Everyone rose to his feet and the
same unending storm of applause was repeated after each of the
six parts . . . At the end of *Blaník* the audience was beside itself
and the people could not bring themselves to take leave of the
composer.[189]

The opening of the National Theatre the previous year had been an
institutional and architectural expression of the close association between
music and nationality in Bohemia, marking the climax of exactly a century
of development. In 1781 Count Franz Anton von Nostitz-Rhineck financed
the construction of a theatre he gave the oxymoronic name Count Nostitz's
National Theatre and emblazoned the dedication 'Patriae et musis' (To the
fatherland and the muses) above the portico. Nostitz was just one of many
Bohemian nobles seeking to regenerate the kingdom's cultural identity
through institutions such as the Royal Society of Bohemia (1784), the Pa-
triotic-Economic Society of the Czech Kingdom (1788), the Society of Patriotic Friends of Art (1796) and the Prague Musical Conservatoire
(1811).[190] Since the Protestant dissidents had been routed by the Habsburg
emperor Ferdinand II at the battle of the White Mountain in 1620, Bohemia had been turned into an exemplar of Catholic, counter-reformatory,
Baroque culture. The Prague of palaces, monasteries and churches that is
so much admired today emerged from this process. Not until the late eighteenth century did growing prosperity, urbanisation, enlightenment and
opposition to the centralising policies of Joseph II encourage a challenge
to its central axioms. Among them was the hegemony of the German
language. After 1620 *anything* written in the Czech language was suspected
of heresy; only Latin and German were deemed suitable for orthodox intercourse. As a result, after a century Czech had virtually disappeared as
a literate language, to be heard only among artisans, servants and peasants.[191]

This was the situation that intellectual nobles like Count Nostitz set
out to change. Their patriotism was Bohemian—that is to say, it was directed toward the kingdom of that name as a geographical, historical and

cultural entity. As such, it had a definite Czech flavour but not exclusively so. Count František Kinský, one of the co-founders of the Royal Society, published a defence of the Czech language in which he proclaimed: 'As a good descendant of Slavs, I have inherited the prejudice that if the mother tongue of a Frenchman is French, and of a German, German, then for a Czech the mother tongue must also be Czech'. But his book appeared in German, as did the *History of the Bohemian Language and Literature* by Josef Dobrovský published in 1792.[192] Gradually, however, the Czech revival reached the tipping point. A moment fraught with symbolic omen was the creation of a National Museum by Count František Kolovrat in 1818. His manifesto, written in German, referred to the new institution as a Patriotic Museum (Vaterländisches Museum), but when Josef Jungmann translated this into Czech, it became the National *Czech* Museum (Národní české museum).[193]

Over the next century the struggle between Czechs and Germans became increasingly bitter, culminating in the establishment of a new Czech(oslovak) state after the First World War and ethnic cleansing of the Germans after the Second. Music had an important part to play in these events, not least because the musical life of Bohemia was especially rich. Already in the eighteenth century, envious foreign observers noted that the kingdom probably exported more musicians than any other part of Europe, including even Italy. They explained this phenomenon by reference to the wealth of the church, the patronage of the nobility, the excellence of the vocal and instrumental instruction available and 'a natural proclivity'.[194] In the nineteenth century, musicians gave the Czechs that crucial ability to imagine themselves as a nation and the cultural self-confidence to turn dreams into action. Very few non-Czechs could name one Czech poet, novelist, painter (with the possible exception of Alfons Mucha) or architect born before 1900, but most educated people have heard of Smetana (born 1824), Dvořák (born 1841) and Janáček (born 1854).

If he was not the greatest composer, the most important of these three for Czech nationalism was Smetana, whose steely integrity in serving the national cause made him a role model even for those who did not like his radical Young Czech politics. In 1861 yet another liberal Bohemian aristocrat, Count Jan Harrach, announced that he was funding two competitions, to find the best opera on a Czech historical subject and the best opera on a popular subject 'taken from the national life of the people'. Only native-born Czechs would be eligible: 'I invite my dear compatriots, wherever they may be, to participate enthusiastically in this Czech enterprise—to produce a real national work that will glorify the Czechs!'[195] Ready and waiting was Smetana, who earlier that year had returned from five years in Sweden with a sense of a patriotic mission: 'My home has rooted itself into my heart so much that only there do I find real contentment. It is to this that I shall sacrifice myself.'[196]

The result was his first opera, *The Brandenburgers in Bohemia*, with a libretto by the journalist Karel Sabina. Set in the late thirteenth century, it is a very thinly disguised assault on foreign occupation and exploitation. The opening lines, sung by Oldřich Rokycanský (described in the *dramatis personae* as 'a bellicose knight and patriot'), set the tone by calling on his fellow countrymen to rise and chase out the foreign troops.[197] The plot of what follows is confused, not to say incoherent, but the nationalist message rings out loud and clear, not least in the closing chorus, which promises that 'good times will again return to us and glory to our Czech fatherland.' Certainly the audience at the premiere on 5 January 1866 was wildly enthusiastic, calling Smetana on stage nine times in the course of the performance.[198]

The audience was not very large, however, because the opera was performed in the Royal Provincial Provisional Theatre at Prague, which was built in 1862 with seating for just 362 people. Not for nothing was it known as the Match-box.[199] The theatre was called provisional because it was intended to serve only until enough money could be raised by public subscription to build a proper national theatre. Unsurprisingly, that took longer than expected. On 16 May 1868 the foundation stone was laid by Smetana with the words 'In music is the life of the Czechs.' This was the feast day of Bohemia's patron saint, John Nepomuk, and the climax of a three-day festival—the Czechs' greatest national celebration between the 1848 revolution and their independence in 1918.[200] Special trains were organised to bring 60,000 visitors to Prague, including members of 148 choral societies. The musical centrepiece was the premiere of *Dalibor*, another opera with a Czech historical theme and music by Smetana. At the end, as the hero Dalibor is stabbed to death, he sings 'Open for me the gates of liberty! I am going to another country!'[201]

The sacralisation of the nation in architectural form eventually reached completion fourteen years later on 11 June 1882 when the new

The Royal Provincial Provisional Theatre at Prague.

theatre was opened, with—of course—another patriotic opera by Smetana. This was *Libuše*, less an opera than a representation of the Czech foundation myth of the ninth century, when the heroine finds a husband in the sturdy peasant Přemysl, thus founding the great Czech dynasty that was to rule Bohemian lands for the next four centuries. In the final scene, Libuše recounts a series of visions in which the glorious if troubled future of the Czechs is revealed. When she reaches the era of the Hussite persecutions, mists begin to rise and her eyes grow dim, but she concludes: 'This much I feel and know in the depths of my heart: my dear Czech people will never perish, they will be able to resist all the horrors of hell!'—'including the Germans and their Austrian Habsburg masters', the audience may well have added to themselves as they rose to their feet to demonstrate their enthusiasm.

The German 'other' was a constant presence in the development of Czech nationalism and Czech music. It was a fine irony that poor Smetana,

František Palacký makes the speech at the laying of the foundation stone of the National Theatre at Prague on 16 May 1868. Smetana is the second on the right of the group standing to the left of Palacký.

who did more than anyone to foster the latter, should have fallen foul of his 'Old Czech' fellow countrymen for being all too influenced by Wagner. In fact, when he was director of the National Theatre repertoire between 1866 and 1872, Smetana deliberately avoided staging any of Wagner's works, despite their popularity, because he found them 'foreign in their downright Germanism' and therefore 'completely unacceptable to a singing nation like the Czechs'.[202]

Although Dvořák, who both venerated and was friendly with Brahms, was much less prone to Germanophobia, Janáček was temperamentally and musically a very different kettle of fish. Born and brought up in Brünn (Brno), he found his way to his own distinctive voice through a process of embracing Moravian folk music while rejecting everything German. Although bilingual, thanks to attendance at a German secondary school (the only one available), he insisted on using Czech whenever possible, writing to his uncle in 1869: 'I have written once or twice—and then burnt the letters, as I don't know whether you are a true Czech or a true German, or half and half. Oh, dear uncle, you don't know how I love the Czechs, and you wouldn't believe how I hate the Germans'.[203] It is some measure of the distorting effect of his national prejudices that he believed tsarist Russia to be a freer country than Austria-Hungary.[204]

Until direct political activity was permitted in the late nineteenth century, culture and especially music allowed the Czechs a medium for national definition, pride and assertion. It was not the only one—the Sokol gymnastic movement was hugely influential, for example—but it did leave the most distinguished and enduring monuments. *Libuše* may never have found its way into the international repertoire, but *The Bartered Bride* (Smetana), *Rusalka* (Dvořák) and *Jenůfa* (Janáček), just to mention three works from a long list of candidates, have made the Czech voice heard across the world. Together with other composers of distinction (Bendl, Foerster, Kàan, Kovařovic, Fibich, for example), the big three exemplified the power of music to express nationalist aspirations and the power of nationalism to influence musical compositions. Even the most cosmopolitan of them, Dvořák, affirmed: 'Whatever I have written in America, England or elsewhere is and always remains Czech music'.[205]

A Life for the Tsar

At least the Czech-speakers of Bohemia had a long tradition of sophisticated music-making to look back to, even if they had to get used to seeing their most gifted musicians Germanising their names and emigrating (as when Jan Václav Stamič became Johann Wenzel Stamitz and moved to the Palatinate). Further to the east, in Russia, art music of any kind was of very recent origin. The Orthodox Church prohibited instrumental music because it adopted an exclusive and literal interpretation of the last line of Psalm 150: 'Let everything that has breath praise the Lord'. Dr. Samuel Collins, who served as physician to Tsar Alexis in the 1660s, described the implications: 'If you would pleas a Russian with Musick, get a consort of Billings-Gate Nightingales, joyn'd with a Flight of Screech-Owls, a nest of Jackdaws, a pack of hungry Wolves, seven Hogs on a windy day, and as many Cats with their Corrivals, and let them sing *Lacrymae* and that will ravish a pair of Russian Luggs, better than all the Musick in *Italy*, light Ayres in France, Marches of England, or the Gigs of Scotland'.[206]

In Russia, music was confined to unaccompanied choral singing in church and folk music outside it. The first orchestral concert was given by twelve German musicians accompanying the duke of Holstein on a visit he made in 1721–22.[207] This new form of recreation was then copied by native nobles as part of their westernising experience. Tsarina Anna's recruiting of Italian instrumentalists to form a court orchestra in the 1730s encouraged the trend. Anna also imported the first opera company, from Leipzig.[208] From there, culture trickled down, albeit through the top layers of Russian society only. By the mid 1740s, advertisements were appearing in the *St. Petersburg Gazette* for concerts organised by native nobles. In 1748, for example, Prince Gagarin announced that the public would be admitted to a concert 'in the Italian, English and Dutch manner' to be held in his palace. Songs would be sung in Italian, Russian, English and German, tickets would cost one ruble each, and anyone decently dressed would be admitted, with only 'drunks, servants and loose women' excluded.[209] These 'musical Wednesdays' of Prince Gagarin became a regular part of the capital's musical scene.

Russian concert culture had a special flavour deep into the nineteenth century. Perhaps its most striking peculiarity was the popularity of orchestras consisting of serfs. Even quite modest landowners trained their serfs as musicians and put them to work in the fields or in the house by day. This was a sensible investment, for not only were the serf-musicians available to entertain the family in the evening, they also represented a marketable asset and could be sold if necessary. Around 1,800 theatres could be found on 173 noble estates, and over 300 serf orchestras.[210] No matter how great their skill and resulting fame, however, the musicians remained at the disposal of their current master. Probably atypical but certainly symbolic was the great whip that Count Kamensky hung in the wings of his private theatre, with which he beat performers during the interval if they had not lived up to his expectations.[211] On the other hand, lucky serfs could be encouraged by a music-loving master; Mikhail Matinsky's owner, Count Yaguzhinsky, for example, sent him to Italy to study music.[212]

Not surprisingly, native-born composers found it difficult to make a mark in this sort of system. Undoubtedly the most successful of all operas composed by a Russian before 1800 was *The Miller, the Sorcerer, the Cheat and the Matchmaker*, with music by Mikhail Matveyevich Sokolovsky and a libretto by Alexander Onisimovich Ablesimov. First performed at Moscow in 1779, it was an immediate success and remained in the repertoire throughout the next century.[213] Yet very little is known about Sokolovsky, not even the year in which he died, and the credit for the music was given by posterity to Yevstigney Ipat'yevich Fomin (1761–1800).[214] The growth of a Russian public for western-style music proved to be a slow business. When the Bolshoi Theatre was fitted out at great expense on the eve of the war of 1812, the governor of Moscow, Count Rostopchin, commented sourly that all he needed now was the money with which to buy 2,000 serfs to serve as the audience.[215]

It was not unusual for rulers to take the lead in musical innovation. What was unusual, if not unique, about Russia was the close association between ruler and nation. Catherine the Great was uncomfortably aware that her German origins—she had been born a princess of Anhalt-Zerbst—made her suspect to the strongly xenophobe Russian nobility. Her husband and predecessor, Peter III, who was half-German, being the son of the duke of Holstein-Gottorp and Peter the Great's daughter, had been deposed and murdered not least because of his enthusiasm for everything Prussian and contempt for everything Russian.[216] So Catherine played the nationalist card for all it was worth: 'Her reign . . . marked the emergence of what might be called "official nationalism", the conscious identification of governmental measures and goals with what were felt to be truly nationalist aspirations', in the words of Hans Rogger.[217] Among other ways she found to stress her identification with her adopted country was the composition of libretti in the Russian language, drawing on folk traditions.[218]

Russia's experience during the Napoleonic wars completed the reversal of the westernising quest begun by Peter the Great at the end of the seventeenth century. So traumatic was the invasion of 1812 that France became the epitome of all that was offensive about western culture. It was 'the land of deception and falsity' (Viazemsky), while Paris was 'the capital of superficial splendour and enchantment' (Karamzin) and 'a city of calculation and egoism' (Glinka), possessing 'only a surface glitter that conceals an abyss of fraud and greed' (Gogol) and characterised by 'vanity, vanity, vanity' (Glinka again).[219] Against the French Revolution's triad of liberty, equality and fraternity, Tsar Nicholas I's minister of education, Serge

Uvarov, advocated orthodoxy, autocracy and nationality. In 1833 he told the tsar that, at a time when order was collapsing all over Europe, 'it was necessary to find the principles which form the distinctive character of Russia, and which belong only to Russia . . . to gather into one whole the sacred remnants of Russian nationality and to fasten them to the anchor of our salvation'.[220]

Russian culture in the nineteenth century was imbued with the notion that it was unique because Russia had taken its Christianity from the unpolluted springs of Byzantium, and so had a mission to regenerate the rest of the world. Among the many examples that might be cited, perhaps the most eloquent was provided by Dostoyevsky in *The Devils:*

> 'Do you know', he [Shatov] began almost menacingly, leaning forward in his chair with flashing eyes and raising the forefinger of his right hand before him (evidently without being aware of it himself)—'do you know who are now the only "god-bearing" people on earth, destined to regenerate and save the world in the name of a new god and to whom alone the keys of life and of the new word have been vouchsafed—do you know which is that people and what is its name?'
>
> 'To judge by your manner I must needs conclude and, I suppose, without delay that it is the Russian people'.
>
> 'And you are already laughing—oh what a tribe!' Shatov again nearly leapt to his feet.[221]

The amazing roll call of Russian writers in the nineteenth century— Pushkin, Lermontov, Herzen, Gogol, Dostoyevsky, Tolstoy, Turgenev, Chekhov—was matched by a simultaneous explosion of musical talent— Glinka, Cui, Rimsky-Korsakov, Musorgsky, Balakirev, Borodin, Tchaikovsky, Rachmaninov. At first, these musicians were in close alliance with the regime. Tsar Nicholas I, his family and his court all attended the premiere of Mikhail Ivanovich Glinka's opera *A Life for the Tsar* (the first Russian opera, in the opinion of Richard Taruskin) in St. Petersburg on 27 November 1836.[222] By all accounts, the epochal nature of the performance was recognised. The *St. Petersburg Gazette* reported: 'All were enthralled with the sounds of the native, Russian national music. Everyone showed complete accord in the expression of enthusiasm which the patriotic content of the opera aroused . . . At the conclusion of the opera the composer was unanimously called to the stage'.[223]

Glinka had succeeded in doing for Russia what Weber had done for Germany in *Der Freischütz:* he had combined the naïveté of folk music with the sophistication of the classical tradition to create a truly national work. This was what the composer and music critic Aleksandr Nikolaevich Serov was trying to express when he wrote: 'I felt the music's stylistic resemblance to our folk songs from its very first sounds, but at the same time I somehow was perplexed. The music was both folklike and not folklike. One could discern very learned and complex forms'.[224] Prince Odoevsky, writing in *Severnaia Pchela* (Northern Bee), believed that the opera marked a watershed in Russian musical history: 'How is one to express the surprise of true music-lovers when from the first act they realised that this opera had answered a question so important to art in general and Russian art in particular, a question, that is, about the existence of Russian opera, *Russian* music, and finally about the existence overall of *folk* music . . . Glinka's opera represents what they have searched for a long time and not found in Europe— *a new element in art.* With its history, a new period begins, *the period of Russian music'.*[225]

Why this opera should have appealed so much to the tsar is not difficult to see. The subject had been suggested to Glinka by Vasiliy Andreyevich Zhukovsky, an official censor and tutor to the crown prince (the future Alexander II).[226] Set in 1613 during a war between Poland and Russia, it tells how a peasant, Ivan Susanin, gives his life for the young tsar Mikhail, the first of the Romanov dynasty, by drawing a Polish murder squad away from their intended victim's hiding place and deep into the forest. When the Poles realise they have been tricked, they try to torture Susanin into leading them to safety, and they kill him when he refuses. But the national flavour is in the music as well as in the libretto. Just as one need only hear a bar or two of Weber's *Der Freischütz* to realise that one is listening to German music, so is the Russian character of *A Life for the Tsar* established by the first sung passage, consisting of an unaccompanied exchange between solo tenor and peasant chorus which sounds as though it comes straight from the Orthodox liturgy.

Ivan Susanin completes the association between ruler and nation by gasping 'Oh my Tsar!' as he expires. And as if that were not enough, Glinka and his four librettists added an epilogue which began: 'Glory, glory to thee our Russian Caesar, Our sovereign given us by God! May thy royal line be immortal! May the Russian people prosper through it.' Glinka also clearly identified the 'other' that was serving as the sounding board for Russian virtues by using dance music, polonaises and mazurkas to depict the Polish enemy. Because the Russians have dominated the Poles for so long, we often forget that during the late medieval and early modern period the relationship was reversed.[227]

The intimate relationship between tsar and musician exemplified by *A Life for the Tsar* could not last. The breakdown came not so much because of the stifling repression imposed by the regime—that was nothing new—as because the despotism proved to be so inefficient. When the Russian armies were rolling back the French invaders in 1812, defeating Napoleon at Leipzig in 1813 and holding a victory parade in Paris in 1814, it was easy to believe in the special mission of Holy Russia and its tsar. But when the despised westerners defeated the Russian armies in the Crimean War a half century later, a severe crisis of confidence ensued. The prolonged period of reform that followed further disrupted the bond between state and society. From this crisis emerged an intelligentsia deeply and increasingly alienated from the regime.[228]

This is not the place to follow the process through to the catastrophe of 1917, but one musical illustration demands to be heard. This is Modest Musorgsky's *Boris Godunov*, regarded by critics and the listening public as the greatest Russian opera. Confusingly but revealingly, it exists in several different versions. The first, completed in 1869, was turned down by the selection committee of the Imperial Theatres Directorate in February 1871, which amounted to a total ban on performance because the theatre was a state monopoly.[229] Objection was taken not to any political offence but to the absence of a leading soprano role. Although Musorgsky could have dealt with this problem easily and quickly, he chose instead to engage in a major rewrite, disappointed by the response to his work from friends and fellow musicians he admired and trusted. His second version was not a compromise or a concession to the censors; it was a positive revision.[230]

The opera still dealt with the decline and fall of the tsar, wracked by guilt at his complicity in the murder of the infant Tsarevich Dmitry, but the identity of his Nemesis is significantly altered. In the original, and also in the play by Pushkin on which it partly was based, Boris Godunov struggled with his conscience and its personification, the Pretender (the 'False

Dmitry'). In the revised version his Nemesis is the Russian people. From being passive and resigned, they become actively hostile—revolutionary even.[231] In his great soliloquy in Act Two, Boris acknowledges the people's wrath:

> With a fervent prayer to God's saints
> I hoped to muffle the sufferings of my soul . . .
> In grandeur and in the glitter of absolute power,
> I, the ruler of Russia, begged for tears to console me . . .
> But then, denunciations:
> Boyars' plotting, intrigues in Lithuania,
> Secret machinations,
> Famine and plague, and fear and devastation . . .
> Like wild beasts the people roam, stricken with disease:
> And Russia groans in hunger and in poverty . . .
> In this affliction dire, sent down by God
> For all my grievous sins a punishment
> They name me cause of all these evil things.
> And curse the name of Boris everywhere![232]

The words sung here by Boris could have come from the lips of Charles I of England in 1649, Louis XVI of France in 1793, and Nicholas II of Russia in 1918, as they awaited their executioners. When the opera was first performed to rapturous applause at the Maryinsky Theatre in St. Petersburg in 1874, this aspect did not pass unnoticed. The prominent critic Nikolay Nikolaevich Strakhov, for example, wrote: 'In Pushkin the general background is our ancient Rus and the entire foundation that sustained her: deep religiosity, family and monastic life, loyalty to the government, the ideal of the Tsar, fidelity to the dynasty . . . But what serves as a background for Mr. Musorgsky?'[233] Musorgsky died of drink in 1882, the year after Tsar Alexander II was assassinated.

As nationalism grew in the nineteenth century, music was both a mirror and a lamp: it reflected the development of nations, and it illuminated and heated that development from within. Many other examples could be chosen—the role of Chopin for Poland, Grieg for Norway, Nielsen for Denmark, Bartók and Kodály for Hungary, Sibelius for Finland, or Charles Ives for the United States, to name just six. A whole chapter could be written about national operas—Stanisław Moniuszko's *Halka* (Poland) or Ferenc Erkel's *Hunyadi Laszló*, for example. Though limitations of space prevent these explorations, a few sentences must be found, in closing, for the amazing multiplication of musicians of Jewish origin—Moscheles, Mendelssohn, Halévy, Meyerbeer, Goldmark, Offenbach, Joachim, Bruch, Mahler, Zemlinsky, Schoenberg, and so on, for this represents an explosion of talent even more impressive than that achieved by Russia. It was part of a much wider Jewish renaissance that included three of the modern world's most influential geniuses: Marx, Einstein and Freud.

Beginning with the granting of civil equality by the National Assembly in France in 1791, Jews started to escape from the ghettos of European cities, and their emancipation proceeded in fits and starts over the next century.[234] But probably just as important was the gradual dissolution of the internal barriers that had confined them to their own closed religious culture. Representative of Jewish liberation was the career of Fromental Halévy (1799–1862), whose father moved from Fürth near Nuremberg to Paris to take advantage of the Revolution's emancipation decrees. Nowhere else in Europe could the infant prodigy Halévy have found such an excellent Conservatoire prepared to admit a Jew, particularly at the tender age of eleven. Trained by Cherubini, Berton and Méhul, he became one of the most successful opera composers of the period.[235]

Music in the twentieth century, assisted by a host of technological changes, continued to be a powerful activist weapon. Amplified, recorded, and reproduced, it could now warm up crowds a hundred thousand strong and reach into millions of homes. The 'Internationale' on the left and the 'Horst Wessel Song' (and other fascist battle hymns) on the right flattered the 'Marseillaise' by imitation. In the twenty-first century, music continues to play an important role in the assertion of national identity. That it has lost none of its mobilising power was demonstrated in the summer of 2003 by the battle of Beirut. As if that unhappy city did not have enough to contend with, on 11 August the news that local hero Melhem Zein had been voted off the Arab Superstar singing contest provoked a riot so serious that the Lebanese army had to be called out: 'Intifada breaks out in studio as anger spills on to the streets', reported a local newspaper.[236] Conspiracy theories were rife, including the rumour that King Abdullah of Jordan had ordered his entire army to vote for the Jordanian contestant, Diana Karzon.

By this time the contest had been going on for four months, with thousands of singers from all over the Middle East being whittled down to just twelve from Algeria, Egypt, Jordan, Lebanon, Syria, the United Arab Emirates, and Palestine. In the final competition, held on 18 August, Diana Karzon faced a Syrian rival, Rowaidah Attiyeh, but managed to scrape home with 52 percent of the total vote of 4.8 million.[237] The showdown was preceded by intense campaigning in both countries, with the nationalist aspect emphasised. A Syrian mobile telephone company, for example, hung posters in the streets of Damascus entreating people to 'Vote for Rowaida Attiyeh. Give your vote to Syria'. The call was heeded by, among others, the merchant Subhan Elewi, who said he voted for Attiyeh 'first because she is Syrian and second because she has a nice voice'. On the other side, in Amman, Tala Qassir told his interviewer: 'Without any doubt, I am voting for Diana, because she is Jordanian and I support my country. Besides that, she has a nice voice and she deserves to win'.[238] The Eurovision Song Contest, staged annually since 1956, is also notoriously disfigured by nationalist prejudice.

Race and Rebellion

Leaving nationalist conflicts, this chapter will be brought to a conclusion with a brief consideration of three ways in which music has played a central role in the liberating process. The first is the civil rights movement in the United States.

If the leaders of the civil rights movement did not achieve all their goals, leaving African Americans subject to many kinds of informal discrimination, nevertheless a revolution undoubtedly occurred in race relations during the second half of the twentieth century. Music was there from the start, for it was through music that the black community found a voice and it was in music that African Americans excelled. Though plenty of whites were involved in jazz, this genre was always perceived—by friend and foe alike—as essentially a black creation. And from the earliest days of jazz, listeners understood that jazz was much more than the music of New Orleans brothels or Chicago dance halls.

In 1931 Duke Ellington wrote: 'The music of my race is something more than the "American idiom". It is the result of our transplantation to American soil, and was our reaction in the plantation days to the tyranny we endured. What we could not say openly we expressed in music, and what we know as "Jazz" is something more than just dance music . . . I think the music of my race is something which is going to live, something which posterity will honour in a higher sense than merely that of the music of the ballroom of today'.[239] Ten years later, by which time his orchestra had accumulated a catalogue of great recordings, he was more emphatic: 'I contend that the Negro is the creative voice of America, is creative America, and it was a happy day in America when the first unhappy slave was landed on its shores . . . It is our voice that sang "America" when America grew too lazy, satisfied and confident to sing'.[240]

Although Ellington was not unique in his musical gifts, he was exceptionally articulate, sophisticated and self-confident, in part the result of a privileged upbringing. Both his musical and social skills made him especially well qualified to make jazz acceptable even to those musical Manichaeans who divided music into good (the classical tradition) and bad (the rest). For the English composer Constant Lambert, for example, even a recording by Louis Armstrong produced only 'exasperation and ennui' after a number of playings, whereas Ellington was 'a real composer, the first jazz composer of distinction, and the first Negro composer of distinction'.[241] Other classical musicians had been quicker to see the potential of jazz—for example, the Swiss conductor Ernest Ansermet, who hailed Sidney Bechet as an 'artist of genius' when he heard him play in the Southern Syncopated Orchestra in 1919, adding: 'What a moving thing it is to meet this very black, fat boy with white teeth and that narrow forehead, who is very glad one likes what he does but who can say nothing of his art, save that he follows his "own way" . . . His "own way" is perhaps the highway the whole world will swing down tomorrow'.[242] Five years later Leopold Stokowski recognised that jazz had come to stay, and he hailed 'the Negro musicians of America' as 'pathfinders into new realms'.[243]

This kind of comment (which could be replicated at will) is more important than it might sound. As African Americans constituted only a minority of the U.S. population, and moreover were often excluded from voting and other political activities by one means or another, they could make progress only by means of white support. Through such a powerful contribution to American culture, the jazz musicians also posted a claim to legal and political equality. And there was another side: as with the Czechs (and any other oppressed nationality), their music helped African Americans to find a distinctive voice, forge their own identity and generate the pride and self-confidence to demand their place in the sun. Along the way, they were given a helping hand by some white musicians. When the most successful band leader in America, Benny Goodman, hired Teddy Wilson in 1935 and Lionel Hampton in 1936 to join him and Gene Krupa to form first his trio and then his quartet, he showed that a mixed-race group could create some of the best small-group jazz ever heard. Wilson claimed later: 'It was a tremendous success. As a matter of fact, it was an asset, racial mixing. The interest in the United States was tremendous, and the public was so for the thing that not one negative voice in any audience did we ever get. Just tremendous enthusiasm. This interracial thing was just wonderful'.[244]

That was almost certainly a rather starry-eyed account. Wilson himself agreed that after a concert Goodman and Krupa went to one hotel and he and Hampton to another, adding: 'We went along with the tide the way it was, because we had opened up a door already, a giant crack, and there was no need of making a fuss'.[245] Although many more boots had to be thrust into that crack before the door could be forced open, a start had been made. Rather belatedly, by the late 1930s the National Association for the Advancement of Colored People (founded in 1909) was beginning to wake up to the potential of jazz and its musicians. Progress remained very slow, with only the occasional individual initiative to suggest change might come. For example, Don Redman in 1944 and Earl Hines in 1945 refused to tour the southern states on the grounds that they would be obliged to perform before segregated audiences.[246]

At this rate, centuries if not millennia would have had to pass before the barriers came down. But as it turned out, the process was accelerated mightily by all the forces making for the explosion of youth culture, notably World War II, consumerism, and demographic shifts. The power of young consumers, both black and white, began to exert itself from the late 1940s. One musical consequence was the growth of 'cross-overs' between the races, greatly encouraged by two kinds of convergence. On the one hand, the blues—the quintessentially African American musical form—developed into something much more palatable to white taste when it moved out of the Mississippi delta as part of the black diaspora to the industrial north. By adding a rhythm section and amplifying their harmonicas and guitars, blues singers such as Big Bill Broonzy, Sonny Boy Williamson, Muddy Waters, John Lee Hooker and Howlin' Wolf made their music both much more conducive to dancing and better able to express the special *Angst* of the big city and the aspirations of its black population.[247] Isaac Hayes, who was to win an Oscar in 1972 for his music for the film *Shaft* (the first African American to win an Oscar in a non-acting category), recalled how the blues became acceptable: 'As a kid in the fifties, I was taught to be *ashamed* of the blues. We thought of it as plantation darkie stuff. And that was miles from where *we* wanted to be.'[248]

A second kind of convergence came from the other side, from young whites who found the electrified urban blues both more exciting rhythmically and more authentic emotionally than the bland popular music churned out by Tin Pan Alley. Much later, Van Morrison begged a few philosophical questions but also summed up a common attitude when he told an interviewer: 'One word sums up the essence of the blues: truth.'[249] Because the airwaves formed one space that could not be segregated, black rhythm and blues (a term coined by Jerry Wexler in 1947) was soon crossing over the racial divide. The black deejay Shelley Stewart claimed: 'Music really started breaking the barriers long before the politics in America began to deal with it. [The races] began to communicate . . . because of the music . . . and the black radio in the black community being accepted and enjoyed . . . by the white community.'[250]

When wedded to white country music, rhythm and blues developed into rock 'n' roll. The great catalyst was, of course, Elvis Presley, whose first recording, 'That's All Right', was thought by many who heard it to be by a black singer. He had first gone to Sun Records in Memphis, Tennessee, in the summer of 1953 to record two songs as a present for his mother. The owner, Sam Phillips, was not present, but his enterprising secretary, Marion Keisker, was so impressed by what she heard that she made an additional copy: 'Over and over I remember Sam saying, "if I could find a white man who had the Negro sound and the Negro feel, I could make a billion dollars".'[251] Elvis Presley certainly generated a billion dollars, and more, but not, alas, for Sam Phillips, who sold the contract to RCA for $35,000 in 1955.

In the authoritative judgment of Berry Gordy, founder of Motown, the most successful black record company, 'In the music business there had long been the distinction between black and white music, the assumption being that R&B was black and Pop was white. But with rock 'n' roll and the explosion of Elvis those clear distinctions began to get fuzzy'.[252] The traffic was not all one-way. Black musicians could also be strongly influenced by predominantly white country music—Chuck Berry, for example. Nevertheless, black rock 'n' roll musicians were in the ascendancy, and most of their white colleagues were prepared to admit it. When Buddy Holly's mother asked him what it felt like to be surrounded by Negroes all the time, he replied: 'Oh, we're Negroes too! We get to feeling that's what we are'.[253] When he played a concert at the Apollo Theatre in New York in August 1957, the audience expected him to be black, because they knew him only through his records. So he created a sensation simply by appearing on stage.[254] In the same vein, Frank Zappa sang on 'Trouble Comin' Every Day' that although he wasn't black, there were many times he wished he could say he wasn't white.[255]

On some occasions musical and social integration went together. Harry Weinger of The Platters, a very popular and influential black group of the late 1950s, claimed that music 'broke down a lot of stereotyped barriers. I credit the music with opening a lot of eyes, ears and doors to a better understanding . . . Because of our music, white kids ventured into black areas. They had a sense of fair play long before the civil rights movements. We were invited into a lot of homes by kids whose fathers looked at us like we were going to steal the goddammed refrigerator'.[256] The white record producer Ralph Bass described the dances he attended in the South: 'They'd put a rope across the middle of the floor. The blacks on one side, whites on the other, digging how the blacks were dancing and copying them. Then, hell, the rope would come down and they'd all be dancing together. And you know it was a revolution. Music did it. We did it as much with our music as the civil rights acts and all of the marches, for breaking the race thing down'.[257] One beneficiary of young whites' enthusiasm for black music was the black deejay Shelley Stewart. In July 1960, when he arrived at Don's Teen Town near Birmingham, Alabama, for his weekly whites-only record session, he was warned by the proprietor that a large gang of Ku Klux Klansmen were waiting outside, ready to launch an assault as soon as he began his act. The reaction of the audience to this news, recorded Stewart,

Chuck Berry (on the right) and fans. On the left is Bo Diddley.

was immediate: 'Those 800 white kids . . . burst out those doors and jumped on the Klan . . . fighting for me'.[258]

The integrating power of music was impressive, especially compared with what had gone before, but it was also limited. If anything, rock 'n' roll intensified white anxieties by its aggressively sexual flavour. Chuck Berry revelled in being 'a brown eyed handsome man' (the title of one of his songs) and grabbed with both hands the advantages it brought him, but his flamboyance cost him dear. After opening his racially integrated Club Bandstand in St. Louis in 1959, he was arrested for taking an underage girl across a state line, charged a $5,000 fine and sentenced to five years in prison. Although the blatantly racist remarks of the presiding judge led to a retrial, he still ended up spending two years in prison and paying a $10,000 fine.[259]

Even an artist as sophisticated and discreet as Nat King Cole was not immune from this kind of resentment. At a whites-only concert at Birmingham, Alabama, in 1956, when he began to sing 'Little Girl', the stage was stormed by a group of men shouting 'Let's go get that coon!' Accompanying him was an English band led by Ted Heath (alas, no relation to the Conservative politician of that name), who sought to calm the situation by launching into 'God Save the Queen'. In vain.[260] For white supremacists, *all* black music was tarred with the same brush. Asa Carter of the North Alabama Citizens' Council asserted that it was only 'a short step . . . from the sly night club technique vulgarity of Cole to the openly animalistic obscenity of the horde of Negro rock 'n' rollers'. He also believed that the National Association for the Advancement of Colored People had a cunning plan to promote sexual integration through the aphrodisiac that was rock 'n' roll, for 'it appeals to the very base of man, brings out the animalism and vulgarity' and so encourages miscegenation.[261]

By this time Alabama was at the centre of the civil rights movement. On 1 December 1955 a black woman in Montgomery, Rosa Parks, was arrested after refusing to give up her seat on a bus to a white man when told to do so by the bus driver. The incident led to a black boycott of the city's buses that triumphed a year later when the Supreme Court declared bus segregation laws unconstitutional. This exemplified the secret of success: a combination of social protest from below with judicial and legislative intervention by the federal government. Almost certainly, the latter would not have acted without the former, so the struggle for legitimacy in the public sphere was crucial. As the historian Tony Badger has written: 'The civil rights movement not only out-sang and out-prayed its opponents, it out-thought them'.[262]

Musicians had been at the fore in the struggle from the start. In 1939 the black diva Marian Anderson was refused permission by the Daughters of the American Revolution to sing in Washington, D.C.'s Constitution Hall, so she moved to the steps of the Lincoln Memorial to give an openair concert. With numerous political figures in the audience, including the first lady, Eleanor Roosevelt, she began with 'My Country 'Tis of Thee'.[263] Twenty-four years later, on 28 August 1963, she was back again, this time singing 'He's Got the Whole World in His Hands' as part of the rally that marked the climax of the great March on Washington for Jobs and Freedom.[264] The day had begun with a concert at the Washington Monument featuring both black and white musicians, including Odetta, Josh White, the Albany Freedom Singers, Bob Dylan and the folk group Peter, Paul and

Mary, whose version of Dylan's civil rights anthem 'Blowin' in the Wind' was then number two on the charts.[265]

The crowd of around a quarter of a million at the Lincoln Memorial for the main event was warmed up by Mahalia Jackson with the gospel classic 'I've Been 'Buked and I've Been Scorned'. By all accounts, the impact on the audience was tremendous: 'The button-down men in front and the old women in back came to their feet screaming and shouting. They had not known that this thing was in them, and that they wanted it touched. From different places and different ways, with different dreams they had come, and now, hearing this sung, they were one'.[266] Martin Luther King Jr. then stepped forward to deliver what was intended to be a short speech. As he was about to finish, Mahalia Jackson called out to him: 'Tell them about your dream, Martin! Tell them about the dream!' He then launched into a visionary passage all the more effective for being improvised, beginning: 'I have a dream that one day this nation will rise up and live out the true meaning of its creed: "We hold these truths to be self-evident, that all men are created equal"'.[267]

As Craig Werner commented: 'If King gave the movement a vision, Mahalia Jackson gave it a voice'.[268] Her own voice was resolutely religious— she refused to sing anything but gospel music despite many alluring offers—but the music of the black church was transported into the secular realm through soul music. The lyrics of Ray Charles' trail-blazing 'I've Got a Woman' of 1954 are as carnal as anything penned by Chuck Berry, but the music came straight out of the church. Not only were all the top soul artists—Wilson Pickett, Percy Sledge, Otis Redding, Aretha Franklin, Marvin Gaye, Gladys Knight—black, their sound was self-consciously black too. Yet many of the session musicians at the Stax studios in Memphis— and all of them at the Muscle Shoals studios in Alabama used by Atlantic, the other main soul recording company—were white.[269]

That did not prevent soul music from becoming a mighty mouthpiece for civil rights as the movement became more militant in the course of the 1960s. 'Respect' (1967) by Aretha Franklin, the Queen of Soul, may be a song about a personal relationship, but 'R-E-S-P-E-C-T' was perceived by millions to spell out a demand made by a whole race. More assertive still was the dominant male soul singer, James Brown. His 'Say It Loud—I'm Black and I'm Proud' at once became the anthem of the Black Power move-

On 28 August 1963 Dr. Martin Luthr King, Jr. listens as Mahalia Jackson sings to a crowd of around a quarter of a million people in front of the Lincoln Memorial immediately before he made his 'I have a dream' speech.

ment. The emphatic repetition of the title's demands culminates with the *cri de coeur:* 'We rather die on our feet, Than keep living on our knees.' Brown was mobilised by the founder of the Afro-American Association, Donald Warden, who commented: 'I've always said that the only thing that unites our race is music.' When Martin Luther King Jr. appeared on television, Warden told Brown, the audience targeted was white, but what the movement needed most was someone who knew how to talk to young black people.[270]

Musical support for the civil rights movement was not confined to rhythm and blues or soul. Jazz musicians also added their voice. Although dismissed by many as an Uncle Tom who had sold out to the entertainment industry, in 1957 Louis Armstrong rejected a proposed tour of the USSR, organised by the State Department's Cultural Exchange Programme, on the grounds that white resistance to school integration in Little Rock, Arkansas, would make it impossible for him to respond to the inevitable questions about the state of civil rights in the United States. He added into the bargain a vehement denunciation of Governor Faubus, who had called in the Arkansas National Guard to prevent the nine black students from entering Central High School, and President Eisenhower, who after some initial hesitation sent federal troops to uphold the court order and protect the students.[271]

Musical protests were made by, among others, Charles Mingus ('Fables of Faubus'), Sonny Rollins ('Freedom Suite'), John Coltrane ('Alabama'), and Max Roach ('We Insist! The Freedom Now Suite'). But the price paid for supporting the cause of civil rights could be heavy. The black singer Harry Belafonte found himself ostracised by Hollywood and excluded from television for more than a decade, but he was defiant: 'There was just no other choice. There was no other army to join. There was no other country to go to. There was no other head of state to appeal to. It was it. It was the day. I felt there was no place else in the world to be other than here.'[272]

Just how crucial was the contribution made by music to the liberation of African Americans obviously cannot be quantified. Yet only the most vehement determinist, who sees integration as the inevitable result of inexorable economic forces, could deny it an important role. The last word can be left to Martin Luther King Jr., who in 1967 told black deejays assembled at Atlanta for the convention of the National Association of Television and Radio Announcers: 'You have paved the way for social and political change by creating a powerful, cultural bridge between black and white. School integration is much easier now that they share a common music, a common language and enjoy the same dances. You introduced youth to that music and created a language of soul and promoted the dances which now sweep across race, class and nation.[273]

But hard times were coming. Dr. King was assassinated in 1968, and in the 1970s and 1980s the limitations of the legal victories achieved by the civil rights movement became painfully apparent.[274] As middle-class whites (and blacks) fled from city centres to exclusive suburban enclaves, many members of the urban black underclass sank ever deeper into poverty, while rates of crime and substance abuse soared.[275] To the hour came the music. Hip-hop and its close relation, rap, expressed and encouraged the intense alienation experienced by young blacks in inner-city ghettos. Rap began in Jamaica when deejays started to improvise their own rhyming verses over the records they were playing.[276] Introduced to the slums of the South Bronx by Caribbean immigrants in the late 1970s, it developed very quickly and spread right across the United States. Drugs, sex, crime and violence in various combinations provided the raw material for most rap songs, which predictably caused outrage to older generations, both black and white.

Representative of rap's concerns are the lyrics of 'Straight Outta Compton' (a slum in South Central Los Angeles) by Niggaz with Attitude. This group brought together six of the most influential rappers of the late 1980s—Eazy-E, Dr. Dre, Ice Cube, MC Ren, Arabian Prince and DJ Yellah. This song revels in their collective image as a 'bad muthafucker' with a well-earned reputation for violence ('More punks I smoke, yo, my rep gets bigger'), sex on demand ('I find a good piece o' pussy, I go up in it') and misogyny ('I'm a call you a bitch or dirty-ass ho'). The album, of the same title, was ranked 144 by *Rolling Stone* magazine on its list of '500 Greatest Albums of All Time'. Niggaz with Attitude achieved 83rd place among the 'The Immortals', the hundred 'greatest [musical] artists of all time' identified by the same journal as part of the celebrations organised in 2004 to mark fifty years of rock 'n' roll. Part of their citation ran: 'Rock & Roll is more about rebellion than guitars. Niggaz with Attitude's *Straight Outta Compton* officially took that baton away from rock: It's the album that made hip-hop the new rock & roll.'[277]

Sex

Whatever one might think of the lyrics and music of the rappers, their ability to strike a responsive chord with their audience cannot be doubted. It would be tempting to regard this as the *ne plus ultra* and call a halt, but one final aspect of music's role in fomenting rebellion and liberation needs to be addressed, however briefly, and that is sex.

The close association between music and sex is as old as time, of course. Among many other landmarks along the way, one of the very first operas—Monteverdi's *The Coronation of Poppea* (1642)—is a highly erotic work. So are Mozart's operas, although not many modern directors seem to be aware of it. Both the text and music of *The Marriage of Figaro*, for example, make it clear that 'the mad day' is going to end with multiple couplings: Figaro and Susannah, Cherubino and Barbarina, the Count and the Countess, even Bartolo and Marcellina. In the nineteenth century, Romanticism, with its emphasis on the emotions, the subconscious and the night, bound the two closer together than ever before. A multiple musical climax in every sense of the word was reached in Act Two of Wagner's *Tristan and Isolde*, complete with postcoital depression. Even more daringly, Act One of *The Valkyrie* (the second part of the *Ring* tetralogy) ends with Siegmund and Sieglinde, brother and sister, about to have sex. Wagner's stage direction states: 'He pulls her to him with furious passion, she sinks on his chest with a cry', adding 'the curtain falls quickly'. ('And about time too!' scribbled an outraged Arthur Schopenhauer in the margin of the copy Wagner had sent him).[278] The association was then continued in operetta, musical comedy and above all cinema. How many films have been made without 'a love interest'? And how many love scenes have transpired without the accompaniment of music? Kissing necessarily silences the embracers, so their emotions have to be expressed with instrumental music.

Popular music has always taken young love and its tribulations as a major theme, but the eruption of a specific youth culture in the second half of the twentieth century brought a revolutionary change in its representation. Put crudely, romance made way for sex. Like film stars, singers had always attracted fans, but rock 'n' roll inspired behaviour that made even Frank Sinatra's bobby-soxers seem tame. The very name had an explicit sexual connotation. Blues singer Trixie Smith sang on a recording of 1922,

'My man rocks me with one steady roll' while Ferdinand Morton (1885–1941) awarded himself the sobriquet Jelly Roll to advertise his sexual prowess.[279]

What had long been a commonplace in black music then exploded into the white world in March 1955 when the film *Blackboard Jungle,* directed by Richard Brooks, was released. As the opening credits roll, a new teacher (played by Glenn Ford) arrives outside North Manual High, making his way to the entrance through groups of rude, hostile, louche, unkempt teenagers. The soundtrack is provided by Bill Haley singing 'Rock around the Clock' with the volume turned up. As James Miller has written: 'In the two minutes and ten seconds it lasted on screen, this combination of image and song defined the cultural essence of [rock 'n' roll]. It would be all about disorder, aggression and sex: a fantasy of human nature running wild to a savage beat'.[280] Probably helped by the accusation by *Time* magazine that the film was playing into the hands of Communist critics of the American way of life, it was a colossal success and Haley's record sold over 6 million copies.[281]

Plump, balding, and not in the first flush of youth, Bill Haley was not the stuff of which rock 'n' roll idols are made. It says a great deal for the raw force of his music that 'Rock around the Clock' made such an impact. Almost simultaneously, however, a much more likely candidate appeared in the shape of Elvis Presley, ten years younger than Haley, with a much better voice and looks to match. He also had charisma, the ability to reduce an audience to hysteria just by appearing on stage. At Kilgore, Texas, in the summer of 1956, the country musician Bob Luman attended a Presley concert:

> This cat came out in red pants and a green coat and a pink shirt and socks . . . and he had a sneer on his face and he stood behind the mic for five minutes I'll bet before he made a move. Then he hit his guitar with a lick and broke two strings . . . So there was these two strings a-dangling, and he hadn't done a thing yet, and these high school girls were screaming and fainting and running up to the edge of the stage, and he started to move his hips real slow like he had a thing for his guitar.[282]

Presley's wild man phase did not last long. His new manager, Colonel Tom Parker, soon had him appearing on television and in the movies, and in the process creating an oxymoronic image of danger and security, simultaneously 'butch god and teddy bear'.[283] 'He's just like a paperback book', said one of his girl fans, 'Real sexy picture on the cover. Only when you get inside, it's just a good story'.[284] The formula had a long future and immense international appeal. Across the Atlantic, a number of enterprising impresarios sought to find an English Elvis, coming up with such wonderfully named candidates as Billy Fury, Cuddly Dudley, Marty Wilde, Vince Eager, Johnny Gentle, Dickie Pride, and Duffy Power. The clear winner was Cliff Richard (*né* Harry Webb), who emerged in 1958 complete with tight trousers, sneer, quiff and sideburns. The television producer Jack Good initiated Richard's metamorphosis into family entertainer: 'Cliff was soon less of a threat than a promise', as the jazz singer George Melly observed.[285]

Melly also found the perfect metaphor to depict the domesticating process:

> Each successive pop music explosion has come roaring out of the clubs in which it was born like an angry young bull. Watching from the other side of the gate, the current Establishment has proclaimed it dangerous, subversive, a menace to youth, and demanded something be done about it. Something is. Commercial exploitation advances towards it holding out a bucketful of recording contracts, television appearances and worldwide fame. Then, once the muzzle is safely buried in the golden mash, the cunning butcher nips deftly along the flank and castrates the animal. After this painless operation, the Establishment realizes it is safe to advance into the field and gingerly pats the now docile creature which can then be safely relied on to grow fatter and stupider until the moment when fashion decides it is ready for the slaughterhouse.[286]

Handsome is as handsome does, Cliff might retort to Melly's further sour observation: 'He is still around, too, an enigma in many ways and apparently ageless'. Those words were written thirty-seven years ago, but in 2007

Cliff was still performing and still recording, having sold around 250 million records in the meantime.

Back in the 1950s, not all rock 'n' rollers succumbed to the temptation to become all-round entertainers. The Beatles retained their integrity by taking a neo-romantic route. An alternative was found by The Rolling Stones, who, far from toning down the raw sexuality of their act, actually sharpened it up. Whether by accident or design, they found a formula with a powerful appeal to the world's adolescents. The kind of teenagers Glenn Ford encountered at North Manual High were everywhere. Mick Jagger did not disguise his (legendary) physical desires with codes of the June-Moon-Spoon variety; he sang, 'I just wanna make love to you' and 'Let's spend the night together', a message reinforced by equally unambiguous body language. The results were spectacular.

The journalist and pop historian Nik Cohn recalls an early Rolling Stones concert in Liverpool: 'After the show, I hung around in the dressing-rooms. The Stones were being ritually vicious to everyone, fans and journalists and hangers-on regardless, and I got bored. So I went down into the auditorium and it was empty, quite deserted, but there was this weird smell. Piss: the small girls had screamed too hard and wet themselves. Not just one or two of them but many, so that the floor was sodden and the stench was overwhelming'.[287]

This is of more than prurient interest. The Rolling Stones had the good fortune to arrive on the scene just as two social developments of immense power began to converge with awesome synergy: the sexual revolution and the clash of generations. The Rolling Stones benefited from this combination—and also gave it further momentum of unquantifiable but undoubted power. For adolescents seeking sexual liberation as part of a rejection of their parents' culture, rock groups like The Rolling Stones were immensely attractive role models. In the popular culture of the past, sex had either been coated in sugary ballads or hinted at slyly (the camera cutting from a kiss to a train rushing through a tunnel). Now it was out there, up front and increasingly in your face. As Flea, bassist of Red Hot Chili Peppers, put it: 'From our viewpoint it's impossible to ignore the correlation between music and sex because, being so incredibly rhythmic as it is, it's very deeply correlated to sex and the rhythm of sex, and the rhythm of your heart pounding and intercourse motions and just the way it makes you feel when you hear it. We try to make our music give you an erection'.[288]

George Bernard Shaw, who died in 1950, famously defined dancing as 'the vertical expression of a horizontal desire legalized by music'.[289] What he would have made of The Rolling Stones and their like challenges the imagination. But rock music has done much more than provide inflammatory lyrics and a beat to support them ('a rancid-smelling aphrodisiac' was Frank Sinatra's comment on Presley's early records).[290] It has taken sex out of the middle-aged, middle-class closet and placed it at the centre of a youth culture that is self-consciously and aggressively hedonistic and amoral. In a seminal article of 1978, the sociologists Simon Frith and Angela McRobbie claimed that 'of all the mass media, rock is the most explicitly concerned with sexual expression. This reflects its function as a youth cultural form: rock treats the problems of puberty, it draws on and articulates the psychological and physical tensions of adolescence, it accompanies the moment when boys and girls learn their repertoire of public sexual behaviour'.[291]

Especially important in this regard, they argue, are 'cock rock' performers like Mick Jagger, Roger Daltrey and Robert Plant—'aggressive, dominating and boastful'.[292] It culminated in what Charles Shaar Murray has memorably termed the 'penile dementia' of heavy-metal rock.[293] In a book cheekily, but it might be thought appropriately, entitled *The Triumph of Vulgarity*, Robert Pattison observed: 'Only someone who has tried to imagine Frank Sinatra performing in a padded G-string can fully appreciate the chasm that separates rock from its pop predecessors'.[294]

Not the least attraction of rock 'n' roll for its practitioners has been the access to easy sex. Where once fans gathered outside a stage door hoping for a crooner's autograph, by the 1960s groupies were competing fiercely for the privilege of offering every possible sexual service to their heroes (but not their heroines—male groupies are not unknown, but rare). From the rich range of possibilities, two will suffice: 'You were at school and nobody wanted to know you. Then you get into a group and you've got thousands of chicks there. There you are with thousands of girls screaming their heads off at you. Man, it's power . . . *phew!*' (Eric Clapton); and 'I'm in this job to exercise my sexual fantasies. When I'm on stage, it's like doing it with twenty thousand of your closest friends' (David Lee Roth of Van Halen).[295]

Needless to say, the musicians themselves played to the gallery. Jimi Hendrix took full advantage of the rumour that his member was of legend-

'Cock Rock': Jimmy Page and Robert Plant of Led Zeppelin in action. The group has sold more than 100 million albums, a total exceeded only by The Beatles and Elvis Presley.

ary size (an enterprising Los Angeles club put Hendrix Super Sausages on its menu), that backstage he had 'pussy for breakfast, dinner and supper', that he had serviced seven groupies in just three hours, and the like.[296] At concerts he would lean over to women in the audience and lap his tongue in simulated cunnilingus.[297] He recounted the following typical on-tour encounter to an interviewer, his coy use of a euphemism only serving to emphasise its casual nature: 'And I get up at 7 o'clock in the morning and I'm really sleepy, and I open the door [of the hotel room] and see someone who really appeals to me, and first of all I ask myself 'What in the world is she doing here? What does she even want?', or something like that. And then she says, 'Uh, may I come in?' And I'm just standing there really digging her . . . and she might be nineteen, twenty, past *that age* . . . so then I'll invite her in for a nap.'[298]

As these episodes reveal, sexual liberation has proved more liberating for men than for women. If it is a cliché to observe that rock is a man's world, it bears repeating. Of course many women have built brilliant and durable careers for themselves, and undoubtedly more of them are making more money than at any previous time. Tina Turner, Annie Lennox and Celine Dion have enjoyed a status just as elevated as any of their male counterparts. But *relatively* their position has deteriorated from the pre-rock days when the likes of Patti Page, Rosemary Clooney and Doris Day shared equal billing with male crooners such as Perry Como, Eddie Fisher and Tony Bennett and conveyed the same sort of message using the same sort of music. *The Rolling Stone Illustrated History of Rock 'n' Roll*, the most comprehensive history available, contains forty-five chapters about named individuals and groups, but only three of them are about women (Aretha Franklin, Janis Joplin and Madonna). The chapter entitled 'The Girl Groups' is just over two pages long and begins with the patronising observation (written by a man, Greil Marcus): 'Of all the genres of rock 'n' roll, girl-group rock is likely the warmest and the most affecting. The style flourished between 1958 and 1963, fallow years for rock 'n' roll, and it flourished for the same reasons much of the rest of the music of the time grew tame, predictable and dull.'[299] A later chapter on 'Women in Revolt' makes the most of Patti Smith, Chrissie Hynde and Sinead O'Connor but can do little to redress the negative balance. Female singers still account for only about a quarter of earnings from rock music, and on concert tours they are paid up to a third less than men with comparable record sales.[300]

If music has proved a double-edged sword in the struggle for women's liberation, it has had an unequivocally positive impact on the simultaneous gay liberation movement. The musical world has long been attractive to homosexuals, in no small part because of its relative tolerance. Once again, Richard Wagner provides a cheering example. When his second wife Cosima was rash enough to criticise the relationship between their friend Paul von Joukowsky and his Neapolitan man-servant Pepino, she incurred the Master's disapproval: 'It is something for which I have understanding, but no inclination,' Wagner said. 'In any case, with all relationships what matters most is what we ourselves put into them.'[301] A simple roll call of some of the more celebrated gay and bisexual musicians in the twentieth century is also revealing: Samuel Barber, Richard Rodney Bennett, Leonard Bernstein, Benjamin Britten, John Cage, Aaron Copland, Peter Maxwell Davies, Lorenz Hart, Hans Werner Henze, Ivor Novello, Peter Pears, Cole Porter, François Poulenc, Ethel Smyth, Stephen Sondheim, Billy Strayhorn, Michael Tilson Thomas, Michael Tippett, and Virgil Thomson, not forgetting Wagner's own son Siegfried.[302]

In the struggle for equality and social justice, the lead in securing legislative change has necessarily been taken by politicians. Where musicians have been in the vanguard is in the simultaneous and more important campaign for social acceptance. As with civil rights for African Americans, no history of the gay movement could be written without a musical dimension. As one activist has written: 'Sharing a taste for music is one of the main glues of gay culture, whether it's nervy nancies in the 50s swooning along to Judy, twirling disco bunnies in 70s clubs shrieking when they recognise the first bars of a Sylvester record or cocky post-modern 90s queerboys playing guessing games about Take That.'[303] Particularly important were discotheques, for the music they created proved to have universal appeal, encouraging crossovers between gay and straight audiences.[304]

So did the growing number of performers who around the same time, in the 1970s, began to experiment with gender-bending. Nothing could have illustrated better the shift in power on the popular music scene from the older generation than the wide acceptance—enthusiasm even—this found. The colossal success enjoyed by the avowedly bisexual David Bowie also encouraged tolerance of gay lifestyles. Writing in *The Face* in 1980, Jon Savage claimed that Bowie's achievement had been 'to open Pandora's box:

by making homosex *attractive* (rather than a snigger) he liberated and brought into the mainstream a whole range of fantasies which had hitherto been repressed. Naturally they came out with great force'.[305] Another boundary was crossed in 1983 with the video accompanying *Relax* by the group Frankie Goes to Hollywood. The lyrics look relatively innocuous, but when sung accompanied by a video filmed in what appeared to be an S and M club on bondage night, the message was unmistakable. It proved too much for the BBC, which promptly banned it—thus ensuring its commercial success (five weeks at number one).

Inside the world of hard rock—traditionally a citadel of uncompromising masculinity—the turning point was the death of Freddie Mercury, the lead singer of Queen, from an AIDS-related illness in November 1991. In the following April, the three survivors, all heterosexual, organised a tribute concert at Wembley Stadium to raise money for the Mercury Phoenix Trust, a charity to raise awareness of the disease. All 72,000 seats available were sold at once and the concert was televised in seventy countries, attracting an audience of more than half a billion, not to mention the untold millions more who experienced it subsequently on video.[306] Re-released as a DVD on the concert's tenth anniversary in 2002, the video went straight to number one in the charts. Although musically uneven, the concert certainly marked mass acceptance of homosexuality by the world of rock music. The presence of George Michael, Elton John, David Bowie and Annie Lennox was perhaps predictable. More indicative of the sea-change in attitude was the appearance of cock-rockers such as Robert Plant, Tony Iommi, Joe Elliott, Slash and Axl Rose. Even more revealing was the conduct of the audience, whose banners and slogans proclaimed Freddie Mercury a martyr, a hero, a god even. This was not so much a concert as a great collective act of redemption—a further demonstration that in the modern world, music is the religion of the masses and the stadium its cathedral.

On the other side of the gender divide, probably less important than the avowedly lesbian musicians has been the gender bending of artists such as Madonna, demonstrating that not only are they not ashamed about, but they positively relish, same-sex physical contacts. Madonna's open-mouth kisses with Britney Spears and Christina Aguilera during their performance at the MTV awards in 2003 probably advanced the cause more effectively than a dozen k.d. lang albums. The same might be said of those 'play gay'

David Bowie as Ziggy Stardust shows that he is in touch with his feminine side.

singers who insist on their heterosexuality but like to flirt with androgynous ambivalence. The most cynical exercise in this regard was the creation of t.A.T.u. by the Russian entrepreneur Ivan Shapovalov in 1999. His gimmick was the pretence that the two singers—Lena Katina and Yulia Volkova—were lesbian lovers, the fact that they were only just over the age of consent (for heterosexual activity) only adding to the spice. He told an eagerly listening *Sun:* 'I got the idea of t.A.T.u. from market research. I saw that most people look up pornography on the Internet and of those, most are looking for underage sex. I saw their needs weren't fulfilled. Later, it turned out, I was right. This is the same as my own desires. I prefer underage girls.'[307] His market research proved to be accurate: t.A.T.u. became an international sensation, the most popular Russian group in history, and sold 5 million copies of their first record. By the time it leaked out that neither girl was lesbian, their reputation had been established and the acceptability of lesbianism had been advanced.[308]

The change in attitude toward homosexuality has been arguably the greatest social change to have occurred in the developed world during the last half-century or so. In 1959 the American pianist Liberace was awarded damages of £8,000 and costs in the High Court in London for a libellous article published three years earlier by the *Daily Mirror,* whose columnist Cassandra had implied that he was homosexual by calling him 'the summit of sex—Masculine, Feminine and Neuter. Everything that He, She and It can ever want' and 'a deadly, winking, sniggering, snuggling, chromium-plated, scent-impregnated, luminous, quivering, giggling, fruit-flavoured, mincing, ice-covered heap of mother love'. Liberace was indeed a homosexual, but that did not stop him from perjuring himself repeatedly in the course of a six-hour cross-examination, denying that he had ever engaged in homosexual acts and proclaiming: 'I am against the practice because it offends convention and it offends society'. His subsequent justification was simple: Cassandra 'cost me many years of my professional career by implying that I am a homosexual . . . It has caused untold agonies and embarrassment and has made me the subject of ridicule . . . In 1956, people were destroyed by that accusation. It hurt me. People stayed away from my shows in droves. I went from the top to the bottom in a very short time, and I had to fight for my life'.[309]

Half-a-century later, on 22 December 2005, another gay pianist, Sir

Madonna shows that she is in touch with her masculine side at the MTV Awards ceremony in 2003.

Elton John, married David Furnish, his long-standing partner, in a civil partnership ceremony at Windsor Guildhall (where earlier in the year the Prince of Wales had married his even longer-standing partner, Camilla Parker-Bowles). The guest list at the reception that followed included celebrities from the worlds of fashion (Donatella Versace, Claudia Schiffer), sports (Michael Vaughan, David Beckham, Greg Rusedski), art (Sam Taylor-Wood), theatre (Sir Anthony Sher, Sir Tim Rice), cinema (Elizabeth Hurley), and of course a large crowd of musicians (Ringo Starr, Ozzy Osbourne, the Scissor Sisters, Bryan Adams, Joss Stone, the Pet Shop Boys, James Blunt, Gary Barlow, Lulu, and so on).

The contrast between the perjury of Liberace and the apotheosis of Sir Elton hardly needs further comment. Sir Elton had already provided the clearest possible sign that the last citadel of the establishment had fallen when he recorded in advance his contribution to the Queen's Jubilee concert from *inside* Buckingham Palace. In 1956, to be thought queer, a poof, a nancy boy or whatever was not just the ultimate stigma, it could also lead to criminal prosecution and imprisonment. According to the *Oxford*

t.A.T.u.—Lena Katina and Yulia Volkova.

English Dictionary, the definition of 'homophobia' was originally a 'fear of men, or aversion towards the male sex'. Its first use to mean 'fear or hatred of homosexuals and homosexuality' did not come until 1969. So rapidly have attitudes changed that today it is axiomatic that being a homophobe places a person outside the pale of civilised society. Although many individuals, groups and impersonal forces have combined to bring this about, it is unthinkable without the participation of musicians, demonstrating once again the liberating power of their art.

Conclusion

For good or ill, music has been transformed in the modern world—and has helped to transform that world. But as I have discovered when inviting comments and questions from the audience after giving public lectures on this topic, many people believe that the history of music during the past century has been anything but a triumphal progress. On the contrary, they assert, music in the classical tradition has disappeared into a stratospheric sonic world of plinks and plonks accessible only by other musicians, while popular music has plumbed ever more subterranean depths of offensive vulgarity. Although I have much sympathy for this alternative scenario, I find that its definition of music is both too elitist and too subjective. In any case, in this book my topic has not been the triumph of serious music, classical music, or even good music (however defined) but the triumph of music *per se.* That much of the music pumped out around the clock through every imaginable medium is found by many to be vacuous, offensive, worthless—and every other pejorative adjective to be found in a thesaurus—is neither here nor there, for my purposes.

The Beatles provide an instructive illustration. Their phenomenal success provoked a reaction of corresponding intensity. Writing in the *New Statesman* in 1964, Paul Johnson exploded with rage at what he called 'this apotheosis of inanity'. He also inadvertently revealed in two ways just why what he called 'the new cult of youth' had developed an 'anti-culture' all of its own. First, he derided with contempt the teenage audiences he had observed on television: 'What a bottomless chasm of vacuity they reveal! The huge faces, bloated with cheap confectionery and smeared with chain store makeup, the open, sagging mouths and glazed eyes, the hands mindlessly drumming in time to the music, the broken stiletto heels, the shoddy, stereotyped, "with-it" clothes: here, apparently, is a collective portrait of a generation enslaved by a commercial machine'. Second, he boasted of the excellence of his own education (Stonyhurst and Magdalen College, Oxford): 'I remember the drudgery of Greek prose and calculus, but I can also remember reading the whole of Shakespeare and Marlowe, writing poems and plays and stories . . . Almost every week one found a fresh idol—Milton, Wagner, Debussy, Matisse, El Greco, Proust—some, indeed, to be subsequently toppled from the pantheon, but all springing from the mainstream of European culture'.[1]

Paul Johnson is happily still with us, and still advertising the depth and range of his personal culture on a weekly basis, although these days he finds the conservative journal *The Spectator* a more congenial organ. It would be interesting to learn his views about The Beatles forty-three years on. He might gain comfort from the following characteristically cynical observation by John Lennon in 1973: 'There's a bloke in England, William Mann, who writes for *The Times* and who wrote the first intellectual article about the Beatles, and after this people began to talk about us in intellectual terms . . . He uses a whole lot of musical terminology and he's a twit. But he made us acceptable to the intellectuals . . . But he is still writing the same rubbish. But he also did us a whole lot of good, because all the intellectuals and middle class people were suddenly saying "Ooh"'.[2] Nothing if not bold, Mann had also described Lennon and McCartney as 'the greatest songwriters since Schubert'.

So who has been proved right, William Mann or Paul Johnson? For all his pretentiousness (a good example being his reference to the 'Aeolian cadence' in The Beatles' song 'Not a Second Time' in 1963), Mann must be the winner.[3] Such a verdict has nothing to do with any subjective assessment of the quality of The Beatles' music but everything to do with durability. As aesthetic criteria go, the ability to appeal to one generation after another commends itself by its objectivity. For all his cynical self-deprecation, Lennon became a cult figure, especially after his murder in 1980. A poll of

600,000 people conducted worldwide twenty years after his death named him the most influential musician of all time, ahead of Johann Sebastian Bach (seventh) and Mozart (tenth). He was also voted best song writer, while The Beatles won the awards for best group and best album (*Sergeant Pepper's Lonely Hearts Club Band*).[4] The Beatles' song 'Yesterday' (1965, composed and sung by Paul McCartney) has been recorded more than 3,000 times by other artists, more than any other song in history. According to the performance rights organisation BMI, by the year 2000 it had been performed in public more than 7 million times, each time providing a royalty for McCartney and Lennon, who was also given official credit.[5]

Nor can it be said that the success of The Beatles and other popular musicians has been at the expense of classical music. Technological advances have made available in several different formats far more versions of a much greater variety of classical music than ever before in history. Until the arrival of the long-playing record, very little 'early music' was available on disc. Beginning in the 1950s, however, an ever-swelling flow of recordings created a new—and very much larger—public for what had previously been very much a minority taste. Noah Greenberg, whose recording of Banchieri madrigals was an unexpected hit in 1953, observed: 'Amazingly enough, it was not the givers of conventional concerts who opened up their programs to the repertory of early music but the record companies—and, for the most part, not the large record companies (who could easily have afforded to do it) but the small ones, who could not afford to hire the virtuoso ensembles and artists needed to sell recordings of the standard repertoire'.[6] By 1981 a discography devoted to early music listed 3,164 different items.[7] Further progress could be charted through the expanding review section of the specialist periodical *Early Music*, founded in 1973. Demonstrating impressive awareness of the potential of new technology, it marked its thirtieth anniversary by starting to post sound clips on the Internet to illustrate articles published in its pages.[8]

In such a rapidly changing world, only the adaptable survive. Sympathy for the casualties, left stranded by the collapse of this orchestra or that record company, has to be balanced by admiration for the enterprise of the beneficiaries. Every time that the 'end of the music industry' is predicted in the face of challenges mounted by Internet downloads or file-sharing, music has found its way back to its place in the sun. Two good examples have been provided recently by Sir John Eliot Gardiner. In the year 2000

Deutsche Grammophon abruptly cancelled the contract to issue record-ings of his *Bach Pilgrimage* of that year, in the course of which he per-formed all 200 of J. S. Bach's church cantatas. His response was to found his own record company named SDG, standing for Soli Deo Gloria (To the Glory of God alone), the words Bach often added to a completed score.[9] The twenty-odd CDs issued so far have been a commercial and artistic tri-umph, as eloquent a tribute as could be imagined to what can be achieved by marrying artistic genius with technological resources. Gardiner has shown another way forward by recording the first part of a concert, at the Cadogan Hall in London in February 2006, and then having the result transferred to CDs in time to be sold to members of the audience as they came out at the end.

Other branches of the creative arts have also benefited from the de-velopments discussed in this book and continue to flourish, although often with paradoxical results. In terms of technological advance, it is architec-ture that has benefited most of all, yet its practitioners enjoy little renown and less respect than musicians. For every new building that captures the public imagination—Renzo Piano and Richard Rogers' Pompidou Centre in Paris, Norman Foster's Gherkin in London, Frank Gehry's Guggenheim Museum in Bilbao—ten thousand more are met with indifference. The same applies to sculpture and sculptors, if not more so. Although books are probably cheaper and can certainly be illustrated more lavishly than at any time in the past, in relative terms the power of the written word and the status of its creators have been in decline since the late nineteenth cen-tury. In particular, the days when poets enjoyed fame and fortune are long gone, as Oxford University Press advertised in 1999 by closing its contem-porary poets list. A comparison of the standing enjoyed by Alfred Lord Tennyson among his contemporaries with the present poet laureate (his name is Andrew Motion) reveals a calamitous decline. The novel is still alive, but novelists have dropped a division or two in public esteem. The gap between Charles Dickens and, say, Martin Amis is better described as a chasm. The over-excited welcome given to J. K. Rowling's Harry Potter se-ries has only served to dramatise the extent to which reading has atrophied. So far, any hopes that digital technology (e-books, for example) might bring a revival of reading have not been fulfilled.

In our postliterate age, the visual arts have come closest to matching the success of music. One simple way of charting the shift in the balance of power between word and image is to compare the change in their relative importance in any newspaper, for it can be summed up very quickly by the formula 'more and more pictures, fewer and fewer words'.[10] Enterprising artists and their agents have been quick to exploit the potential of new technology, building their own websites to advertise their wares. In the same way that YouTube has allowed musicians to cut out the middlemen and go straight to their audience, the Saatchi Gallery's Your Gallery is allowing aspiring painters to beam their creations across the world.[11] Actual (as opposed to virtual) galleries have also done well—the Tate Modern in London attracted nearly five million visitors in 2006, and the Museum of Fine Arts in Boston is undergoing a huge expansion. At the very top of the slippery pole, artists are probably better paid than at any time in human history: *Red-Haired Man on a Chair* by Lucian Freud fetched $8,200,000 at auction, Damien Hirst's *Lullaby Water* claimed £3,700,000, and Charles Saatchi paid Tracey Emin £150,000 for *My Bed*. The list goes on.

Yet even when every record-breaking auction price has been logged and every concession about the ubiquity of images has been granted, the visual arts are unable to mount much of a challenge to music's lonely eminence. At the heart of the imbalance is the nature of the respective genres. No matter what medium they employ, all artists seek to create an artefact that is unique, that cannot be reproduced. A wealthy patron might give a million pounds or more for an original painting, but not a brass farthing for a photograph of the same. So, in what Walter Benjamin called the age of mechanical reproduction, art is necessarily handicapped if not hobbled.[12] Moreover, even if the artefact does not disappear into the vault of a bank or onto the wall of a closely guarded private dwelling, it has to be viewed in a gallery. Below the level of high art, virtually all images have a very short life span. The one or two that achieve classic status—the Athena poster of a girl in a tennis dress scratching her bare bottom, which sold two million copies, springs readily to mind—are the exceptions that prove the rule. Yet the hordes of musical equivalents—'Itsy Bitsy Teenie Weenie Yellow Polka Dot Bikini' (1960) will serve as well as any—have turned out to have amazing staying power despite the stupefying banality of both lyrics and music.

A much more serious challenge has been mounted by the moving images of cinema and television. The medium has benefited as much as music from technological innovation, while its stars have achieved comparable status, popularity and wealth. They have also played an important role in promoting social and political change. Yet music necessarily enjoys two advantages. First, it is far more interactive. Only a minuscule number of those who watch film or television can ever hope to become active participants as actors or presenters. On the other hand, only the tone deaf are disqualified from making music of some kind. In the twentieth and twenty-first century, the falling cost of musical instruments and the introduction of mass instruction techniques such as the Suzuki method have combined to make active music-making more widespread than ever before. The decline in the manufacturing of traditional pianos has been more than offset by the rapid expansion of instruments old and new. The rewards that await entrepreneurs able to adapt to changing market conditions have been exemplified by the meteoric growth of the Japanese Yamaha corporation after 1945 to become the biggest manufacturer of musical instruments in the world.

Second, the relationship between music and the moving image has been mutually beneficial but unequal. As we have seen, cinema and television were less a threat than an opportunity for music and musicians. In the last few years this has been demonstrated yet again by the phenomenal success of the talent show *Pop Idol* and its various spinoffs (*American Idol, Germany Seeks a Superstar, The X-Factor* and so on), first televised in 2001. From Albania to Bolivia, from Afghanistan to Serbia, the format has proved irresistible: in more than fifty countries across the globe hundreds of thousands of aspiring singers of all ages, shapes and sizes have been prepared to queue for hours just to audition. Millions more pay to phone, text or email their votes. In the course of the various heats for the *American Idol* competition in 2006, more than 500 million votes were cast, the final alone attracting 63 million (the highest vote total achieved by an American president was Ronald Reagan's 54.5 million in 1984).[13] And that is the adamantine, irreducible fact: music can exist without the moving image, but the moving image cannot exist without music.

As this book has tried to show, to the age came the art form. The development of the public sphere and the resulting transformation of cultural places and spaces; secularisation and the corresponding sacralisation of culture; the romantic revolution; the ever-accelerating pace of technological innovation; the eruption of youth culture during the second half of the twentieth century—all combined to propel music to pole position among both the creative and the performing arts, in terms of status, influence and material reward. None of these forces looks like going into reverse in the foreseeable future. This may be bad news for latter-day Paul Johnsons, diverted from studying Greek and calculus or writing 'poems and plays and stories', but it is good news for music.

Chronology

As my investigation of the triumph of music has been organised under five thematic headings, it may be helpful to have a chronological table listing the main events and works mentioned in the main text. A second column has been added to provide a more general historical context.

1612 Claudio Monteverdi is dismissed by the duke of Mantua and moves to Venice	1602 Death of Elizabeth I of England
	1618 Thirty Years War begins
1642 Monteverdi, *The Coronation of Poppea*	1642 Civil War in Britain
	1643 Accession of Louis XIV
1660 Lully becomes Composer of the King's Chamber Music	1660 Restoration of Charles II in England
1662 Cavalli's *Ercole* is the last Italian opera to be performed in France for 67 years	1661 Louis XIV's personal rule begins
1665 Louis XIV dismisses his Italian musicians	
1669 Foundation of the Royal Academy of Music in France	1667 War of Devolution in the Spanish Netherlands; Pascal, *Pensées*; Spinoza, *Tractatus theologico-politicus*
1672 First public concert (in London)	1672 Franco-Dutch War (to 1678)
1680s Public concerts begin in Leipzig	1681 French occupy Strasburg
1681 Lully buys an office conferring immediate hereditary nobility	1682 Ménestrier claims that France has replaced Italy as the cultural hegemon of Europe
	1683 Turkish siege of Vienna relieved
	1685 Louis XIV revokes the Edict of Nantes and expels Protestants; James II succeeds to the English throne

1687 Lully dies a very rich man	1687 Newton, *Principia mathematica* 1688 Glorious Revolution in England 1689 Nine Years War begins
	1694 Bank of England established
1700 Bartolomeo Cristofori invents the piano	1700 Great Northern War begins (to 1721)
	1701 War of the Spanish Succession begins (to 1714) 1703 Peter the Great starts construction of St. Petersburg 1704 Battle of Blenheim
1713 Three Choirs Festival begins in England	1714 First international treaty to be drafted in French rather than Latin 1715 Death of Louis XIV; Jacobite rising in Britain
1717 J. S. Bach is imprisoned by the duke of Weimar	1717 Establishment of a Grand Lodge in London begins the modern history of freemasonry
1719 Augustus the Strong of Saxony and Poland builds the largest opera house north of the Alps to celebrate his marriage alliance with the Habsburgs	1719 Daniel Defoe, *Robinson Crusoe*
	1721 Montesquieu, *Persian Letters*
1723 J. S. Bach moves to Leipzig 1725 Series of Concerts Spirituels begin in Paris 1726 Academy of Ancient Music founded in London 1728 John Gay, *The Beggar's Opera* 1729 Bach, *St. Matthew Passion*	1725 Death of Peter the Great 1726 Jonathan Swift, *Gulliver's Travels*
1737 San Carlo opera house at Naples is completed 1738 Life-size statue of Handel is installed in the Vauxhall pleasure-garden in London	1737 Consecration of the Church of St. Charles (Karlskirche) in Vienna 1738 John Wesley's conversion experience begins the history of Methodism

1775 Hanover Square Rooms opened in London

1776 Declaration of American Independence; Adam Smith, *The Wealth of Nations*; Gibbon, *The History of the Decline and Fall of the Roman Empire*

1780 The Grand Théâtre is opened at Bordeaux
1781 Count Nostitz's National Theatre is opened in Prague; Mozart is booted out of the service of the archbishop of Salzburg; new concert hall—the Gewandhaus—opened in Leipzig

1780 Gordon Riots in London
1781 British defeated at Yorktown; Kant, *Critique of Pure Reason*

1783 Treaty of Versailles recognises American independence; Russia annexes the Crimea

1784 Handel Commemoration concerts in London
1786 Mozart, *The Marriage of Figaro*
1787 Mozart is appointed Court Composer to the Emperor Joseph II; writes *Don Giovanni*

1786 Death of Frederick the Great
1787 Assembly of Notables meets at Versailles, initiating the terminal crisis of the old regime in France
1788 Louis XVI agrees to summon the Estates General
1789 Fall of the Bastille; promulgation of the Declaration of the Rights of Man and the Citizen

1790 Joseph II dies, is succeeded by his brother Leopold II; Burke, *Reflections on the Revolution in France*
1791 Thomas Paine, *The Rights of Man*

1792 Wars of the French Revolution begin
1793 Terror begins in France
1794 Fall of Robespierre; Terror ends
1795 Third Partition expunges Poland from the map
1798 Wordsworth and Coleridge, *Lyrical Ballads*; Alois Senefelder invents lithography
1799 Napoleon Bonaparte seizes power in France

1791 Mozart, *The Magic Flute*; *La Clemenza di Tito*; Haydn's first visit to London; Mozart dies and is buried in an unmarked grave; Singing Academy founded in Berlin
1792 Claude-Joseph Rouget de l'Isle writes and composes the *Marseillaise*
1794 Haydn's second visit to London
1795 William Parsons is the first musician to be knighted in Great Britain
1798 Haydn, *The Creation*

1800 *The Miller, the Sorcerer, the Cheat and the Matchmaker*; music by Mikhail Matveyevich Sokolovsky and libretto by Alexander Onisimovich Ablesimov

1804 First performance of Beethoven's Third Symphony (*Eroica*) in Prince Lobkowitz's palace in Vienna

1808 Apotheosis of Haydn with a performance of *The Creation* in Vienna; Beethoven's marathon concert at the Theater an der Wien in Vienna
1809 Haydn dies in French-occupied Vienna with a guard of honour at his door

1810 First choral festival in Germany (at Frankenhausen); Gabriel-Joseph Grenié begins to manufacture 'free reed' organs
1812 The 'incident at Teplitz' when Beethoven snubs the imperial family

1814 Heinrich David Stölzel demonstrates a horn with valves in Berlin

1820s Conductors begin to use the baton, read from a full score and do not play an instrument during performances
1821 Karl Friedrich Schinkel's new play house, incorporating a concert room, is opened on the Gendarmenmarkt in Berlin; premiere of Carl Maria von Weber's romantic opera *Der Freischütz* in Berlin
1824 Franz Liszt gives his first public concert, in Vienna, at the age of 12; Stendhal hails Rossini as 'a new Napoleon'

1827 Beethoven dies and is given a magnificent funeral
1828 Niccolò Paganini begins his sensational concert tours; Odeon concert hall designed by Leo von Klenze opened in Munich

---

1804 Napoleon proclaims himself emperor

1805 Battles of Trafalgar, Austerlitz
1806 Napoleon reorganises Germany; Holy Roman Empire formally ends; Prussia is defeated at the double battle of Jena and Auerstedt
1808 Rising in Spain against Napoleonic rule

1809 Austria again defeated by Napoleon

1812 Goya, *The Disasters of War*; Napoleon's invasion of Russia ends in disaster
1813 Napoleon is defeated at Leipzig and loses control of Germany
1814 Napoleon abdicates and is exiled to Elba
1815 Napoleon defeated at Waterloo and exiled to St. Helena
1819 Schopenhauer, *The World as Will and Idea*; Géricault, *The Raft of the Medusa*
1819 Karlsbad Decrees imposes repressive regime in Germany

1821 Death of Napoleon; Hegel, *Philosophy of Right*

1824 Death of Byron; Delacroix, *Massacre at Chios*

1825 Manzoni, *I Promessi Sposi*
1827 Joseph Niepce produces photographs on asphalt-coated plates

1829 Mendelssohn stages the 'centenary' performance of Bach's *St. Matthew Passion* at Leipzig

1831 Theobald Boehm begins to develop improved fingering system for the flute; Vincenzo's Bellini, *Norma*

1834 Liszt snubs King Louis-Philippe
1835 Wilhelm Wieprecht and J. G. Moritz patent the tuba
1836 Mikhail Ivanovich Glinka, *A Life for the Tsar*

1838 Louis Jullien begins his series of popular concerts in London
1839 Etienne François Périnet of Paris patents the cylindrical piston valve

1840 Johann Nikolaus Becker, *Rhine Song*; Liszt humiliates Tsar Nicholas I
1842 Alexandre-François Debain patents the harmonium; Henry Bishop the first musician to be knighted by a reigning monarch in the United Kingdom; the apotheosis of Liszt in Berlin
1845 First brass band competition organised, at Burton Constable near Hull
1846 Adolphe Sax patents the saxophone

1849 Verdi, *La Battaglia di Legnano*; Wagner flees into exile after participating in the abortive revolution at Dresden

1850 Jenny Lind embarks on a series of concerts in the USA that earn a huge fortune
1852 Charles Morton founds the first music hall in London
1853 Wagner's musical revelation at La Spezia

1830 Revolution in France and Belgium and attempted revolutions in several other parts of Europe; Delacroix, *Liberty Leading the People*; Victor Hugo, *Ernani*; Stendhal, *Scarlet and Black*

1832 Great Reform Act in Great Britain; Mazzini founds Young Italy; Hambach Festival, radical German demonstration
1834 Prussian Customs Union (Zollverein) founded

1837 Accession of Queen Victoria; electric telegraph patented
1838 Chartist Movement begins

1840 Napoleon's ashes returned from St. Helena
1841 Ludwig Feuerbach, *The Essence of Christianity*
1842 Hong Kong ceded to Britain; Gogol, *Dead Souls*

1845 Great Famine begins in Ireland
1846 Polish revolt in Galicia
1848 Revolution in France and attempted revolutions in several other parts of continental Europe; Marx and Engels, *The Communist Manifesto*
1849 Counter-revolution successful everywhere

1852 Louis Napoleon Bonaparte proclaimed Emperor Napoleon III
1853 Crimean war begins

1854 Wagner reads Schopenhauer's *The World as Will and Representation* for the first time	1854 Wagner reads Schopenhauer's *The World as Will and Representation* for the first time
1856 Peace of Paris ends Crimean War; Indian Mutiny; Sinn Fein founded in Ireland	1856 Berlioz's treatise on the art of conducting
1859 Wars of Italian Unification begin	1858 Charles Hallé begins his series of popular concerts in Manchester
1861 Victor Emmanuel II assumes title of King of Italy; emancipation of serfs in Russia	1861 Count Harrach's competition for the best opera on a Czech historical subject; Jules Étienne Pasdeloup begins his series of popular concerts in Paris
1866 War between Austria and Prussia; Dostoevsky, *Crime and Punishment*	1866 First performance of Smetana, *The Brandenburgers in Bohemia*
1869 Opening of the Suez Canal	1869 First version of Modest Musorgsky, *Boris Godunov*; Musikverein opened in Vienna; Wagner's treatise on the art of conducting
1870 Franco-Prussian War	1875 New opera house in Paris designed by Charles Garnier is opened; Smetana, *From the Woods and Meadows of Bohemia*
1871 Proclamation of the German Empire	
1875 German Social Democratic Party founded	1876 First complete performance of Wagner, *The Ring of Nibelung*, at Bayreuth in the presence of the German Emperor
	1877 Thomas Edison invents the phonograph
1882 British occupy Egypt and the Sudan; Gottlieb Daimler builds petrol engine	1882 First performance of *Parsifal* at Bayreuth; first performance of Smetana, *Ma Vlast*; the National Theatre in Prague is opened with a performance of Smetana, *Libuše*
1883 Nietzsche, *Thus Spake Zarathustra*	1883 Death of Wagner
	1884 New Gewandhaus opened at Leipzig
	1887 Emile Berliner patents the gramophone
1895 Birth of cinema	
1902 Lenin, *What Is to Be Done?*	1902 Enrico Caruso records ten arias for The Gramophone Company

Music	Events	
		1905 Revolution in Russia
1917 The Original Dixieland Jazz Band makes the first jazz recording	1914 First World War begins	
	1917 Revolution in Russia	
	1918 First World War ends	
1919 Hammersmith Palais de Danse opens	1919 Versailles Peace Settlement	
	1920 First regular radio broadcast	
	1922 First European radio station (BBC) begins broadcasting; Mussolini comes to power	
1924 Electrical recording introduced	1924 Death of Lenin	
1925 Edmund Meisel's score for Sergei Eisenstein, *The Battleship Potemkin*		
1927 First jukebox	1927 'Talking' films	
	1929 Wall Street crash	
1933 Fred Astaire and Ginger Rogers appear in *Flying Down to Rio*	1933 Hitler comes to power	
1935 Teddy Wilson joins the Benny Goodman Trio	1936 Spanish Civil War begins	
1938 First Pirate Radio Ship	1938 Germany annexes Austria	
1939 Marian Anderson's concert at the Lincoln Memorial	1939 The Second World War begins with the German invasion of Poland	
1941 Les Paul develops the first solid-body electric guitar	1941 Germany invades the Soviet Union; Japan attacks Pearl Harbor	
	1945 The Second World War ends	
1947 Wynonie Harris, 'Good Rockin' Tonight'	1947 British rule in India ends	
1948 Les Paul invents multi-tracking; Vinyl LP first demonstrated	1948 Berlin airlift	
1950 Leo Fender markets the Broadcaster	1950 Korean War begins	
1953 Elvis Presley visits Sun Records in Memphis, Tennessee; Leo Fender markets the first solid-body electric bass guitar	1953 Death of Stalin	
1954 First transistor radio; Leo Fender markets the Stratocaster	1954 French surrender at Dien Bien Phu	
1956 Elvis Presley records 'Heartbreak Hotel'	1956 Hungarian insurrection suppressed by Soviet forces; Suez Crisis	

1962 The Beatles record 'Love Me Do'
1963 Introduction of the music cassette by Philips; Mahalia Jackson sings at the Lincoln Memorial
1964 Bob Dylan introduces The Beatles to marijuana; John Coltrane records *A Love Supreme*; Harold Wilson, then leader of the opposition, presents awards to The Beatles as Showbusiness Personalities of 1963
1965 Bob Dylan goes electric; The Beatles perform at Shea Stadium in New York; The Beatles discover LSD
1966 *Sergeant Pepper's Lonely Hearts Club Band*; Harold Wilson, now prime minister, officiates at the reopening of the Cavern Club in Liverpool
1967 Aretha Franklin, 'Respect'

1979 Sony Walkman first marketed

1981 MTV begins transmissions
1985 The Live Aid concerts are watched on television by c. 2 billion people

1990s The three tenors (Pavarotti, Domingo, Carreras) earn vast sums from stadium concerts
1997 Tony Blair invites Noel Gallagher of Oasis to a party at 10 Downing Street

2001 First iPod

2003 Bono is admitted to the Légion d'Honneur by President Jacques Chirac; The Battle of Beirut over the Arab Superstar singing competition

---

1964 Labour Party wins the general election
1965 Escalation of Vietnam War

1973 American forces withdraw from Vietnam

1980 Soviet forces invade Afghanistan

1988 Soviet forces withdraw from Afghanistan
1989 Berlin wall dismantled and Soviet Union begins to collapse
1990 Unification of Germany
1997 Labour Party wins general election

2001 9/11 attack on the World Trade Center, New York; USA and UK begin war in Afghanistan

2003 USA and allies invade Iraq

2005 Bono is named Person of the Year by *Time*; 3.8 billion people watch the Live 8 concerts, it is claimed; YouTube goes online

2006 Concert by The Rolling Stones at Copacabana Beach, Rio de Janeiro, is attended by more than a million people

2007 100 millionth iPod sold; Bono is given an honorary knighthood by Tony Blair

2007 Tony Blair resigns as prime minister, replaced by Gordon Brown

2008 Barack Obama and Hillary Clinton compete to become the Democratic Party's nominee for president of the USA

Further Reading

As full references are given in the footnotes, I have not repeated everything here. I have confined myself to those books and articles I found especially helpful and which will help the interested reader to take the subject further. The first port of call should be always *The New Grove Dictionary of Music and Musicians*, an invaluable tool and which is now accessible on line and is constantly being updated. The German equivalent—*Die Musik in Geschichte und Gegenwart*—is also very helpful.

Abrams, M. H. *The Mirror and the Lamp: Romantic Theory and the Critical Tradition*. Oxford, 1953.

Adamson, John. The making of the Ancien Régime court 1500–1700. In *The Princely Courts of Europe*, ed. J. Adamson. London, 1999.

Adorno, Theodor. On jazz. In *Essays on Music*, ed. T. Adorno, selected with an introduction, commentary and notes by Richard Leppert. Berkeley, 2002.

Aseyev, A. N. *Russky dramatichesky teatr ot ego istokov do kontsa XVIII veka*. Moscow, 1977.

Aulard, François-Alphonse. La Marseillaise et le Réveil du peuple. In *Études et leçons sur la Révolution française*, vol. I. Paris, 1914.

Badger, Anthony J. Different perspectives on the civil rights movement. *History Now* 8 (June 2006).

Bailbé, Joseph-Marc, et al. (eds.). *La Musique en France à l'époque romantique (1830–1870)*. Paris, 1991.

Balet, Leo, and E. Gerhard. *Die Verbürgerlichung der deutschen Kunst, Literatur und Musik im 18. Jahrhundert*. Strasbourg, 1936.

Barbier, Pierre, and France Vernillat. *Histoire de France par les chansons*, vol. II: *Mazarin et Louis XIV*. Paris, 1956.

Barth, Herbert, Dietrich Mack, and Egon Voss (eds.). *Wagner: A Documentary Study*. London, 1975.

Beales, Derek. Religion and culture. In *The Short Oxford History of Europe: The Eighteenth Century*, ed. T. C. W. Blanning. Oxford, 2000.

———. Mozart and the Habsburgs. In idem, *Enlightenment and Reform in Eighteenth-century Europe*. London, 2005.

Beauvert, Thierry. *Opera Houses of the World*. London, 1996.

Bekker, Paul. *Das deutsche Musikleben*. Berlin, 1919.

Berry, Mark. *Treacherous Bonds and Laughing Fire: Politics and Religion in Wagner's Ring*. Aldershot, 2005.

Black, John. *The Italian Romantic Libretto: A Study of Salvadore Cammarano.* Edinburgh, 1984.

Blanning, T. C. W. *The Culture of Power and the Power of Culture: Old Regime Europe 1660–1789.* Oxford, 2002.

——. The commercialisation and sacralisation of culture. In *The Oxford Illustrated History of Modern Europe,* ed. T. C. W. Blanning. Oxford, 1996.

Blanning, Tim. *The Pursuit of Glory: Europe 1648–1815.* London, 2007.

Blaukopf, Kurt. *Musik im Wandel der Gesellschaft. Grundzüge der Musiksoziologie.* Munich and Zürich, 1982.

Braun, Rudolf, and David Guggerli. *Macht des Tanzes—Tanz der Mächtigen. Hoffeste und Herrschaftszeremoniell 1550–1914.* Munich, 1993.

Braunbehrens, Volkmar. *Mozart in Vienna.* Oxford, 1991.

Brauneis, Walther. 'Composta per festeggiare il sovvenire di un grand uomo': Beethovens *Eroica* als Hommage des Fürsten Franz Joseph Maximilian von Lobkowitz für Louis Ferdinand von Preußen. *Österreichische Musikzeitschrift* 12 (1998).

Brenet, Michel. *Les Concerts en France sous l'ancien régime.* Paris, 1900; reprinted New York, 1970.

Breuning, Gerhard von. *Memories of Beethoven: From the House of the Black-Robed Spaniards,* ed. Maynard Solomon. Cambridge, 1992.

Brophy, James. *Popular Culture and the Public Sphere in the Rhineland, 1800–1850.* Cambridge, 2007.

Brown, Clive. *Louis Spohr: A Critical Biography.* Cambridge, 1984.

Buckman, Peter. *Let's Dance: Social, Ballroom and Folk Dancing.* New York, 1978.

Burger, Ernst. *Franz Liszt: A Chronicle of His Life in Pictures and Documents.* Princeton, 1989.

Burrows, Donald. *Handel: Messiah.* Cambridge, 1991.

Cairns, David (ed.). *The Memoirs of Hector Berlioz.* London, 1969.

Carnegy, Patrick. *Wagner and the Art of the Theatre.* New Haven, 2006.

Carse, Adam. *The Orchestra in the Eighteenth Century.* Cambridge, 1940.

Chanan, Michael. *Musica Practica: The Social Practice of Western Music from Gregorian Chant to Postmodernism.* London and New York, 1994.

Charlton, David (ed.). *E. T. A. Hoffmann's Musical Writings: Kreisleriana, The Poet and the Composer, Music Criticism.* Cambridge, 1989.

Cheshikhin, Vsevolod'. *Istoriya russkoy opery (s 1674 po 1903 g.),* 2nd ed. St. Petersburg, 1905.

Cohn, Nik. *Awopbopaloobop alopbamboom: Pop from the Beginning.* London, 1970.

Cole, Michael. *The Pianoforte in the Classical Era.* Oxford, 1998.

Comini, Alessandra. *The Changing Image of Beethoven: A Study in Mythmaking.* New York, 1987.

Cook, Nicholas. *Music: A Very Short Introduction*. Oxford, 1998.

Cooke, Deryck. *I Saw the World End: A Study of Wagner's Ring*. London, 1979.

Cooke, Mervyn. *Jazz*. London, 1998.

Cooke, Mervyn, and David Horn (eds.). *The Cambridge Companion to Jazz*. Cambridge, 2002.

Corner, John (ed.). *Popular Television in Britain: Studies in Cultural History*. London, 1991.

David, Hans T., and Arthur Mendel. *The New Bach Reader: A Life of Johann Sebastian Bach in Letters and Documents*, revised and expanded by Christoph Wolff. New York, 1999.

Davies, Hunter. *The Beatles: The Authorised Biography*. London, 1968.

Day, Timothy. *A Century of Recorded Music: Listening to Musical History*. London, 2000.

DeCurtis, Anthony, and James Henke (eds.). *The Rolling Stone Illustrated History of Rock 'n' Roll*. London, 1992.

Dent, Edward. *The Rise of Romantic Opera*, ed. Winton Dean. Cambridge, 1976.

Deutsch, Otto Erich. *Mozart: A Documentary Biography*. Stanford, 1965.

Didier, Béatrice. *La Musique des lumières. Diderot—L'Encyclopédie—Rousseau*. Paris, 1985.

Dieckmann, Friedrich. *Richard Wagner in Venedig*. Leipzig, 1983.

Dörffel, Alfred. *Geschichte der Gewandhausconcerte zu Leipzig vom 25. November 1791 bis 25. November 1881*. Leipzig, 1884.

Driver, Jim (ed.). *The Mammoth Book of Sex, Drugs and Rock 'n' Roll*. London, 2001.

Duhamel, Jean-Marie. *La Musique dans la ville de Lully à Rameau*. Lille, 1994.

Dylan, Bob. *Chronicles*, vol. I. New York, 2004.

Eberly, Philip K. *Music in the Air: America's Changing Tastes in Popular Music, 1920–1980*. New York, 1982.

Ehrlich, Cyril. *The Music Profession in Britain since the Eighteenth Century: A Social History*. Oxford, 1985.

———. *The Piano: A History*, rev. ed. Oxford, 1990.

Elkin, Robert. *The Old Concert Rooms of London*. London, 1955.

Emerson, Caryl, and Robert William Oldani. *Modest Musorgsky and Boris Godunov: Myths, Realities, Reconsiderations*. Cambridge, 1994.

Erismann, Hans. *Richard Wagner in Zürich*. Zürich, 1987.

Fantel, Hans. *Johann Strauss, Father and Son, and Their Era*. Newton Abbot, 1971.

Fiaux, Louis. *La Marseillaise, son histoire dans l'histoire des français depuis 1792*. Paris, 1918.

Figes, Orlando. *Natasha's Dance: A Cultural History of Russia*. London, 2002.

Fontaine, Gérard. *Palais Garnier: le fantasme de l'Opéra*. Paris, 1999.

Forbes, Elliot (ed.). *Thayer's Life of Beethoven*, rev. ed. Princeton, 1969.

Forsyth, Michael. *Buildings for Music: The Architect, the Musician, and the Listener from the Seventeenth Century to the Present Day*. Cambridge, Mass., 1985.

Freydank, Ruth. *Theater in Berlin von den Anfängen bis 1945*. Berlin, 1988.

Friedlander, Paul. *Rock 'n' Roll: A Social History*. Boulder, 1996.

Friedländer, Saul, and Jörn Rüsen (eds.). *Richard Wagner im Dritten Reich*. Munich, 2000.

Frith, Simon, and Andrew Goodwin (eds.). *On Record: Rock, Pop and the Written Word*. London, 1990.

Frith, Simon, Will Straw, and John Street (eds.). *The Cambridge Companion to Pop and Rock*. Cambridge, 2001.

Fürstenau, Moritz. *Zur Geschichte der Musik und des Theaters am Hofe zu Dresden*, vol. II. Dresden, 1862.

Geiringer, Karl. *Haydn: A Creative Life in Music*. London, 1982.

Gelatt, Roland. *The Fabulous Phonograph: The Story of the Gramophone from Tin Foil to High Fidelity*. London, 1956.

Gronow, Pekka, and Ilpo Saunio. *An International History of the Recording Industry*. London and New York, 1998.

Gutman, Robert W. *Richard Wagner: The Man, His Mind and His Music*. London, 1968.

Hanslick, Eduard. *Geschichte des Concertwesens in Wien*, 2 vols. Vienna, 1869.

Hanson, Alice M. *Musical Life in Biedermeier Vienna*. Cambridge, 1985.

Harris, John. *The Last Party: Britpop, Blair and the Demise of English Rock*. London and New York, 2003.

Helm, E. E. *Music at the Court of Frederick the Great*. Norman, 1960.

Herbert, Trevor, and John Wallace (eds.). *The Cambridge Companion to Brass Instruments*. Cambridge, 1997.

Hildebrandt, Dieter. *Pianoforte: A Social History of the Piano*. New York, 1988.

Hirshon, Stanley P. Jazz, segregation, and desegregation. In *A Master's Due: Essays in Honor of David Herbert Donald*, ed. William J. Cooper, Jr., Michael F. Holt, and John McCardell. Baton Rouge and London, 1985.

Hollis, Helen Rice. *The Piano: A Pictorial Account of Its Ancestry and Development*. Newton Abbot, 1975.

Ingham, Richard (ed.). *The Cambridge Companion to the Saxophone*. Cambridge, 1998.

Isherwood, Robert M. *Music in the Service of the King: France in the Seventeenth Century*. Ithaca and London, 1973.

Johnson, James H. Musical experience and the formation of a French musical public. *Journal of Modern History* 64, 2 (1992).

———. *Listening in Paris: A Cultural History*. Berkeley and Los Angeles, 1995.

Johnson, Paul. *The Birth of the Modern: World Society 1815–1830*. London, 1991.

Kahn, Ashley. *A Love Supreme: The Creation of John Coltrane's Classic Album.* London, 2002.

Kemp, Peter. *The Strauss Family: Portrait of a Musical Dynasty.* Tunbridge Wells, 1985.

Kenney, William Howland. *Recorded Music in American Life: The Phonograph and Popular Memory, 1890–1945.* New York and Oxford, 1999.

Kimbell, David. *Verdi in the Age of Italian Romanticism.* Cambridge, 1981.

———. *Italian Opera.* Cambridge, 1991.

Kirchner, Bill (ed.). *The Oxford Companion to Jazz.* Oxford, 2000.

Klenke, Dietmar. *Der singende 'deutsche Mann': Gesangvereine und deutsches Nationalbewußtsein von Napoleon bis Hitler.* Münster, 1998.

Koenigsberger, H. G. Music and religion in modern European history. In *The Diversity of History: Essays in Honour of Sir Herbert Butterfield,* ed. J. H. Elliott and H. G. Koenigsberger. London, 1970.

Kureishi, Hanif, and Jon Savage (eds.). *The Faber Book of Pop.* London, 1995.

Landon, H. C. Robbins (ed.). *Haydn: Chronicle and Works* (5 vols.), vol. I: *The Early Years 1732–1765.* London, 1976–1980.

Landon, H. C. Robbins, and David Wyn Jones. *Haydn: His Life and Music.* London, 1988.

Landon, H. C. Robbins, and John Julius Norwich. *Five Centuries of Music in Venice.* London, 1991.

Large, Brian. *Smetana.* London, 1970.

Lehmann, Dieter. *Russlands Oper und Singspiel in der zweiten Hälfte des 18. Jahrhunderts.* Leipzig, 1958.

Levasheva, O. E. Nachalo russkoy opery. *Istoriya russkoy msuzyki,* vol. 3: *XVIII vek, chast' vtoraya.* Moscow, 1985.

Loesser, Arthur. *Men, Women and Pianos: A Social History.* London, 1955.

Loth, Arthur. *Le Chant de la Marseillaise, son véritable auteur.* Paris, 1886; new edition ed. Pierre Brière-Loth, Paris, 1992.

Lowinsky, Edward E. Musical genius: evolution and origins of a concept. *Musical Quarterly* 50 (1964).

Luckett, Richard. *Handel's Messiah: A Celebration.* London, 1992.

Lyttelton, Humphrey. *I Play as I Please: The Memoirs of an Old Etonian Trumpeter.* London, 1954.

Magee, Bryan. *Aspects of Wagner,* rev. ed. Oxford, 1988.

———. *Wagner and Philosophy.* London, 2000.

Martland, Peter. *Since Records Began: EMI, the First 100 Years.* London, 1997.

Marwick, Arthur. *The Sixties: Cultural Revolution in Britain, France, Italy, and the United States c. 1958–c. 1974.* Oxford, 1998.

Mason, Laura. *Singing the Revolution: Popular Culture and Politics 1787–1799.* Ithaca and London, 1996.

Mauron, Marie. *La Marseillaise.* Paris, 1968.

McKinnon, James (ed.). *Man and Music: Antiquity and the Middle Ages.* London, 1990.

McVeigh, Simon. *Concert Life in London from Mozart to Haydn.* Cambridge, 1993.

Mead, Christopher Curtis. *Charles Garnier's Paris Opéra: Architectural Empathy and the Renaissance of French Classicism.* Cambridge, Mass., and London, 1991.

Melly, George. *Revolt into Style: The Pop Arts in the 50s and 60s.* Oxford, 1989.

Metzger, Heinz-Klaus, and Rainer Riehn (eds.). *Richard Wagner, Parsifal, Musik-Konzepte,* vol. 5. Munich, 1982.

Miller, James. *'Flowers in the dustbin': The Rise of Rock and Roll 1947–1977.* New York, 1999.

Miller, Simon (ed.). *Music and Society: The Last Post.* Manchester, 1993.

Milligan, Thomas B. *The Concerto and London's Musical Culture in the Late Eighteenth Century.* Epping, 1983.

Millington, Barry. *Wagner.* London, 1984.

Millner, Frederick L. *The Operas of Johann Adolf Hasse.* Ann Arbor, 1979.

Montagu, Jeremy. *The World of Baroque and Classical Musical Instruments.* Newton Abbot, 1979.

———. *The World of Romantic and Modern Musical Instruments.* Newton Abbot, 1981.

Mundy, John. *Popular Music on Screen: From Hollywood Musical to Music Video.* Manchester, 1999.

Murray, Charles Shaar. *Crosstown Traffic: Jimi Hendrix and the Rock 'n' Roll Revolution.* New York, 1989.

Naegele, Verena. *Parsifals Mission. Der Einfluß Richard Wagners auf Ludwig II. und seine Politik.* Cologne, 1995.

Neubauer, John. *The Emancipation of Music from Language: Departure from Mimesis in Eighteenth Century Aesthetics.* New Haven and London, 1986.

Newcomb, Horace (ed.). *Encyclopedia of Television,* 2nd ed., vol. 3 (New York and London, 2004).

Nott, James J. *Music for the People: Popular Music and Dance in Interwar Britain.* Oxford, 2002.

Ogren, Kathy J. *The Jazz Revolution: Twenties America and the Meaning of Jazz.* Oxford, 1989.

Orlova, Alexandra. *Glinka's Life in Music: A Chronicle.* Ann Arbor and London, 1988.

Ozouf, Mona. *Festivals and the French Revolution.* Cambridge, Mass., 1988.

Padel, Ruth. *I'm a Man: Sex, Gods and Rock 'n' Roll.* London, 2000.

Palmer, Robert. *Dancing in the Street: A Rock and Roll History.* London, 1996.

Palmer, Tony. *All You Need Is Love: The Story of Popular Music.* London, 1976.

Parker, Roger. *Leonora's Last Act: Essays in Verdian Discourse.* Princeton, 1997.

Pattison, Robert. *The Triumph of Vulgarity: Rock Music in the Mirror of Romanticism.* Oxford, 1987.

Perger, Richard von. *Geschichte der k.k. Gesellschaft der Musikfreunde in Wien.* Vienna, 1912.

Pestelli, Giorgio. *The Age of Mozart and Beethoven.* Cambridge, 1984.

Phillips-Matz, Mary Jane. *Verdi: A Biography.* Oxford, 1993.

Pierre, Constant. *Les Hymnes et chansons de la Révolution.* Paris, 1904.

Pintér-Lück, Éva. Norma-Bellini. In *Opera—Composer—Works—Performers,* ed. Sigrid Neef. Cologne, 1999.

Place, Adelaïde de. *La Vie musicale en France au temps de la Révolution.* Paris, 1989.

Porter, Cecelia Hopkins. *The Rhine as Musical Metaphor: Cultural Identity in German Romantic Music.* Boston, 1996.

Porter, Eric. *What Is This Thing Called Jazz? African American Musicians as Artists, Critics, and Activists.* Berkeley, 2002.

Porter, Lewis. *John Coltrane: His Life and Music.* Ann Arbor, 1998.

Powell, Ardal. *The Flute.* New Haven and London, 2002.

Prendergast, Roy M. *Film Music: A Neglected Art,* 2nd ed. New York, 1992.

Priestley, Bryan. *John Coltrane.* London, 1987.

Prinz, Ulrich. *Johann Sebastian Bachs Instrumentarium. Originalquellen—Besetzung—Verwendung.* Stuttgart, 2005.

Quander, George (ed.). *Apollini et Musis. 250 Jahre Opernhaus Unter den Linden.* Frankfurt am Main and Berlin, 1992.

Raeburn, Michael, and Alan Kendall (eds.). *Heritage of Music,* vol. I: *Classical Music and Its Origins.* Oxford, 1989.

———. *Heritage of Music,* vol. II: *The Romantic Era.* Oxford, 1989.

———. *Heritage of Music,* vol. III: *The Nineteenth Century Legacy.* Oxford, 1990.

Raphaël, Gaston. *Le Rhin allemand, Cahiers de la Quinzaine, 19.* Paris, 1903.

Raynor, Henry. *A Social History of Music from the Middle Ages to Beethoven.* London, 1972.

Reiss, Werner. *Johann Strauss Meets Elvis. Musikautomaten aus zwei Jahrhunderten.* Stuttgart, 2003.

Restle, Konstantin (ed.). *Faszination Klavier. 300 Jahre Pianofortebau in Deutschland.* Munich, 2000.

Ringer, Alexander (ed.). *The Early Romantic Era: Between Revolutions, 1789 and 1848.* London, 1990.

Rosselli, John. From princely service to the open market: Singers of Italian opera and their patrons 1600–1850. *Cambridge Opera Journal* 1, 1 (1989).

———. *Music and Musicians in Nineteenth Century Italy.* London, 1991.

Russell, Dave. *Popular Music in England, 1840–1914.* Manchester, 1987.

Rust, Frances. *Dance in Society: An Analysis of the Relationship between the Social Dance and Society in England from the Middle Ages to the Present Day.* London, 1969.

Salmen, Gabriele, and Walter Salmen. *Musiker im Porträt,* vol. III: *Das 18. Jahrhundert.* Munich, 1983.

Salmen, Walter. *Johann Friedrich Reichardt. Komponist, Schriftsteller, Kapellmeister und Verwaltungsbeamter der Goethezeit.* Freiburg in Breisgau and Zürich, 1963.

Samson, Jim (ed.). *The Late Romantic Era: From the Mid-nineteenth Century to the First World War.* London, 1991.

———. *The Cambridge History of Nineteenth Century Music.* Cambridge, 2002.

Sassoon, Donald. *The Culture of the Europeans from 1800 to the Present.* London, 2006.

Savage, Jon. *Time Travel: Pop, Media and Sexuality.* London, 1996.

Schleuning, Peter. *Das 18. Jahrhundert. Der Bürger erhebt sich.* Hamburg, 1984.

Schmidt-Görg, Joseph, and Hans Schmidt (eds.). *Ludwig van Beethoven.* Hamburg, 1969.

Schneider, L. *Geschichte der Oper und des Koeniglichen Opernhauses in Berlin.* Berlin, 1842.

Scholes, Percy A. (ed.). *An Eighteenth-century Musical Tour in Central Europe and the Netherlands. Being Dr Charles Burney's Account of His Musical Experiences.* Oxford, 1959.

Schönzeler, Hans-Hubert. *Dvořák.* London and New York, 1984.

Schwab, Heinrich. *Konzert. Öffentliche Musikdarbietung vom 17. bis 19. Jahrhundert.* Leipzig, 1971.

Shapiro, Harry. *Waiting for the Man: The Story of Drugs and Popular Music,* rev. ed. London, 1999.

Shaw, George Bernard. The perfect Wagnerite. In *Major Critical Essays,* ed. Michael Holroyd. London, 1986.

Sheehan, James J. *German History 1770–1866.* Oxford, 1989.

Shore, Michael. *The Rolling Stone Book of Rock Video.* London, 1985.

Simon, Jacob (ed.). *Handel: A Celebration of His Life and Times.* London, 1985.

Smith, Richard. *Seduced and Abandoned: Essays on Gay Men and Popular Music.* London, 1995.

Smith, Ruth. *Handel's Oratorio and Eighteenth Century Thought.* Cambridge, 1995.

Solomon, Maynard. *Mozart: A Life.* London, 1995.

Somfai, László. *Joseph Haydn: His Life in Contemporary Pictures.* London, 1969.

Southern, Eileen. *The Music of Black Americans: A History,* 2nd ed. New York, 1983.

Spencer, Stewart (ed.). *Wagner Remembered.* London, 2000.

Spohr, Louis. *Autobiography.* London, 1865.

Spotts, Frederic. *Bayreuth: A History of the Wagner Festival.* New Haven and London, 1994.

Steinberg, Michael P. (eds.). *Beethoven and His World.* Princeton, 2000.

Steinhauser, Monika. *Die Architektur der Pariser Oper. Studien zu ihrer Ent-*

stehungsgeschichte und ihrer architekturgeschichtlichen Stellung. Munich, 1969.

Stendhal. *Life of Rossini,* trans. Richard N. Coe. London, 1956.

Stowell, Robin (ed.). *The Cambridge Companion to the Violin.* Cambridge, 1992.

Stravinsky, Igor. *An Autobiography.* London, 1975.

Strunk, Oliver (ed.). *Source Readings in Music History,* rev. ed. by Leo Treitler. New York and London, 1998.

Sugden, John. *Niccolo Paganini: Supreme Violinist or Devil's Fiddler?* Neptune City, N.J., 1980.

Symes, Colin. *Setting the Record Straight: A Material History of Classical Recording.* Middletown, 2004.

Taruskin, Richard. Musorgsky vs. Musorgsky: The versions of *Boris Godunov. Nineteenth Century Music* 8 (1984–1985).

——. *Defining Russia Musically: Historical and Hermeneutical Essays.* Princeton, 1997.

——. *The Oxford History of Western Music,* 6 vols. Oxford, 2005.

Temperley, Nicholas (ed.). *The Blackwell History of Music in Britain,* vol. 5: *The Romantic Age 1800–1914.* Oxford, 1988.

Thomas, Tony. *Music for the Movies.* Los Angeles, 1997.

Thompson, Allison (ed.). *Dancing through Time: Western Social Dance in Literature, 1400–1918: Selections.* Jefferson, N.C., and London, 1998.

Tiersot, Julien. *Histoire de la Marseillaise.* Paris, 1915.

Tralage, J. N. du. *Notes et documents sur l'histoire des théâtres de Paris.* Paris, 1880.

Trynka, Paul (ed.). *The Beatles: Ten Years that Shook the World.* London, 2004.

Tucker, Mark (ed.). *The Duke Ellington Reader.* New York, 1993.

Tyrrell, John. *Czech Opera.* Cambridge, 1988.

Van Orden, Kate. *Music, Discipline and Arms in Early Modern France.* Chicago and London, 2005.

Vovelle, Michel. La Marseillaise: war or peace. In *Realms of Memory: Constructions of the French Past,* ed. Pierre Nora, vol. III: *Symbols.* New York, 1998.

Wagner, Richard. *My Life.* Cambridge, 1983.

Waksman, Steve. *Instruments of Desire: The Electric Guitar and the Shaping of Musical Experience.* Cambridge, Mass., 1999.

Walker, Alan. *Franz Liszt: The Virtuoso Years 1811–1847,* rev. ed. London, 1989.

——. *Franz Liszt: The Weimar Years 1848–1861.* London, 1989.

——. *Franz Liszt: The Final Years 1861–1886.* London, 1997.

Walter, Friedrich. *Geschichte des Theaters und der Musik am kurpfälzischen Hofe.* Leipzig, 1898.

Ward, Brian. *Just My Soul Responding: Rhythm and Blues, Black Consciousness and Race Relations.* London, 1998.

Warner, Timothy. *Pop Music: Technology and Creativity: Trevor Horn and the Digital Revolution.* Aldershot, 2003.

Warrack, John. *Carl Maria von Weber,* 2nd ed. Cambridge, 1976.

Weber, Max. *The Rational and Social Foundations of Music,* ed. Don Martindale and Johannes Riedel. Carbondale, Ill., 1958.

Weber, Solveig. *Das Bild Richard Wagners. Ikonographische Bestandsaufnahme eines Künstlerkults,* 2 vols. Mainz, 1993.

Weber, William. Learned and general musical taste in eighteenth century France. *Past and Present* 89 (1980).

——. *The Rise of Musical Classics in Eighteenth Century England.* Oxford, 1992.

——. *Music and the Middle Class: The Social Structure of Concert Life in London, Paris and Vienna between 1830 and 1848.* Aldershot, 2004.

—— (ed.). *The Musician as Entrepreneur 1700–1914: Managers, Charlatans and Idealists.* Bloomington and Indianapolis, 2004.

Weiss, Piero, and Richard Taruskin (eds.). *Music in the Western World: A History in Documents.* New York and London, 1984.

Wellesz, Egon, and Frederick Sternfeld (eds.). *The New Oxford History of Music,* vol. VII: *The Age of Enlightenment 1745–1790.* Oxford, 1973.

Werner, Craig. *A Change Is Gonna Come: Music, Race and the Soul of America.* Edinburgh, 1998.

Wheeler, Tom. *The Stratocaster Chronicles: Celebrating 50 Years of the Fender Strat.* Milwaukee, 2004.

Wicke, Peter. *Rock Music: Culture, Aesthetics and Sociology.* Cambridge, 1990.

Williams, Adrian (ed.). *Portrait of Liszt by Himself and His Contemporaries.* Oxford, 1990.

Williams, Chris (ed.). *Bob Dylan in His Own Words.* London, 1993.

Wokler, Robert. *La Querelle des Bouffons* and the Italian liberation of France: A study of revolutionary foreplay. *Eighteenth-Century Life* 11, 1 (1987).

Wolff, Christoph. *Johann Sebastian Bach: The Learned Musician.* Oxford, 2002.

Zaslaw, Neal. *Mozart's Symphonies: Context, Performance Practice, Reception.* Oxford, 1989.

Zaslaw, Neal (ed.). *The Classical Era: From the 1740s to the End of the Eighteenth Century.* London, 1989.

Zemanová, Mirka. *Janáček: A Composer's Life.* London, 2002.

Zöchling, Dieter (ed.). *Die Chronik der Oper.* Gütersloh and Munich, 1996.

Notes

Introduction

1. George III succeeded in 1760 but his jubilee was celebrated as the fiftieth year of his reign began. This was just as well, as in the following year he succumbed to permanent dementia.
2. *The Sunday Times*, 9 June 2002.
3. *The Times*, 6 June 2002.
4. Forty-one songs were performed at the concert, but only a selection was included on the DVD.

1. Status

1. Ludwig II to Richard Wagner after attending the dress rehearsals of *The Ring of the Nibelung* at Bayreuth in August 1876.
2. Piero Weiss and Richard Taruskin (eds.), *Music in the Western World: A History in Documents* (New York and London, 1984), pp. 25, 28.
3. Oliver Strunk (ed.), *Source Readings in Music History*, rev. ed. by Leo Treitler (New York and London, 1998), p. 326.
4. Weiss and Taruskin (eds.), *Music in the Western World*, p. 108.
5. Quoted in H. G. Koenigsberger, 'Music and religion in modern European history', in *The Diversity of History: Essays in Honour of Sir Herbert Butterfield*, ed. J. H. Elliott and H. G. Koenigsberger (London, 1970), p. 51.
6. Richard Taruskin, *The Oxford History of Western Music* (6 vols.), Vol. 1: *The Earliest Notations to the Sixteenth Century* (Oxford, 2005), pp. 758–760.
7. Part II, Section 2 Member VI, Subsection 3: 'Music a remedy'.
8. Jacques Attali, *Noise: The Political Economy of Music* (Manchester, 1985), p. 12. For other examples of Muslim hostility to music and musicians, see Hans Engel, *Die Stellung des Musikers im arabisch-islamischen Raum* (Bonn, 1987), pp. 91–101.
9. Book VIII.
10. Strunk (ed.), *Source Readings in Music History*, p. 142.
11. Alec Harman, 'Medieval and renaissance music', Part One in *Man and His Music: The Story of Musical Experience in the West*, new ed. by Alec Harman, Anthony Milner, and Wilfrid Mellers (London, 1988), p. 12.
12. Christopher Page, 'Court and city in France, 1100–1300', in *Man and*

Music: Antiquity and the Middle Ages, ed. James McKinnon (London, 1990), pp. 201, 208.

13. Michael Long, 'Trecento Italy,' in ibid., pp. 254, 262.

14. Patrick Macey, 'Josquin des Prez,' in *The New Grove Dictionary of Music and Musicians,* 2nd ed., 29 vols., ed. Stanley Sadie (London, 2001), XIII, pp. 200–206.

15. Weiss and Taruskin (eds.), *Music in the Western World,* pp. 181–184.

16. Henry Raynor, *A Social History of Music from the Middle Ages to Beethoven* (London, 1972), p. 291.

17. Christoph Wolff, *Johann Sebastian Bach: The Learned Musician* (Oxford, 2002), p. 184.

18. Raynor, *A Social History of Music,* p. 292.

19. Thomas Bauman, 'Courts and municipalities in North Germany,' in *The Classical Era: From the 1740s to the End of the Eighteenth Century,* ed. Neal Zaslaw (London, 1989), p. 242.

20. L. Schneider, *Geschichte der Oper und des Koeniglichen Opernhauses in Berlin* (Berlin, 1842), Beilagen, 17.

21. O. von Riesemann (ed.), 'Eine Selbstbiographie der Sängerin Gertrud Elizabeth Mara,' *Allgemeine Musikalische Zeitung* X (11 August–29 September 1875), pp. 561, 564, 577.

22. Kurt Blaukopf, *Musik im Wandel der Gesellschaft. Grundzüge der Musiksoziologie* (Munich and Zürich, 1982), p. 118.

23. Ibid.

24. Karl Geiringer, *Haydn: A Creative Life in Music* (London, 1982), p. 62.

25. H. C. Robbins Landon (ed.), *Haydn: Chronicle and Works* (5 vols.), vol. I: *The Early Years 1732–1765* (London, 1976–1980), pp. 350–352.

26. H. C. Robbins Landon and David Wyn Jones, *Haydn: His Life and Music* (London, 1988), pp. 118–119.

27. Landon and Jones, *Haydn: His Life and Music,* p. 169. Nor was the Prince amused when Haydn got ideas above his station by teaching himself to play the baryton.

28. Geiringer, *Haydn,* p. 59.

29. Quoted in David Andrew Threasher, 'Franz Joseph Haydn (1732–1809) Symphonies nos. 40–54,' in the booklet accompanying *Haydn symphonies nos. 40–54,* by the Austro-Hungarian Orchestra, conducted by Adam Fischer, vol. 3, Nimbus NI 5530/4 (1997).

30. László Somfai, *Joseph Haydn. Sein Leben in zeitgenössischen Bildern* (Budapest, 1966), p. 57.

31. Landon (ed.), *Haydn: Chronicle and Works,* II: *Haydn at Esterháza 1766–1790,* p. 737.

32. Ibid., pp. 741, 745.

33. Landon and Jones, *Haydn: His Life and Music,* p. 175.

34. Ibid., p. 180.

35. C. F. Pohl, *Joseph Haydn*, vol. I (Berlin, 1875), p. 112; Landon and Jones, *Haydn: His Life and Music*, p. 118.

36. I have discussed the rise of the public sphere in greater detail in 'The rise of the public sphere', Part II in *The Culture of Power and the Power of Culture: Old Regime Europe 1660–1789* (Oxford, 2002).

37. Donald W. Krummel, 'Publishing', in *The New Grove Dictionary of Music and Musicians*, ed. Sadie, XX, p. 366.

38. Ibid. See also Raynor, *A Social History of Music*, p. 331.

39. Hans-Martin Fleske, 'Breitkopf und Härtel', in *The New Grove Dictionary of Music and Musicians*, ed. Sadie, IV, pp. 309–311. In its review of musical developments in eighteenth-century Germany, the *Allgemeine Musikalische Zeitung* hailed Breitkopf as the man whose invention put music within reach of the common man: 'Bemerkungen über die Ausbildung der Tonkunst in Deutschland im achtzehnten Jahrhundert', 19 (4 February 1801), p. 324.

40. Landon (ed.), *Haydn: Chronicle and Works*, I, pp. 591–598.

41. Ulrich Leisinger, 'Haydn's keyboard music', in the booklet accompanying Christine Schornsheim, *Joseph Haydn, Piano sonatas—complete recording* (Capriccio 49 404).

42. There is a good reproduction in Michael Raeburn and Alan Kendall (eds.), *Heritage of Music*, vol. I: *Classical Music and Its Origins* (Oxford, 1989), p. 297. It is also significant that the Duke should choose to have himself depicted holding a score and leaning against a harpsichord (or perhaps fortepiano).

43. Landon (ed.), *Haydn: Chronicle and Works*, II, p. 595.

44. Ibid., p. 596.

45. Ibid., p. 447 n. 5.

46. Derek Beales, 'Religion and culture', in *The Short Oxford History of Europe: The Eighteenth Century*, ed. T. C. W. Blanning (Oxford, 2000), p. 149.

47. Ibid., p. 368.

48. Donald Burrows, 'Handel; his life and work', in *Handel*, ed. Simon, p. 17.

49. The original is now to be found in the Victoria and Albert Museum. There is a good reproduction in David H. Solkin, *Painting for Money: The Visual Arts and the Public Sphere in Eighteenth-Century England* (New Haven, 1993), p. 113.

50. There is a good reproduction in Joseph Burke, *English Art 1714–1800* (London, 1976), plate 50B.

51. John Mainwaring, *Memoirs of the Life of the Late George Frederic Handel. To which is added, A Catalogue of His Works, and Observations upon Them* (London, 1760).

52. William Coxe, *Anecdotes of George Frederick Handel and John Christopher Smith* (London, 1799), p. 31.

53. Landon and Jones, *Haydn: His Life and Music*, p. 229.

54. Landon (ed.), *Haydn: Chronicle and Works*, III, p. 49. The 'grand overture' was a symphony, probably no. 96.

55. Ibid., p. 56.

56. Landon and Jones, *Haydn: His Life and Music*, p. 237. As we have seen, it is impossible to estimate Haydn's salary precisely because a good deal of his remuneration was paid in kind.

57. Ibid., p. 252.

58. Ground plans of the concert-hall at Eisenstadt, the music room at Esterháza, the Hanover Square Rooms, and the concert-hall attached to the King's Theatre in the Haymarket can be found in Michael Forsyth, *Buildings for Music: The Architect, the Musician, and the Listener from the Seventeenth Century to the Present Day* (Cambridge, Mass., 1985), p. 39. The music room at Esterháza was about one half the size of the Hanover Square Rooms.

59. 'A note for volume ten of the Haydn symphonies', recording by Derek Solomons and L'Estro Armonico, CBS Masterworks, M3T 4211. Trumpeters and timpani players could be added from the military establishment when required.

60. For information on the size of orchestras in the eighteenth century, see Peter Schleuning, *Das 18. Jahrhundert. Der Bürger erhebt sich* (Hamburg, 1984), p. 144, and Adam Carse, *The Orchestra in the Eighteenth Century* (Cambridge, 1940), *passim*.

61. Landon and Jones, *Haydn*, p. 271.

62. Landon (ed.), *Haydn: Chronicle and Works*, I, p. 343.

63. Lázló Somfai, 'Haydn at the Esterházy court', in *The Classical Era: From the 1740s to the End of the Eighteenth Century*, ed. Neal Zaslaw (London, 1989), p. 268.

64. Especially when they are performed by Derek Solomons and L'Estro Armonico, using period instruments and employing an orchestra of the original size. Alas, only the recordings of symphonies 26, 48, and 49 ever found their way on to CDs, although many more were once available on LPs and cassettes. These revelatory performances are well worth seeking out.

65. Landon (ed.), *Haydn: Chronicle and Works*, V, pp. 360–362.

66. James Webster, 'Joseph Haydn', in *The New Grove Dictionary of Music and Musicians*, ed. Sadie, XI, p. 190.

67. Giorgio Pestelli, *The Age of Mozart and Beethoven* (Cambridge, 1984), p. 143.

68. Emily Anderson (ed.), *The Letters of Mozart and His Family*, 3rd ed. (London, 1985), pp. 716–717.

69. Ibid., p. 743.

70. Volkmar Braunbehrens, *Mozart in Vienna* (Oxford, 1991), pp. 133–139.

71. Ibid., p. 63.

72. Eduard Hanslick, *Geschichte des Concertwesens in Wien*, 2 vols. (Vienna, 1869), I, p. 38.

73. Mozart to his father, 22 December 1781, in Anderson (ed.), *The Letters of Mozart*, p. 789. Also quoted in Maynard Solomon, *Mozart: A Life* (London, 1995), p. 287.

74. Mozart to his father, 21 December 1782, in Anderson (ed.), *The Letters of Mozart*, p. 832. Also quoted in Volkmar Braunbehrens, *Mozart in Vienna* (Oxford, 1991), p. 134.

75. Solomon, *Mozart*, pp. 291–292. A complete list can be found in Anderson (ed.), *The Letters of Mozart*, pp. 870–872. See also Neal Zaslaw, *Mozart's Symphonies: Context, Performance, Practice, Reception* (Oxford, 1989), p. 376.

76. Braunbehrens, *Mozart in Vienna*, pp. 118–119.

77. Ibid., p. 141, 363–368.

78. Maynard Solomon, *Mozart: A Life* (London, 1995), pp. 498–499.

79. H. C. Robbins Landon (ed.), *Beethoven: A Documentary Study* (London, 1970), p. 244.

80. Richard Wagner, *My Life* (Cambridge, 1983), p. 30.

81. Tilman Seebass, 'Lady Music and her protégés. From musical allegory to musicians' portraits,' *Musica Disciplina* (1988), p. 24.

82. Ludwig Finscher, Rolf Ketteler, and Jörg Jewanski, 'Musik und bildende Kunst: Der Komponist als Objekt,' *Musik in Geschichte und Gegenwart*, vol. VI, cols. 775–776.

83. Quoted in H. C. Robbins Landon and John Julius Norwich, *Five Centuries of Music in Venice* (London, 1991), p. 87.

84. Conrad Freyse, *Bachs Antlitz. Betrachtungen und Erkenntnisse zur Bach-Ikonographie* (Eisenach, 1964), pp. 15–16.

85. Jacob Simon (ed.), *Handel: A Celebration of His Life and Times* (London, 1985), p. 33.

86. Gabriele Salmen and Walter Salmen, *Musiker im Porträt*, vol. III: *Das 18. Jahrhundert* (Munich, 1983), p. 162.

87. Somfai, *Joseph Haydn. Sein Leben in zeitgenössischen Bildern*, p. 215.

88. Otto Erich Deutsch, *Mozart: A Documentary Biography* (Stanford, 1965), p. 417; Volkmar Braunbehrens, *Mozart in Vienna* (Oxford, 1991), pp. 418–424.

89. Christopher H. Gibbs, 'Performances of grief: Vienna's response to the death of Beethoven,' in *Beethoven and His World*, ed. Scott Burnham and Michael P. Steinberg (Princeton, 2000), p. 227.

90. Thomas Nipperdey, *Deutsche Geschichte 1800–1866. Bürgerwelt und starker Staat* (Munich, 1983), p. 539.

91. 'Wien im April 1827. Beethovens Bestattung,' *Berliner Allgemeine Musikalische Zeitung*, ed. A. Marx, 1827, no. 21, p. 167.

92. Elliot Forbes (ed.), *Thayer's Life of Beethoven*, rev. ed. (Princeton, 1969), pp. 1053–1055, reprints the fullest contemporary report.

93. Simon (ed.), *Handel,* pp. 232–233.

94. Forbes (ed.), *Thayer's Life of Beethoven,* pp. 170–171.

95. Landon (ed.), *Beethoven: A Documentary Study,* p. 47.

96. Alessandra Comini, *The Changing Image of Beethoven: A Study in Myth-making* (New York, 1987), pp. 16–17.

97. Hanslick, *Geschichte des Concertwesens in Wien,* I, p. 38.

98. Cyril Ehrlich, *The Piano: A History,* rev. ed. (Oxford, 1990), p. 17.

99. Herbert Schneider, 'Die Popularisierung musikdramatischer Gattungen in der Tanzmusik,' in *Atti del XIV Congresso della Società Internazionale di Musicologia: Trasmissione e recezione delle forme di cultura musicale,* vol. 1: *Round Tables,* ed. Angelo Pompilio et al. (Turin, 1990), p. 445.

100. *Allgemeine Musikalische Zeitung* 93 (20 November 1822), p. 737.

101. Stendhal, *Life of Rossini,* trans. Richard N. Coe (London, 1956), p. 30.

102. Ibid, p. 407.

103. *Allgemeine Musikalische Zeitung* 94 (22 November 1820), pp. 746–747.

104. Alice M. Hanson, *Musical Life in Biedermeier Vienna* (Cambridge, 1985), pp. 103–104.

105. Forbes (ed.), *Thayer's Life of Beethoven,* p. 1046.

106. Quoted in Hanson, *Musical Life in Biedermeier Vienna,* p. 66.

107. Ibid., p. 67.

108. Quoted in Paul Johnson, *The Birth of the Modern: World Society 1815–1830* (London, 1991), p. 126.

109. Stendhal, *Life of Rossini,* p. 1.

110. Johnson, *The Birth of the Modern,* p. 128.

111. 'Rossini,' *The Musical World,* xxv, 2 September 1836, p. 191.

112. Max Weber, 'Politics as a vocation,' in *From Max Weber: Essays in Sociology,* new ed., ed. H. H. Gerth and C. Wright Mills (London, 1991), pp. 78–79.

113. Jean Tulard, *Napoléon ou le mythe du sauveur* (Paris, 1977), p. 150.

114. Ibid, p. 107.

115. Heinrich Panofka, 'Correspondenz, Paris September 1834 (Paganini),' *Neue Leipziger Zeitschrift für Musik,* I, 53, 2 October 1834, p. 212.

116. Quoted in Edward Neill, 'Niccolò Paganini,' in *The New Grove Dictionary of Music and Musicians,* ed. Sadie, XVIII, p. 890.

117. John Sugden, *Niccolò Paganini: Supreme Violinist or Devil's Fiddler?* (Neptune City, N.J., 1980), p. 80.

118. Alan Walker, *Franz Liszt: The Virtuoso Years 1811–1847,* rev. ed. (London, 1989), p. 168.

119. Joseph-Marc Bailbé et al. (eds.), *La Musique en France à l'époque romantique (1830–1870)* (Paris, 1991), p. 203.

120. Quoted in James H. Johnson, *Listening in Paris: A Cultural History* (Berkeley and Los Angeles, 1995), p. 267.

121. Sugden, *Niccolò Paganini,* p. 42.

122. To Eckermann, quoted in Ibid. p. 43.

123. Michael Raeburn and Alan Kendall (eds.), *Heritage of Music*, vol. II: *The Romantic Era* (Oxford, 1989), p. 180.

124. Quoted in Bailbé, *La Musique en France à l'époque romantique*, p. 202.

125. Paul Smith, 'Niccolo Paganini,' *Revue et Gazette musicale de Paris*, 18, 50 (14 December 1851), p. 404.

126. Frederic Ewen (ed.), *The Poetry and Prose of Heinrich Heine* (New York, 1948), pp. 620–621.

127. Adrian Williams (ed.), *Portrait of Liszt by Himself and His Contemporaries* (Oxford, 1990), p. 51. Liszt mistakenly attributed these words to Michelangelo.

128. Ibid., p. 17.

129. Ibid., p. 41.

130. Ibid., pp. 49, 84, 123, 146.

131. Walker, *Franz Liszt: The Virtuoso Years 1811–1847*, p. 374.

132. Williams (ed.), *Portrait of Liszt*, p. 189.

133. Walker, *Franz Liszt: The Virtuoso Years 1811–1847*, p. 288.

134. Ibid., p. 221.

135. Ibid., p. 146.

136. Ibid., p. 289. I once employed a variation of this tactic myself, at a conference at the German Historical Institute in Paris, with equally gratifying results.

137. Williams (ed.), *Portrait of Liszt*, p. 102. This comment was used by the diplomat Philipp von Neuman after witnessing Liszt's relaxed attitude when paying a visit to Princess Metternich, wife of the Austrian Chancellor.

138. Ibid. p. 106.

139. Walker, *Franz Liszt: The Virtuoso Years 1811–1847*, p. 149.

140. Ibid., pp. 190–197.

141. Ewen (ed.), *The Poetry and Prose of Heinrich Heine*, p. 634.

142. Ibid., p. 135.

143. Ernst Burger, *Franz Liszt: A Chronicle of His Life in Pictures and Documents* (Princeton, 1989), p. 160. There are many other fine examples to be found in this excellent volume.

144. Williams (ed.), *Portrait of Liszt*, pp. 440, 442.

145. Walker, *Franz Liszt: The Virtuoso Years 1811–1847*, p. 287.

146. Quoted in John Deathridge and Carl Dahlhaus, *The New Grove Wagner* (London, 1984), p. 60.

147. Quoted in Frederic Spotts, *Bayreuth: A History of the Wagner Festival* (New Haven and London, 1994), p. 68.

148. Barry Millington, *Wagner* (London, 1984), p. 94.

149. *L'Art Musical*, 15, 33 (17 August 1876) p. 263.

150. Quoted in Alan Walker, *Franz Liszt: The Final Years 1861–1886* (London, 1997), p. 351.

151. Bryan Magee, *Aspects of Wagner,* rev. ed. (Oxford, 1988), p. 33.

152. Solveig Weber, *Das Bild Richard Wagners. Ikonographische Bestand-saufnahme eines Künstlerkults,* 2 vols (Mainz, 1993).

153. Quoted in Nicholas Cook, *Music: A Very Short Introduction* (Oxford, 1998), p. 37.

154. Hanslick, *Geschichte des Concertwesens in Wien,* p. 62.

155. *The Oxford English Dictionary,* 2nd ed., vol. III, ed. J. A. Simpson and E. S. C. Weiner (Oxford, 1989), p. 693.

156. David Cairns (ed.), *The Memoirs of Hector Berlioz* (London, 1969), p. 196.

157. Leon Botstein, 'Conducting,' in *The New Grove Dictionary of Music and Musicians,* ed. Sadie, VI, pp. 264–270.

158. Hans Erismann, *Richard Wagner in Zürich* (Zürich, 1987), p. 61.

159. Stewart Spencer (ed.), *Wagner Remembered* (London, 2000), p. 222.

160. Erismann, *Richard Wagner in Zürich,* p. 62.

161. '"Well, I should like to be a LITTLE larger, sir, if you wouldn't mind," said Alice: "three inches is such a wretched height to be." "It is a very good height indeed!" said the Caterpillar angrily, rearing itself upright as it spoke (it was exactly three inches high).' Lewis Carroll, *Alice in Wonderland.*

162. Stewart Spencer (ed.), *Wagner Remembered,* p. 91. Sir Adrian Boult, when asked why he did not conduct without a score like Karajan and other stars, replied: 'unlike them, I can read it.'

163. Alan Walker, *Franz Liszt: The Weimar Years 1848–1861* (London, 1989), p. 261 n. 101.

164. http://en.wikipedia.org/wiki/The_Three_Tenors.

165. Bruce Carr, 'Theatre music: 1800–34,' in *The Blackwell History of Music in Britain,* vol. 5: *The Romantic Age 1800–1914,* ed. Nicholas Temperley (Oxford, 1988), p. 291.

166. John Harris, 'Poll position,' in *The Beatles: Ten Years That Shook the World,* ed. Paul Trynka (London, 2004), p. 109.

167. Paul Johnson, 'The menace of Beatlism,' *New Statesman* (28 February 1964), reprinted in *The Faber Book of Pop,* eds. Hanif Kureishi and Jon Savage (London, 1995), pp. 195–198; Hunter Davies, *The Beatles: The Authorised Biography* (London, 1968), p. 212.

168. George Melly, *Revolt into Style: The Pop Arts in the 50s and 60s* (Oxford, 1989), p. 82.

169. It can be safely conjectured that on this occasion Sir Paul did not smoke marijuana in a toilet at the Palace, as he reportedly did in 1965.

170. John Harris, *The Last Party: Britpop, Blair and the Demise of English Rock* (London and New York, 2003), p. xiii.

171. Ibid., p. 156.

172. Ibid., p. 345.

173. Ibid., p. 357.

174. Ibid., p. 356.

175. Miranda Sawyer, 'Police, nudity, furious punters and taking out U2,' *The Guardian,* 6 May 2005.

176. *New Musical Express,* 5 July 2006.

177. http://en.wikipedia.org/wiki/Do_They_Know_It's_Christmas.

178. Peter Wicke, *Rock Music: Culture, Aesthetics and Sociology* (Cambridge, 1990), p. viii; http://en.wikipedia.org/wiki/Live_Aid.

179. Paul Vallely, 'Can rock stars change the world?' *The Independent,* 16 May 2006, p. 43.

180. http://en.wikipedia.org/wiki/Live_8.

181. Paul Vallely, 'The Missionary,' *The Independent,* 13 May 2006, p. 41.

182. Anthony Barnes, 'Arise Sir Bono!' Ibid., 24 December 2006, p. 3.

183. Vallely, 'The Missionary,' p. 41.

2. *Purpose*

1. David Charlton (ed.), *E. T. A. Hoffmann's Musical Writings: Kreisleriana, The Poet and the Composer, Music Criticism* (Cambridge, 1989), p. 96. Cf. Lamartine's belief that 'music is the literature of the heart, it takes up communication where words stop,' quoted in L. M. Gottschalk, 'La musique, le piano et les pianistes,' *La France Musicale,* 24, 45 (4 November 1860), p. 433.

2. This argument is developed in much greater depth and detail in Paul Bekker, *Das deutsche Musikleben* (Berlin, 1919), a musicological classic. See especially pp. 3–20.

3. Werner Sombart, *Luxury and Capitalism* (Ann Arbor, 1967), p. 72.

4. Jean-François Solnon, *La Cour de France* (Paris, 1987), p. 363.

5. John Adamson, 'The making of the Ancien Régime court 1500–1700,' in *The Princely Courts of Europe,* ed. John Adamson (London, 1999), pp. 15–17.

6. Peter Burke, *The Fabrication of Louis XIV* (New Haven, 1992), p. 65.

7. Elizabeth Hyde, *Cultivated Power: Flowers, Culture and Politics in the Reign of Louis XIV* (Philadelphia, 2005), *passim.* In just four years the royal nursery at Paris (one of many) delivered 18,000,000 tulips and other bulbs; ibid., p. 160.

8. Antoine Schnapper, 'The King of France as collector in the seventeenth century,' in *Art and History: Images and Their Meaning,* ed. Robert I. Rotberg and Theodore K. Rabb (Cambridge, 1988), p. 195.

9. Rebecca Harris-Warrick, 'Magnificence in motion: stage musicians in Lully's ballets and operas,' *Cambridge Opera Journal* 6, 3 (1994), p. 195.

10. Quoted in Rudolf Braun and David Guggerli, *Macht des Tanzes—Tanz der Mächtigen. Hoffeste und Herrschaftszeremoniell 1550–1914* (Munich, 1993), pp. 123–124.

11. Solnon, *La Cour de France,* p. 408.

12. Michel Antoine, *Louis XV* (Paris, 1989), p. 147.

13. Braun and Guggerli, *Macht des Tanzes—Tanz der Mächtigen,* p. 145.

14. Solnon, *La Cour de France,* p. 411.

15. Ibid., p. 412.

16. Robert M. Isherwood, *Music in the Service of the King: France in the Seventeenth Century* (Ithaca and London, 1973), pp. 133–134.

17. Donald Jay Grout, 'Some forerunners of the Lully opera,' *Music and Letters* 22 (1941), p. 1.

18. There is an excellent summary of the Lully operatic tradition in Cynthia Verba, *Music and the French Enlightenment: Reconstruction of a Dialogue 1750–1764* (Oxford, 1993), pp. 12–13.

19. James R. Anthony, 'Jean-Baptiste Lully,' in *The New Grove Dictionary of Music and Musicians,* 20 vols., ed. Stanley Sadie (London, 1980), XI, p. 317.

20. Neal Zaslaw, 'Lully's orchestra,' in *Jean-Baptiste Lully. Actes du Colloque/Kongressbericht Saint-Germain-en-Laye—Heidelberg 1987,* ed. Jérome de La Gorce and Herbert Schneider (Laaber, 1990), Neue Heidelberger Studien zur Musikwissenschaft, vol. 18, p. 540.

21. Henry Prunières, *La Vie illustre et libertine de Jean-Baptiste Lully* (Paris, 1929), pp. 221–227.

22. Solnon, *La Cour de France,* p. 411; Anthony, 'Jean-Baptiste Lully,' p. 315.

23. James R. Anthony, 'Michel-Richard Delalande,' in *The New Grove Dictionary of Music and Musicians,* ed. Sadie, XIV, pp. 139–140.

24. Jean-Marie Apostolides, *Le Roi-machine. Spectacle et politique au temps de Louis XIV* (Paris, 1981), pp. 30–31.

25. Nicole Ferrier-Caverivière, *L'Image de Louis XIV dans la littérature française de 1660 à 1715* (Paris, 1981), p. 371 n. 71.

26. Alain Rey, 'Linguistic absolutism,' in *A New History of French Literature,* ed. Denis Hollier (Cambridge, Mass., 1989), p. 12.

27. A *da capo* aria (literally 'from the beginning') is an aria in three parts, the third being a repetition of the first and the second presenting a contrast in tempo and usually in melody.

28. Dennis Libby, 'Italy: two opera centres,' in *The Classical Era: From the 1740s to the End of the Eighteenth Century,* ed. Neal Zaslaw (London, 1989), pp. 17–18; Egon Wellesz and Frederick Sternfeld, *The New Oxford History of Music,* vol. VII: *The Age of Enlightenment 1745–1790* (Oxford, 1973), p. 8.

29. Ibid., p. 30.

30. Stefan Kunze, 'Die opera seria und ihr Zeitalter' in *Colloquium 'Johann Adolf Hasse und die Musik seiner Zeit,'* ed. Friedrich Lippman (Siena, 1983), Veröffentlichungen der musikgeschichtlichen Abteilung des Deutschen Historischen Instituts in Rom (n.p., 1987), pp. 5–8.

31. Ibid., p. 222.

32. Friedrich Walter, *Geschichte des Theaters und der Musik am kurpfälzischen Hofe* (Leipzig, 1898), p. 99.

33. Percy A. Scholes (ed.), *An Eighteenth-century Musical Tour in Central*

Europe and the Netherlands. Being Dr Charles Burney's Account of His Musical Experiences (Oxford, 1959), p. 38.

34. Peter Schleuning, *Das 18. Jahrhundert. Der Bürger erhebt sich* (Hamburg, 1984), p. 62.

35. E. E. Helm, *Music at the Court of Frederick the Great* (Norman, 1960), p. 71.

36. John A. Rice, *W. A. Mozart, La Clemenza di Tito* (Cambridge, 1991), p. 45.

37. Ruth Smith, *Handel's Oratorio and Eighteenth Century Thought* (Cambridge, 1995), p. 170.

38. Jean-Marie Duhamel, *La Musique dans la ville de Lully à Rameau* (Lille, 1994), p. 67.

39. Until recently it was believed that the first performance had taken place in 1729.

40. Hans T. David and Arthur Mendel (eds.), *The New Bach Reader: A Life of Johann Sebastian Bach in Letters and Documents* (New York and London, 1998), p. 327.

41. The website dedicated to Bach's vocal music lists 117 complete recordings, including twenty since 2000. http://www.bach-cantatas.com/IndexVocal.htm#BWV244.

42. *The Dublin Journal*, 10 April 1742, quoted in Donald Burrows, *Handel: Messiah* (Cambridge, 1991), p. 18.

43. Ibid., pp. 47–49. In fact he had been born in 1685.

44. Eduard Hanslick, *Geschichte des Concertwesens in Wien*, 2 vols. (Vienna, 1869), vol. I, p. ix.

45. Hugh Arthur Scott, 'London's earliest public concerts', *Musical Quarterly* 22 (1936), p. 454. The definition of a concert is taken from Heinrich Schwab, *Konzert. Öffentliche Musikdarbietung vom 17. bis 19. Jahrhundert* (Leipzig, 1971), p. 6.

46. Michel Brenet, *Les Concerts en France sous l'ancien régime* (Paris, 1900; reprinted New York, 1970), p. 119; Hanslick, *Geschichte des Concertwesens in Wien*, I, p. xiv.

47. Brenet, *Les Concerts en France sous l'ancien régime*, p. 117.

48. Karl Czok, 'Zur Leipziger Kulturgeschichte des 18. Jahrhunderts', in *Johann Sebastian Bach und die Aufklärung*, ed. Reinhard Szekus (Leipzig, 1982), p. 26.

49. Alfred Dörffel, *Geschichte der Gewandhausconcerte zu Leipzig vom 25. November 1791 bis 25. November 1881* (Leipzig, 1884), p. 3.

50. Horst Thieme (ed.), *Leipzig. Streifzüge durch die Kulturgeschichte*, 2nd ed. (Leipzig, 1990), p. 198.

51. Dörffel, *Geschichte der Gewandhausconcerte*, pp. 19–20.

52. Roger North, *Memoires of Musick Being Some Historico-criticall Collections of That Subject* (1728), ed. Edward F. Rimbault (London, 1846), p. 117.

53. Simon McVeigh, *Concert Life in London from Mozart to Haydn* (Cam-

bridge, 1993), pp. 6, 53, has written 'It should not be thought that commercial modes of organisation . . . implied a bourgeois cultural leadership . . . Modern musical taste was undoubtedly formed by aristocratic patrons in the fashionable end of town' and 'Modern concert life was not a bourgeois creation, and concert life only expanded into the City in later emulation, in the same way as the bourgeois bought gentility in the form of pianos and daughters' lessons.'

54. Goethe to his mother, 11 August, 1785; *Goethes Werke*, hrsg. im Auftrage der Großherzogin Sophie von Sachsen, 133 vols. (Weimar, 1887–1912), V, pp. 178–181.

55. I have discussed this issue in greater detail in *The Culture of Power and the Power of Culture: Old Regime Europe 1660–1789* (Oxford, 2002), pp. 161–180.

56. John Rosselli, 'From princely service to the open market: singers of Italian opera and their patrons 1600–1850', *Cambridge Opera Journal* 1, 1 (1989), p. 12.

57. J. N. du Tralage, *Notes et documents sur l'histoire des théâtres de Paris* (Paris, 1880), pp. 85–87.

58. James H. Johnson, *Listening in Paris: A Cultural History* (Berkeley and Los Angeles, 1995), p. 24.

59. Ibid., p. 30.

60. Frances Burney, *Evelina, or The History of a Young Lady's Entrance into the World*, ed. Margaret Anne Doody (London, 1994), p. 116.

61. Quoted in Anna Verena Westermayr, 'The 1784 Handel Commemoration: the conduct and interpretation of a spectacle' (unpublished master's thesis, University of Cambridge, 1996), p. 42. It is likely that the practice of standing was initiated by George II at the first London performance in 1743: Richard Luckett, *Handel's Messiah: A Celebration* (London, 1992), p. 175.

62. Richard Scheel, 'Feste und Festspiele', in *Die Musik in Geschichte und Gegenwart*, ed. Ludwig Finscher, vol. IV (Kassel and Basel, 1955), p. 108.

63. William Weber, *The Rise of Musical Classics in Eighteenth Century England* (Oxford, 1992), p. 142.

64. 'Die Begründung der teutschen Musikfeste', *Allgemeine Musikalische Zeitung*, xxxviii, 17 (1836), p. 266.

65. Edward Dent, *The Rise of Romantic Opera*, ed. Winton Dean (Cambridge, 1976), p. 184.

66. Jean-Jacques Rousseau, *The Confessions*, ed. J. M. Cohen (London, 1953), p. 321.

67. Maurice Tourneux (ed.), *Correspondance littéraire, philosophique et critique par Grimm, Diderot, Raynal, Meister, etc.*, vol. II (Paris, 1877), p. 312; *Journal et mémoires du marquis d'Argenson*, ed. E. J. B. Rathery, vol. VIII (Paris, 1867), pp. 13, 20.

68. Quoted in William Weber, 'Learned and general musical taste in eighteenth century France', *Past and Present* 89 (1980), p. 73, and Duhamel, *La Musique dans la ville,* p. 47, respectively.

69. Rousseau, *The Confessions,* p. 180.

70. Ibid., p. 327.

71. Jean-Jacques Rousseau, *The Discourses and Other Early Political Writings,* ed. Victor Gourevitch (Cambridge, 1997), p. 6.

72. Ibid., p. 16.

73. Maurice Cranston, *Jean-Jacques: The Early Life and Works of Jean-Jacques Rousseau 1712–1754* (Harmondsworth, 1987), p. 232.

74. Rousseau, *The Confessions,* p. 17.

75. Ibid., p. 262.

76. Ibid., p. 190.

77. Ibid., p. 354.

78. Raymond Trousson, 'J.-J. Rousseau et son œuvre dans la presse périodique allemande de 1750 à 1800', *Dix-huitième siècle* 1 (1969), pp. 289–306.

79. Christian Daniel Schubart, *Deutsche Chronik* lxxii (5 December 1774), p. 574.

80. Johann Georg Meusel, 'Ueber das Kunstgefühl. Ursachen seines Mangels und seiner Verstimmung', *Miscellaneen artistischen Inhalts* (1780), iii, p. 11.

81. Quoted in W. D. Robson-Scott, *The Literary Background of the Gothic Revival in Germany* (Oxford, 1965), p. 59, and Isaiah Berlin, *Against the Current: Essays in the History of Ideas* (London, 1979), p. 10.

82. Hans Günter Ottenberg (ed.), *Der Critische Musicus an der Spree. Berliner Musikschrifttum von 1748 bis 1799* (Leipzig, 1984), p. 15.

83. David Charlton (ed.), *E. T. A. Hoffmann's Musical Writings,* p. 96. He added: 'music reveals to man an unknown realm, a world quite separate from the outer sensual world surrounding him, a world in which he leaves behind all precise feelings in order to embrace an inexpressible longing.'

84. John Neubauer, *The Emancipation of Music from Language: Departure from Mimesis in Eighteenth Century Aesthetics* (New Haven and London, 1986), p. 5.

85. M. H. Abrams, *The Mirror and the Lamp: Romantic Theory and the Critical Tradition* (Oxford, 1953), p. 23.

86. Quoted in ibid., pp. 21, 48.

87. Edward Young, *Conjectures on Original Composition, in a Letter to the Author of Sir Charles Grandison* (London, 1759), pp. 26–27.

88. Ibid., p. 28.

89. Robson-Scott, *The Literary Background of the Gothic Revival in Germany,* p. 58.

90. Herbert Dieckmann, 'Diderot's conception of genius', *Journal of the History of Ideas* 2, 2 (1941), p. 151.

91. Edward E. Lowinsky, 'Musical genius: evolution and origins of a concept,' *Musical Quarterly* 50 (1964), p. 326.

92. Johann Wolfgang von Goethe, *Dichtung und Wahrheit*, pt. 2, bk. 8.

93. L. D. Ettlinger, 'Winckelmann,' in *The Age of Neo-classicism*, The Fourteenth Exhibition of the Council of Europe (London, 1972), pp. xxxiii–iv.

94. James J. Sheehan, *German History 1770–1866* (Oxford, 1989), p. 329.

95. Gerhard von Breuning, *Memories of Beethoven: From the House of the Black-robed Spaniards,* ed. Maynard Solomon (Cambridge, 1992), pp. 109–110. There are several slightly differing versions. This one seems the most authoritative, for Breuning recorded that the lines were written down 'as Grillparzer transmitted them to my father at his personal request, and as I copied them then and there.'

96. For example, his letter to Vocke of 22 May 1793, reprinted in Donald W. MacArdle and Ludwig Misch (eds.), *New Beethoven Letters* (Norman, Okla., 1957), p. 6, in which he quotes a passage from Schiller's *Don Carlos*.

97. Joseph Kerman and Alan Tyson, *The New Grove Beethoven* (London, 1983), pp. 53, 76–77.

98. Quoted in Maynard Solomon, *Beethoven* (London, 1977), p. 316. I have adjusted the translation for 'Wissenschaft' from 'science' to 'scholarship,' since 'science' has connotations of the 'natural sciences,' which Beethoven certainly did not intend.

99. Paul Johnson, *The Birth of the Modern: World Society 1815–1830* (London, 1991), p. 125.

100. This has been reprinted many times, for example in H. C. Robbins Landon, *Beethoven: A Documentary Study* (London, 1975), p. 86.

101. Ibid., p. 97.

102. Ibid., p. 94.

103. Walther Brauneis, '"Composta per festeggiare il sovvenire di un grand uomo": Beethovens *Eroica* als Hommage des Fürsten Franz Joseph Maximilian von Lobkowitz für Louis Ferdinand von Preußen,' *Österreichische Musikzeitschrift* 12 (1998), p. 7.

104. Alan Walker, *Franz Liszt: The Virtuoso Years 1811–1847,* rev. ed. (London, 1989), p. 417.

105. Norbert Stich, 'String quartets. String quintet,' in *Ludwig van Beethoven,* eds. Joseph Schmidt-Görg and Hans Schmidt (Hamburg, 1969), p. 105.

106. Walker, *Franz Liszt: The Virtuoso Years,* p. 227.

107. Franz Liszt, 'Lettre d'un bachelier ès musique,' *Revue et Gazette musicale de Paris,* IV, 29 (16 July 1837), pp. 239–241.

108. Hugh Arthur Scott, 'London concerts from 1700 to 1750,' *Musical Quarterly* 24 (1938), pp. 201–202.

109. Thomas Nipperdey, *Wie das Bürgertum die Moderne fand* (Berlin, 1988), p. 35.

110. Quoted in T. C. W. Blanning, 'The commercialisation and sacralisation

of culture,' in *The Oxford Illustrated History of Modern Europe*, ed. T. C. W. Blanning (Oxford, 1996), p. 135.

111. Alan Walker, *Franz Liszt: The Weimar Years 1848–1861* (London, 1989), pp. 272–273.

112. Jacob Grimm and Wilhelm Grimm, 'Philister,' in *Deutsches Wörterbuch*, vol. 7 (Leipzig, 1889), col. 1826.

113. For example, 'Bemerkungen über die Ausbildung der Tonkunst in Deutschland im 18ten Jahrhundert,' *Allgemeine Musikalische Zeitung* 19 (4 February 1801), p. 322; 'Andeutungen über Kunst, Dilettantism und Kritik,' *Allgemeine Musikalische Zeitung mit besonderer Rücksicht auf den österreichischen Kaiserstaat* 19 (4 September 1819), p. 565; *Berliner Allgemeine Musikalische Zeitung* 24 (14 June 1826), p. 187; 'Jetziger Zustand der Musik in Berlin,' *Neue Leipziger Zeitschrift für Musik* I, 34 (28 July 1834), p. 136.

114. Joseph d'Ortigue, 'Des sociétés philharmoniques dans le Midi de la France,' *Gazette musicale de Paris* I, 48 (30 November 1824), p. 383.

115. A useful phrase invented by Klaus Lankheit. He was using it with reference to the visual arts, but it applies to music just as well. Klaus Lankheit, *Revolution und Restauration* (Baden-Baden, 1965), p. 9.

116. Franz Liszt, 'De la situation des artistes et de leur condition dans la société,' *Gazette musicale de Paris* II, 19 (10 May 1835); 20 (17 May 1835); 30 (26 July 1835); 35 (30 August 1835); 41 (11 October 1835).

117. Liszt, 'Lettre d'un bachelier ès musique,' pp. 239–241.

118. Quoted in Alan Walker, *Franz Liszt: The Final Years 1861–1886* (London, 1997), p. 354.

119. Adrian Williams (ed.), *Portrait of Liszt by Himself and His Contemporaries* (Oxford, 1990), pp. 197, 424.

120. Richard Wagner, *My Life* (Cambridge, 1983), trans. Andrew Gray, ed. Mary Whittall, p. 499. This is by far the best English translation available but, disgracefully, does not have an index.

121. *Tristan and Isolde*, Act II.

122. Quoted in Robert W. Gutman, *Richard Wagner: The Man, His Mind and His Music* (London, 1968), p. 20.

123. Richard Wagner, *Sämtliche Schriften und Dichtungen*, 5th ed., 12 vols. (Leipzig, n.d.), vol. III, p. 38.

124. Quoted in Herbert Barth, Dietrich Mack, and Egon Voss (eds.), *Wagner: A Documentary Study* (London, 1975), p. 199.

125. There is a good account of the early stages of the Bayreuth Festival in Frederic Spotts, *Bayreuth: A History of the Wagner Festival* (New Haven and London, 1994), ch. 1.

126. For two particularly penetrating analyses of *The Ring*, see Deryck Cooke, *I Saw the World End: A Study of Wagner's Ring* (London, 1979), and Mark Berry, *Treacherous Bonds and Laughing Fire: Politics and Religion in Wagner's Ring* (Aldershot, 2005).

127. Williams (ed.), *Portrait of Liszt*, p. 614.

128. Verena Naegele, *Parsifals Mission. Der Einfluß Richard Wagners auf Ludwig II. und seine Politik* (Cologne, 1995), pp. 27–28.

129. Udo Bermbach, 'Liturgietransfer. Über einen Aspekt des Zusammenhangs von Richard Wagner mit Hitler und dem Dritten Reich' in *Richard Wagner im Dritten Reich,* eds. Saul Friedländer and Jörn Rüsen (Munich, 2000), pp. 43–45. Bermbach writes with special insight and cogency about Wagner; it is very regrettable that so little of his work is accessible to Anglophone readers.

130. Bryan Magee, *Wagner and Philosophy* (London, 2000), p. 129.

131. Wagner, *My Life,* p. 510.

132. Bryan Magee, *The Philosophy of Schopenhauer* (Oxford, 1983), pp. 348–349. The volume contains a substantial separate essay entitled 'Schopenhauer and Wagner.'

133. Ibid., p. 349.

134. Quoted in Barth, Mack, and Voss (eds.), *Wagner: A Documentary Study,* p. 241.

135. Quoted in Friedrich Dieckmann, *Richard Wagner in Venedig* (Leipzig, 1983), p. 214.

136. Quoted in Constantin Floros, 'Studien zur *Parsifal*-Rezeption,' in *Richard Wagner, Parsifal, Musik-Konzepte,* vol. 5, eds. Heinz-Klaus Metzger and Rainer Riehn (Munich, 1982), p. 15.

137. Although this is the figure usually given, Mozart wrote many more—the recording of the symphonies by the Academy of Ancient Music directed by Christopher Hogwood includes the forty-one symphonies plus twenty-seven other symphonic works on nineteen CDs—Editions de Oiseau-Lyre, 452 496-62.

138. Heinz Becker, 'Johannes Brahms,' in *The Nineteenth Century Legacy,* eds. Michael Raeburn and Alan Kendall (Oxford, 1990), p. 196.

139. In a letter to the members of the musical association on the island of Rügen: H. C. Robbins Landon, *Haydn: Chronicle and Works,* vol. V: *Haydn: The Late Years* (London, 1977), p. 233.

140. *The Musical World* xix, 36 (5 September 1844), p. 291; Williams (ed.), *Portrait of Liszt,* p. 224.

141. Weber, *The Rise of Musical Classics in Eighteenth Century England,* p. 6.

142. McVeigh, *Concert Life in London from Mozart to Haydn,* pp. 21–24.

143. Igor Stravinsky, *An Autobiography* (London, 1975; first published in French in 1935), p. 115.

144. Ibid., pp. 53–54.

145. Ibid., p. 20.

146. Ibid., p. 175.

147. *A Love Supreme* is currently available on Impulse 0602498840139 and also in a 'deluxe edition' which includes a recording of the only known live performance. In both cases, the original liner notes are included.

148. Quoted in Bryan Priestley, *John Coltrane* (London, 1987), p. 52.

149. Quoted in Ashley Kahn, *A Love Supreme: The Creation of John Coltrane's Classic Album* (London, 2002), p. xv.

150. Quoted in Lewis Porter, *John Coltrane: His Life and Music* (Ann Arbor, 1998), p. 232.

151. Ibid., p. 231.

152. Ibid.

153. Quoted in Kahn, *A Love Supreme*, p. xxii. Not everyone agreed, of course. When Coltrane died in 1967, Philip Larkin wrote an obituary for *The Daily Telegraph* so vituperative that it could not be published at the time: 'to squeak and gibber for sixteen bars is nothing; Coltrane could do it for sixteen minutes, stunning the listener into a kind of hypnotic state in which he read and re-read the sleeve note and believed, not of course that he was enjoying himself, but that he was hearing something significant . . . I regret Coltrane's death, as I regret the death of any man, but I can't conceal the fact that it leaves in jazz a vast, blessed silence.' Quoted in Mervyn Cooke, *Jazz* (London, 1998), p. 152.

154. Ibid., p. 171.

155. Tony Palmer, *All You Need Is Love: The Story of Popular Music* (London, 1976), p. 249.

156. Dave Marsh, 'Eric Clapton,' in *The Rolling Stone Illustrated History of Rock 'n' Roll*, ed. Anthony DeCurtis and James Henke (London, 1992), p. 407.

157. There is a revealing discussion by two former members of the Yardbirds of Clapton's deification in the BBC series 'Dancing in the Streets' in the episode entitled 'Crossroads,' once available on video—BBCV 5896—but alas long deleted.

158. Rupert Steiner, 'Rock star rolls in Ferrari,' *The Sunday Times* (23 February 2003). This article was occasioned by Clapton personally taking delivery of his new £400,000 Ferrari Enzo from the factory at Maranello. Steiner also reported that in the financial year 1999–2000 his company Marshbrook had paid him £8,800,000; that his total disclosed earnings for the past ten years amounted to £67,000,000; and that the sixty concerts performed in 2002 had grossed £28,000,000.

159. Bob Dylan, *Chronicles*, vol. I (New York, 2004), p. 51. As this quintessentially romantic effusion suggests, Robert Pattison's claim that 'nineteenth century romanticism lives on in the mass culture of the twentieth century, and the Sex Pistols come to fulfil the prophecies of Shelley' is not so preposterous as it might seem. Robert Pattison, *The Triumph of Vulgarity: Rock Music in the Mirror of Romanticism* (Oxford, 1987), p. xi.

160. Chris Williams (ed.), *Bob Dylan in His Own Words* (London, 1993), p. 30.

161. James Miller, *'Flowers in the Dustbin': The Rise of Rock and Roll 1947–1977* (New York, 1999), pp. 227–228. Cf. George Melly, writing in 1970: 'I now suspect it was the influence of Bob Dylan which secured their [The

Beatles'] release from the prison of commercial pop . . . [they] simply followed his example in trusting their own memories and feelings as the source for their music. It was, however, their *own* past they turned to.' George Melly, *Revolt into Style: The Pop Arts in the 50s and 60s* (Oxford, 1989), p. 85.

162. Harry Shapiro, *Waiting for the Man: The Story of Drugs and Popular Music*, rev. ed. (London, 1999), pp. 116–117.

163. Another possible adaptation of Marx's dictums to suit the modern world is, of course: 'it is opiates that are the opiate of the people.'

3. Places and Spaces

1. Hellmut Lorenz (ed.), *Geschichte der bildenden Kunst in Österreich*, vol. 4: *Barock* (Munich, 1999), p. 260. There are excellent illustrations of the exterior and interior respectively on pp. 88 and 116.

2. Hans Sedlymayr, 'Die Schauseite der Karlskirche in Wien,' in *Kunstgeschichtliche Studien für Hans Kauffmann*, ed. Wolfgang Braunfels (Berlin, 1956), pp. 263–264.

3. Thomas DaCosta Kaufmann, *Court, Cloister and City: The Art and Culture of Central Europe 1450–1800* (London, 1995), p. 300.

4. Sedlymayr, 'Die Schauseite der Karlskirche in Wien,' p. 268 n. 15.

5. Thomas Hochradner, 'Johann Joseph Fux,' in *Die Musik in Geschichte und Gegenwart*, ed. Ludwig Finscher, Personenteil, vol. 7 (Kassel, 2002), p. 318.

6. Hilde Haiger-Pregler, 'Höfisches und nichthöfisches Theater in Paris und Wien,' in *J.J. Fux-Symposium Graz '91*, ed. Rudolf Flotzinger (Graz, 1992), pp. 49–50.

7. Egon Wellesz, *Fux* (Oxford, 1965), pp. 42–43.

8. Frederick L. Millner, *The Operas of Johann Adolf Hasse* (Ann Arbor, 1979), p. 6.

9. Moritz Fürstenau, *Zur Geschichte der Musik und des Theaters am Hofe zu Dresden*, vol. II (Dresden, 1862), pp. 142–143.

10. Although of poor quality, there is a full reproduction of the painting in Dieter Zöchling (ed.), *Die Chronik der Oper* (Gütersloh and Munich, 1996), p. 33.

11. Michael Forsyth, *Buildings for Music: The Architect, the Musician, and the Listener from the Seventeenth Century to the Present Day* (Cambridge, Mass., 1985), p. 88.

12. Marguerite Countess of Blessington, *The Idler in Italy*, 3 vols. (London, 1839–1840), II, p. 253.

13. Fürstenau, *Zur Geschichte der Musik und des Theaters am Hofe zu Dresden*, p. 140.

14. Dennis Libby, 'Italy: two opera centres,' in *The Classical Era: From the*

1740s to the End of the Eighteenth Century, ed. Neal Zaslaw (London, 1989), p. 24.

15. James H. Johnson, 'Musical experience and the formation of a French musical public,' *Journal of Modern History* 64, 2 (1992), p. 195.

16. Sydney Lady Morgan, *Italy,* 2 vols. (London, 1821), I, p. 44.

17. Millner, *The Operas of Johann Adolf Hasse,* p. 6.

18. H. C. Robbins Landon and David Wyn Jones, *Haydn: His Life and Music* (London, 1988), p. 174.

19. Charles Saunders, *A Treatise on Theatres* (London, 1790), pp. 64, 71.

20. Louis Spohr, *Autobiography* (London, 1865), p. 259.

21. Morgan, *Italy,* I, p. 97.

22. F.-G. Pariset, 'Les beaux-arts de l'âge d'or,' in *Histoire de Bordeaux,* ed. C. Higounet, vol. V: *Bordeaux au XVIIIe siècle,* ed. François-Georges Pariset (Bordeaux, 1968), pp. 608–609.

23. Robert Latham and William Matthews (eds.), *The Diary of Samuel Pepys,* vol. VI: *1665* (London, 1972), p. 242.

24. Roger North, *Memoires of Musick being some historico-criticall collections of that subject* (1728), ed. Edward F. Rimbault (London, 1846), pp. 111–112.

25. Christoph Wolff, *Johann Sebastian Bach: The Learned Musician* (Oxford, 2002), p. 352.

26. Eugen K. Wolf, 'The Mannheim court,' in *The Classical Era,* ed. Neal Zaslaw (London, 1989), p. 213.

27. Jan Larue, 'Der Hintergrund der klassischen Symphonie,' in Schwab, *Konzert.,* p. 104.

28. Charles Burney, *The Present State of Music in Germany, the Netherlands and the United Provinces,* 2 vols. (London, 1775), I, p. 95.

29. Emily Anderson (ed.), *The Letters of Mozart and His Family,* 3rd ed. (London, 1985), p. 355.

30. Quoted in Wolf, 'The Mannheim court,' pp. 226–227.

31. Clive Brown, *Louis Spohr: A Critical Biography* (Cambridge, 1984), p. 12.

32. Ibid., p. 48.

33. Tim Healey, 'Dogs and tumults,' http://www.thisislimitededition.co .uk/item.asp?category=History&ID=599.

34. Robert Elkin, *The Old Concert Rooms of London* (London, 1955), p. 92; Thomas B. Milligan, *The Concerto and London's Musical Culture in the Late Eighteenth Century* (Epping, 1983), p. 1.

35. L. Schneider, *Geschichte der Oper und des Koeniglichen Opernhauses in Berlin* (Berlin, 1842), p. 21.

36. Walter Rösler, 'Die Canaillen bezahlet man zum Plaisir,' in *Apollini et Musis. 250 Jahre Opernhaus Unter den Linden,* ed. George Quander (Frankfurt am Main and Berlin, 1992), p. 14.

37. O. von Riesemann (ed.), 'Eine Selbstbiographie der Sängerin Gertrud Elizabeth Mara,' *Allgemeine Musikalische Zeitung,* X (11 August–29 September, 1875), p. 546.

38. Leo Balet and E. Gerhard, *Die Verbürgerlichung der deutschen Kunst, Literatur und Musik im 18. Jahrhundert* (Strasbourg, 1936), p. 71.

39. Dieudonné Thiébault, *Mes Souvenirs de vingt ans de séjour à Berlin; ou Frédéric le Grand, sa famille, sa cour, son gouvernement, son académie, ses écoles, et ses amis littérateurs et philosophes,* 3rd ed., 4 vols. (Paris, 1813), II, p. 209.

40. Percy A. Scholes (ed.), *An Eighteenth-Century Musical Tour in Central Europe and the Netherlands. Being Dr. Charles Burney's Account of his Musical Experiences* (Oxford, 1959), pp. 164, 207.

41. Forsyth, *Buildings for Music,* p. 104.

42. Rösler, 'Die Canaillen bezahlet man zum Plaisir,' p. 18.

43. On Frederick as Musician, see E. E. Helm, *Music at the Court of Frederick the Great* (Norman, 1960), *passim;* Helmuth Osthoff, 'Friedrich der Große als Komponist,' *Zeitschrift für Musik* 103, 2 (1936); and Helmuth Osthoff, 'Friedrich II. als Musikliebhaber und Komponist,' in *Friedrich der Große,* ed. Erhard Bethke (Gütersloh, 1985).

44. Peter Gay, *The Enlightenment: An Interpretation,* vol. 1: *The Rise of Modern Paganism* (London, 1967), p. 100; Winfried Böhm, 'Bildungsideal, Bildungswesen, Wissenschaft und Akademien,' in *Friedrich der Große,* ed. Bethke, p. 186.

45. Adolf Rosenberg, 'Friedrich der Große als Kunstsammler,' *Zeitschrift für bildende Kunst,* new series, 4 (1893), p. 209.

46. James J. Sheehan, *Museums in the German Art World: From the End of the Old Regime to the Rise of Modernism* (New York, 2000), p. 21.

47. Ibid., p. 22.

48. Ibid., p. 26.

49. Peter Mandler, 'Art in a cool climate: the cultural policy of the British state in European context, c. 1780–c. 1850,' in *Unity and Diversity in European Culture c. 1800,* ed. Tim Blanning and Hagen Schulze, Proceedings of the British Academy, vol. 134 (Oxford, 2006), pp. 106–107.

50. Ruth Freydank, *Theater in Berlin von den Anfängen bis 1945* (Berlin, 1988), p. 112.

51. Ingeborg Allihn, Eveline Bartlitz, Joachim Jaenecke, and Marion Sommerfeld, 'Berlin,' in *Die Musik in Geschichte und Gegenwart,* Sachteil, vol. I (Kassel, 1994), col. 1435.

52. Michael Schwarzer, 'The social genesis of public theater in Germany,' in *Karl Friedrich Schinkel 1781–1841: The Drama of Architecture,* ed. John Zukowsky (Chicago, 1994), p. 62.

53. Norbert Miller, 'Der musikalische Freiheitskrieg gegen Gaspare Spontini. Berliner Opernstreit zur Zeit Friedrich Wilhelms III.,' in *Preußen—Ver-*

such einer Bilanz, 5 vols., ed. Manfred Schlenke, vol. 4: *Preußen—Dein Spree-Athen. Beitrage zu Literatur, Theater und Musik in Berlin*, ed. Hellmuth Kühn (Hamburg, 1981), *passim*.

54. John Warrack, *Carl Maria von Weber*, 2nd ed. (Cambridge, 1976), p. 250.

55. Gottfried Eberle, *200 Jahre Sing-Akademie zu Berlin. 'Ein Kunstverein für die heilige Musik'* (Berlin, 1991), p. 44.

56. Ibid., pp. 50, 64–65.

57. *Leipziger Tageblatt*, 12 December 1884, reprinted in Wolfgang Schneider (ed.), *Leipzig. Streifzüge durch die Kulturgeschichte*, 2nd ed. (Leipzig, 1995), p. 391.

58. Robin Middleton and David Watkin, *Neoclassical and Nineteenth Century Architecture* (New York, 1980), p. 406.

59. Heinrich Habel, *Das Odeon in München und die Frühzeit des öffentlichen Konzertsaalbaus* (Berlin, 1967), pp. 1–16, 49.

60. Eduard Hanslick, *Geschichte des Concertwesens in Wien*, 2 vols (Vienna, 1869), vol. I, pp. 144–147; 'Über den Verein der Musikfreunde in Wien und das damit verbundene Conservatorium,' *Allgemeine Musikalische Zeitung* 46 (13 November 1833), pp. 757–764.

61. This is the concert hall from which the New Year's Day concert of the Vienna Philharmonic Orchestra is televised. There is an excellent collection of contemporary photographs in Renate Wagner-Rieger (ed.), *Die Wiener Ringstrasse—Bild einer Epoche. Die Erweiterung der Inneren Stadt Wien unter Kaiser Franz Joseph*, vol. I (Vienna, 1969), illustrations 41 a–j. More accessible are the excellent modern colour photographs to be found in Rolf Toman (ed.), *Wien. Kunst und Architektur* (Cologne, 1999), pp. 206–207. Hansen was one of Hitler's favourite architects, as his early architectural drawings reveal.

62. Richard von Perger, *Geschichte der k.k. Gesellschaft der Musikfreunde in Wien* (Vienna, 1912), p. 114.

63. Herbert Barth, Dietrich Mack, and Egon Voss (eds.), *Wagner: A Documentary Study* (London, 1975), p. 199. This excellent source book also contains many contemporary illustrations of Bayreuth.

64. To the mayor of Bayreuth, Friedrich Feustel, 12 April 1872, ibid., p. 220.

65. Patrick Carnegy, *Wagner and the Art of the Theatre* (New Haven, 2006), pp. 72–74. There are many excellent illustrations in Manfred Kiesel (ed.), *Das Richard Wagner Festspielhaus Bayreuth* (Cologne, 2007).

66. Barth, Mack, and Voss (eds.), *Wagner*, p. 242.

67. Forsyth, *Buildings for Music*, p. 166.

68. Monika Steinhauser, *Die Architektur der Pariser Oper. Studien zu ihrer Entstehungsgeschichte und ihrer architekturgeschichtlichen Stellung* (Munich, 1969), p. 13.

69. Quoted in Christopher Curtis Mead, *Charles Garnier's Paris Opéra: Ar-*

chitectural Empathy and the Renaissance of French Classicism (Cambridge, Mass., and London, 1991), p. 120.

70. Quoted in ibid., p. 127.

71. Quoted in Steinhauser, *Die Architektur der Pariser Oper*, p. 106.

72. *The Musical Times*, 1 February 1875.

73. *The Musical Standard*, n.s., vol. VIII, no. 545, 9 January 1875.

74. Good-quality reproductions can be found in Gérard Fontaine, *Palais Garnier: le fantasme de l'Opéra* (Paris, 1999), pp. 232, 265.

75. Frederic Spotts, *Bayreuth: A History of the Wagner Festival* (New Haven and London, 1994), p. 51.

76. Ibid.

77. Steinhauser, *Die Architektur der Pariser Oper*, p. 50.

78. A good visual review of these and other opera houses can be found in Thierry Beauvert, *Opera Houses of the World* (London, 1996).

79. Donald Sassoon, *The Culture of the Europeans from 1800 to the Present* (London, 2006), p. 566.

80. Ibid., p. 1358.

81. George Bernard Shaw, 'The perfect Wagnerite', in *Major Critical Essays*, ed. Michael Holroyd (London, 1986), p. 299.

82. James H. Johnson, *Listening in Paris: A Cultural History* (Berkeley and Los Angeles, 1995), p. 259.

83. Richard Wagner, *My Life*, ed. Mary Whittall (Cambridge, 1983), pp. 174–175.

84. Johnson, *Listening in Paris*, pp. 259, 264.

85. *Revue Musicale*, 'Correspondance', 18 May 1830, p. 115.

86. Elizabeth Bernard, 'Musique et communication. Les formes du concert', in *La Musique en France à l'époque romantique (1830–1870)*, ed. Joseph-Marc Bailbé et al. (Paris, 1991), p. 90.

87. Simon McVeigh, *Concert Life in London from Mozart to Haydn* (Cambridge, 1993), p. 69.

88. Percy M. Young, 'Orchestral music', in *The Blackwell History of Music in Britain*, ed. Nicholas Temperley, vol. 5: *The Romantic Age 1800–1914* (Oxford, 1988), pp. 358–359.

89. *The Musical World*, 7 February 1839, p. 77.

90. Ibid., 30 January 1845, pp. 49–50.

91. Quoted in ibid., p. 49.

92. 'Jullien's monster concert', ibid., 26 June 1845, p. 303.

93. 'Jullien's *Concerts Monstres*', ibid., 2 June 1849, p. 349.

94. Joel Sachs, 'London: the professionalisation of music', in *Man and Music: The Early Romantic Era between Revolutions, 1789 and 1848*, ed. Alexander Ringer (London, 1990), p. 226.

95. Nicholas Temperley, 'Ballroom and drawing-room music', in *The Romantic Age*, ed. Temperley, p. 115.

96. Ibid., 9 June 1849.

97. Ibid., 4 November 1848, p. 718.

98. John Rink, 'The profession of music,' in *The Cambridge History of Nineteenth Century Music*, ed. Jim Samson (Cambridge, 2002), pp. 63–64.

99. William Weber, *Music and the Middle Class: The Social Structure of Concert Life in London, Paris and Vienna between 1830 and 1848* (Aldershot, 2004), p. 19. The figure for London is probably an underestimate, as it does not include the many suburban concerts not mentioned in the press.

100. A. Laudely, 'Pasdeloup,' *L'Art Musicale* 26, 8 (30 April 1887), pp. 121–122. Jean-Jacques Eigeldinger, '1830–1870. Eléments d'une trajectoire musicale,' in *La Musique en France à l'époque romantique (1830–1870)*, ed. Joseph-Marc Bailbé et al., p. 18.

101. Michel Brenet, *Les Concerts en France sous l'ancien régime* (Paris, 1900; reprinted New York, 1970), p. 209.

102. Jules Ruelle, 'Concert populaire du Cirque. Réouverture et Wagnérisme,' *L'Art Musical* 14, 44 (2 November 1876), p. 349. Ruelle habitually referred to Wagner as 'Son Incommensurabilité.'

103. Laudely, 'Pasdeloup,' p. 122.

104. Oscar Commettant, 'Concerts populaires de musique classique,' *L'Art Musical*, 2, 3 (19 December 1861), p. 19.

105. Cyril Ehrlich, *The Music Profession in Britain since the Eighteenth Century: A Social History* (Oxford, 1985), p. 63.

106. Quoted in Dave Russell, *Popular Music in England, 1840–1914* (Manchester, 1987), p. 68.

107. 'Des associations musicales,' *L'Art Musical* 1, 25 (17 June 1838), pp. 1–2.

108. Quoted in Hanns-Werner Heister, 'Konzertwesen,' *Die Musik in Geschichte und Gegenwart*, Sachteil, vol. 5 (Kassel, 1996), col. 694.

109. Rebecca Harris-Warrick, 'Ballroom dancing at the court of Louis XIV,' *Early Music* 14 (1986), p. 41.

110. Ibid., p. 146.

111. Quoted in Harris-Warrick, 'Ballroom dancing at the court of Louis XIV,' p. 41.

112. Derek Carew, 'The consumption of music,' in *The Cambridge History of Nineteenth Century Music*, ed. Samson, p. 251.

113. Peter Buckman, *Let's Dance: Social, Ballroom and Folk Dancing* (New York and London, 1978), pp. 108–110.

114. Quoted in Nicholas Temperley, 'Ballroom and drawing-room music,' in *The Romantic Age 1800–1914*, ed. Temperley, p. 109.

115. Carew, 'The consumption of music,' p. 255.

116. Allison Thompson (ed.), *Dancing through Time: Western Social Dance in Literature, 1400–1918: Selections* (Jefferson, N.C., and London, 1998), p. 137.

117. Carew, 'The consumption of music,' p. 254.

118. Quoted in Hans Fantel, *Johann Strauss, Father and Son, and Their Era* (Newton Abbot, 1971), pp. 43–44.

119. Ibid., p. 256.

120. Peter Kemp, *The Strauss Family: Portrait of a Musical Dynasty* (Tunbridge Wells, 1985), p. 139.

121. Dave Russell, *Popular Music in England, 1840–1914* (Manchester, 1987), p. 74.

122. Dave Russell, 'Morton, Charles (1819–1904),' in *Oxford Dictionary of National Biography* (Oxford, 2004) (http://www.oxforddnb.com/view/article/50957, accessed 18 Sept. 2006).

123. Cyril Ehrlich, *The Music Profession in Britain since the Eighteenth Century*, pp. 57–58.

124. Russell, *Popular Music in England*, pp. 76–77.

125. Quoted in ibid., p. 92. McGlennon's own emphasis.

126. Richard Middleton, 'Popular music of the lower classes,' in *The Romantic Age 1800–1914*, ed. Temperley, pp. 80–87.

127. Russell, *Popular Music in England*, p. 80.

128. Ibid., p. 36.

129. Sassoon, *The Culture of the Europeans*, p. 803.

130. Roy M. Prendergast, *Film Music: A Neglected Art*, 2nd ed. (New York, 1992), p. 5.

131. John Mundy, *Popular Music on Screen: From Hollywood Musical to Music Video* (Manchester, 1999), p. 17.

132. Tony Thomas, *Music for the Movies* (Los Angeles, 1997), p. 38.

133. Ibid., pp. 39–40.

134. Prendergast, *Film Music*, pp. 16–17.

135. Thomas, *Music for the Movies*, p. 40.

136. Prendergast, *Film Music*, p. 35.

137. Sassoon, *The Culture of the Europeans*, p. 792. The Palladium at Midsomer Norton, alas long since closed, was surely not alone in offering its patrons double seats in the back row.

138. Quoted in Frances Rust, *Dance in Society: An Analysis of the Relationship between the Social Dance and Society in England from the Middle Ages to the Present Day* (London, 1969), p. 81.

139. Quoted in ibid., p. 89.

140. Ibid., p. 93.

141. I owe this information to Donald Sassoon, who conveyed it in the course of a contribution to an Ameurus Conference at Dresden on 19 May 2007.

142. Adam Sherwin, 'Stones gig at rugby's HQ kicks up storm,' *The Times*, 4 December 2002.

143. Ibid.; the source quoted is *Fortune* magazine.

144. Tom Phillips, 'Rio rolls towards Stones' biggest bang,' *The Guardian*, 14 February 2006, p. 19.

145. Nicholas Wapshott, 'It's not only rock and roll . . .', *The Sunday Telegraph*, 11 September 2005, p. 8.

146. Ian Burrell, 'Rock revival fuels record sales of live concert tickets', *The Independent*, 12 January 2004, p. 7.

4. Technology

1. 'Charbon acoustique. Gaz musical', *Le Ménestrel* IV, 50 (25 June 1837).

2. Michael Cole, *The Pianoforte in the Classical Era* (Oxford, 1998), p. 3. This provides the most detailed and convincing account of the early history of the piano. A facsimile of the inventory is reprinted in Konstantin Restle (ed.), *Faszination Klavier. 300 Jahre Pianofortebau in Deutschland* (Munich, 2000), p. 82, together with a portrait of Cristofori and a photograph of one of the three surviving pianos made by him.

3. Leo Balet and E. Gerhard, *Die Verbürgerlichung der deutschen Kunst, Literatur und Musik im 18. Jahrhundert* (Strassburg, 1936), p. 364.

4. Jeremy Montagu, *The World of Baroque and Classical Musical Instruments* (Newton Abbot, 1979), p. 70.

5. Hans T. David and Arthur Mendel, *The New Bach Reader: A Life of Johann Sebastian Bach in Letters and Documents*, revised and expanded by Christoph Wolff (New York, 1999), p. 365.

6. Christoph Wolff, *Johann Sebastian Bach: The Learned Musician* (Oxford, 2001), p. 427.

7. Cole, *The Pianoforte in the Classical Era*, p. 1.

8. H. C. Robbins Landon and David Wyn Jones, *Haydn: His Life and Music* (London, 1988), p. 167.

9. Ulrich Leisinger, 'Haydn's keyboard music', in the booklet accompanying Christine Schornsheim, Joseph Haydn, Piano sonatas—complete recording (Capriccio 49 404).

10. Ibid., p. 33.

11. Stephen Roe, 'Johann (John) Christian Bach', *Grove Music Online*, ed. L. Macy, www.grovemusic.com (accessed 11 July 2007).

12. Ibid.

13. Béatrice Didier, *La Musique des lumières. Diderot—L'Encyclopédie—Rousseau* (Paris, 1985), p. 264.

14. Cole, *The Pianoforte in the Classical Era*, ch. 3.

15. Ibid., pp. 86–87.

16. This includes the Shudi firm which Broadwood joined in 1761, becoming a partner nine years later.

17. Derek Adlam and Cyril Ehrlich, 'Broadwood', in *The New Grove Dictionary of Music and Musicians*, 2nd ed., 29 vols., ed. Stanley Sadie (London, 2001), IV, pp. 411–412.

18. Cole, *The Pianoforte in the Classical Era*, pp. 133–140.

19. Ibid., p. 136.

20. Emily Anderson (ed.), *The Letters of Mozart and His Family*, 3rd ed. (London, 1985), pp. 327–328.

21. Elliot Forbes (ed.), *Thayer's Life of Beethoven*, rev. ed. (Princeton, 1969), pp. 694–695.

22. H. C. Robbins Landon, *Beethoven: A Documentary Study* (London, 1970), p. 195.

23. Anne Rousselin-Lacombe, 'Piano et pianistes', in *La Musique en France à l'époque romantique (1830–1870)*, ed. Joseph-Marc Bailbé et al. (Paris, 1991), p. 145.

24. Quoted in Cole, *The Pianoforte in the Classical Era*, p. 217.

25. Gunther Joppig, 'Biedermeierliches in der Musik', in *Biedermeiers Glück und Ende . . . die gestörte Idylle 1815–1848*, ed. Hans Ottomeyer (Munich, 1987), p. 225.

26. Alan Walker, *Franz Liszt: The Virtuoso Years 1811–1847*, rev. ed. (London, 1989), pp. 285–286.

27. Quoted in Kurt Blaukopf, *Musik im Wandel der Gesellschaft. Grundzüge der Musiksoziologie* (Munich and Zürich, 1982), p. 96.

28. Dieter Hildebrandt, *Pianoforte: A Social History of the Piano* (New York, 1988), p. vii.

29. Paul Johnson, *The Birth of the Modern: World Society 1815–1830* (London, 1991), p. 130.

30. Volkmar Braunbehrens, *Mozart in Vienna* (Oxford, 1991), p. 147.

31. John Rosselli, *Music and Musicians in Nineteenth Century Italy* (London, 1991), p. 114.

32. Quoted in Colin Heywood, 'Society', in *The Short Oxford History of Europe: The Nineteenth Century*, ed. T. C. W. Blanning (Oxford, 2000), p. 52.

33. Daniel Heartz, *Haydn, Mozart and the Viennese School 1740–1780* (New York and London, 1995), p. 56. However, Cyril Ehrlich has claimed that it was Johann Christian Bach who gave the first public performance on a piano, in London in 1768: Cyril Ehrlich, *The Piano: A History*, rev. ed. (Oxford, 1990), p. 13.

34. Alice M. Hanson, *Musical Life in Biedermeier Vienna* (Cambridge, 1985), p. 118.

35. Henri Blanchard, 'Coup d'œil musical sur les concerts de la semaine et de la saison', *Revue et Gazette musicale de Paris* XII, 1 (12 January 1845).

36. 'Sur l'industrie musicale', *Gazette musicale de Paris*, ix (25 December 1830), pp. 198–200.

37. Rousselin-Lacombe, 'Piano et pianistes', p. 129.

38. Ehrlich, *The Piano*, p. 68.

39. Ibid., p. 71.

40. Cyril Ehrlich, *The Music Profession in Britain since the Eighteenth Century: A Social History* (Oxford, 1985), p. 71.

41. F. W. J. Hemmings, *Culture and Society in France 1789–1848* (Leicester, 1987), p. 295.

42. Émile Zola, *Nana*, ed. Douglas Parmeé (Oxford, 1992), p. 81.

43. Elizabeth Gaskell, *North and South* (London, 1994), pp. 1, 112.

44. *L'Art Musical*, I, 2 (13 December 1860), p. 12.

45. *La Critique Musicale. Journal complet de toutes les branches de l'art* I, 1 (1 November 1846), p. 5.

46. François Fétis, 'Soirées musicales de quatuors et de quintetti', *Revue Musicale*, 1 (February 1827), p. 37; Friedrich August Kanne, 'Über das Fortepiano-Spiel', *Allgemeine Musikalische Zeitung mit besonderer Rücksicht auf den österreichischen Kaiserstaat* 45 (7 November 1818), p. 409.

47. Rousselin-Lacombe, 'Piano et pianistes', p. 129.

48. Jeremy Montagu, *The World of Romantic and Modern Musical Instruments* (Newton Abbot, 1981), p. 34.

49. Malou Haine, 'Les facteurs d'instruments de musique à l'époque romantique', in *La Musique en France à l'époque romantique (1830–1870)*, ed. Joseph-Marc Bailbé et al. (Paris, 1991), p. 104; Ehrlich, *The Piano*, p. 32; Helen Rice Hollis, *The Piano: A Pictorial Account of Its Ancestry and Development* (Newton Abbot, 1975), p. 110.

50. Quoted in Arthur Loesser, *Men, Women and Pianos: A Social History* (London, 1955), p. 338.

51. Blaukopf, *Musik im Wandel der Gesellschaft*, pp. 88–90.

52. F. Danjou (ed.), *Revue de la musique religieuse, populaire et classique* (Paris, 1845), I, p. 165. He also called Liszt 'the Alexander, the Napoleon, the Cæsar of pianists.'

53. Max Weber, *The Rational and Social Foundations of Music*, ed. Don Martindale and Johannes Riedel (Carbondale, Ill., 1958), p. 124.

54. Hildebrandt, *Pianoforte*, p. 2.

55. Ulrich Prinz, *Johann Sebastian Bachs Instrumentarium. Originalquellen—Besetzung—Verwendung* (Stuttgart, 2005).

56. 'Bemerkungen über die Ausbildung der Tonkunst in Deutschland im 18. Jahrhundert', *Allgemeine Musikalische Zeitung* 16 (14 January 1801), p. 263.

57. Thomas Hiebert, 'The horn in the baroque and classical periods', *The Cambridge Companion to Brass Instruments*, ed. Trevor Herbert and John Wallace (Cambridge, 1997), pp. 103–104.

58. Simon Wills, 'Brass in the modern orchestra', in *The Cambridge Companion to Brass Instruments*, ed. Herbert and Wallace, p. 158.

59. Ardal Powell, *The Flute* (New Haven and London, 2002), pp. 68, 121–122.

60. Adam Carse, *The Orchestra in the Eighteenth Century* (Cambridge, 1940), p. 38.

61. Landon and Jones, *Haydn*, p. 255.

62. Montagu, *The World of Baroque and Classical Musical Instruments*, pp. 110–112; John Dilworth, 'The violin and bow—origins and development,' in *The Cambridge Companion to the Violin*, ed. Robin Stowell (Cambridge, 1992), p. 21.

63. Simon McVeigh, 'The violinists of the baroque and classical periods,' in *The Cambridge Companion to the Violin*, ed. Stowell, p. 46.

64. Montagu, *The World of Romantic and Modern Musical Instruments*, p. 11.

65. 'Musikzustand und musikalisches Leben in Wien,' *Cäcilia, eine Zeitschrift für die musikalische Welt* I, 1 (1824).

66. 'Quelques considérations sur l'état actuel de la musique,' *Le Dilettante. Journal de musique, de littérature, de théâtres et de beaux-arts* I, 2 (13 October 1833) and I, 6 (10 November 1833).

67. Philip Bate and Ludwig Böhm, 'Theobald Boehm,' in *New Grove Dictionary of Music and Musicians*, ed. Sadie, III, pp. 777–778.

68. Ibid. See also Powell, *The Flute*, ch. 9.

69. Montagu, *The World of Romantic and Modern Musical Instruments*, ch. 3.

70. Quoted in Thomas Liley, 'Invention and development,' in *The Cambridge Companion to the Saxophone*, ed. Richard Ingham (Cambridge, 1998), p. 3.

71. Ibid., p. 1.

72. Ibid., p. 18.

73. Quoted in ibid., p. 14.

74. Montagu, *The World of Romantic and Modern Musical Instruments*, p. 82.

75. Ibid., p. 77. This page includes a convenient chronology of the major changes between 1815 and 1839.

76. Arnold Myers, 'Design, technology and manufacture since 1800,' in *The Cambridge Companion to Brass Instruments*, ed. Herbert and Wallace, pp. 115–116.

77. 'Exposition universelle de Londres,' *Revue et Gazette musicale de Paris* 18, 46 (16 November 1851), p. 369.

78. Trevor Herbert, 'Brass bands and other vernacular brass traditions,' in *The Cambridge Companion to Brass Instruments*, ed. Herbert and Wallace, p. 177.

79. Dave Russell, *Popular Music in England 1840–1914: A Social History* (Manchester, 1987), p. 162.

80. Ibid., p. 170.

81. Ibid., p. 162.

82. Ibid., p. 188.

83. John Brewer, *The Pleasures of the Imagination: English Culture in the Eighteenth Century* (London, 1997), p. 553.

84. Bernarr Rainbow, 'Parochial and nonconformist church music', in *The Blackwell History of Music in Britain*, vol. 5: *The Romantic Age 1800–1914*, ed. Nicholas Temperley (Oxford, 1988), pp. 144–151.

85. Montagu, *The World of Romantic and Modern Musical Instruments*, p. 41.

86. Malou Haine, 'Les facteurs d'instruments de musique à l'époque romantique', in *La Musique en France à l'époque romantique*, ed. Bailbé et al., p. 105.

87. *Revue de la musique religieuse, populaire et classique*, I, p. 11. He returned to the same theme a year later: II, p. 78.

88. Hans Klotz and T. Wohnhaas, 'Walcker', in *New Grove Dictionary of Music and Musicians*, ed. Sadie, XXVII, p. 7.

89. Gustav Bock (ed.), *Neue Berliner Musikzeitung* 28 (9 July 1851), p. 215.

90. Roland Gelatt, *The Fabulous Phonograph: The Story of the Gramophone from Tin Foil to High Fidelity* (London, 1956), p. 10. This excellent study also includes a helpful chronology.

91. Peter Martland, *Since Records Began: EMI, the First 100 Years* (London, 1997), p. 23.

92. Timothy Day, *A Century of Recorded Music: Listening to Musical History* (London, 2000), p. 2.

93. Ibid., p. 11.

94. Gelatt, *The Fabulous Phonograph*, p. 137.

95. Colin Symes, *Setting the Record Straight: A Material History of Classical Recording* (Middletown, 2004), p. 40.

96. Gelatt, *The Fabulous Phonograph*, pp. 28, 145. Some idea of Edison's own elegant taste can be gleaned from his request that 'I'll Take You Home Again, Kathleen' be sung at his funeral: William Howland Kenney, *Recorded Music in American Life: The Phonograph and Popular Memory, 1890–1945* (New York and Oxford, 1999), p. 9.

97. Day, *A Century of Recorded Music*, p. 2.

98. Noel Malcolm, 'An unsung cultural revolution' (a review of Day, *A Century of Recorded Music*), *The Sunday Telegraph*, 10 December 2000, p. 13.

99. Symes, *Setting the Record Straight*, p. 28.

100. Quoted in Martland, *Since Records Began*, p. 58.

101. Gelatt, *The Fabulous Phonograph*, p. 81.

102. Quoted in Martland, *Since Records Began*, p. 56.

103. Ibid., p. 59.

104. Gelatt, *The Fabulous Phonograph*, pp. 153, 169.

105. James J. Nott, *Music for the People: Popular Music and Dance in Interwar Britain* (Oxford, 2002), pp. 17, 32.

106. Day, *A Century of Recorded Music*, p. 5; Gelatt, *The Fabulous Phonograph*, p. 86.

107. Pekka Gronow and Ilpo Saunio, *An International History of the Recording Industry* (London and New York, 1998), p. 33.

108. Ehrlich, *The Music Profession in Britain,* p. 118.

109. Nott, *Music for the People,* p. 1.

110. Ehrlich, *The Music Profession in Britain,* pp. 209–210.

111. Quoted in Gelatt, *The Fabulous Phonograph,* pp. 232–233.

112. Malcolm, 'An unsung cultural revolution', p. 13.

113. David Sager, 'History, myth and legend: the problem of early jazz', in *The Cambridge Companion to Jazz,* ed. Mervyn Cooke and David Horn (Cambridge, 2002), pp. 270, 279; for the Original Dixieland Jazz Band, see http://www.redhotjazz.com/odjb.html.

114. David Horn, 'The identity of jazz', in *The Cambridge Companion to Jazz,* ed. Cooke and Horn, p. 27.

115. E. J. Hobsbawm ('Eric Newton'), *The Jazz Scene,* new ed. (London, 1989), p. 112. Philip Larkin wrote of these 1920s recordings: 'It is tempting to say that one could do without any twentieth century artist sooner than Louis Armstrong, for while the rest were pulling their media to pieces, Armstrong was giving jazz its first definitive voice, one that changed the character of popular music down to the present day.' Richard Palmer and John White (eds.), *Larkin's Jazz: Essays and Reviews 1940–84* (London, 2001), p. 115.

116. It can be found at www.grovemusic.com/shared/views/article.html?section=jazz.015400.2.

117. Humphrey Lyttelton, *I Play as I Please: The Memoirs of an Old Etonian Trumpeter* (London, 1954), p. 34.

118. Donald Sassoon, *The Culture of the Europeans from 1800 to the Present* (London, 2006), p. 1128.

119. Quoted in Philip K. Eberly, *Music in the Air: America's Changing Tastes in Popular Music, 1920–1980* (New York, 1982), p. 17.

120. Ibid., pp. 25, 34. As Avner Offer has observed, radio and television, which consumed time, diffused much more rapidly than domestic appliances such as vacuum cleaners or washing machines, which saved time: 'the time saved by one set of appliances was consumed by the other.' Avner Offer, *The Challenge of Affluence: Self-control and Well-being in the United States and Britain since 1850* (Oxford, 2006), p. 170.

121. Nott, *Music for the People,* p. 59.

122. Ibid., p. 61.

123. Ehrlich, *The Music Profession in Britain since the Eighteenth Century,* p. 212.

124. Sassoon, *The Culture of the Europeans,* p. 1142.

125. Ibid., pp. 71, 79, 82.

126. Martland, *Since Records Began,* p. 142. Martland doubts this but provides no figures.

127. Ibid., p. 46.

128. Gronow and Saunio, *An International History of the Recording Industry,* p. 68.

129. Henry Pleasant, 'Bing Crosby,' in *The New Grove Dictionary of Music and Musicians,* ed. Sadie, VI, p. 721.

130. http://en.wikipedia.org/wiki/Bing_Crosby.

131. John Mundy, *Popular Music on Screen: From Hollywood Musical to Music Video* (Manchester, 1999), p. 180.

132. Quoted in Humphrey Burton, 'Television: concerts and recital relays and recordings,' in *The New Grove Dictionary of Music and Musicians,* ed. Sadie, XXV, p. 234.

133. Quoted in Tom McCourt and Nabell Zuberi, 'Music on television,' in *Encyclopedia of Television,* 2nd ed., vol. 3, ed. Horace Newcomb (New York and London, 2004), p. 1570.

134. Lawrence Welk with Bernice McGeehan, *Wunnerful, wunnerful! The Autobiography of Lawrence Welk* (Englewood Cliffs, N.J., 1971), p. 257. Even by the standards of the genre, this is a wonderfully wholesome and saccharine book.

135. http://en.wikipedia.org/wiki/Lawrence_Welk.

136. I especially recommend the video of 'The Wiggles—The Movie,' which I have now had to watch so often that I know it off by heart.

137. Arthur Marwick, *The Sixties: Cultural Revolution in Britain, France, Italy and the United States c. 1958–c. 1974* (Oxford, 1998), p. 36.

138. Quoted in Iain Brailsford, 'History repeating itself: were post-war American youngsters ripe for harvest?' www.kingston.ac.uk/cusp/Lectures/Brailsfordpaper.doc.

139. Ibid.

140. Werner Reiss, *Johann Strauss Meets Elvis. Musikautomaten aus zwei Jahrhunderten* (Stuttgart, 2003), p. 68.

141. Ibid., p. 255.

142. James Miller, *'Flowers in the dustbin': The Rise of Rock and Roll 1947–1977* (New York, 1999), p. 25; published in the United Kingdom in 2000 as *Almost Grown: The Rise of Rock and Roll* with the same pagination.

143. Ibid., p. 37.

144. Quoted in Robert Palmer, *Dancing in the Street: A Rock and Roll History* (London, 1996), p. 19.

145. Gelatt, *The Fabulous Phonograph,* p. 223.

146. Ibid., p. 232.

147. Reiss, *Johann Strauss Meets Elvis,* p. 273.

148. www.etedeschi.ndirect.co.uk/tr.radio.history.htm.

149. Robert Pattison, *The Triumph of Vulgarity: Rock Music in the Mirror of Romanticism* (Oxford, 1987), pp. 214–215.

150. The promisingly entitled book written and compiled by Paul du Gay, Stuart Hall, Linda James, Hugh Mackay, and Keith Negus, *Doing Cultural Studies: The Story of the Sony Walkman* (London, 1997), was designed for an Open University course and so is more about theory than practice. It does

however contain the following majestic observation by Iain Chambers, which, alas, is all too typical of a certain kind of writing about popular music: 'As part of the equipment of modern nomadism it [the Walkman] contributes to the prosthetic extension of our bodies, perpetually "on the move", caught up in a decentred diffusion of languages, experiences, identities, idiolects and histories that are distributed in a tendentially global syntax' (p. 141).

151. *The Independent*, 27 April 2007, p. 19.

152. http://news.sky.com/skynews/article/0,,30200–1263084,00.html?f =rss.

153. Michael Chanan, *Musica Practica: The Social Practice of Western Music from Gregorian Chant to Postmodernism* (London and New York, 1994), p. 15.

154. Miller, 'Flowers in the Dustbin,' pp. 141, 214.

155. John Hill, 'Television and pop: the case of the 1950s,' in *Popular Television in Britain: Studies in Cultural History*, ed. John Corner (London, 1991), pp. 90–91, 96.

156. Severin Carrell, 'MTV discovers the flip side to all that sex,' *The Independent on Sunday*, 16 July 2006, p. 9.

157. It can be found at http://www.youtube.com/watch?v=cmjuGIVyP4Q.

158. Quoted in Michael Shore, *The Rolling Stone Book of Rock Video* (London, 1985), p. 14.

159. Johnny Davis, 'The beat goes on,' *The Independent Review*, 22 February 2005, p. 2.

160. Ian Burrell, 'Internet killed the video star,' *The Independent*, 2 August 2006, p. 10. See also Bella Thomas, 'What the poor watch on TV,' *Prospect* (January 2003), p. 48.

161. Theodor Adorno, 'On Jazz,' in T. Adorno, *Essays on Music*, selected with an introduction, commentary and notes by Richard Leppert (Berkeley, Los Angeles and London, 2002), pp. 470–491.

162. 'How much amplifier power do I need?,' www.crownaudio.com/amp_htm/amp_info/how_much_power.htm.

163. John Vasey, *Concert Tour Production Management: How to Take Your Show on the Road* (Boston, 1998), p. 81.

164. www.missoulian.com/articles/2006/10/04/news/local/news02.txt.

165. Simon Frith, Will Straw and John Street (eds.), *The Cambridge Companion to Pop and Rock* (Cambridge, 2001), p. 166.

166. Gelatt, *The Fabulous Phonograph*, p. 220.

167. Gronow and Saunio, *An International History of the Recording Industry*, p. 150.

168. Paul Théberge, '"Plugged in": technology and popular music', in *The Cambridge Companion to Pop and Rock*, ed. Frith, Straw and Street, p. 9.

169. Paul Trynka (ed.), *The Beatles: Ten Years that Shook the World* (London, 2004), p. 242.

170. Quoted in Peter Wicke, *Rock Music: Culture, Aesthetics and Sociology* (Cambridge, 1990), p. 15.

171. Quoted in Timothy Warner, *Pop Music: Technology and Creativity: Trevor Horn and the Digital Revolution* (Aldershot, 2003), p. 22.

172. Trevor Pinch and Frank Trocco, *Analog Days: The Invention and Impact of the Moog Synthesizer* (Cambridge, Mass., 2002), p. 7.

173. Ibid., p. 28.

174. Ibid., p. 132.

175. Ibid., p. 66.

176. Quoted in Steve Waksman, *Instruments of Desire: The Electric Guitar and the Shaping of Musical Experience* (Cambridge, Mass., 1999), p. 39.

177. Ibid., p. 43.

178. Quoted in Miller, 'Flowers in the Dustbin,' p. 40.

179. Andy Gill, 'Strat's the way to do it,' *The Independent*, Arts and Books Review, 24 September 2004.

180. Ibid.

181. Ibid.

182. *The Independent*, 4 November 2006. Clapton donated the instrument to the auction, the proceeds of which went to his 'Crossroads' charity in Antigua.

183. Tom Wheeler, *The Stratocaster Chronicles: Celebrating 50 Years of the Fender Strat* (Milwaukee, 2004), p. 122.

184. *The Independent*, 3 February 2006, p. 16.

185. *The Daily Telegraph*, 24 October 2005, p. 11.

186. David Sinclair, 'Bedroom superstar,' *The Independent*, 7 April 2006, p. 16.

187. It can be found at www.youtube.com/watch?v=fN4fIRjMf-M.

188. http://en.wikipedia.org/wiki/YouTube.

189. Louise Jury, 'Golden age of home-grown music fuelled by downloads,' *The Independent*, 6 January 2007, p. 20.

5. Liberation

1. Thomas Carlyle, *History of Friedrich II of Prussia Called Frederick the Great*, vol. 5 (London, 1865), pp. 259–260. Carlyle gives a more literal translation, but I have preferred the version usually sung in English churches.

2. G. B. Volz (ed.), *Die Politischen Testamente Friedrichs des Grossen* (Berlin, 1920), pp. 184–185.

3. Andreas Dörner, *Politischer Mythos und symbolische Politik. Sinnstiftung durch symbolische Formen am Beispiel des Hermannmythos* (Opladen, 1995), p. 188.

4. Siegmar Keil, '"Nun danket alle Gott"—ein Kirchenlied als Inspirationsquell,' *Die Tonkunst online*, 0510 (1 October 2005), p. 1.

5. Barbara W. Tuchman, *August 1914* (London, 1962), p. 80.

6. Christopher Clark, *Iron Kingdom: The Rise and Downfall of Prussia* (London, 2006), p. 657.

7. *The Letters and Speeches of Oliver Cromwell, with Elucidations by Thomas Carlyle*, ed. S. C. Lomas, vol. II (London, 1904), p. 100.

8. Kate van Orden, *Music, Discipline and Arms in Early Modern France* (Chicago and London, 2005), p. 19.

9. Reinhold Koser and Hans Droysen (eds.), *Briefwechsel Friedrichs des Großen mit Voltaire*, 3 vols., Publikationen aus den K. Preußischen Staatsarchiven, vols. 81, 82, 86 (Leipzig, 1908–1909, 1911), I, 71–72.

10. *Des moeurs, des coutumes, de l'industrie, des progrès de l'esprit humain dans les arts et dans les sciences, Oeuvres de Frédéric le Grand*, 30 vols. (Berlin, 1846–1856), vol. I, p. 224.

11. K. Biedermann, *Fredrich der Große und sein Verhältniß zur Entwicklung des deutschen Geisteslebens* (Brunswick, 1859), p. 5.

12. Quoted in E. E. Helm, *Music at the Court of Frederick the Great* (Norman, 1960), p. 73. I have discussed the question of Frederick's alleged Francophilia in 'Frederick the Great and German culture,' in *Royal and Republican Sovereignty in Early Modern Europe: Essays in Honour of Ragnhild Hatton's Eightieth Birthday*, ed. G. C. Gibbs, Robert Oresko, and Hamish Scott (Cambridge, 1996), pp. 527–550.

13. Percy A. Scholes (ed.), *An Eighteenth-Century Musical Tour in Central Europe and the Netherlands. Being Dr. Charles Burney's Account of his Musical Experiences* (Oxford, 1959), p. 167.

14. Helm, *Music at the Court of Frederick the Great*, p. 129.

15. O. von Riesemann (ed.), 'Eine Selbstbiographie der Sängerin Gertrud Elizabeth Mara,' *Allgemeine Musikalische Zeitung* X (11 August–29 September 1875), p. 533.

16. Quoted in Helm, *Music at the Court of Frederick the Great*, pp. 71, 73.

17. Walter Salmen, *Johann Friedrich Reichardt. Komponist, Schriftsteller, Kapellmeister und Verwaltungsbeamter der Goethezeit* (Freiburg in Breisgau and Zürich, 1963), pp. 38, 43.

18. Noel Malcolm, 'My country, old or young?' (review of Adrian Hastings, *The Construction of Nationhood: Ethnicity, Religion and Nationalism* (Cambridge, 1997)), *The Sunday Telegraph*, 30 November 1997, p. 13.

19. I have discussed this further in *The Pursuit of Glory: Europe 1648–1815* (London, 2007), pp. 305–321.

20. ('*Hispanus flet, dolet Italus, Germanus boat, Flander ululat, & solus Gallus cantat.*') Charles de Saint-Denis, seigneur de Saint-Evrémond, 'Sur les opera, a Monsieur de Bouquinquant,' in *Oeuvres meslées*, vol. XI (Paris, 1684) and reprinted in François Lesure (ed.), *Textes sur Lully et l'opéra français* (Geneva, 1987), p. 105.

21. Robert M. Isherwood, *Music in the Service of the King: France in the Seventeenth Century* (Ithaca and London, 1973), pp. 133–134.

22. *Comparaison de la musique italienne et de la musique française,* 2nd ed., 3 vols. (Brussels, 1705–1706; reprinted in facsimile, Geneva, 1972), III, p. 202.

23. Ibid., vol. I, p. 90.

24. Pierre Bourdelot and Pierre Bonnet, *Histoire de la musique et de ses effets* (Amsterdam, 1725; reprinted in facsimile, Graz, 1966), pp. 293–295.

25. Ibid., pp. 291, 299–300. For other examples of French hostility to Italian music, see Michel Brenet, *Les Concerts en France sous l'ancien régime* (Paris, 1900; reprinted New York, 1970), pp. 150–152.

26. Marc-Antoine Laugier, *Sentiment d'un harmoniphile sur différens ouvrages de musique* (Amsterdam, 1756; reprinted in facsimile, Geneva, 1972), p. 80. On the modern title page of the reprint, it is stated that the work, which appeared anonymously, was written by A. J. Labbet and A. Léris, but in the catalogue of the University Library in Cambridge, it is firmly stated: 'for this work, often attributed to A. J. Labbet and A. de Léris, but really by M. A. Laugier, see LAUGIER (Marc Antoine).'

27. *Der musikalische Patriot,* III, 3 August 1741, p. 19.

28. Jean-Marie Duhamel, *La Musique dans la ville de Lully à Rameau* (Lille, 1994), p. 47.

29. Quoted in ibid., p. 47.

30. Adelaïde de Place, *La Vie musicale en France au temps de la Révolution* (Paris, 1989), p. 60.

31. For an excellent concise account of the affair, see Robert Wokler, '*La Querelle des Bouffons* and the Italian liberation of France: a study of revolutionary foreplay,' *Eighteenth-Century Life* 11, 1 (1987). I have discussed it in greater detail in *The Culture of Power and the Power of Culture: Old Regime Europe 1660–1789* (Oxford, 2002), ch. 8.

32. Jean-Jacques Rousseau, *The Confessions,* ed. J. M. Cohen (London, 1953), p. 358.

33. Friedrich Melchior Grimm, *Le petit prophète de Boehmischbroda* (Paris, 1753).

34. Rousseau, *Lettre sur la musique française.* This is reprinted in Denise Launay (ed.), *La Querelle des bouffons,* 3 vols. (Geneva, 1973), vol. I. An English translation of part of it can be found in Oliver Strunk (ed.), *Source Readings in Music History,* rev. ed. by Leo Treitler (New York and London, 1998), pp. 895–908. The passage quoted is on p. 908.

35. Rousseau, *Confessions,* p. 359.

36. Abbé Pellegrin, *Dissertation sur la musique françoise et italienne,* in Launay, ed., *La Querelle des bouffons,* III, p. 33; [de Rochemont], *Reflexions d'un patriote sur l'opéra françois, et sur l'opéra italien, qui présentent le Parallele du goût des deux Nations dans les beaux Arts,* in ibid., pp. 24, 81–82.

37. Pellegrin, *Dissertation,* in ibid., pp. 16, 19, 27, 47; [de Rochemont], *Reflexions,* in ibid., pp. 42, 80–83.

38. *Réponse du Coin du Roi au Coin de la Reine,* I, pp. 1–2.

39. [P. Castel], *Réponse critique d'un académicien de Rouen, à l'académicien de Bordeaux, sur le plus profond de la musique,* in ibid., p. 51.

40. [P. Castel], *Lettres d'un académicien de Bordeaux,* in ibid., pp. 3–4.

41. [V.T.H.S.V.], *Lettre de M.M. . . . du Coin du Roi, à MM. du Coin de la Reine, sur la nouvelle Piece, intitulée . . . La Servante Maitresse,* in ibid., pp. 12, 18.

42. [de Rochemont], *Réflexions d'un patriote,* in ibid., pp. 48–50.

43. This quaintly outdated opinion was quoted by Ernest Gellner in *Nations and Nationalism* (Oxford, 1983), p. 51. However, I have been unable to find this line in my copy of the novel. Gellner added: 'and every high culture now wants a state, and preferably its own.'

44. The actual phrase dates only from 1914 but the prejudice had existed since time out of mind: Stephen Banfield, 'The artist and society,' in *The Blackwell History of Music in Britain,* vol. 5: *The Romantic Age 1800–1914,* ed. Nicholas Temperley (Oxford, 1988), p. 11.

45. *Allgemeine Musikalische Zeitung* IV, 50 (8 September 1802), p. 805; V, 12 (15 December 1802), p. 194.

46. Ibid., VII, 29 (17 April 1805), p. 472.

47. *The Spectator,* new ed. (London, n.d.), 18 (21 March 1711), p. 33.

48. Michael Greenhalgh, 'King Arthur,' in the booklet accompanying the recording by Alfred Deller, the Deller Consort and Choir and the King's Musick, Harmonia Mundi HMX 2901531, p. 6.

49. John Dryden, *King Arthur or The British Worthy: A Dramatick Opera,* ed. Dennis Arundell (Cambridge, 1928), p. 65.

50. Ibid., p. 60.

51. Paul Hammond, 'Dryden, John (1631–1700),' *Oxford Dictionary of National Biography* (Oxford, 2004); online edition www.oxforddnb.com/view/article/8108 (accessed 5 February 2007). The libretto of 1691 was very likely based on an earlier draft of 1684, written before his conversion.

52. Dryden, *King Arthur,* p. 21.

53. Ibid., p. 62.

54. Ibid., p. 63.

55. Dennis Arundell, 'Introduction,' in ibid., pp. vii–viii.

56. Ibid., p. 60.

57. *The Works of James Thomson, with his last corrections and improvements,* 4 vols. (London, 1766), III, p. 244.

58. Ibid., p. 253.

59. Jonathan Keates, 'Thomas Arne's *Alfred:* an opera born of patronage and patriotism,' *BBC Music Magazine,* June 1997.

60. Matthew Kilburn, 'Frederick Lewis, prince of Wales (1707–1751),' *Oxford Dictionary of National Biography* (Oxford, 2004); online edition www.oxforddnb.com/view/article/10140 (accessed 6 February 2007). See also Alan D. McKillop, 'The early history of Alfred,' *Philological Quarterly* 41, 1 (1962).

61. I have discussed this further in *The Pursuit of Glory: Europe 1648–1815* (London, 2007), pp. 443–444.

62. Robert D. Hume, 'The Beggar's Opera', in *The New Grove Dictionary of Opera*, ed. Stanley Sadie (New York, 1992), I, pp. 374–377.

63. Percy A. Scholes, *The Oxford Companion to Music*, 10th ed. (Oxford, 1970), pp. 408–413.

64. I have discussed it in greater detail in *The Culture of Power and the Power of Culture*, pp. 275–277.

65. Roy Palmer (ed.), *The Oxford Book of Sea Songs* (Oxford, 1986).

66. Quoted in Michael Dobson, *The Making of a National Poet: Shakespeare, Adaptation and Authorship, 1660–1769* (Oxford, 1992), p. 204 n. 27.

67. Pierre Barbier and France Vernillat, *Histoire de France par les chansons*, vol. II: *Mazarin et Louis XIV* (Paris, 1956), pp. 90, 115, 117.

68. Ibid., p. 97.

69. Ibid., vol. III: *Du Jansénisme au siècle des lumières* (Paris, 1957), p. 140.

70. Quoted in Michel Antoine, *Louis XV* (Paris, 1989), p. 852.

71. Roger Bickart, *Les Parlements et la notion de souveraineté nationale au dix-huitième siècle* (Paris, 1932), p. 110.

72. Claude Duneton, *Histoire de la chanson française*, vol. II: *De 1780 à 1860* (Paris, 1998), p. 39. On the problems of censoring songs that were not written down, see Annette Keilhauer, *Das französische Chanson im späten Ancien Régime* (Hildesheim, 1998), pp. 55–56.

73. François Moureau, 'Stratégie chansonnie de la Révolution *francaise*', *The French Review* 62, 6 (1989), p. 968.

74. Laura Mason, *Singing the Revolution: Popular Culture and Politics 1787–1799* (Ithaca and London, 1996).

75. Pierre Barbier and France Vernillat, *Histoire de France par les chansons*, vol. IV: *La Révolution* (Paris, 1957), p. 78.

76. Robert Brécy, *The Revolution in Song* (Paris, 1988), p. 55.

77. Barbier and Vernillat, *Histoire de France par les chansons*, IV, p. 82.

78. Quoted in Brécy, *The Revolution in Song*, p. 55.

79. Mason, *Singing the Revolution*.

80. Ibid.

81. I have discussed this very important change in *The French Revolutionary Wars 1787–1802* (London, 1996), pp. 46–47, 55.

82. He was born just 'Rouget'—the aristocratic-sounding suffix 'de l'Isle' had been added in 1776 to get him into a military college: Julien Tiersot, *Histoire de la Marseillaise* (Paris, 1915), p. 5.

83. This story has been told many times, invariably based on Rouget de l'Isle's own account in the preface to his *Cinquante chants français* of 1825. My own account is drawn mainly from Hervé Luxardo, *Histoire de la Marseillaise* (Paris, 1989), pp. 19–24.

84. Ibid., p. 16; Duneton, *Histoire de la chanson française*, II, p. 126.

85. Julien Tiersot, *Histoire de la Marseillaise* (Paris, 1915), pp. 39–40.

86. David Bell, 'Aux origines de la 'Marseillaise': L'Adresse à la nation angloise de Claude-Rigobert Lefebvre de Beauvray', *Annales historiques de la Révolution francaise* 299 (1995), pp. 75–76.

87. Arthur Loth in *Le Chant de la Marseillaise son véritable auteur* (first published 1886, new edition ed. Pierre Brière-Loth, Paris, 1992) claimed to show that the melody had appeared five years before, the French Revolution in an oratorio, *Esther*, by Jean-Baptiste Lucien Grisons, who probably got it from somewhere else himself.

88. Tiersot, *Histoire de la Marseillaise*, p. 44.

89. Luxardo, *Marseillaise*, pp. 34–37.

90. Tiersot, *Histoire de la Marseillaise*, p. 57.

91. Louis Fiaux, *La Marseillaise, son histoire dans l'histoire des français depuis 1792* (Paris, 1918), p. 33.

92. Mona Ozouf, *Festivals and the French Revolution* (Cambridge, Mass., 1988), p. 81.

93. Ibid., p. 38; Tiersot, *Histoire de la Marseillaise*, p. 70.

94. Marie Mauron, *La Marseillaise* (Paris, 1968), p. 58.

95. Quoted in John A. Lynn, *The Bayonets of the Republic: Motivation and Tactics in the Army of Revolutionary France 1791–94* (Urbana and Chicago, 1984), p. 151.

96. David A. Bell, *The First Total War* (Boston and New York, 2007), p. 145.

97. Ibid., p. 162; Hermann Wendel, *Die Marseillaise* (Zürich, 1936), p. 40.

98. Michel Vovelle, 'La Marseillaise: war or peace', in *Realms of Memory: Constructions of the French Past*, ed. Pierre Nora, vol. III: *Symbols* (New York, 1998), p. 40.

99. Ibid., p. 41.

100. The marquis de Bouillé had achieved notoriety by brutally repressing mutinies at Metz and Nancy in 1790, becoming a symbol of counter-revolution. He planned the abortive attempt by the royal family to escape in June 1791 and emigrated when it failed.

101. Luxardo, *La Marseillaise*, pp. 99–100.

102. They can be found at http://chnm.gmu.edu/revolution/d/626/. The first verse runs: French people, people of brothers,/ Can you watch, without shuddering in horror,/ As crime unfurls its banners/ Of Carnage and Terror?/ You suffer an atrocious horde, Of assassins and brigands,/ Soiling with its savage breath,/ The lands of the living!

103. François-Alphonse Aulard, 'La Marseillaise et le Réveil du peuple', in Aulard, *Études et leçons sur la Révolution française*, vol. I (Paris, 1914), pp. 242–248. On counter-revolutionary songs, see Simone Wallon, 'La chanson des rues contre-révolutionnaires en France de 1790 à 1795', in *Orphée*

phrygien: les musiques de la Révolution, ed. Jean-Rémy Julien and Jean-Claude Klein (Paris, 1989), pp. 137–153.

104. Pierre, *Les Hymnes et chansons de la Révolution,* p. 13.

105. Aulard, 'La Marseillaise et le Réveil du peuple,' pp. 261–264.

106. Jacques Godechot, 'Nation, patrie, nationalisme et patriotisme en France au XVIIIe siècle,' *Annales historiques de la Révolution française* 43 (1971), pp. 496–498.

107. David Cairns (ed.), *The Memoirs of Hector Berlioz* (London, 1969), p. 133.

108. Gaston Raphaël, *Le Rhin allemand,* Cahiers de la Quinzaine, 19 (Paris, 1903), p. 11.

109. Michael Paul Driskel, 'Singing the *Marseillaise* in 1840: the case of Charlet's censored prints,' *The Art Bulletin* 69, 4 (1987), p. 605.

110. Richard Wagner, *My Life* (Cambridge, 1983), p. 399. Wagner mistakenly believed that Sunday was the 7th of May.

111. Wagner had already used the *Marseillaise* to express opposition to the other major German power, Austria. In 1834, aged twenty-one, he had persuaded a group of drinking companions at the Black Horse Inn at Prague 'to bellow the *Marseillaise* loudly out into the night.' The consequence was a summons to an interrogation at the local police station: ibid., p. 85.

112. It is now available on a DVD from Studio Canal, ref. 196 828–9.

113. David Kimbell, *Italian Opera* (Cambridge, 1991), p. 326.

114. Ibid., p. 394.

115. John Rosselli, *Music and Musicians in Nineteenth Century Italy* (London, 1991), p. 56.

116. David Kimbell, *Verdi in the Age of Italian Romanticism* (Cambridge, 1981), p. 22; John Black, *The Italian Romantic Libretto: A Study of Salvadore Cammarano* (Edinburgh, 1984), p. 5.

117. Quoted in Rosselli, *Music and Musicians,* pp. 70–71.

118. Kimbell, *Italian Opera,* p. 418; Rosselli, *Music and Musicians,* p. 61.

119. Ibid., pp. 70, 115.

120. Derek Beales and Eugenio F. Biagini, *The Risorgimento and the Unification of Italy* (London, 2002), p. 33.

121. Quoted in Kimbell, *Italian Opera,* p. 392.

122. Ibid.

123. Ibid., p. 493.

124. Dennis Libby, 'Italy: two opera centres,' in *The Classical Era: From the 1740s to the End of the Eighteenth Century,* ed. Neal Zaslaw (London, 1989), p. 15.

125. Stendhal, *Life of Rossini* (London, 1956), p. 30.

126. Edward Dent, *The Rise of Romantic Opera* (Cambridge, 1976), p. 114.

127. Ibid., p. 28.

128. Ibid., p. 467.

129. Wolfgang Altgeld, *Das politische Italienbild der Deutschen zwischen Aufklärung und europäischer Revolution von 1848* (Tübingen, 1984), p. 189.

130. Quoted in Kimbell, *Italian Opera*, p. 355.

131. Dent, *The Rise of Romantic Opera*, p. 116.

132. Jonathan Keates, *The Siege of Venice* (London, 2005), p. 15.

133. Ibid., p. 351.

134. Éva Pintér-Lück, 'Norma-Bellini,' in *Opera—Composer—Works—Performers*, ed. Sigrid Neef (Cologne, 1999), p. 29.

135. Harold Acton, *The Last Bourbons of Naples (1825–1861)* (London, 1961), p. 81.

136. Ibid.

137. Black, *The Italian Romantic Libretto*, p. 104.

138. Ibid., p. 118.

139. Mary Jane Phillips-Matz, *Verdi: A Biography* (Oxford, 1993), p. 79.

140. Ibid., p. 765.

141. Roger Parker, *Leonora's Last Act: Essays in Verdian Discourse* (Princeton, 1997), p. 20.

142. Kimbell, *Italian Opera*, p. 494. John Rosselli, however, wrote: 'The alleged close bond between early nineteenth century Italian opera and liberal nationalism is one of those clichés that go marching on in the face of the evidence': *Music and Musicians in Nineteenth Century Italy*, p. 65.

143. Phillips-Matz, *Verdi*, p. 388. The poet Giovanni Prati, who recorded this scene, did not reveal whether Cavour was able to hit the high C at the aria's climax.

144. 'Bemerkungen über die Ausbildung der Tonkunst in Deutschland im achtzehnten Jahrhundert,' *Allgemeine Musikalische Zeitung*, 15 (7 January 1801), p. 242; 16 (14 January 1801), p. 259.

145. Emily Anderson (ed.), *The Letters of Mozart and His Family*, 3rd ed. (London, 1985), pp. 522, 564, 587–588.

146. Ibid., pp. 531–533.

147. Quoted in R. R. Palmer, *Twelve Who Ruled: The Year of the Terror in the French Revolution* (Princeton, 1970), p. 320.

148. Quoted in T. C. W. Blanning, *Reform and Revolution in Mainz, 1743–1803* (Cambridge, 1974), p. 323.

149. Speech of 7 May 1794, quoted in T. J. Reed, *The Classical Centre: Goethe and Weimar 1775–1832* (Oxford, 1986), p. 183 n. 30.

150. Augusta Wedler-Steinberg (ed.), *Körners Werke*, vol. I (Berlin, n.d.), p. 6.

151. 'Gedanken über Musik,' *Museum der eleganten Welt* I, 4 (13 January 1836), p. 56.

152. J. Fesky, 'Allerlei über den Standpunct der heutigen Musik. Teutsche, französische und italienische Musik,' *Cäcilia* XVII (1835), pp. 225–226.

153. Schubart, *Deutsche Chronik* XL (18 May 1775), p. 314.

154. Alice M. Hanson, *Musical Life in Biedermeier Vienna* (Cambridge, 1985), p. 65.

155. Franz Stoepel (ed.), *Münchener Allgemeine Musik-Zeitung* XX (16 February 1828), p. 310.

156. John Warrack (ed.), *Carl Maria von Weber: Writings on Music* (Cambridge, 1981), p. 332. See also John Warrack, *Carl Maria von Weber,* 2nd ed. (Cambridge, 1976), pp. 94–99.

157. J. Fesky, 'Allerlei über den Standpunkt der heutigen Musik. Teutsche, französische und italienische Musik,' *Cäcilia* XVII (1835), pp. 222, 225.

158. Adolph Bernhard Marx (ed.), *Berliner Allgemeine Musikalische Zeitung* 21 (23 May 1827), p. 165.

159. Ibid., 43 (27 October 1824), p. 372.

160. Schubart, *Deutsche Chronik* XL (18 May 1775), p. 314.

161. 'Zustand der Musik in England, besonders in London,' *Allgemeine Musikalische Zeitung* 12 (15 December 1802), p. 193.

162. Ibid., XLI, 18 (1 May 1839), pp. 348–349.

163. Marx (ed.), *Berliner Allgemeine Musikalische Zeitung* 2 (14 January 1824), p. 12.

164. Carl Friedrich Cramer, *Magazin der Musik* (Hamburg, 1783–1786; reprinted Hildesheim and New York, 1971), II, 2 (1784), p. 1059.

165. Ibid., II, 1 (1784), p. 590.

166. *Allgemeine Musikalische Zeitung* 15 (7 January 1801), p. 241.

167. *Cäcilia,* XVII (1835), p. 287.

168. Thomas Nipperdey, *Deutsche Geschichte 1800–1866. Bürgerwelt und starker Staat* (Munich, 1983), p. 480.

169. F. S. Gassner (ed.), *Zeitschrift für Deutschlands Musik-Vereine und Dilettanten* (Karlsruhe, 1841), p. 168.

170. Clive Brown, *Louis Spohr: A Critical Biography* (Cambridge, 1984), p. 62.

171. G. Schilling (ed.), *Jahrbücher des deutschen Nationalvereins für Musik und ihre Wissenschaft* (Karlsruhe, 1839–1842), 19 (8 August 1839), p. 152.

172. Richard Scheel, 'Feste und Festspiele,' in *Die Musik in Geschichte und Gegenwart,* IV (Kassel and Basel, 1955), p. 110.

173. Gertrude Cepl-Kaufmann and Antje Johanning, *Mythos Rhein: zur Kulturgeschichte eines Stromes* (Darmstadt, 2003), pp. 168–178.

174. Translation by Sarah Hanbury-Tenison, in Hagen Schulze, *The Course of German Nationalism from Frederick the Great to Bismarck 1763–1867* (Cambridge, 1991), p. 65.

175. Gassner (ed.), *Zeitschrift für Deutschlands Musik-Vereine und Dilettanten,* p. 107.

176. *Allgemeine Musikalische Zeitung* 9 (3 March 1841), p. 191. Within a year, the poem had been set to music well over a hundred times: Cecelia Hopkins Porter, *The Rhine as Musical Metaphor: Cultural Identity in German Romantic Music* (Boston, 1996), pp. 229–237.

177. Schilling (ed.), *Jahrbücher des deutschen Nationalvereins für Musik und ihre Wissenschaft*, 11 (18 March 1841), p. 85.

178. Hans Hattenhauer, *Geschichte der deutschen Nationalsymbole: Zeichen und Bedeutung*, 2nd ed. (Munich, 1990), pp. 62–68.

179. James Brophy, *Popular Culture and the Public Sphere in the Rhineland, 1800–1850* (Cambridge, 2007), p. 91.

180. Ibid., p. 90.

181. 'Über die hohe Bedeutung der Musik in der Gegenwart', *Neue Zeitschrift für Musik* XVI, 43 (27 May 1842), p. 169.

182. Gassner (ed.), *Zeitschrift für Deutschlands Musik-Vereine und Dilettanten*, p. 223.

183. *La France Musicale*, IV, 16 (18 April 1841), pp. 133–135.

184. L. Bischoff (ed.), *Rheinische Musik-Zeitung für Kunstfreunde und Künstler* (Cologne, 1850) I, 16 (19 October 1850), p. 126.

185. Dietmar Klenke, *Der singende 'deutsche Mann': Gesangvereine und deutsches Nationalbewußtsein von Napoleon bis Hitler* (Münster, 1998), p. 63.

186. Ibid.

187. Benedict Anderson, *Imagined Communities: Reflections on the Origin and Spread of Nationalism*, rev. ed. (London, 1991), p. 6.

188. Brian Large, *Smetana* (London, 1970), pp. 3, 43.

189. Quoted in Ibid., p. 268.

190. Derek Sayer, *The Coasts of Bohemia: A Czech History* (Princeton, 1998), pp. 54–55.

191. Ibid., pp. 49–50.

192. Ibid., p. 56.

193. Ibid., p. 53.

194. 'Über den Zustand der Musik in Böhmen', *Allgemeine Musikalische Zeitung* 28 (9 April 1800), p. 488; Johann Friedrich Reichardt, *Briefe eines aufmerksamen Reisenden die Musik betreffend*, 2 vols. (Frankfurt and Leipzig, 1774–1776), II, pp. 124–130.

195. Large, *Smetana*, pp. 141–142.

196. Ibid., p. 120.

197. Translation from the booklet accompanying the recording conducted by Jan Hus Tichý on Supraphon 11 1804-2 612.

198. Large, *Smetana*, p. 145.

199. John Tyrrell, *Czech Opera* (Cambridge, 1988), p. 24.

200. Ibid., p. 41.

201. Translation from the booklet accompanying the complete recording conducted by Josef Krips on Myto Records MCD 924.65. If anything, the plot is even more incoherent than that of *The Brandenburgers in Bohemia*.

202. Large, *Smetana*, p. 209.

203. Mirka Zemanová, *Janáček: A Composer's Life* (London, 2002), p. 20.

204. Ibid.

205. Hans-Hubert Schönzeler, *Dvořák* (London and New York, 1984), p. 153.

206. Quoted in Malcolm Burgess, 'A survey of the stage in Russia from 1741 to 1783, with special reference to the development of the Russian theatre' (unpublished Ph.D. diss., University of Cambridge, 1953), p. 1.

207. A. M. Sokolova, 'Kontsertnaya zhizn', *Istoriya russkoy muzyki* III (Moscow, 1985), p. 244.

208. Dieter Lehmann, *Russlands Oper und Singspiel in der zweiten Hälfte des 18. Jahrhunderts* (Leipzig, 1958), p. 22 n. 4.

209. Ibid., p. 247.

210. Orlando Figes, *Natasha's Dance: A Cultural History of Russia* (London, 2002), p. 39.

211. B. N. Aseyev, *Russky dramatichesky teatr ot ego istokov do kontsa XVIII veka* (Moscow, 1977), p. 304.

212. Vsevolod' Cheshikhin, *Istoriya russkoy opery (s 1674 po 1903 g.)*, 2nd ed. (St. Petersburg, 1905), p. 52.

213. Ibid., p. 47.

214. Richard Taruskin, 'Mikhail Matveyevich Sokolovsky,' in *The New Grove Dictionary of Music and Musicians*, ed. Sadie, IV, p. 41.

215. S. Frederick Starr, 'Russian art and society 1800–1850,' in *Art and Culture in Nineteenth Century Russia*, ed. Theofanis George Stavrou (Bloomington, Ind., 1983), p. 96.

216. Claus Scharf, '"La Princesse de Zerbst Catherinisée": Deutschlandbild und Deutschlandpolitik Katharinas II.,' in *Deutsche und Deutschland aus russischer Sicht. 18. Jahrhundert: Aufklärung*, ed. Dagmar Herrmann (Munich, 1992), p. 285.

217. Hans Rogger, *National Consciousness in Eighteenth Century Russia* (Cambridge, Mass., 1960), p. 34.

218. O. E. Levasheva, 'Nachalo russkoy opery,' *Istoriya russkoy muzyki*, vol. 3. *XVIII vek, chast' vtoraya* (Moscow, 1985), p. 10.

219. Figes, *Natasha's Dance*, pp. 65–66; Alexandra Orlova, *Glinka's Life in Music: A Chronicle* (Ann Arbor and London, 1988), pp. 422, 614. There are plenty more condemnations of Paris to be found in this latter collection. Glinka appears to have disliked Paris even more than Richard Wagner did. Part of the reason for his virulent Francophobia may have been childhood memories of his home being overrun and looted by Napoleon's soldiers in 1812.

220. Nicholas V. Riasanovsky, *A Parting of the Ways: Government and the Educated Public in Russia 1801–55* (Oxford, 1976), p. 107.

221. Fyodor Dostoyevsky, *The Devils*, trans. David Magarshack (London, 1971), p. 253.

222. Richard Taruskin, 'A Life for the Tsar,' in *The New Grove Dictionary of Opera*, ed. Sadie, II, pp. 1261–1264.

223. Orlova, *Glinka's Life in Music*, pp. 136–137.

224. Ibid., p. 141.

225. Ibid., p. 143. This invaluable anthology includes a number of other similar comments by contemporaries.

226. Richard Taruskin, *Defining Russia Musically: Historical and Hermeneutical Essays* (Princeton, 1997), p. 27.

227. Geoffrey Hosking, *Russia: People and Empire 1552–1917* (Cambridge, Mass., 1997), p. 28.

228. Riasanovsky, *A Parting of the Ways*, pp. 255–256.

229. Richard Taruskin, 'Boris Godunov,' in *The New Grove Dictionary of Opera*, ed. Sadie, I, pp. 552–559.

230. Richard Taruskin, 'Musorgsky vs. Musorgsky: the versions of *Boris Godunov*,' *Nineteenth Century Music* 8 (1984–1985), pp. 91–118, 245–272.

231. Ibid., pp. 114, 256, 260.

232. This translation is a combination of that given in ibid., p. 114, and in Caryl Emerson and Robert William Oldani, *Modest Musorgsky and Boris Godunov: Myths, Realities and Reconsiderations* (Cambridge, 1994), pp. 204–205.

233. Ibid., p. 150.

234. Jacob Katz, *Out of the Ghetto: The Social Background of Jewish Emancipation, 1770–1870* (Cambridge, Mass., 1973), *passim.*

235. Artur Holde, *Jews in Music* (London, 1959), pp. 62–63.

236. *The Sunday Times,* 17 August 2003.

237. Nicholas Blanford, 'Battle of the divas brings harmony to the Arab world,' *The Times,* 20 August 2003, p. 14.

238. www.cbsnews.com/stories/2003/08/18/world/main568959.shtml.

239. Mark Tucker (ed.), *The Duke Ellington Reader* (New York, 1993), p. 59.

240. Ibid., p. 146.

241. Ibid., p. 128.

242. Quoted in Kathy J. Ogren, *The Jazz Revolution: Twenties America and the Meaning of Jazz* (Oxford, 1989), p. 162. The description of Bechet is mystifying, as he was not 'very black' but a Creole.

243. Ibid., p. 7.

244. Stanley Hirshon, 'Jazz, Segregation, and Desegregation,' in *A Master's Due: Essays in Honor of David Herbert Donald*, edited by William J. Cooper Jr. et al. (Baton Rouge and London, 1985), p. 235.

245. Ibid.

246. Eric Porter, *What Is This Thing Called Jazz? African American Musicians as Artists, Critics, and Activists* (Berkeley, 2002), p. 85.

247. Eileen Southern, *The Music of Black Americans: A History,* 2nd ed. (New York, 1983), pp. 493–494.

248. Brian Ward, *Just My Soul Responding: Rhythm and Blues, Black Consciousness and Race Relations* (London, 1998), p. 40.

249. The interview was with a French journalist, Hugo Cassavetti, and can be found at: www.harbour.sfu.ca/~hayward/van/reviews/1997april .html.

250. Ward, *Just My Soul Responding*, p. 128.

251. Quoted in Anthony DeCurtis and James Henke (eds.), *The Rolling Stone Illustrated History of Rock 'n' Roll* (London, 1992), p. 27.

252. Craig Werner, *A Change is Gonna Come: Music, Race and the Soul of America* (Edinburgh, 1998), p. 17.

253. Ward, *Just My Soul Responding*, p. 115.

254. Ruth Padel, *I'm a Man: Sex, Gods and Rock 'n' Roll* (London, 2000), p. 159.

255. Werner, *A Change Is Gonna Come*, p. 164.

256. Ibid., pp. 125, 128.

257. Ward, *Just My Soul Responding*, p. 130.

258. Ibid., p. 128.

259. Robert Christgau, 'Chuck Berry,' in *The Rolling Stone Illustrated History of Rock 'n' Roll*, eds. DeCurtis and Henke, p. 64.

260. Ward, *Just My Soul Responding*, p. 95.

261. Ibid., p. 104.

262. Anthony J. Badger, 'Different Perspectives on the Civil Rights Movement,' *History Now* 8 (June 2006).

263. Werner, *A Change Is Gonna Come*, p. 9.

264. In 1955 Marian Anderson was the first black singer to appear at the Metropolitan Opera House in New York. During the next two decades she was followed by Shirley Verrett, Grace Bumbry, Jessye Norman, Leontyne Price, Leona Mitchell, and Kathleen Battle.

265. www.abbeville.com/civilrights/washington.asp.

266. Ibid.

267. The full text can be found in many places, for example James Melvin Washington (ed.), *A Testament of Hope: The Essential Writings of Martin Luther King, Jr.* (New York, 1986), pp. 217–220.

268. Werner, *A Change Is Gonna Come*, p. 4.

269. Robert Palmer, *Dancing in the Street: A Rock 'n' Roll History* (London, 1996), p. 80.

270. Ward, *Just My Soul Responding*, p. 389.

271. Dan Morgenstern, 'Louis Armstrong,' in *The Oxford Companion to Jazz*, ed. Bill Kirchner (Oxford, 2000), pp. 118–119.

272. Quoted in Ward, *Just My Soul Responding*, p. 323.

273. Quoted in ibid., p. 232.

274. Palmer, *Dancing in the Street*, p. 95. On the BBC television programme for which this book was written, there is a particularly revealing interview with the white guitarist Steve Cropper about the effect of King's assassination on interracial musical cooperation.

275. Badger, 'Different perspectives on the civil rights movement.'

276. Pekka Gronow and Ilpo Saunio, *An International History of the Recording Industry* (London and New York, 1998), p. 204.

277. www.rollingstone.com/news/story/5939212/the_immortals. 'Sergeant Pepper's Lonely Hearts Club Band' was ranked as the number one record and The Beatles the number one group. These were peer reviews, involving fifty-five 'top musicians, historians, industry executives and critics.'

278. William Ashton Ellis, *The Life of Richard Wagner*, vol. IV (London, 1904), p. 442.

279. James Miller, *'Flowers in the Dustbin': The Rise of Rock and Roll 1947–1977* (New York, 1999), p. 84.

280. Ibid., pp. 87–88.

281. Ibid., p. 93. According to the sleeve of the VHS recording—ISBN 0-7928-3244-2—the film was withdrawn from the Venice Film Festival at the request of the American ambassador Clare Boothe Luce on the grounds that it presented too unflattering a picture of American secondary education.

282. Quoted in Paul Friedlander, *Rock 'n' Roll: A Social History* (Boulder, Colo., 1996), p. 42.

283. Sue Wise, 'Sexing Elvis,' in *On Record: Rock, Pop and the Written Word*, ed. Simon Frith and Andrew Goodwin (London, 1990), p. 396.

284. Quoted in Nik Cohn, *Awopbopaloobop Alopbamboom: Pop from the Beginning* (London, 1970), p. 26.

285. George Melly, *Revolt into Style: The Pop Arts in the 50s and 60s* (Oxford, 1989), p. 56. This book was first published 1970.

286. Ibid., p. 37.

287. Cohn, *AwopBopaLooBop aLopBamBoom*, p. 64.

288. Mat Smith, 'Phallus or fallacy,' *The Melody Maker*, 12 March 1988; reprinted in Jim Driver (ed.), *The Mammoth Book of Sex, Drugs and Rock 'n' Roll* (London, 2001), p. 348.

289. Quoted by George Melly in an article on the twist and discotheques in *The New Statesman*, 23 March 1962.

290. Quoted in Miller, *'Flowers in the Dustbin,'* p. 169.

291. Simon Frith and Angela McRobbie, 'Rock and sexuality,' in *On Record: Rock, Pop and the Written Word*, ed. Simon Frith and Andrew Goodwin (London, 1990), p. 371.

292. Ibid., p. 374.

293. Charles Shaar Murray, *Crosstown Traffic: Jimi Hendrix and the Rock 'n' Roll Revolution* (New York, 1989), p. 58.

294. Robert Pattison, *The Triumph of Vulgarity: Rock Music in the Mirror of Romanticism* (Oxford, 1987), p. 115.

295. Ruth Padel, *I'm a Man*, pp. 295, 311.

296. Ibid.

297. Murray, *Crosstown Traffic*, p. 69 [*sic*].

298. Quoted in Ibid., p. 71.

299. DeCurtis and Henke (eds.), *The Rolling Stone Illustrated History of Rock 'n' Roll*, pp. 189–191.

300. John Harlow, 'Beyoncé joins the big boys with £30m tour deal,' *The Sunday Times*, 14 March 2004, p. 31.

301. Martin Gregor-Dellin and Dietrich Mack (eds.), *Cosima Wagner's Diaries*, vol. II: *1878–1883* (London, 1980), p. 631. Entry for 25 February 1881.

302. http://en.wikipedia.org/wiki/Category:Gay_musicians.

303. Andy Medhurst, preface to Richard Smith, *Seduced and Abandoned: Essays on Gay Men and Popular Music* (London, 1995), p. xvi.

304. Alexander Laski, 'The politics of dancing—gay disco and postmodernism,' in *Music and Society: The Last Post*, ed. Simon Miller (Manchester, 1993), pp. 115–117.

305. Jon Savage, *Time Travel: Pop, Media and Sexuality* (London, 1996), p. 114.

306. Laura Jackson, *Queen: The Definitive Biography* (London, 1999), pp. 225–229. See also the booklet accompanying the DVD set.

307. www.thesun.co.uk/article/0,,2003061831,00.html. The odd spelling of 't.A.T.u.' was due to the existence of another group called 'Tatu.' Shapovalov let it be known that the word was a Russian abbreviation for 'this girl loves that girl.'

308. Both girls turned up at the Gay Pride rally in Moscow on 26 May 2007, an action that was as courageous as it was well-publicised. After being pelted with eggs, they were whisked away by their entourage: www.pinknews.co.uk/news/articles/2005-4495.html.

309. This information is taken from an extract from Darden Asbury Pyron's biography *Liberace: An American Boy*, which can be found at www.press.uchicago.edu/Misc/Chicago/686671.html.

Conclusion

1. Paul Johnson, 'The Menace of Beatlism,' *New Statesman* 18 February 1964; reprinted in Hanif Kureishi and Jon Savage (eds.), *The Faber Book of Pop* (London, 1995), pp. 195–198.

2. Quoted in Peter Wicke, *Rock Music: Culture, Aesthetic and Sociology* (Cambridge, 1990), pp. 23–24.

3. Paul Trynka (ed.), *The Beatles: Ten Years that Shook the World* (London, 2004), p. 248.

4. Matt Wells, 'How Robbie headed Amadeus in the race to be music's man of the millennium,' *The Guardian*, 8 November 1999.

5. http://en.wikipedia.org/wiki/Yesterday_(song). Although in fact the song was written by McCartney alone, Lennon and McCartney share the credit.

6. Quoted in Harry Haskell, *The Early Music Revival: A History* (London, 1988), p. 109. An honourable exception was Deutsche Grammophon's 'Archiv' series.

7. Trevor Croucher, *Early Music Discography: From Plainsong to the Sons of Bach,* 2 vols. (London, 1981), p. vi.

8. John Milsom, 'Soundclips and *Early Music*,' *Early Music* 31, 1 (2003), p. 3.

9. It has been noticed that 'SDG' might also be read as an acronym for 'Sod Deutsche Grammophon.'

10. There is admittedly at least one exception: the grim German daily *Frankfurter Allgemeine Zeitung.*

11. http://www.saatchi-gallery.co.uk/yourgallery/.

12. Walter Benjamin, 'The work of art in the age of mechanical reproduction,' in idem *Illuminations* (London, 1970): 'Even the most perfect reproduction of a work of art is lacking in one element; its presence in time and space, its unique existence at the place where it happens to be.' I owe this insight to Eric Hobsbawm who delivered it during the course of an intervention at an Ameurus conference at Dresden on 19 May 2007. He added that the visual arts had declined during the course of the twentieth century, especially during its second half, and would continue to do so during the twenty-first.

13. http://www.advanced-television.com/2006/news_archive_2006/may29_jun2.htm#pop.

Illustration Credits

Party at the Palace—the Queen's Jubilee Concert, 3 June 2002. (AP Photo / Steve Holland)

Brian May performs 'God Save the Queen' at the opening of the Jubilee Concert, 3 June 2002. (PA Photos)

Breitkopf and Härtel thematic catalogue (1763). (Breitkopf & Härtel KG)

The Duke of Alba by Goya (1795). (Erich Lessing / Art Resource, NY)

Franz Joseph Haydn by J. E. von Mansfeld. (The Art Archive / Museum der Stadt Wien / Alfredo Dagli Orti)

Handel by Louis François Roubiliac. (Victoria & Albert Museum, London / Art Resource, NY)

Handel Monument by Louis François Roubiliac, Westminster Abbey. (Michael Jenner / Alamy)

Apotheosis of Haydn on 27 March 1808 by Balthasar Wigand. (The Art Archive / Museum der Stadt Wien / Alfredo Dagli Orti)

Monteverdi by Bernardo Strozzi (1640). (Erich Lessing / Art Resource, NY)

Johann Sebastian Bach by Elias Gottlob Haussmann (1746). (Erich Lessing / Art Resource, NY)

George Frederick Handel by Thomas Hudson (1756). (© Private Collection / The Bridgeman Art Library)

Mozartkugel advertisement. (FAN Travelstock / Alamy)

Beethoven by Franz Klein (1812). (Beethoven-Haus, Bonn)

Beethoven's funeral procession in 1827 by Franz Stober. (Erich Lessing / Art Resource, NY)

Niccolo Paganini by J. A. D. Ingres (1819). (Réunion des Musées Nationaux / Art Resource, NY)

Paganini by Ferdinand-Victor-Eugène Delacroix (1831). (The Phillips Collection, Washington, DC)

French caricature of Franz Liszt. (Interfoto)

Franz Liszt concert at Berlin in 1842. (The Granger Collection, New York)

Franz Liszt, lithograph, by Josef Kriehuber (1846). (The Art Archive / Museum der Stadt Wien / Alfredo Dagli Orti)

Emperor William I driven through the streets of Bayreuth (1876). (Reuter Wagner Museum, Eisenach)

Wagner with Emperor William I in Bayreuth at the opening of the Festival Theatre (1876). (Münchner Stadtmuseum, Munich)

Harold Wilson harassed by the Beatles (1964). (Kent Gavin / Getty Images)

Tony Blair with Noel Gallagher of Oasis (1997). (AP Photo / Rebecca Naden)

Bono and Bob Geldof with Tony Blair (2003). (AP Photo / Roger Allen / Daily Mirror Pool)

Performance of *The Princess of Elis* by Molière within *The Pleasures of the Enchanted Isle,* engraving by Israel Silvestre (1664). (© Roger-Viollet / The Image Works)

Town plan of Mannheim in the mid-eighteenth century. (Reiss-Engelhorn-Museen, Mannheim / Jean Christen)

Gewandhaus, Leipzig, by Felix Mendelssohn-Bartholdy (1837). (Bildarchiv Preussischer Kulturbesitz / Art Resource, NY)

La Petite Loge by Jean-Michel Moreau (1783). (Victoria & Albert Museum, London / Art Resource, NY)

Apollo Belvedere, Vatican. (Clifford Boehmer / Harvard University Press)

Title page of Beethoven's Third Symphony, *Eroica.* (Erich Lessing / Art Resource, NY)

Festival Theatre at Bayreuth. (Courtesy Bernd Mayer, Bayreuth)

Closing moments of the first performance of *Parsifal* at Bayreuth by Paul von Joukowsky (1882). (The Granger Collection, New York)

John Coltrane (1964). (AP IMAGES)

Sixties icon Eric Clapton is defiled.

Teatro Regio, Turin, during a performance of *Arsace* by Pietro Domenico Olivero (1740). (The Art Archive / Museo Civico Turin / Gianni Dagli Orti)

Bayreuth: the margrave's box in the Margrave's Opera House, by Giuseppe and Carlo Galli Bibiena (1744–48). (INTERFOTO Pressebildagentor / Alamy)

Haydn directs a performance at the opera house at Esterháza. (The Granger Collection, New York)

Interior of La Scala, Milan. (The Art Archive / Museo Teatrale alla Scala Milan / Alfredo Dagli Orti)

The Rittersaal in the Electoral Palace, Mannheim (1730). (Photographie Robert Häusser, Mannheim)

Electoral Palace, Mannheim (1725). (The Granger Collection, New York)

The Hanover Square Rooms, London (1843). (Courtesy of Monir Tayeb and Michel Austin [www.hberlioz.com])

Opera House Knobelsdorff Theatre, Berlin, built by Frederick the Great, engraving by J. Rosenberg (1778). (The Art Archive)

National Theatre on the Gendarmenmarkt, Berlin (ca. 1810). (Bildarchiv Preussischer Kulturbesitz / Art Resource, NY)

Schauspielhaus on the Gendarmenmarkt, Berlin. (The Granger Collection, New York)

Concert hall in the Schauspielhaus, Berlin. (Bildarchiv Preussischer Kulturbesitz / Art Resource, NY)

The original appearance of the main hall of the Musikverein, Vienna. (Copyright Wien Museum)

Detail of *Mountebanks and Promenaders on the Pont au Change, Paris,* ca. 1790, watercolor on paper by French School (18th century). (© Musée de la Ville de Paris, Musée Carnavalet, Paris, France / Lauros / Giraudon / The Bridgeman Art Library)

Claude-Joseph Rouget de l'Isle Sings His 'Battle Hymn for the Army of the Rhine' by Isidore Pils (1849). (Snark / Art Resource, NY)

La Marseillaise by Nicolas Toussaint Charlet (1840). (Cabinet des Estampes, Manuscrits occidentaux, Bibliothèque nationale de France)

At the Advance Post by Georg Friedrich Kersting (1814). (Bildarchiv Preussischer Kulturbesitz / Art Resource, NY)

Title page of Smetana's tone poem 'From Bohemia's Woods and Meadows' (1875). (© British Library Board. All Rights Reserved [h.3913.n(4)])

The Royal Provincial Provisional Theatre at Prague. (National Museum Prague: Theatre Division)

František Palacký at the laying of the foundation stone of the National Theatre, Prague. (Zlata Praha, 1868)

Chuck Berry, Bo Diddley, and fans. (© Annie Leibovitz / Contact Press Images)

Mahalia Jackson sings to a crowd at the Lincoln Memorial (Bob Parent / Getty Images); Crowd gathered at the Lincoln Memorial for Martin Luther King's 'I have a dream' speech (Bob Gomel / Getty Images)

Jimmy Page and Robert Plant. (© Neal Preston / CORBIS)

David Bowie as Ziggy Stardust. (© Hulton-Deutsch Collection / CORBIS)

Madonna with Britney Spears and Christina Aguilera (2003). (Scott Gries / Getty Images)

t.A.T.u.—Lena Katina and Yulia Volkova. (AP Photo / Jasper Juinen)

Index